Mao Tse-tung in Opposition

1927–1935

JOHN E. RUE

With the assistance of S. R. Rue

Published for
the Hoover Institution on War, Revolution and Peace
by Stanford University Press, Stanford, California

The Hoover Institution on War, Revolution and Peace, founded at Stanford University in 1919 by the late President Herbert Hoover, is a center for advanced study and research on public and international affairs in the twentieth century. The views expressed in its publications are entirely those of the authors and do not necessarily reflect the views of the Hoover Institution.

Stanford University Press
Stanford, California

Printed in the United States of America
ISBN 0-8047-0222-5
Original edition 1966
Last figure below indicates year of this printing:
89 88 87 86 85 84 83 82 81 80

To Mulford Q. Sibley
friend, scholar, and patriot

TO THE READER

It is well known that the pioneering scholarship on the documents of the Kiangsi period has been done by Professor Hsiao Tso-liang. He has thoroughly gone through the documents for the period and has demonstrated keen perception in the choice of those he has excerpted and translated. As my many citations to him convey, it would have been impossible for me to have written as fully on this period without the aid of his work.

Much more than is indicated in the footnotes, the part of this book dealing with the Kiangsi period is heavily dependent on the data of Professor Hsiao's *Power Relations within the Chinese Communist Movement, 1930–1934, a Study of Documents* (Seattle: University of Washington Press, 1961) and of his unpublished manuscript *The Land Revolution in China, 1930–1934, a Study of Documents,* with translations of documents. Unfortunately, specific references to these works were omitted in various cases.

I am more than pleased to acknowledge my indebtedness to Professor Hsiao's work, as he has justifiably requested.

J. E. R.

Acknowledgments

This volume has been so long in the making that it is impossible for me to adequately express my gratitude to all who have helped me. Among those who have so graciously given of both criticism and encouragement are some to whom I am particularly indebted. Werner Levi, John Turner, Richard Mather, and Mulford Sibley read the manuscript in its more difficult stages and made valuable suggestions for its improvement, as did the anonymous reader for Stanford University Press. Robert C. North, Karl Wittfogel, and C. S. Chao were helpful in clarifying a number of historical and philosophical problems for me. Dennis Doolin has been unfailingly generous and resourceful in helping me with matters of translation, location of material, and interpretation of data. Eugene Wu and David Tseng also made translations for me from the Chinese, as did Noel Voge and Marin Pundeff from the Russian. Paul Hoffman, Harold Quigley, and especially Mulford Sibley were encouraging when I was disheartened.

I am indebted to the Hoover Institution at Stanford University for the use of its excellent Chinese collection, for the helpfulness of its staff, and for its financial assistance. The Stanford Studies of the Communist System, headed by Jan F. Triska, also gave me financial support during the year in which this manuscript was completed. While most of my research was done at the Hoover Library, I am also grateful for the assistance I received from librarians at the University of Minnesota Library and the Hill Reference Library in St. Paul, and those at the interlibrary loan desks at Reed College and San Fernando Valley State College.

Don Ryan and Nancy Fouquet drew the maps; Lois Tretiak painstakingly proofread the text and prepared the index; and Chris Keller assisted in proofreading. The small army of typists who made legible the various drafts of my manuscript included Lila Pineles, Sandra

Rogers, Jean Hunt, Marion Kost, Mary Campbell, Mary Johnson, and Mary Ann West.

All quotations from the English edition of *Mao Tse-tung: Selected Works* are used by permission of International Publishers Co., Inc.; those from Edgar Snow's *Red Star Over China* (copyright 1938, 1944, by Random House, Inc.) by permission of its publisher, Grove Press, Inc. The translations by Karl Wittfogel and C. Martin Wilbur of excerpts from the CCP Central Committee's Resolution on Political Discipline of November 1927, and the excerpt from Stuart Schram's translation of Mao's letter of August 20, 1927, to the CCP Central Committee are used by permission of the *China Quarterly*.

Perhaps my greatest debt is to Mao Tse-tung—one of the master politicians of our era, a subtle thinker who adapted the Marxism of old Europe to the demands of the Chinese revolution, a shrewd strategist and charismatic leader who succeeded in reuniting China after almost half a century of turmoil. His life story has occupied my scholarly endeavors for a decade.

J.E.R.

Contents

The reader is invited to consult the Chronology, pp. 341–52.

Maps

Abbreviations

A-B Corps	Anti-Bolshevik Corps
BIC	Bureau of Investigation Collection
CCP	Chinese Communist Party
CEC	Central Executive Committee
CFWH	*Cheng-feng wen-hsien (Party Rectification Papers)* [12]
CPSU	Communist Party of the Soviet Union
ECCI	Executive Committee of the Communist International
HC	*Mao Tse-tung Hsüan-chi* [83]
HC (*Hsü-pien*)	*Hsüan-chi (supplement)* [86]
ICC	International Control Commission (of the Comintern)
KMT	Kuomintang
NPSS	New People's Study Society
NTTC	*Nung-ts'un tiao-ch'a (Rural Survey)* [87]
OGPU	Secret police of the Soviet Union
RSOC	Snow, *Red Star over China*
RSQHP	"Resolution on Some Questions in the History of Our Party"
SSC	Shih Sou Collection
SW	*Selected Works of Mao Tse-tung*

Bracketed numbers refer to entries in the Chinese Sources section of the Bibliography. When capitalized, the word "Soviet" refers to the Soviet Union; in lower case it refers to soviets in China.

From the talented brush of Chang Kia-ngau, this calligraphy is read "Ching-kang-shan t'ung-chih ti t'ien-hsia." This we translate "The world of the comrades of Ching-kang Mountain."

When Mao Tse-tung was under house arrest in Yü-tu, Kung Ch'u brought him a chicken and some wine. While eating and drinking, they reminisced of their first meeting on Ching-kang Mountain. Long after sunset the two old comrades continued to drink the wine in the darkened courtyard. When Kung Ch'u was about to leave, Mao Tse-tung suddenly sighed and said, "Alas, this is no longer the world of the comrades of Ching-kang-shan."

Mao Tse-tung in Opposition

CHAPTER I

Introduction

Mao Tse-tung's rise to power is a well-known fact for which there is no sufficient explanation. He is unique among Communist leaders who rose to power in the Stalinist era, for even before he took power there was at the core of his ideological position a challenge to Stalin's authority to determine the ideological correctness of positions on all issues of theory and policy directly affecting the Chinese Communist Party, a repugnance for Stalin's methods of controlling non-Soviet parties, and a rejection of the use of terror as a method for maintaining orthodoxy in Communist parties everywhere.

Mao's methods of overcoming erroneous lines in the CCP were in complete contradiction to the methods developed by the leaders of the Communist Party of the Soviet Union during the Stalinist era. Mao developed his ideas on inner-party education in the wake of the great purges in the Soviet Union. Those ideas were not an imitation of Stalin's practice, but a reaction against it. Mao made it clear during the first party rectification movement in 1942–44 that he intended to overcome the ideological weaknesses of certain leading Chinese Communist intellectuals who had once been his opponents without resorting to a "killing cure." The rectification of thought, in his eyes, was preferable to physical extermination.

After Khrushchev's denunciation of the cult of the individual in 1956 Mao apparently moved toward the old Stalinist position on many issues, but he was not a Stalinist in the years immediately prior to Stalin's death. Prominent members of the Chinese Central Committee had by that time asserted that Mao had creatively developed his own brand of Marxism-Leninism—and that he had arrived at his special ideological position not by starting from Stalin's interpretation of dialectical and historical materialism, but by independently applying the universal principles of Marxism-Leninism to an analysis of Chinese history and the problems of modern China. His theses on the Chinese revolution, and the role the CCP could play in it, were developed in opposition to the lines taken by leaders of the Chinese Politburo before 1935, who followed the line of the Comintern. After 1927, and especially after 1929, the Comintern line was the Stalinist line.

Recognition of Mao's Power and Authority in China and Moscow

Mao rose to power within two closely linked political systems: the Chinese Communist Party and the Comintern. Constitutionally, the CCP was subordinate to the directing center of the Comintern, and the leading organs of the CCP, like those of all other national parties belonging to the International (with the sole exception of the CPSU), were closely controlled and supervised from Comintern headquarters in Moscow. In fact, before 1927 no non-Soviet party was more completely supervised by the Central Committee of the CPSU and the Comintern than the Chinese party. In the 1920's the Comintern apparatus was not a monolithic structure; it was riddled by factional disputes among the supporters of the Russian party leaders struggling for Lenin's mantle. Between 1927 and 1930, in Stalin's fight with Trotsky and the Left and Right Oppositions in the CPSU, his men seized control of the Comintern apparatus directing all non-Soviet parties.

Under the Stalinist regime developed in the 1930's, the system for inspection and control of foreign party leaders was gradually tightened. At the height of the great purges in the USSR the old-line inspectors in the Comintern apparatus were replaced by the Soviet secret police.[1] Only after June 1941, when the Soviet party leaders were devoting all their time to the war, were the controls over some non-Soviet party leaders relaxed. The Chinese party chieftains isolated in Yenan were probably among those whom the Soviet apparatus found it difficult to control under wartime conditions. After the demise of the Comintern in 1943, supervision of foreign parties was officially taken over by a bureau of the Central Committee of the CPSU.

When World War II ended, the Soviet apparatus was again in a position to exert pressure on Chinese party leaders. After the People's Government was set up in Peking in 1949, the Central Committee of the CPSU was able to apply all the tactical devices initially developed to control the satellite regimes of Eastern Europe. Pressure

1 Numbers refer to Notes, pp. 315–40. Notes at the foot of the page are keyed to the text by letters. Complete authors' names, titles, and publication data for notes of both kinds are to be found in the Bibliography, pp. 355–69.

to conform to Soviet standards, both in conduct and in theory, was probably at its greatest during the years between Mao's visit to Moscow in December 1949 and Stalin's death in 1953.

Mao's rise to power coincided with the consolidation of Stalin's dictatorship over all state and party organs controlled by the Kremlin, with the construction of the monolithic totalitarian state in the Soviet Union, and with the establishment of an officially prescribed ideology—Marxism-Leninism, dialectical and historical materialism —that could be altered only by the tremendous organizing, mobilizing, and transforming guidance of the dictator in Moscow. Mao fought his way to the chairmanship of the CCP in the face of continuous and determined opposition from Chinese party leaders appointed and supervised by agencies of the Comintern. He consolidated his power over the party in spite of everything its former leaders could do to overthrow him. He developed his political, organizational, and military lines in opposition to the lines the Stalinists expounded when they were in command of the central organs of the CCP: he developed his ideological line in his struggle to maintain his position of leadership on the Central Committee. So by 1945 Mao had few ideological commitments to Stalin. After that year relations between the two were dictated by their relative power positions. Mao, as the leader of the party controlling the weaker state, occasionally had to bow to the authority of Moscow, but even under great pressure he maintained intact the essential features of his special position.

A careful examination of the revised edition of his works, which was published between 1951 and 1953, will illustrate the many problems Mao faced in denying the correctness of certain aspects of Stalin's theory and practice to a Chinese audience while simultaneously maintaining officially correct and cordial relations with the omniscient dictator in the Kremlin. Such an examination is of general interest as an example of the use of sophisticated verbal camouflage by relatively weak groups who need to conceal their opposition status under the conditions created by a tightly disciplined and highly centralized international party regime. It is also of more immediate interest in the light of the present Sino-Soviet rift. If it can be shown that the recent disputes have roots running back into the Stalinist era, and that Moscow has intermittently challenged Mao's political power and ideological orthodoxy since he first took a position of his own, we may be better able to understand the present struggle for political and ideological supremacy between Moscow and Peking.

By his own testimony, from 1927 until 1935 Mao was opposed to the line that the Comintern directed the Chinese party to follow.[2] In

January 1935, Mao and his supporters took over the Secretariat and the Revolutionary Military Commission of the Central Committee at an enlarged meeting of the Politburo at Tsun-yi, Kweichow (the Tsun-yi Conference).[3] From that time until late in 1938, Mao was de facto chairman of the CCP Politburo. Only late in 1938, however, was his leadership of that body publicly acknowledged by Moscow: the earliest Soviet acknowledgment of his party position so far discovered is the article on Mao in the 1938 edition of the *Bol'shaia Sovetskaia Entsiklopediia*.[4]

Between 1938 and 1945, Mao developed his special ideological position in a struggle with Wang Ming, the leader of the party's Stalinist faction, over united front strategy. The struggle grew in scope and intensity until the entire past history of the CCP was involved.[5] In its course, Mao redesigned the educational program for higher cadres in the CCP and then extended the new program to the whole of the CCP.[6] This struggle, which culminated in the party rectification movement, was also marked by a direct comparison of the methods of leadership advocated by Mao and by Stalin.

In April 1945, after this contest came to an end, the victorious Maoists convened the Seventh Congress of the CCP. Seven years after Moscow had first recognized his leadership, Mao was ready to advance his claim to unique ideological authority for the Chinese party. The Congress was called only after the conclusion of the first party rectification movement, and after the Seventh Plenum of the Central Committee (elected at the Sixth Congress in 1928) had approved the Maoist interpretation of the inner-party struggle between the correct and erroneous lines between July 1927, when the first great revolution failed, and January 1935, when the Tsun-yi Conference was held.[7] This Congress accepted the claim that Mao's thought or ideology made original and creative contributions to the science of Marxism-Leninism. The claim was embodied in the Preamble to the new Party Constitution adopted by the Congress, which also gives a succinct statement of Mao's theses on the Chinese revolution.

The Seventh Congress was Mao's Congress of Victors. He had overcome all his enemies in the Chinese party. There was no one left for him to fight. The comrades who had supported him throughout his long, devious struggle were to become the party's leaders in its final drive for power. The Seventh Congress readily accepted Mao's political, military, and organizational line as the sole correct one: all that remained was to gain acceptance for his special ideological views. This job fell to Liu Shao-ch'i. In his speech to the Congress on the new Party Constitution, Liu developed the theme that Mao had made new, original, and creative contributions to the universal science of Marxism-Leninism.[8]

After the Seventh Congress Mao's power rested on two closely related factors. One was control of the party apparatus; the other was the belief of other leaders of the Chinese party that his political line was correct and that his thought was the best representative of Marxist-Leninist ideology in China.[9]

Before the death of Stalin no Soviet source acknowledged any of the claims put forward at the Seventh Congress for the originality and creativity of Mao's thought; in fact the Seventh Congress itself was ignored by the Soviet press.[10] As leader of the Communist world movement, Stalin jealously guarded his ideological authority. He was unwilling to delegate final ideological authority to any other Communist party leader either in the Soviet Union or abroad. During the Stalinist era any political line advanced by any Communist leader had to be traced back to some position Stalin had allegedly taken under similar circumstances and its orthodoxy illustrated with profuse quotations from Stalin's writings. Soviet authorities would not acknowledge that a line advocated by lesser party leaders was correct unless these requirements were fulfilled. To do otherwise would endanger the unity of the Communist camp and the primacy of the Soviet Union within the camp; moreover, it would be an affront to Stalin.[11]

Neither Mao nor his supporters on the Central Committee have adhered to this procedure. Liu's exposition of Mao's thought is almost barren of quotes from Stalin justifying Mao's position, and in Mao's published works there are almost no quotes from Stalin or any other indications that Mao's views are derived directly or indirectly from those of Stalin. In the few instances in which Mao does attempt to show that his theses follow from Stalin's, a careful reading suggests that in fact they do not, and that he has used Stalin's theses either as a camouflage for his previous opposition or as a dialectical irony.

Revision of Mao's Works After His Visit to Moscow

In 1949, when Mao went to Moscow to meet Stalin for the first time, there were many problems to be settled between them. Not the least of these was the problem of Mao's ideological pretensions. Would Mao and his supporters continue to insist that his ideology was correct, that his theses on the Chinese revolution were an independent and creative addition to Marxism-Leninism? Would he somehow manage to evade the issue and avoid a direct clash with Stalin? Or would he be forced to submit publicly to Stalin's ideological authority even in those matters most deeply affecting his power and prestige in the Central Committee of the CCP?

A revision of Mao's works was begun after his return to Peking in 1950. Numerous additions, omissions, revisions, and corrections were made before their publication under the title *Hsüan-chi* (*Selected Works*) in 1951–53. (Hereafter the Chinese edition will be referred to as HC, the English as SW.) This revision represents the greatest length to which Mao was willing to go in publicly yielding to Stalin's ideological and political authority.

Mao had four evident reasons for revising his works. First, he wished to eliminate the most obvious of the theoretical errors in his early works. He had begun to write in Communist journals long before he had mastered the main concepts of Marxist-Leninist theory, and many of his early articles contained gross theoretical errors he had no desire to see in print again. Second, he wished to assert that some of the ideas he had proposed to the Central Committee before 1935 had been correct and useful even though they had initially been rejected. Third, he wanted to close all avenues by which his old rivals could attack him for his resistance to disciplinary measures and evasion of Politburo orders before 1935. The events of those years had to be edited and construed in such a way as to justify his activities. Fourth, he wanted to play down the fact that the CCP had shifted its locus of ideological authority from Moscow to Peking. Mao still agreed with Stalin on most of the fundamentals of Marxism-Leninism, and he did not wish to undermine the officially cordial relations between Stalin and himself by calling attention to old differences.

Very few of the writings Mao published before 1935 were considered eligible for inclusion in the authorized version of HC published after he returned from Moscow in 1950: ten short pieces occupying only 152 pages in the English version, all of which were retitled, cut, rearranged, or otherwise extensively modified before the author pronounced them worthy of inclusion. In the judgment of one scholar with broad experience in translating Mao's works, "The texts included in the *Selected Works* have been subjected to such numerous and profound changes by the author that one cannot accept even a single sentence as being identical with what Mao had actually written without checking it against the original version."[12] Why did Mao think these works so important that he not only included them in HC, but took a good deal of trouble in revising them as well?

The answer is that it was in these works that Mao took his first steps toward developing an independent theory of his own. Of course, he was in opposition to the party line when he wrote them. Each and every one of these ten early works was condemned by responsible CCP leaders shortly after it was written, and several of them were held up as horrid examples of Mao's theoretical deficiencies. When Mao persisted in asserting his strange, un-Marxist notions, he was reprimanded, and when he implemented his ideas on tactics in the face of opposition from higher authorities in the party, he was dismissed from one or more of his responsible party positions. Hence a new interpretation of the inner-party disputes of 1927–35 had to be established before Mao's works of these years could be published —a new line had to be taken on the course the party should have followed at the time these articles were written.

This feat was accomplished when Mao rewrote the party's history from his own perspective. The earliest version of the new history, attributed to Mao himself, is now dated 1944. It was written to refute the version of inner-party conflict formulated by Wang Ming and Po Ku, the leaders of the Russian Returned Students (the 28 Bolsheviks), whom the Maoist faction had overthrown at the Tsun-yi Conference.[a]

[a] The Russian Returned Students (the 28 Bolsheviks) had been students at Sun Yat-sen University in Moscow. Most of them went to Russia in 1926 and, except for short tours of duty as interpreters for delegations of visiting Russians, did not return to China until the spring of 1930. In the fratricidal strife between the Stalinists and the United Opposition only these 28 students consistently sided with the Stalinist faction. When the first group of Chinese students arrived in Moscow to enter the new Sun Yat-sen University, Stalinists, Trotskyites, and Zinovievites all were represented on the faculty and in the administration. Karl Radek, a Trotskyite, was the rector and Pavel Mif, a Stalinist, the second-ranking administrator. After Radek was expelled from the CPSU in late 1927, Mif took over as rector and at the same time became chief of the Chinese section of the Far Eastern Bureau of the Comintern. In early 1930 this group returned to China in a mission led by Mif and became known as the Returned Students. After a short but decisive struggle against Li Li-san, Ch'ü Ch'iu-pai, Teng Chung-hsia, and Ho Meng-hsiung, they took over the CCP Politburo at the Fourth Plenum of the Central Committee (January 1931). The factions they drove from power at the Fourth Plenum initially referred to them as "Stalin's China Section" (Hsiao, p. 125). Later, after Wang Ming had written his short pamphlet on bolshevizing the CCP, they were nicknamed the 28 Bolsheviks.

No complete list of the 28 has ever been published. Ch'en Shao-yü (Wang Ming) and Ch'in Pang-hsien (Po Ku) were the acknowledged leaders of the clique. Other members who have been positively identified are Shen Tse-min, Wang Chia-hsiang, Chang Wen-t'ien (also known as Lo Fu and Szu Mei), Ho Tzu-shu, Wu Liang-p'ing, Liang Pai-t'ai, Chu Jui, Tso Ch'üan, Hsü Meng-ch'iu, Ch'en Hui-ch'ing (Mme. Teng Fa), and Ch'en Chang-hao. Three wives may also have been among the members: Meng Ch'ing-shu (Mme. Ch'en Shao-yü), Liu Ying (Mme.

The New History

In the "Resolution on Some Questions in the History of Our Party" (hereafter cited as RSQHP), Mao lays down his interpretation of the history of the CCP from early 1927 until the Tsun-yi Conference of January 1935. After a short attack on the right deviation of Ch'en Tu-hsiu, he turns to a long analysis of the errors of the three left lines followed by the CCP Politburos under Ch'ü Ch'iu-pai from November 1927 to April 1928; under Li Li-san from June 1929 to September 1930; and under Wang Ming, Po Ku, and the other Returned Students from January 1931 to January 1935.

While Mao declares that he opposed all three left lines, he does not attack their leading exponents with equal vehemence: Li Li-san, Wang Ming, and Po Ku are the only comrades he attacks by name. He refrains from associating the name of Ch'ü Ch'iu-pai with the first left line,[b] and defends the policies adopted by the Politburo under Ch'ü's leadership at the Third Plenum (September 1930). In his analysis of the policies adopted by that Plenum Mao illustrates his anti-Comintern bias, for the faction that seized power in September 1930 did so in spite of the opposition of Pavel Mif, the Comintern agent who attended the Plenum.

The leaders of the two previous Politburos had been approved by the Comintern or one of its agents before they took power. Their policies bore the imprint of that body and in certain crucial periods Stalin himself directed their work by telegram. Ch'ü and Li fell when they failed to implement the line of the Comintern or when their theoretical analyses diverged from the current Stalinist line, or both. After a short and bitter struggle in the fall of 1930, Moscow imposed its chosen men to lead the new CCP Politburo—Pavel Mif's protégés, Wang Ming and Po Ku, and the other 28 Bolsheviks.

There is no evidence that this faction ever resisted the Comintern

---

Chang Wen-t'ien), and Liu Chien-hsien (Mme. Ch'in Pang-hsien). Thus we can positively identify thirteen of the 28. If the three wives followed the same line as their husbands while in Moscow, they may also be included, bringing the total number identified to sixteen. Someone called Wei Jen (which is almost certainly a pseudonym) wrote for the group (Hsiao, p. 374). If Wei is not a pseudonym for someone already on the list, the total number identified comes to seventeen, leaving eleven persons as yet unnamed.

[b] Perhaps in deference to Ch'ü's status as a party martyr (he was killed by the Nationalists in 1935). It is also at least possible that Ch'ü, although the party's official leader, opposed the first left line, which was imposed on the party by Stalin's agent, Heinz Neumann, in November 1927. Solid evidence on Ch'ü's ideas in late 1927 is not available.

line, or that their theoretical analyses diverged at any time from the Stalinist line. Although Po Ku and other members of the faction were removed from the Politburo by the Maoist faction at Tsun-yi, Wang Ming continued in Stalin's favor at least until the end of 1937, and possibly until 1940. No analysis of the errors of the Returned Students drawn up in Moscow has ever come to light. If such a document ever existed, Mao almost surely would have used it to justify his seizure of power at Tsun-yi. After all, if Moscow approved of his overthrowing the Returned Students, Mao had no reason to conceal it.

In RSQHP Mao condemns Wang Ming and Po Ku not because they disagreed with the Comintern line, but because they disagreed with him. The three left lines were not to the left of the Comintern line, but to the left of Mao's theses on the Chinese revolution. In RSQHP, the center from which right and left deviate is not Stalin, but Mao. Nor is Mao's condemnation couched in the familiar terminology generally employed in the Communist world in reviewing the political errors of fallen leaders. Both content and style are uniquely his own.

Because Mao has shifted the locus of authority from Stalin to himself, the periods he identifies as those in which the left lines were dominant should be interpreted as the periods of greatest tension between Mao and the CCP Politburo. According to this reading Mao was in opposition or under attack, or both, for 68 of the 89 months between August 1927 and January 1935. Even the remaining 21 months were not free from tension, for the periods when the extreme left line became dominant may coincide with occasions when Mao was reprimanded for his political errors or when organizational measures were taken to deprive him of prestige and power in the party hierarchy. RSQHP states emphatically that the most acute conflict between the Maoist faction and the Politburo led by Wang Ming and Po Ku developed during the soviet period in the South (January 1931 to January 1935). Since this was the faction Mao displaced at Tsun-yi, the emphasis could be misleading; the period of greatest tension between Mao and the Comintern may well have occurred earlier.

According to Chang Kuo-t'ao, who was one of Mao's rivals for control of the CCP after 1935 and who left the party in 1938, Mao was expelled from the Central Committee three times and reprimanded eight times before 1935. Chang does not date the reprimands, but he does state that Mao was expelled from the Central Committee for the first time in late 1923 or early 1924, for the second time at the November Plenum of 1927, and for the third time a few months after the Fifth Plenum in January 1934.[13] Kung Ch'u, a member of Mao's Front Committee in the Ching-kang Mountains and a Red Army commander who left the CCP during the Long March, confirms Chang's story and says Mao was expelled from the Central Committee for the third time and sent to the Yü-tu prison in August 1934.[14]

The precise accusations leveled against Mao in late 1923 or early 1924 are still unknown, although we know that Li Li-san later accused him of working so closely with the Kuomintang right wing before his expulsion that he became "Hu Han-min's secretary." Mao's expulsion at the November 1927 Plenum is now fully documented. Shortly thereafter Li Li-san, this time with Stalin's prompting, accused him of representing the "localism and conservatism of peasant consciousness," i.e., of modeling himself on the Russian Social Revolutionaries.[15] When the 28 Bolsheviks reached out to reorganize the CCP in the soviet districts in 1931, they condemned Mao's egalitarian land reform policies as representing a rich peasant line that confused class relations, labeled his military policies "guerrillaism," ridiculed his political mass line for its ideological poverty, narrow empiricism, and pragmatic opportunism, and accused him of negligence for not having developed a strong proletarian base.[16] These accusations were repeated in the appendix to the new edition of Wang Ming's *Liang t'iao lu-hsien (The Two Lines)*, which was republished in Moscow in March 1932 with the full authority of the Comintern behind it.[17] Shortly thereafter the CCP Politburo accused the Maoists of "right opportunism," conciliation toward the Li Li-sanists, double-dealing, following the rich peasant line, and being responsible for Lo Ming's line. These struggles culminated in Mao's third expulsion from the Central Committee and his imprisonment in Yü-tu.[18]

The accusations of "peasant consciousness," "right opportunism," etc., that Li, Wang, and Po brought against Mao were not woven out of thin air. Considering the Comintern line at the time these accusations were made, they were perfectly justified. From 1927 to 1935 the Chinese Politburos followed the Comintern line as closely as they could. The accusations they raised against Mao were in fact replies to theses he had proposed, or actions he had initiated, without consulting the party center, and in defiance of its line.

Mao, then, really was in opposition to the Moscow line on China in the periods identified in RSQHP, even when Stalin was personally responsible for guiding China policy. Therefore, when he prepared his new interpretation of party history before the Seventh Congress, he not only had to overcome the ideological authority of Wang Ming, but he also had to devise a theoretical scheme that would allow him to assert that his theses had been correct even though when first advanced they had been opposed by both the Chinese Politburo and the Executive Committee of the Comintern (ECCI). His rewriting of party history, moreover, had to be acceptable to the Central Committee of the CCP, for only with its support could he obscure those issues which might cause an open clash between Stalin and himself. RSQHP accomplished these goals. It linked together all of Mao's deviations before 1935, identified them with his theory of new democracy, condemned those who opposed his views in the past, and asserted his right to lead the CCP. In RSQHP Mao laid the ideological foundation for his Congress of Victors.

CHAPTER II

The Beginning of Mao's Party Career

The Maoist Reconstruction of the History of the CCP

The Maoist cult—the worship of Mao's ideology—grew out of a reaction to the doctrinaire, mechanical imposition of Stalin's formulas in revolutionary China. In the ensuing struggle Stalin's best known disciples were eliminated from all positions of power in the CCP. Mao's astonishing triumph in this dangerous inner-party struggle led neither to a split in the Chinese party nor to a reign of terror. It did lead to a cautious reconstruction of the history of the CCP and its relations with the Comintern. Mao's modification of party history began soon after the Comintern was abolished in 1943, and was given its first definitive form shortly before the Seventh National Congress of the CCP.

On April 20, 1945, immediately before the opening of this Congress, the Seventh Enlarged Plenum of the Central Committee adopted Mao's "Resolution on Some Questions in the History of Our Party" (RSQHP).[1] This work was not published until February 1953, eight years after it was adopted and one month before Stalin's death. If the essay in its published form is accepted at face value, Mao's claim in 1945 that he had relied on Stalin's guidance in developing his theories of the Chinese revolution was an irony disguised in dialectic. In the sections of RSQHP dealing with his own military and organizational lines, Mao neither quotes from Stalin nor cites him as his authority. In the section dealing with ideological questions he does quote from Stalin, but without mentioning his name in the text.[2] Both the context and the unique manner in which the citation is given in the footnotes lead us to the conclusion that Mao had little respect for Stalin's foresight; moreover, his treatment of Stalin's political theses on the Chinese revolution and Stalin's ideological contributions to Marxism-Leninism is cautiously derogatory when it is not outright damning.

Mao does claim that his political line originates in three of Stalin's general propositions:

1. In China the main enemies of progress are feudalism and imperialism, and the main ally of the proletariat is the peasantry.[3]

2. One of the most important and distinctive aspects of the Chinese revolutionary struggle is that the forces of both revolution and counterrevolution are armed.[4]

3. Correct tactical direction in attack and defense must be based upon a correct analysis of the situation, correct forms of struggle, and correct forms of organization.[5]

Mao introduces Stalin's propositions with such innocuous phrases as "in line with Comrade Stalin," "Comrade Stalin said," and "as Comrade Stalin pointed out."[6] Throughout the whole of RSQHP he uses only one flattering adjective to describe Stalin's theses or statements—"clever" or "shrewd."[7] On the other hand, he makes no bones about the superiority of his own analyses of situations and his own judgments on tactical matters—he boldly declares that correct application of revolutionary theory is "best exemplified by Comrade Mao Tse-tung's direction of the Chinese revolutionary movement."[8]

Mao's attitude toward Stalin and all his works is made much more explicit in the Chinese text of HC than in the English translation. The Chinese version of RSQHP, for example, contains material omitted from the English. Consideration of this material will help us determine Mao's views on the relations between Stalin's theses and his own—views Mao was willing to publish for a Chinese but not for a foreign audience.

In RSQHP Mao writes that from 1921 to 1927, and especially from 1924 to 1927, "the great anti-imperialist and anti-feudal revolution of the Chinese people, under the correct guidance of the Communist International, and under the influence of the impulse given and the organizational work accomplished by the Chinese Communist Party's correct leadership, achieved rapid development and great victories."[9] In other words, the Comintern's guidance was correct *until* 1927.[10] But while its guidance was correct throughout the pre–1927 period, the directives issued by the Comintern and by Stalin in the first six months of that year were only clever and very numerous; never does Mao say they were correct.

Mao does state, however, that his own opinions were correct during the first six months of 1927, and he does not say at this point that his proposals were based on or identical with Stalin's directives. Although he points out that the CCP was guided and directed by

Stalin and the Comintern until the defeat of the Revolution in July 1927, he does not acknowledge any help or guidance from either Stalin or the Comintern after that date.[11]

Mao uses the literary device of parallel prose to point out the differences or contradictions between his theses and Stalin's, and between his position and his opponents'. He also uses it to contrast the correct line he was espousing with the erroneous lines followed by the leadership of the CCP in various periods before 1935. In the two sentences that introduce the first two paragraphs of Part II of RSQHP (see Table 1), Mao subtly contrasts the guidance of the Chinese revolution

TABLE 1

Two Parallel Sentences from the "Resolution on Some Questions in the History of Our Party"

*Part II, paragraph 1, sentence 1**	*Part II, paragraph 2, sentence 1†*
In the first period of China's new-democratic revolution, i.e. during 1921–27, and especially during 1924–27,	In the ten years from the defeat of the revolution in 1927 to the outbreak of the Anti-Japanese War in 1937,
thanks to the correct guidance of the Communist International and to the influence it exerted and to the impulse given and the agitation and organizational work done under the Chinese Communist Party's correct leadership,	the Chinese Communist Party, and the Chinese Communist Party was alone in this,
the great anti-imperialist and anti-feudal revolution of the Chinese people made rapid progress and scored great victories.	despite the counterrevolutionary reign of intense terror, continued with perfect solidarity to hold aloft the great banner of anti-imperialism and anti-feudalism and led the broad masses of workers, peasants, soldiers, revolutionary intellectuals and other revolutionary masses to wage great political, military and ideological struggles.

*Mao, SW, IV, 172.

†Mao, SW, IV, 173; HC, III, 956–57. This is my translation. Only two phrases vary from the translation in SW. In the second part of the sentence, the Chinese has "and the Chinese Communist Party was alone in this" where SW has "and it alone." In the second to the last phrase, the Chinese has "other revolutionary masses" where SW has "other revolutionary people."

by the Comintern from 1924 to 1927 (first paragraph) with its guidance by the CCP from 1927 to 1937 (second paragraph). The second clauses of the two sentences may be read as parallel and contrasting. Note that Mao omits any mention of guidance from the Comintern between the end of July 1927 and the beginning of the Anti-Japanese War. From 1924 to 1927, the CCP carried on its organizational and agitational work on the basis of directives from the Comintern. After 1927, the CCP had to work out its own political and ideological lines. If we compare what Mao writes about the work and struggle of the CCP in the two periods, we see that political, military, and ideological contests occurred in the Chinese party only in the second period. In these contests Mao neither claims nor disclaims help or direction from Stalin or the Comintern: he simply ignores them. Of course, he could hardly affirm that the Comintern's guidance had been correct in those years while still rejecting the lines followed by the party's leaders of the same period without falling into a desperate contradiction.

The clue to Mao's reconstruction of history is to be found in the treatment accorded to Mao and his ideas by the leaders of the CCP and the Comintern before the Maoists seized power in the Secretariat of the CCP at the Tsun-yi Conference in January 1935. In the long years of struggle before that date Mao was frequently out of favor with the dominant faction in the CCP Politburo. As we have seen, Chang Kuo-t'ao reports that Mao was expelled from the Central Committee three times between 1924 and 1935,[12] and Kung Ch'u records that Mao was imprisoned on the orders of the Politburo in the summer of 1934 because of his independent action at the time the Nationalist Nineteenth Route Army revolted in Fukien.[13] Mao himself has publicly acknowledged only one expulsion from the Politburo or Central Committee, a decision to that effect made by the enlarged meeting of the Politburo on November 15, 1927.[14]

It is probable that decisions of the CCP Politburo to reprimand or expel Mao were usually approved by the Comintern apparatus. In some cases the initial move may have originated in the Far Eastern Bureau of the Comintern in Moscow or with the ECCI's representatives or responsible instructors in China. The practice of the Comintern, like that of all Communist parties, was based on the principle of democratic centralism. In this formula centralism played a greater role than democracy. Each national party composed a national section of the Comintern. Formally, Central Committees of national sections were elected by lower bodies, but elections were usually manipulated so that the dominant faction in the CPSU retained control. The Comintern's decisions were binding on all Central Committees. Members could not resign from a Central Committee without permission from the ECCI, nor could a Central Committee expel members without ECCI confirmation. But the ECCI had unhampered authority to expel entire sections, groups, or individuals. In addition, it could and did send representatives and instructors to guide the work of the national sections. The prerogatives of these representatives and instructors were determined by the ECCI. Representatives had the right to participate in meetings at all levels and to speak against the majority of any committee that dared oppose the Comintern line.

Only two routes for appeal against decisions of the ECCI or its instructors were legally available. Party members subject to disciplinary measures could lodge complaints against their Central Committees with the International Control Commission. Under ordinary circumstances such an appeal would be ineffective. They could also appeal to the next World Congress of the International. Opposition factions in both the Russian and other parties attempted this at early Congresses, but never gained a favorable decision. After 1928, few such appeals were attempted.[15]

Since the central apparatus of the Comintern was located in Moscow and subordinate to the CPSU, any purge of the CPSU was accompanied by a similar purge of the Comintern. After the bolshevization of all Comintern sections, the purges extended outward from Moscow to the Politburos of other Communist parties. Mao's first expulsion from the CCP Politburo may have resulted from Stalin's attempt to bolshevize the CCP.

Stalin and the Comintern

The Third International was founded in Moscow in March 1919. Lenin, Trotsky, and Bukharin wrote the major theses accepted by the International's First Congress, and Zinoviev became its first President. Stalin may have been present, but he did not take part in the official proceedings. All voting delegates represented European parties, although there were a few Orientals in attendance. Korea and China were represented by men co-opted from among the leaders of the few resident Oriental workers whom the Bolsheviks had organized. Problems concerning the creation of new Oriental Communist parties were not under consideration.[16] The First Congress satisfied itself with only a skeletal organization, since everyone anticipated that a great revolution would soon erupt in Germany and that the next congress would meet in Berlin. It was not to be.

When the Second Congress met a year later in Moscow, the Bolsheviks had already won the civil war. The Red Army was marching toward Warsaw. Hopes for revolution in Europe were still running high, but Lenin feared the sectarianism of the new Communist parties. He therefore proposed that European Communists not only break away from the old Social Democratic parties, but also be ready to penetrate trade unions and participate in parliamentary activities in order to woo the proletariat away from its reform-socialist or petty-bourgeois political affiliations.

The delay of the European revolution indicated that attention should be given to methods of undermining capitalist power in the colonial half of the world. The Second Congress considered the problem of creating Communist parties in the East at great length, and ultimately adopted Lenin's basic thesis: the Comintern must create regular Communist parties in colonial and semicolonial countries, and these Communist parties must collaborate with bourgeois-democratic parties so long as the latter remain anti-imperialistic. M. N. Roy, an Indian nationalist revolutionary, proposed in a set of counter-theses that the new Communist parties should collaborate with national revolutionary parties in the common struggle against imperialism, but at the same time must oppose the bourgeoisie on class issues. The Dutch Communist Hendricus Sneevliet (known as "Maring"), who had recently organized the Communist Party of Indonesia and was by this time already in contact with Sun Yat-sen, suggested a third alternative: Marxists should join nationalist parties and build Communist factions within them. They should use these organizations to reach the masses, and when the inevitable split came should take as many members as possible with them into the Communist party. All three postures were taken in setting forth Comintern positions on the proper relationship between the CCP and the KMT during the 1920's.

Lenin and Roy disagreed on the relative importance of Asia's peasantry, proletariat, and bourgeoisie in the anti-imperialist struggle. Lenin, who had had some experience in organizing soviets in relatively backward areas in Russia, stressed the need for peasant soviets in colonial countries to struggle against the imperialist power, which supported landlords and other feudal remnants. Since, by Marxist definition, a peasant economy was bourgeois, it followed that Lenin supported bourgeois-democratic movements in the colonial countries. Roy saw less need for collaboration with bourgeois nationalists; as an urban intellectual, he emphasized building new Communist parties among the emerging proletariat in backward countries. But both comrades agreed that the Communists must always maintain an independent existence for their own organizations. Lenin was then advocating that European Communists break with the old Social Democratic parties of the Second International, and he was not about to contradict his own policy by subordinating Communist organizations to bourgeois parties in the colonies.

Lenin laid down the major premises underlying his theses on national and colonial problems in his opening speech to the Second Congress:

> The imperialist war drew the dependent peoples into world history; it is one of our most important tasks to find out how we should set about organizing the soviet movement in the noncapitalist countries. Soviets are possible there too; *they will not be workers' soviets, but soviets of peasants, or of laboring people.* . . . The second congress must work out practical instructions for making the work which has up to now been carried on among hundreds of millions of people in an unorganized fashion organized, uniform, and systematic.[17]

The world war, Lenin argued, had divided the world into oppressed and oppressing nations. Soviet Russia was the natural leader of the oppressed. Nonetheless, the great majority of people in oppressed nations were peasants, and a peasant economy—always and everywhere—was characterized by bourgeois-capitalist relations. Thus all existing national movements in the colonies had a bourgeois character. The true center of the struggle against imperialism, therefore, was in Europe, with its developed proletariat. The oppressed nations could bypass the capitalist stage of development only if the revolution succeeded first in the imperialist countries of the West.[18]

Roy, on the other hand, believed it was possible for the imperialist system to collapse in the colonies before capitalism collapsed in Europe. Russian capitalism had not yet reached its highest stage of development when the Russian proletariat, in alliance with the poor peasantry, had successfully overthrown the old order. The Communists could duplicate this feat in Asia by giving support to the struggle of the poorest peasantry and the proletariat, not by emphasizing alliance with existing national movements made up largely of urban bourgeois democrats (Roy differed from Lenin in wanting to organize only the *poorest* of the peasants). He also argued that in India rapid industrial development promoted by the war had given rise to a new proletariat, whose interests conflicted with those of India's middle-class nationalists. It followed that in India the Comintern should concentrate on the proletariat and the poor peasantry, supporting bourgeois nationalists only as long as they remained genuinely revolutionary.[19]

The differences between the two comrades were compromised by a verbal expedient, though Lenin's view was basically adopted. In the theses reported out of committee, Roy's term "national revolutionary" was substituted for Lenin's "bourgeois-democratic"; i.e., the Communists would support those anti-imperialist movements that were in fact revolutionary movements. The revised theses urged that revolutionary tendencies in peasant movements be encouraged, and that closer ties be established "between the west European Communist proletariat and the revolutionary peasant movement in the East."[20] This meant that peasant soviets might be organized in backward countries under the control of imperialist powers and be used as one of the weapons in the struggle against imperialism. There is even a hint in the theses that peasant soviets could be created to reinforce the fervor of liberation movements in the colonies before Communist parties in the West could organize proletarian parties in the East.[21] A crucial paragraph in the theses reads:

> It is particularly important to support the peasant movement in the backward countries against the landlords and all forms and survivals of feudalism. Above all, efforts must be made to give the peasant movement as revolutionary a character as possible, organizing the peasants and all the exploited wherever possible in soviets, and thus establish as close a tie as possible between the west European Communist proletariat and the revolutionary peasant movement in the East, in the colonies and backward countries.[22]

Lenin's theses on national and colonial questions undoubtedly reflected the experience of the Russian Communists in dealing with nationality questions within the borders of the old Tsarist empire. In Russian Central Asia, for example, where most Bolsheviks were Russians and Russians were an extremely small, privileged colonial minority, the Communists soon discovered that local nationalist leaders supported them only until they made the first moves toward overthrowing the existing economic order, to which local leaders responded by throwing out all Russians, including the Bolsheviks. The Soviet government then turned for allies to the local workers and peasants and began to attack the leaders of the bourgeois nationalist movements. The first institutions used to subvert bourgeois leaders were local soviets of the "toiling masses," hastily organized under the tutelage of Stalin's Commissariat of Nationalities. Those working in the Russian government knew that the organization of peasant soviets was in part fictitious, devised chiefly to give a gloss of popular approval to Moscow's destruction of autonomous national political institutions in the Russian east.[23]

The peasants and nomadic peoples of Central Asia — Uzbeks, Tadjiks, Turcomen, and Cossacks — certainly opposed the peasant soviets organized by the Turkestan Soviet Government in Tashkent, for its policies and actions undermined and destroyed old Islamic institutions in order to benefit the new Russian overlords. Like their Great Russian counterparts, the peasants of Central Asia (as well as those of North Caucasia, Transcaucasia, and the Ukraine) repeatedly rebelled against the arbitrary and excessive requisitions of food for the Red Army. In spite of sharp racial antagonism between the Russian settlers and the native peasantry, common economic and political grievances led to several unstable alliances between Moslem insurgents (the Basmachi led by Enver Pasha) and groups of Russian settlers in joint demands for freedom of speech, press, education, and trade, for abolition of the Chekas and the political commissars, and for an end to the state grain monopoly. Under the banner of Pan-Islam, the Moslem peasants of Central Asia continued their struggle against the new Soviet power until 1922, when the death of Enver Pasha left the movement leaderless. These Central Asian soviets were not instituted by the native peasants, but were forced on them by the Cheka in order to provision and supply the Russian Red Army. It is hardly surprising that after this experience with peasant soviets, most Russian Bolsheviks viewed Roy's plea for support of the toiling peasant masses only as a propaganda gesture that might win over some radical revolutionary leaders to the struggle against British and French power in India and the Middle East.[24]

As far as Lenin was concerned, nationalist leaders opposed to the British or French imperialists had to be used, even if they were opposed to Communism. When the proletarian revolution in Europe was victorious, Communist parties in power would call for national self-determination in their former colonies and assist newly formed Communist parties there to overthrow their landlords as well as the weak modern bourgeoisie. If the revolution in Europe came soon enough, peasant soviets and soviet governments might exist in some backward countries even before Communist parties could be organized, but Roy's notion that the Asian masses ought to rise against imperialism *before* the European proletariat could destroy its own capitalists was visionary. As Conrad Brandt has suggested, when Lenin called for a broad coalition of Communists with all nationalist groups in the colonies *and* for peasant soviets, he was thinking of successive stages of development rather than presenting mutually exclusive alternatives.[25] In 1920, Lenin and Trotsky still shared the belief that revolution in Europe was about to erupt and the world Communist order about to emerge. History still seemed to be developing in accordance with Trotsky's theory of permanent revolution. Lenin expected the world revolution to follow Trotsky's idea of what should have occurred in Russia after 1905: first a coalition with all national revolutionaries against the old order, then soviets of peasants and workers to ensure power for the Communist party in a victorious proletarian revolution. But by the time the great debate on the Chinese revolution broke out in 1927, Stalin and Trotsky were treating the two ideas as mutually exclusive. Trotsky saw soviets as the only possible means of saving the revolution, while Stalin insisted on continuing the broadest possible anti-imperialist alliance with all groups in the Kuomintang. Both men claimed to be followers of Lenin, and each relied on his own exegesis of Lenin's 1920 theses on the national and colonial question. Lenin, however, was no Leninist. His theses, devised to solve the tactical problems of 1920, were ill-suited to become guides for action in 1927, by which time hope for immediate revolution in Europe had faded and the political situation in China had made the two policies contradictory.

China itself did not figure in the debates at the Second Congress, but Maring, G. N. Voitinsky, and Yang Ming-chai were sent to China as Comintern representatives after the Congress ended. Maring was by that time a member of the ECCI. He represented Java, and was the only Far Eastern member of the Committee elected at the Second Congress except for the Korean, Pak. As a full member of the ECCI, Maring outranked Stalin, who was then only a candidate member. While Stalin certainly had more power than any non-Russian member of the ECCI, he was not yet using it to influence Comintern policy or personnel.[26]

In addition to Lenin's theses on the national and colonial question, the Second Congress also adopted his Twenty-one Conditions of admission to the Comintern, which were designed to split the Social Democratic parties in Europe. Lenin wanted to create truly revolutionary national parties, organized around a single world center. Each national section was to be an active and responsible part of a single whole whose purpose was to promote world revolution.

When Maring, Voitinsky, and Yang reached China, they brought with them the revolutionary hopes of the time and a formula for organizing new Communist parties. They were also searching among Chinese nationalist revolutionaries for possible allies who might be useful in the Soviet effort to undermine the power of the imperialists in the Far East, especially the Japanese, whose army was still occupying eastern Siberia and Manchuria. To extend and consolidate Soviet power over the whole of the former Tsarist empire, Chinese nationalists were of more immediate use than future Communists. Maring's suggestion that Chinese Marxists should join nationalist groups and build up Communist fractions within them probably accorded with Lenin's view of a proper course of action. Radical nationalist parties had to be strengthened before a viable Communist party could hope to split off from them.

Maring, Voitinsky, and Yang were neither intimates nor protégés of Stalin. Until Lenin's first stroke in 1922, Stalin and his close associates had very little to do with the appointment of emissaries sent to China by agencies of the International or the Soviet state. Most decisions concerning the International were made by Lenin and Zinoviev, and major decisions on the conduct of the civil war and Soviet foreign policy were made by Lenin and Trotsky. Stalin's activities were largely confined to internal matters in the Commissariat of Nationalities. After 1922, as General Secretary of the CPSU, he took a larger part in formulating foreign policy. His influence within the Comintern, however, remained limited as long as he was allied with Zinoviev against Trotsky. He gained control over the Comintern gradually, by the same means he had used to achieve power in the central organs of the CPSU—infiltration by his adherents into the bureaucratic apparatus superficially controlled by his enemies. Even before his break with the left opposition, Stalin was able to place enemies of his enemies in Comintern organs. He began to infiltrate the Comintern apparatus when the OGPU men Peter Stuchka and Josef Unschlicht were appointed to the International Control Commission in 1923. This was the ideal agency for ridding the Comintern of Trotskyism, for its major functions were to guard against Comintern deviations from the party line and to audit the accounts of all foreign sections. Stalin used his appointees to the ICC much as he had earlier used his appointees to the control commissions of the CPSU in fighting Trotskyites in the internal Soviet apparatus. Having successfully infiltrated the ICC with his own henchmen, he wrested from Zinoviev and Bukharin full control of the Comintern apparatus.[27]

In 1924 Stalin's men actively intervened in the Fifth World Congress of the Comintern, forcing it to declare that the organizational experience of the CPSU held universal implications for other Communist parties and that henceforth they must all pattern their organizational structure on the Russian model. Expressed in the slogan of "bolshevization," this meant that the regime of party secretaries Stalin had so recently imposed on the CPSU must be extended and that all territorial organization must give way to a system based on the factory cell. Taken together, these changes tended to reduce the importance of democratic procedures and to place the centralized administrative machine of each party in the hands of Comintern representatives, who in turn imposed Stalin's wishes.[28] From this time onward, quarrels among the members of the Russian Central Committee were quickly reflected in factional alignments in the Comintern. As the Stalinist faction increased its power within the CPSU, group after group was expelled from non-Soviet parties until only Stalinists remained. This process was completed more quickly in European parties with a Social Democratic tradition than in Asiatic parties created *de novo* by the Comintern.

In China, the process of bolshevization began in 1924, but very little was accomplished in the next three years because, as a fraction inside the KMT, the CCP did not have sufficient autonomy to bolshevize its organizational structure. Factional struggles in the CPSU were first reflected in China by changes in personnel: new Comintern representatives to the CCP, new Soviet military advisers for the KMT, new diplomats at the Soviet Embassy in Peking. These changes had little effect on the CCP, in which factions had been precipitated by indigenous issues before the struggle in Moscow made itself felt. Participation in the Nationalist Revolution engaged the members of the CCP in many passionate controversies concerned solely with China and internal Chinese politics. Russian politics seemed remote and irrelevant. It was only after the collapse of the United Front that Ch'en Tu-hsiu, who led the CCP until 1927, discovered that he agreed with Trotsky. Lesser figures in the CCP undoubtedly shared his experience.

Unlike the CCP, the Chinese Communist Youth Corps was only partially inside the KMT; it could therefore be reorganized along Russian Bolshevik lines before the CCP itself. The process began in

1924 under the direction of Jen Pi-shih, and in the following years the Youth Corps became more radical, more proletarian, and less willing to subordinate itself to the exigencies of collaboration with the KMT.[a] Those youth leaders who had been exposed to education in Moscow were more familiar with Russian factional controversies than many of their party elders, and when the KMT expelled the CCP in 1927, some of them were ready to label their ousted superiors in the CCP with epithets borrowed from the Russian factional controversy.[29]

Mao Tse-tung, the Non-Bolshevik Revolutionary

The great complexity of Chinese politics, the strenuous activities in which most members of the CCP were engaged within the KMT, and the factional strife in the Soviet Union after Lenin's death all made it very difficult for Chinese Communists to gain a broad comprehension of Marxism and to act like disciplined members of a Leninist-type party. Mao, for example, though an active revolutionary throughout the 1920's, was much too busy to master the fundamental Marxist categories. He was a revolutionary before he became a Communist. A natural leader of men, he found it difficult to subordinate himself to the strict party discipline inherent in a Leninist democratic centralist regime. Even after he absorbed the basic elements of Marxist thought and understood the use of the democratic centralist system in conducting inner-party disputes, he remained a revolutionary whose entire being was focused on the problem of victory for the Communists in China. He could not bring himself to subordinate the interests of the Chinese revolution to the interests of the Soviet state or the world revolutionary movement as Stalin perceived them. Mao's success must be attributed to his single-mindedness in pursuing his goal, and in his single-mindedness lies the basis for the present split in the world Communist movement. The end of the story was foreshadowed, although it could not be foretold, in its beginnings.

According to the growing Maoist legend, Mao had grasped the fundamentals of dialectical materialism before he was graduated from Hunan First Normal School in 1918. Mao himself has never been guilty of such an assertion. In his interviews with Snow in 1936, he declared of those early years, "I was then an idealist. . . . My mind

[a] Jen Pi-shih, for instance, supported Ch'en Tu-hsiu's desire to break with the KMT before Stalin and Borodin were willing to countenance such a break. Thus, willy-nilly, he associated himself with a man and a position that were soon labeled Trotskyite.

was a curious mixture of ideas of liberalism, democratic reformism, and Utopian Socialism. I had somewhat vague passions about 'nineteenth-century democracy,' Utopianism, and old-fashioned liberalism, and I was definitely anti-militarist and anti-imperialist."[30]

Mao absorbed a powerful dose of idealism under the tutelage of Yang Ch'ang-chi, who was his ethics teacher at First Normal and who later became his father-in-law. Yang was a disciple of the English philosopher T. H. Green. As the textbook for his senior class he used Friedrich Paulsen's neo-Kantian *System der Ethik,* as translated into Chinese by Ts'ai Yüan-p'ei, the anarchist chancellor of Peking National University.[31] "The Power of the Mind," an essay for which Mao received the highest mark in Yang's class, illustrates how deeply he was imbued with the ethical idealism of his teacher and how far he had to go to become a materialist:

> I say: the concept is reality, the finite is the infinite, the temporal is the intemporal, imagination is thought, I am the universe, life is death, death is life, the present is the past and the future, the past and the future are the present, the small is the great, the *yin* is the *yang,*[b] the high is the low, the impure is the pure, the thick is the thin, the substance is the words, that which is multiple is one, that which is changing is eternal.[32]

The dialectic running through this essay, which is written in classic parallel prose, appears to be deeply rooted in Chinese philosophy and heavily influenced by Hegelian and Kantian concepts, but shows no trace of Marxist emphasis on the importance of social classes and political systems.

Although not a precocious Marxist or Leninist, Mao rebelled against both parental and political authority with the fervor common to young intellectuals of his time. As an adolescent he resisted a marriage arranged by his father in the traditional fashion and refused to live with his wife. Also against his father's wishes, he left home to enter a modern school in a nearby county (hsien). He rejected his mother's Buddhism while still in middle school. He cut off his queue, the symbol of Chinese submission to the Manchu dynasty, at least a year before the fall of the dynasty. He joined the revolutionary army as soon as the Republican Revolution broke out in 1911. When Ch'en Tu-hsiu's journal *La Jeunesse* appeared in 1915, Mao was among the first to respond to its appeal. He objected to the effeteness of the traditional Chinese scholar and became an ardent advocate of physical education. His first published article, written in the traditional Chi-

[b] *Yin* and *yang* are complementary opposites in Chinese: weak-strong, female-male, soft-hard, moon-sun, dark-light, etc.

nese style, appeared in *La Jeunesse* on April 1, 1917. In it Mao appears as a nationalist, objecting to the Confucian stress on filial piety as an obstacle to the creation of national patriotism and a strong national army.[33]

Soon after the Republican Revolution Mao became one of the leaders of the rebellious student movement in Ch'angsha. A model student, quiet, older than most of his classmates, he was capable of defending himself and others, willing to speak out boldly against the injustices and brutalities that occasionally marred relations between students and teachers. Shortly after he was enrolled at First Normal, he helped a fellow student to cancel an arranged marriage by pleading the case with the headmaster. In 1915, he drafted a student manifesto accusing the headmaster of mismanaging the school's funds, and he would have been expelled for this rash act if four of his teachers had not intervened to save him. National political affairs led to another student protest in 1916, when news of President Yüan Shih-k'ai's ill-fated attempt to found a new dynasty reached Ch'angsha. On that occasion, Mao openly distributed pamphlets written against the president by Liang Ch'i-ch'ao. Soon afterward, when war between North and South was precipitated by Yüan's death, Mao organized the students to defend the school buildings. When marauding Northern troops occupied the school, Mao and other students borrowed rifles from a neighboring police station and, by surrounding the school at night and shouting that Southern troops had entered the city, convinced the Northerners to surrender and return the school to its regular occupants. Hunan had but one year of peace while Mao attended First Normal. In those troubled years, when all too frequently schools were occupied by soldiers and school funds pilfered by warlords, Mao's ability, courage, and self-control marked him as a leader among the students and won for him the respect of his teachers.[34]

From 1915 to 1918, Mao was an officer of the Ch'angsha Student Association, an organization through which he came in contact with all the politically active students in the provincial capital. He served as its secretary from 1915 to 1917 and became its general director in 1918, his last year at First Normal.[35] He found the interests and political inclinations of the students in this organization too diverse for unified action, however, and in the spring of 1917 he attempted to organize a group interested in physical education and patriotic work. According to Mao, three and a half students responded. The three were Lo Chang-lung, a future CCP leader expelled as a rightist in 1931, and two ultra-reactionaries whom he does not name. The "half" response was from Li Li-san, de facto leader of the CCP from 1928 to 1930, who soon decided he was not interested.[36]

In the following year Mao did successfully organize such a group, the Hsin-min hsüeh-hui (New People's Study Society), dedicated to "strengthening Chinese society through strengthening Chinese youth."[37] Many of the seventy or eighty members Mao recruited into this tightly knit organization soon became prominent in the CCP, and some later became part of the basic inner core of the Maoist faction. Among the NPSS's members were Ts'ai Ho-shen, Lo Chang-lung, Hsiang Chin-yü, Hsia Hsi, Hsiao Chen, Yeh Li-yün, Kuo Liang, and Ho Shu-heng (Ho Hsien-hon), all of whom were killed or expelled from the CCP before 1935; and Liu Shao-ch'i, Jen Pi-shih, Li Fu-ch'un, Wang Jo-fei, T'eng Tai-yüan, Li Wei-han, Li Li-san, Hsiao Ching-kuang, Ts'ai Ch'ang, and Hsiao Chu-chang (Emi Hsiao), all of whom were in the highest echelons of the CCP in 1945. Hsü T'e-li, a teacher at First Normal and later a prominent elder in the CCP, was among the patrons of the group, and Yang Ch'ang-chi, Mao's future father-in-law, was one of its chief sponsors.[38]

Similar radical student organizations were springing up all over China in 1918. Among the most important of those that later contributed members to the CCP were the Chou-wu hsüeh-hui (Awakening Society) in Tientsin, organized by Chou En-lai, Teng Ying-ch'ao, Ma Chün, and Sun Hsiao-ch'ing; and the Social Welfare Society in Wuhan, founded by Yün Tai-ying (Wen Teh-ying), Lin Piao, and Chang Hao (Lin Yü-nan).[39] There is no evidence that these organizations were inspired by the Russian Revolution or by Marxist organizers. Their purpose was to protest Japanese encroachments on Chinese territory during the First World War, to struggle against warlords who had sold out Chinese national interests to foreign imperialists, and to further the building of a new, strong, modern China. Their members were much more excited about remaking China and fitting themselves for the difficult times ahead than about events occurring in faraway Petrograd and Moscow.

Shortly after Mao's NPSS was formed, its founders graduated from First Normal and began to look for ways to continue their education. At this time several KMT leaders with anarchist sympathies and connections in France organized a work-study program, which enabled Chinese students without funds to finance European educations by working part-time in factories. Ts'ai Ho-shen went to Peking to find out about this organization and wrote back that members of the NPSS could qualify by coming to Peking and studying French. Many of the group did so, Mao among them. While he did not master French or go abroad, he considerably extended his circle of revolutionary acquaintances in Peking. Perhaps his most important acquaintance was Li Ta-chao, chief librarian of Peking National University and later a founder of the CCP, who gave him a job in the University library. Mao joined two student groups at the University, the Journalism and Philosophy Societies, in one or the other of which he met Chang Kuo-t'ao, one of the first members of the CCP (expelled in 1938); T'an P'ing-shan, a founder of the CCP expelled in November 1927; Ch'en Kung-po, another founder of the CCP, who left the party in 1923 and later became an adherent of Wang Ching-wei and a pro-Japanese traitor; Shao P'iao-p'ing, a versatile journalist executed by Chang Tso-lin in 1926; and Tuan Hsi-p'eng, first chairman of the All-China Student Federation in 1919 and leader of the KMT Anti-Bolshevik Corps in Kiangsi province after 1927.[40] Mao also met more prominent men, notably Ch'en Tu-hsiu and Hu Shih, but neither deigned to talk to a poor student who spoke only an uncultured southern dialect. Mao's best friends in Peking were anarchists, including his three roommates, Ch'ang K'ung-ti, Hsiung Kuang-ch'u, and Hsiao Yü, and another student, Chü Hsün-pei (Chü Sheng-pai), who influenced him most deeply. None of these students ever became Communists. They were advocates of mass action, mass education, and even revolution, but as anarchists they rejected political office for themselves and regarded all government and property as evil forces originating in usurpation and theft.[41] Introduced by these students to the books of Kropotkin, Bakunin, and Tolstoy, Mao became more radical and began to search more deeply for the roots of social evil and political injustice.[42] Mao left Peking in February 1919, after a stay of seven months. On his way home he passed through Shanghai, where he watched several of his best friends embark for France to take part in the work-study program. When he arrived in Hunan he founded a new student journal, the *Hsiang-chiang p'ing-lun* (*Hsiang River Review*), and he later took over and reorganized another journal, *Hsin Hunan* (*New Hunan*). Hunanese students were then agitating against Chang Ching-yao, the warlord governor of Hunan and a member of the pro-Japanese Anhwei faction. In December, Mao helped to organize a strike against the governor by students and teachers, as a result of which his journal and all student organizations were suppressed, and Mao himself was forced to flee to Peking. Chang Ching-yao executed much too freely for a man of Mao's stature to remain safely in the province after openly opposing him.[43]

The views Mao expressed in his Hunan journals were anti-militarist, anti-imperialist, and anti-foreign, but still not Marxist. His conversion to Marxism came only after his return to Peking. Throughout this second visit to the capital, Mao was under the personal influence of Li Ta-chao, who was rapidly moving toward a Marxist position. This is the time at which Mao himself began to seriously study Marxist ideas and consciously consider himself a Marxist, the time at which he read Marx's *Communist Manifesto,* Kautsky's *Class Struggle,* and Kirkupp's *History of Socialism.*[44] His Marxism, however, was not the Marxism of Lenin, whose works he had not yet read. He knew nothing of democratic centralism or Lenin's theories of the role of the party in relation to the proletariat. Kirkupp was an old-fashioned English Fabian. Kautsky opposed Lenin's red terror as well as his concept of the proletarian dictatorship.

Mao joined one of the first Marxist study circles in Peking, but his major concern was still the problem of ridding his home province of Chang Ching-yao.[c] This problem was solved for him in June 1920, when the Chihli faction[d] among the northern warlords came to power. Chang was forced to flee Hunan, and Mao returned home. Chang was replaced as governor by T'an Yen-k'ai, an old associate of Sun Yat-sen's who had been Hunan's first Republican governor in 1912. When Mao returned, T'an was reviving the educational system, which had been wiped out after the student strike the year before. Yi P'ei-ch'i, a local scholar appointed by T'an to head the First Normal School, assembled a new faculty and invited Mao to teach Chinese literature and head First Normal's primary school. Mao held this post from 1920 until the end of the school year in 1922.

It was late in the summer of 1920 when Mao arrived in Ch'angsha from Shanghai, where he had stayed for several months after leaving Peking. He brought with him translations of Communist literature, and in the fall he began to distribute it through the Wen-hua shu-tien (Culture Bookstore), which he established for that purpose. His

[c] He also joined the Young China Association, an extremely nationalistic student organization that opposed the Anhwei faction in the Peking government. Chang Wen-t'ien, later a leader of the 28 Bolsheviks, was also a member of the Young China Association at the time.

[d] The Chihli faction was allegedly pro-British. Wu P'ei-fu was its dominant figure during the 1920's. The province of Chihli is now called Hopeh; the name was changed when the capital was moved from Peking to Nanking in 1928.

bookshop dealt regularly with a similar enterprise in Wuhan run by Yün Tai-ying. In October 1920, Mao received a charter for the Socialist Youth Corps and established its first branch in Hunan. He and Ho Shu-heng, who had remained in Ch'angsha to run the affairs of the NPSS, personally recruited the society's most radical members into the Youth Corps. At the same time NPSS members in France, who had been in correspondence with their comrades in China, formed another Youth Corps unit. The first cell of the CCP in Hunan was formed soon afterward by separately organizing those members of the Youth Corps whom Mao considered most reliable. In June 1921, after the first cells of the Youth Corps and the CCP were established in Hunan, Mao and Ho Shu-heng went to Shanghai to attend the First Congress of the CCP, where Mao became one of the party's founders.[45]

Although by that time he considered himself a Marxist, he had probably still not read any of Lenin's major works. Since he knew no foreign language, his whole knowledge of Marxism and Communism was mediated through Chinese translations and personal contacts. He was by no means a theoretician and had nothing to do with formulating the theses of the First Congress. Ch'en Tu-hsiu, the comrade elected to lead the new party, still viewed him as a provincial nationalist, concerned solely with Hunan. The CCP and Youth Corps cells he recruited in Hunan consisted almost entirely of his fellow students, his own pupils, former teachers, intimate friends, and members of his family. He had few or no contacts as yet with the proletariat of Hunan; he scorned the peasantry and despised the village life from which he had emerged. He had nevertheless created from these personal sources the nucleus of the Maoist faction that was one day to rule China. Individual members of this Hunanese faction were later to appear in France, Moscow, Peking, Shanghai, and Canton as prominent leaders of the CCP. For the next five years, however, they formed a self-centered provincial clique, a marginal group in the CCP. It was not until 1926 that Mao's faction became important. In that year, when Hunan suddenly and explosively became the center of the most radical peasant movement in China, it was Mao's Hunanese Communists who precipitated the final break with the KMT and sealed the failure of Stalin's first major attempt to direct a revolutionary national movement outside the Soviet Union.

Mao's Affiliations in the CCP

Almost all the first members of the CCP were students. For the nucleus of the party, the first Comintern organizers wisely sought out intellectuals of national repute who had already shown an interest in Marxism and the Russian Revolution. Li Ta-chao and Ch'en Tu-hsiu, joint founders of the CCP, were famous educators and journalists, leaders of the iconoclastic, modernizing, anti-Japanese May Fourth Movement. Their first converts to revolutionary Marxism were students caught up in the modernist movement, striving to emancipate themselves from narrow family and provincial loyalties.

These old forms of Chinese social relations, however, did not die out easily. The traditional preeminent status of scholars, the persisting respect for elders, the old provincial scholars' guilds, and the finely graduated status system that classified students according to the year in which they passed examinations all tended to perpetuate the old forms of Chinese social relations even in the most radical, modern organizations. Students could create a society of equals most easily among those who had graduated in the same year from the same university. If a school drew students from all provinces, its graduates could find comrades throughout China; but if the school was a provincial academy, its graduates tended to form only provincial cliques. Traditional guild organizations perpetuated these cliques. Wherever students went, guild houses—organized on provincial or even hsien lines—provided lodging and food to those with proper introductions. As a poor student, Mao could not afford to live in the wealthy Hunan guild houses, and as a modern nationalist he sought friends from other provinces. Nevertheless, most of his intimate friends in Peking and Shanghai were from Hunan. Even though Hunan First Normal School possessed a national reputation, its students were recruited entirely from Hunan. The graduates of First Normal in 1918 and the members of the NPSS accordingly have a special significance, because in this social setting they were inevitably the group with which Mao's ties were closest. It was natural that Mao drew the first recruits to the Socialist Youth Corps and the first CCP branch in Hunan from among them. Most of Mao's intimates in the first party branches in other provinces were Hunanese of his student generation and members of the NPSS as well.

The Chinese social tradition required younger members of the CCP to look up to their elders in the party, particularly the men who had recruited them, as elder brothers rather than as equal comrades. But when party elders acted in a paternal or patriarchal manner, Mao was among the first to rebel, as he had rebelled against his father. Ch'en Tu-hsiu, a great scholar and an astute politician, never gained Mao's affection. Mao's chosen elder in the CCP was Li Ta-chao, who had been kind to him in Peking and had stimulated his first interest in Marxism. Li had two other claims to Mao's respect: he was a leader of the Young China Association, of which Mao was a member, and he had connections in the northern government, which controlled Hunan most of the time.

Mao's ties with Li and the Peking Communist cell were tightened by the fact that three of the first members of the Peking cell were from Hunan: Teng Chung-hsia, Liu Jen-ch'ing, and Lo Chang-lung. Liu and Lo were also members of the NPSS. Chou Fu-hai, who represented the Communist groups in Japan at the First Congress, was also from Hunan, but not a member of the NPSS; Mao's ties with him were never close. Li Ta, who joined in Shanghai, was from Hunan. Li, who was head of the Propaganda Bureau until 1923, left the CCP when it entered the KMT; Mao's relations with him have not been recorded. Mao's ties with the first groups formed in Canton, Tsinan, Wuhan, and T'aiyüan were less intimate because no Hunanese were members of those groups. Five out of the twelve representatives to the First Congress were Hunanese, representing Peking, Japan, and Shanghai as well as Hunan.[e]

All the members of the first cell Mao organized in Hunan were Hunanese, and the great majority were members of the NPSS: Mao himself, Ho Shu-heng, Hsia Hsi, Hsia Ming-han, Ch'en Yu-k'uei, Kuo Liang, Chiang Meng-chou, Hsiao Shu-fan, Lin Tsu-han, and Mao's brother, Mao Tse-min.[46] Most of these early comrades were slaughtered by the Nationalists after 1927, but Mao and Lin survived to be elected to the 1945 Central Committee.

In addition to Peking, the major strongholds of the Hunanese in the nascent CCP were France and the Soviet Union. Hunan contributed more students to the work-study group in France than any other province. The NPSS was one of the best organized of the Hunanese groups, and by 1920 it had become one of the most active groups among student workers in France. Mao's most intimate friend, Ts'ai Ho-shen (together with his wife, Hsiang Chin-yü, his sister, Ts'ai Ch'ang, and her husband, Li Fu-ch'un), Li Wei-han (also known as Lo Mai or Lo Man), Lo Hsüeh-tsan, Kuo Nung-chen, Ho Ch'ang-kung, and Chang K'un-ti (all members of the NPSS) joined with Chou En-lai, Li Li-san, Ch'en Yi, Wang Jo-fei, Jen Cho-hsüan (Yeh Ch'ing), Chao Shih-yen (Shih Yang), Ch'en Yen-nien, Ch'en Chao-nien, Teng Hsiao-p'ing, and Wu Yü-chang to form the first Chinese

[e] Various sources disagree on how many delegates attended. For a discussion of this point see Appendix A, "Note on the Delegates to the First Congress of the CCP and on the Party's Membership at the Time."

Socialist Youth Corps in France.[47] Ten of these founders of the Socialist Youth Corps in France survived to become members of the 1945 CCP Central Committee; four of them—Ts'ai Ch'ang, Li Fu-ch'un, Li Wei-han, and Ho Ch'ang-kung—were members of the NPSS, and Li Li-san was also from Hunan. The other survivors were drawn from three provinces: Chou En-lai from Hopeh; Wang Jo-fei from Kweichow; and Teng Hsiao-p'ing, Wu Yü-chang, and Ch'en Yi from Szechwan.

The second foreign center where students from Hunan congregated was Moscow. When the Communist University for Toilers of the East (KUTV) was established in Moscow in 1921 under the jurisdiction of Stalin's Commissariat of Nationalities, the first Chinese students to enroll were Liu Shao-ch'i, Jen Pi-shih, Hsiao Ching-kuang, Lo I-nung, and P'eng Shu-chih. They had attended the Comintern-sponsored foreign-language school in Shanghai in 1920 and joined the Socialist Youth Corps before they left China. Liu, Jen, and Hsiao were from Hunan and members of Mao's NPSS. Lo I-nung later worked with Mao in the peasant movement. P'eng Shu-chih took a different political course and achieved prominence before the others. After he returned to China he became Ch'en Tu-hsiu's favorite Russian interpreter. (He was expelled with Ch'en from the Central Committee in 1927 and followed him out of the CCP in 1929.[48]) Ch'ü Ch'iu-pai, a newsman employed by a Peking daily, arrived in Moscow one year before KUTV was established. His Russian was good, and he was employed as the first Russian-Chinese translator in KUTV. Ch'ü and the five students joined the CCP in Moscow and were among the founders of the main branch of the CCP in the Soviet Union.[49] The friendly relations established between Liu, Jen, Hsiao, Lo, and Ch'ü in Moscow were of great value to Mao in later years when Ch'ü became the dominant figure in the CCP.

Liu Shao-ch'i was among the first of the students in Moscow to leave KUTV. At the end of the first year he returned to Hunan, where he worked in the labor movement until 1923. Liu was undoubtedly the first of the Russian returned students to give Mao his impressions of Moscow, Russians, and the work-style of school administrators in the capital of the revolution.[50]

The Party of the Proletariat

The small group of intellectuals who gathered at the First Chinese Communist Party Congress set themselves one major goal: to become the party of the proletariat. To this end they organized a Trade

Union Secretariat, and within a year more than half of the CCP worked under its jurisdiction.

Before 1920, most Chinese workers were organized in guilds controlled by merchants. Sun Yat-sen's Revolutionary Party and the anarchists were the only political groups that had organized workers in China, and the unions they sponsored were largely confined to craftsmen in Canton and Hong Kong, and to Chinese merchant seamen the world over. The inspiration for building effective modern labor organizations in China originated in France among the 120,000 workers the Chinese government had sent there as part of its contribution to the war effort. A Labor Federation of Chinese Workers was established in France in January 1920, and returned workers' associations were organized in Shanghai and Canton the same year. Many of the 3,000-odd work-study students in France joined the French association. They could have made up nearly half its total membership of 6,000, and some of them must have been among the organization's leaders. As a result, many of the students returning to China from France between 1920 and 1924, as well as some of those returning from Russia, knew something about modern union organization.[51]

Mao began to organize the workers of Hunan in 1921. He led a delegation of students to Chao Heng-t'i, the governor of Hunan, informed him that they were socialists, and secured permission to organize labor unions. Then he set to work to organize Ch'angsha. He also made at least one short trip to the mines in the P'ing-hsiang and Liu-yang districts in the mountains east of the city. Li Li-san returned from France in late 1921, joined the Trade Union Secretariat in Hupeh, and soon afterward performed the extraordinary feat of organizing the Han-yeh-p'ing Company, the major iron and steel works in Wuhan. Although Li's Han-yeh-p'ing Union had its headquarters in Wuhan, it was this union with which the miners on the Kiangsi-Hunan border became affiliated.[52] Liu Shao-ch'i returned from Moscow early in 1922, and was sent to work among the coal miners of An-yüan and P'ing-hsiang. Liu assisted Li in organizing the first strike there in that year and was one of the the major leaders in the sympathy strike that followed Wu P'ei-fu's massacre of the railroad workers on the P'ing-han line in early 1923.

The first conflicts between Li Li-san and Mao probably centered on the question of union organization. Li's Han-yeh-p'ing Union was an industrial union, whereas Mao, as head of the Trade Union Secretariat in Hunan, was organizing the workers of Ch'angsha in city-wide craft unions. Liu Shao-ch'i, who had organized the miners of An-yüan, was caught in the middle. According to most later reports, the An-yüan miners were devoted to Li Li-san but were organized like Mao's unions, on anarcho-syndicalist lines. The An-yüan union, isolated on the mountainous Hunan-Kiangsi border, remained powerful long after most other North Chinese unions were suppressed.

Li Li-san and Liu Shao-ch'i continued to work in the area until 1924, when Li went to Moscow and Liu to Canton.[53] The mines were closed down in 1925 and the unions collapsed. The 100,000 miners who lost their jobs left the area as militant unionists. When the Northern Expedition reached Hunan in 1926, these former miners became the hard core of the armed workers' pickets in Ch'angsha, Hankow, and other cities of central China. These jobless Han-yeh-p'ing miners who had been organized by Mao, Li, and Liu were the first contingent of the lumpenproletariat to join China's Red Armies. They joined Yeh T'ing's Independent Division (the only division in the Nationalist armies made up exclusively of Communists and members of the Socialist Youth Corps), and took part in the Nanch'ang Uprising, Mao's Autumn Harvest Uprisings, and P'eng Teh-huai's uprising of 1928. Several years afterward, when Mao and Li became rival leaders of the CCP, both comrades had a claim on the loyalties of the members of the first and strongest Red union in central China, many of whom had since joined the Red Armies.[54]

Mao's work in union organization was interrupted when he went to Shanghai to attend the Second Congress of the CCP in the summer of 1922. According to Snow, Mao missed the Congress because he could find no comrades in Shanghai and "forgot the name of the place where it was to be held."[55] But there is a mystery here. Mao had an excellent reason for attending this particular Congress: he was at that time a leader of the movement to expel Chao Heng-t'i from Hunan, and the Congress's support in this enterprise would have been important to him.[f] Moreover, according to one recent report, soon after Mao arrived in Shanghai he had an interview with Maring, the Comintern delegate to the CCP. Having spoken his mind to Maring, he returned to Hunan without attending the Congress. In other words, he *had* met at least one comrade in Shanghai, and therefore assuredly knew where the Congress was held. The leaders of the Congress may well have decided beforehand not to sponsor the drive

[f] Chao had executed several workers the previous winter, and Mao had taken advantage of Chao's resulting unpopularity to build up strength for the Communists among the first labor unions in Hunan. (Snow, RSOC, pp. 158–59.)

against Chao Heng-t'i in Hunan, and therefore reprimanded Mao and refused to allow him to attend.[g]

This report is supported by some circumstantial evidence. Chao was a subordinate of Wu P'ei-fu, and Wu was still protecting Communist labor organizers in North China. The Trade Union Secretariat would presumably have been quite willing to sacrifice a small group of workers in Hunan in order to protect its rapidly growing strength in North China.

No support was available from Maring, either, for he did not believe that the CCP could build a firm proletarian base in China without allying itself with one of the radical democratic parties. Since there were few radical democrats in China outside Sun Yat-sen's revolutionary group, Maring was pushing the CCP toward alliance with the KMT. At the Hangchow Plenum in August, he suggested that CCP members join the KMT and work within it to win over the masses. Comrades working in the Trade Union Secretariat objected because labor unions controlled by Communists were still growing throughout North China under the patronage of Wu P'ei-fu. Ch'en Tu-hsiu also objected—he disliked Sun Yat-sen and had been working with Ch'en Chiung-ming, who had driven Sun out of Canton a year before. But Maring insisted, invoking Comintern discipline, and finally the CCP leaders capitulated and agreed to negotiate with Sun. Maring and Ch'en then met with Sun and worked out a tentative agreement allowing individual members of the CCP to join the KMT on the condition that they agree to obey Sun and follow his principles. Li Ta-chao publicly joined the KMT before the end of the year.

At the same time, presumably as a part of his agreement with Ch'en and Maring, Sun began to appoint secret reorganization committees with power to expel members of the KMT who refused to follow his directives.[56] Tung Pi-wu, an old KMT member and secretly a Communist, became the head of the reorganization committee for Hupeh. Wu Yü-chang played a similar role in Szechwan. Mao Tse-tung, Hsia Hsi, and Lin Po-chü, all Communists, were selected to reorganize the KMT in Hunan. This arrangement gave the CCP a special position in the Hunan KMT after 1922. Mao's reorganization committee was able to purge KMT members opposed to the entry of the Communists in the first reorganization, and by the time the First KMT Congress met in January 1924 it had turned the Hunan KMT into a radical underground party. Tung in Hupeh and Wu in Szechwan worked

[g] Confidential personal communication to me from a source I consider completely reliable.

to achieve similar results. Their efforts received initial approval from Sun, who employed T'an P'ing-shan, a Cantonese Communist labor leader, as his secretary in charge of reorganization.[57]

Communists in Hunan who were opposed to the new alliance, especially labor leaders like Li Li-san, soon began to attack Mao for neglecting the proletariat. Most Communists refused to join the KMT before Wu P'ei-fu suppressed the great railroad workers' strike in February 1923 and forced Communist organizers out of North China.

In the meantime, Maring's initiative had been approved by the Comintern, and a Soviet envoy, Adolf Joffe, having failed to open diplomatic relations with the Peking government, had negotiated an agreement with Sun that promised Soviet assistance to the KMT in its efforts to achieve a united, independent China. The CCP's entry into the KMT and the KMT's alliance with the Soviet Union can be considered, at least in retrospect, a Trotskyite policy. Maring left the service of the Comintern soon after Trotsky was dismissed from the War Commissariat, and Joffe, who committed suicide in 1927 in despairing protest against the purge of the United Opposition, never returned to China after 1923. The minority among the Chinese Communists who had supported Maring and Joffe against the majority led by Ch'en Tu-hsiu were suspect long after the Zinoviev-Stalin and Bukharin-Stalin combinations reaffirmed the Soviet policy of alliance with the KMT. Mao, who had supported Maring against the majority in 1922, soon suffered for his prescience.

Labor unions continued to flourish in Hunan until the spring of 1923, when Chao Heng-t'i, following the lead of Wu P'ei-fu, suppressed the great strike in the An-yüan coal fields and then ordered Mao's arrest. Mao hurriedly departed for Shanghai, where he worked for the Central Committee of the CCP until the end of the year, except for a trip to Canton in June to attend the Third Congress of the CCP.[58] According to later accounts Mao and Ch'ü Ch'iu-pai were responsible with Maring for the resolutions adopted at this Congress.[59]

The First Expulsion

Mao's first expulsion from the Politburo occurred in the fall of 1924. The Third Congress, in June 1923, had endorsed the entry of CCP members into the KMT. At that time Ch'en Tu-hsiu, acting under the orders of the Comintern, also pushed through a resolution to the effect that the CCP should share control of the labor movement with the KMT. Strong opposition to this resolution was led by Chang

Kuo-t'ao, then head of the Orgburo and the Trade Union Secretariat. In the first vote on this question Mao sided with Chang against Ch'en and Maring. After the opposition had lost by a one-vote margin, Mao shifted his vote to the side of the Comintern majority. He received his reward shortly after this Congress: in December 1923 he replaced Chang as head of the Orgburo. A month later he attended the First Congress of the KMT in Canton and was elected an alternate member of the Central Executive Committee. Then he returned to Shanghai to work with Wang Ching-wei and Hu Han-min, the KMT leaders there. Mao became so close to Hu Han-min that he was attacked by Communist party committees in Ch'angsha, Peking, and Hankow for displaying rightist proclivities. Under pressure, he allegedly resigned from both the KMT Central Executive Committee and the CCP Orgburo on the pretext of ill health, and returned to Hunan to recuperate shortly before the Fourth Congress of the CCP (January 1925). In fact, he was expelled from the Central Committee.[60]

One cause of Mao's "ill health" is apparent. Shortly after the Third Congress, the Comintern reversed its position on sharing control of the labor movement with the KMT. At the same time, Maring was recalled from China and replaced by Voitinsky.[h] Voitinsky not only cooperated with Ch'en Tu-hsiu in removing men whom Maring had promoted, but also repudiated Maring's views on CCP tactics within the KMT. Maring had instructed members of the CCP to join the KMT to broaden their influence among the masses while preparing to split the KMT at the first convenient opportunity. This tactic required that the Communists, in alliance with the KMT left wing, drive out the right wing and take over control of the KMT party organization. Voitinsky rejected this view. He insisted that the KMT should be split into right, left, and center. The Communists should work with the left wing but not recruit all its members into the CCP, as Maring had advocated. This would only drive many to the center and isolate the Communists. By cooperating with the left KMT, the center could be neutralized and the alliance with the right wing maintained as long as possible. At the same time, Voitinsky agreed that in order to remain a proletarian party, the CCP must organize the labor movement outside the KMT. The Comintern apparatus, under the control of Zinoviev and Stalin, supported this new interpretation of united front tactics in China.

Mao remained in the Orgburo after this shift in tactics, but Chang

[h] Within the year, Maring left the Communist Party to become the leader of the Left Socialists in Holland.

Kuo-t'ao regained some of his former prestige.[61] Enmity between the two dates from this episode. Mao's reputation as a member of the right wing can also be traced back to the time he gained his position on the Orgburo with the assistance of men who were to become Trotskyites. When Li Li-san later attacked Mao as "Hu Han-min's secretary," he was reminding his colleagues of this period in Mao's party career.[62]

CHAPTER III

The Destruction of the United Front

Mao Turns to the Peasantry

After retiring to Hunan in late 1924, Mao began to organize peasant associations near his home in Hsiang-t'an. He had first become interested in the organization of the peasant movement while he was in charge of the party's Orgburo in Shanghai. Organizing peasant associations in the colonies was one of the techniques devised by the Comintern to attract support for the USSR after the failure of the uprisings of 1923 in Germany and the recession of the active revolutionary movements in Europe. To this end, the Peasant International (Krestintern) was founded and held its first international congress in 1924, while Mao was still head of the Orgburo.[1] In the Far East, the Krestintern worked closely with the Communist Trade Union International (the Profintern).

The first serious effort to organize the Chinese peasantry was made in 1924, when the Communist-led Conference of Transport Workers of the Pacific decided to organize the peasants of Kwangtung because the coastal blockade against British goods, which had been instituted by the Nationalist government in support of the Hong Kong strike, could not be fully effective without the peasants' support.[2] Peasant organization proceeded slowly until May 1925, when the KMT held its First Peasant Congress in Canton. The resolutions of that congress emphasized that the "struggle must be concentrated in the city because the political center is located in the city; therefore, the working class must strive to lead the peasants to participate in this struggle."[3] At that time the peasant associations were not yet a well-organized force, even in Kwangtung province. But after the suppression of the strikes at the end of the summer of 1925, which left the rightists in control of the cities, students rushed out to work in the villages. By the end of the year, criticisms of the excesses of the peasant movement were already being expressed by both KMT and CCP leaders.[4]

When the First Peasant Congress was held, Mao was still in retirement, suffering from diplomatic indisposition at his home in Hsiang-t'an, but shortly afterward he actively began to organize the peasants of Hsiang-t'an and Hsiang-hsiang, some forty miles southwest of Ch'angsha. His efforts did not at first attract the attention of the authorities, but Chao Heng-t'i, his old enemy, became aware of his renewed activity when Mao went to Ch'angsha in June to take part in a demonstration precipitated by the May 30th incident (when British police fired on Chinese demonstrators supporting strikers in Shanghai). Chao issued an order for Mao's arrest, forcing him to flee Hunan and go to Canton, where he was invited to become Wang Ching-wei's secretary in the KMT Propaganda Department. In that capacity he edited *Political Weekly*, the official journal of the KMT, and even served for a short time as deputy head of the department in Wang's absence (in October 1925).[5] By the time Mao arrived in Canton, the peasant movement in Kwangtung was developing into an active militant force. Mao's interest in the Krestintern grew, and he participated when the CCP fraction in the KMT Propaganda Department worked out demands for radical agrarian reforms in the villages of Kwangtung.

The peasant associations in Kwangtung had been under Communist control since they were first organized in Hai-lu-feng by P'eng P'ai in 1922. Until late 1925, the peasant unions in Hai-lu-feng held a very special position because the area was controlled by the anti-Nationalist warlord Ch'en Ch'iung-ming. When the Nationalist army launched the First Eastern Expedition against Ch'en in 1925, the peasants of Hai-lu-feng demanded and received a 25 percent reduction in rents. Radical reforms in Hai-lu-feng served the KMT well; they undermined landlord power in territories held by the KMT's warlord enemies. No sizable opposition to the radical peasant movement in eastern Kwangtung developed among the more conservative landowning elements in the Canton organization of the KMT before 1925 because their own lands and rents were not directly threatened.[6] Thus Communists could support the radical slogans of the Hai-lu-feng peasant unions without endangering their position in the KMT, even though they dared not publicly support even rent reductions in the areas directly under KMT control.[7]

Wang Ching-wei, Mao's superior in the KMT Propaganda Department and a leader of the KMT left wing, certainly did not support peasant radicalism in 1925, and with good reason. The May 30th incident in Shanghai had provoked another general strike in Hong Kong. One hundred thousand strikers had moved in a body from Hong Kong to Canton, where they picketed to enforce the blockade against British imports. They demanded and received pay from the KMT provincial government and support from the Revolutionary Army for their activities.

The government badly needed funds to support the strikers, and those funds could come only from the landlords. But reductions in rent meant less money in the landlords' hands. Mao was aware of this simple fact, and in spite of his initial success in organizing peasant associations in Hunan he was primarily oriented toward the proletariat. The peasant movement was a useful ally, but it had not become the main revolutionary force in China. The best use of the peasant movement was still to undermine the warlord enemies of the Nationalists, provide troops for the revolutionary armies, and assist the workers in guarding the coasts to prevent the smuggling of guns to conservative traitors and the remnant armies still at their disposal in Kwangtung.

The KMT had such a low estimate of the peasants that it was difficult to find any prominent Nationalists willing to work in the Peasant Department. Communists accordingly held many influential posts in the Peasant Department of the Central Executive Committee (CEC) of the KMT in Kwangtung from the time the department was founded in February 1924 until after Chiang Kai-shek's coup in March 1926. The first head of the department was the Communist Lin Tsu-han, who had assisted Mao in the first reorganization of the KMT in Hunan. He was succeeded in 1925 by P'eng Su-ming, Li Chang-ta, and Huang Chü-su (all Communists), Liao Chung-k'ai (a non-Communist, assassinated in August 1925), and Ch'en Kung-po (who by that time had left the CCP). After the Second KMT Congress, in January 1926, Lin Tsu-han again became head of the department. When Chiang Kai-shek forced all Communists out of high office in the united KMT in May 1926, Kan Nai-kuang took over the department, which subsequently became disorganized and ineffective. Still another Communist, T'an P'ing-shan, served briefly as head of the department under the left KMT government in the spring of 1927.[8] Since the head of the Peasant Department frequently held other, more demanding KMT positions, the most powerful man in the department was usually the secretary. Only Communists held that post; P'eng P'ai was the first secretary and Lo Ch'i-yüan the second.[a] Al-

[a] After the Sixth Congress of the CCP, P'eng P'ai became the head of the CCP Politburo's Peasant Department. He was killed in the summer of 1929. His replacement, Lo Ch'i-yüan, remained head of the department until February 1931, when he was executed by the KMT at Lung-hua.

most all the department's organizers were Communists. Finally, the principals of the institute for training peasant leaders were Communists throughout the six-term history of the institute.[9] P'eng P'ai, Yüan Hsiao-hsien, T'an Chih-t'ang, and Lo Ch'i-yüan held that position during its first five terms. Mao himself was principal in the last term, May to October 1926.

Stalin Shifts to the Right

Throughout 1925 Comintern policy toward the Chinese revolution drifted steadily toward the left. The chief advisers to the KMT and the CCP—General Galen, Borodin, and Voitinsky—had been appointed to their positions before Lenin's death, at a time when Trotsky was Commissar for War and Zinoviev was Chairman of the ECCI. By the end of 1925, however, Stalin had split with the left wing in the CPSU and allied himself with Bukharin, who replaced Zinoviev in the ECCI. "Socialism in one country"—the primacy of Soviet state interests over those of the international revolution—now became the watchword of Soviet policy in China. It appeared to the new coalition in the Politburo that the capitalist system had stabilized itself, and that the time had come to regularize diplomatic relations with the imperialist powers. The Comintern could continue to assist revolutionary movements abroad, but not to the extent of endangering the economic recovery and foreign trade of the Soviet Union.[10]

In December 1925, after Stalin's triumph over Zinoviev and Kamenev, the Comintern apparatus aligned its policy with the interests of the Soviet state even more completely than before. The Comintern journal enunciated a simple criterion by which the policy of the CCP might be judged:

> The policy of the USSR has already converted the first stage of the proletarian dictatorship into a political ally of the Chinese liberation movement by giving to China powerful support in her struggle. The CCP should accordingly strive to take eventual account of the position of the USSR by bringing its tactics into line with the tactics of the RKP [Russian Communist Party].[11]

The line on China at this time was that the revolution would not succeed in the near future, and that the Comintern and the CCP should therefore seek to confine the activities of the KMT to Kwangtung, discourage the campaign against the warlords in the north, and maneuver carefully within the KMT to move it slowly to the left. In other words, the CCP should busy itself waiting for an auspicious change in the world situation.

As 1925 drew to a close, the KMT consolidated its hold on Kwangtung, eliminated the last threat from Ch'en Ch'iung-ming's army in the east, brought the warlords of Kwangsi, to the west, into the Nationalist camp, and negotiated a secret agreement with T'ang Sheng-chih, an officer in Chao Heng-t'i's Hunan army who was preparing a revolt within Wu P'ei-fu's army in Central China. After Sun's death in Peking in March, the Kwangtung KMT leaders had moved toward the left. In September Hu Han-min, Mao's old comrade in Shanghai, hurriedly departed for Moscow after being implicated in the assassination of Liao Chung-k'ai, the most sturdy non-Communist leftist in the KMT. Borodin and Chiang Kai-shek then eliminated Hsü Chung-chih, the last of the older generation of Sun Yat-sen's Cantonese warlord supporters. The leaders of the KMT right wing responded to this leftward trend in November. Meeting at Sun Yat-sen's grave in the Western Hills outside Peking, they voted to expel the Communists and Wang Ching-wei (the new leader of the left wing) from the KMT, dismiss Borodin, and dissolve the left-dominated KMT Political Council in Canton.[12]

At about the same time, the Soviet advisers in Canton began to take control of the KMT military apparatus. Russians took over the Navy and Aviation Bureaus. A Russian intelligence agent, Victor Rogachev, became head of the General Staff Communication Department and urgently requested that it be designated the chief administrative organ of the Revolutionary Army. Kisanko, a high-ranking commissar of the Soviet Red Army who had arrived in Canton in October 1925 to replace Galen as chief of the Soviet advisory group, supported Rogachev's initiatives and further attempted to place Soviet advisers in all policy-making posts in the Revolutionary Army.[b] He also picked a quarrel with Borodin, attacking him for trying to

[b] No information about Kisanko's identity has been found in Soviet sources. F. F. Liu identifies him as A. S. Bubnov, who was then a member of the Central Committee of the CPSU and head of Political Administration (PUR) of the Soviet Red Army. (F. F. Liu, *A Military History of Modern China,* Princeton, N.J.: Princeton University Press, 1956, p. 23.) According to E. H. Carr, this identification is undoubtedly an error. Kisanko arrived in Canton in late October, and replaced Galen on November 1, 1925. He was placed under house arrest by Chiang Kai-shek during the March 20 coup. Chiang then demanded that Kisanko, his deputy Rogachev, and eight other Soviet advisers who were personally hostile to Chiang be immediately withdrawn. The two most powerful Russians in Canton at the time, Soloviev and Kubiak, acceded to Chiang's demand. (Soloviev was a counselor of the Soviet Embassy in Peking; Kubiak was Secretary of the Far Eastern Bureau of the CPSU and leader of a delegation to the KMT from the Central Control Commission of the CPSU.) Kisanko and Rogachev left Canton on the night of March 24, 1926. Bubnov probably was not in Canton during this period, although he may have been in Canton earlier, before taking over the Political Administration of

influence the civilian organs of the KMT, which were then dominated by the left, and for trying to play the military and civilian wings of the party against each other. Kisanko also began to send messages to the Soviet Ambassador in Peking accusing Borodin of carelessness in using the secret Soviet military code.[13]

Kisanko and Rogachev must be identified with the rising Stalinist faction in the Soviet military establishment. Their maneuvers against Borodin within the Soviet advisers' group tended to increase the tensions between the civilian wing of the KMT, led by Wang Ching-wei, and the military officers, among whom Chiang Kai-shek now emerged as the dominant figure. At the same time, their maneuvers in Revolutionary Army headquarters alienated Chiang and his Whampoa cadets from the Cantonese military leaders and increased the tension between Communists and non-Communists among the Whampoa cadets.[c] Evidently the aim of the new Soviet advisers was to make Chiang their puppet and isolate him from his Chinese supporters. Had they succeeded, Chiang would have become so dependent on Soviet aid that he could not have begun his drive to the north without Russian consent.

But the Stalinists underestimated their man. Borodin, although he

---

the Soviet Red Army. He visited Canton at least once in 1926, probably in May or June, returning with a recommendation that Moscow support the Northern Expedition. (Carr, *Socialism in One Country*, III, Part 2, 728*n1*, 761, 777–80.)

[c] The Whampoa Academy was founded in 1923 on the outskirts of Canton to train politically reliable officers for the KMT Army. Chiang Kai-shek was appointed its head, and General Vassili Blücher (known as Galen) acted as his chief military adviser and chief of staff. Galen held this post from 1923 until November 1925, when he was replaced by Kisanko, and again, at Chiang's request, from the summer of 1926 until August 1927. Some forty Soviet officers taught in the academy. Chou En-lai was appointed Chiang's deputy political commissar, and also acted as chief of the military committee of the CCP Kwangtung Regional Committee. Under his direction, cadets with Communist sympathies were organized as the League of Military Youth. In May 1926 the conservatives expelled members of the League from the academy. Most of the Communists joined Yeh T'ing's Independent Division during the Northern Expedition, while others made themselves available for picketing or joined the armed units of the peasant associations. In early 1926 the academy was reorganized and renamed the Central Political and Military Academy. In 1927 it was moved to Wuhan, where it fell under the influence of the left KMT. After the collapse of the United Front it was moved again, to Nanking.

The Whampoa cadet faction in the CCP can be defined as those Communists who graduated from the Whampoa Academy before May 1926. The great majority had been members of the League of Military Youth. As professional officers, most of them objected to Mao's guerrilla tactics, and few were won over to his military point of view before 1935. Lin Piao was the first and for a long time the only Maoist in the faction. Chou En-lai was its acknowledged leader, and he usually led the CCP Military Committee until 1935. Chou argued against Mao's theories of guerrilla warfare until at least 1938, and probably was not completely won over until the first party rectification movement in 1942–43.

disliked Chiang, was a better judge of his willfulness, his ability, and his political acumen. Aware that Chiang resented the Stalinists' efforts to control him, Borodin was wary of forcing him into a position where he could preserve his autonomy only by breaking with the Russians.

While the Soviet advisers were attempting to gain control of the KMT military, the Comintern was urging the CCP to consolidate its hold on the revolutionary mass movements in Kwangtung, expand its membership there, and create a party capable of taking over control from the KMT at the local level. The CCP had already organized many workers in Canton, but the new CCP members were almost all concentrated in the KMT's central administrative organs. Few were available to take over KMT hsien party organs, to say nothing of party headquarters in other provinces. The Communists could capture power in China from within the KMT only if they could consolidate their control of the KMT at all levels before the revolutionary movement expanded beyond the narrow confines of Kwangtung. The Comintern therefore instructed them to discourage the idea of a Northern Expedition until they had a disciplined mass party at their disposal.[14]

Communist influence was strong in the central headquarters of the KMT. T'an P'ing-shan was in charge of the KMT Organization Department, and 26 of the 29 persons working under him were Communists. Mao, as Wang Ching-wei's secretary, controlled much of the daily business of the Propaganda Department. Three of the five men running the KMT political training classes were Hunanese Communists: Mao, Lin Tsu-han, and Li Fu-ch'un. Lin was in charge of the Peasant Department as well. There were Communist secretaries in the Labor, Youth, Overseas, Merchants', and Women's Departments, and the chief secretary at central party headquarters was a Communist. At the Second KMT Congress, in January 1926, the Communists numbered approximately one-fifth of the Central Executive Committee and one-third of its Standing Committee. Communists were also quickly penetrating the political departments of the First Army. But they held only a thin layer of high-level positions, for there were fewer than 2,000 Communists in all China who had been in the party for a year or more.[15]

At the Second KMT Congress Chiang Kai-shek demanded that plans be drawn up immediately for a Northern Expedition. Borodin, supported by the Communists and part of the left KMT faction, refused to give his consent, which was necessary to obtain Soviet aid.[16]

Soviet embroilment in the politics of North China had created a need to restrain the Nationalists in the south. For some months the Soviet-supported warlord in North China, Feng Yü-hsiang, had been fighting a losing war against the Japanese-supported warlord of Manchuria, Chang Tso-lin, and his ally Wu P'ei-fu, the most powerful warlord supporting the Peking government. Chang was also becoming increasingly belligerent toward the Soviet Union. By early March 1926 Feng's defeat seemed imminent, as did war between Chang and the USSR, and the whole Soviet position in Manchuria and North China was in danger. At this point the CPSU Politburo appointed a special commission to consider Far Eastern policy. Trotsky chaired the commission, an indication that he and Stalin had not yet split over China.[17] After considering the commission's report, the Politburo agreed that the distribution of power in North China must be maintained in its current state. In order to do this, Feng and his National Revolutionaries were to cease their activities in the north for the moment. Japan's de facto control over southern Manchuria was to be recognized. So was Chang's control over northern Manchuria, in return for an agreement on his part not to move against the south.

The Politburo wanted at all costs to avoid giving the impression that the Soviet Union was about to divide China into spheres of influence, in the old imperialist manner. Revolutionary, anti-imperialist propaganda was therefore encouraged; agreement to the new tactics was sought from the CCP and the KMT. But while denying that China was again to be divided up, the Politburo in fact treated each autonomous area as a political entity and the Republican government in Peking as the mere shadow it was fast becoming. These Politburo decisions implied that the Soviet Union would not encourage any move by the Nationalist armies beyond the borders of Kwangtung and Kwangsi. Stalin himself formulated this position explicitly in an amendment to the commission's resolution on China policy: "The Canton government should in the present period decisively reject the thought of military expeditions of an offensive character, and, in general, of any such proceedings as may encourage the imperialists to embark on military action."[18] Evidently no one among the Politburo members believed that Chiang Kai-shek would dare embark on a military expedition without the approval of his Soviet advisers. Obviously they had misjudged their man, who had secretly been preparing his way for several months. While the Politburo meeting was still in session, Chiang arrested his Soviet advisers and cleared the way for military action.

A month before Mao was to give his report to the Second KMT Congress, Communist labor organizers fleeing from Hunan had brought him news that Chao Heng-t'i had sent an armed regiment into An-yüan to break the miners' strike. The Communist director of the union had been shot, many miners killed, and the union suppressed. Burning with rage, Mao immediately left for CCP headquarters in Shanghai to organize a campaign against Chao.[19] To his dismay, however, Ch'en Tu-hsiu refused to sponsor his campaign. The Central Committee of the CCP, falling in line with the Comintern, had just voted to confine the KMT movement to Kwangtung, and Ch'en presumably reasoned that a campaign against Chao would look too much like encouragement for Chiang Kai-shek and the right wing of the KMT, who were then demanding immediate preparations for the Northern Expedition. It was at this time that Mao wrote "The Class Basis of Chao Heng-t'i, and the Tasks Before Us" and his "Analysis of the Different Classes of Chinese Society." Neither article, according to Mao, was acceptable to Ch'en, who refused to publish them in *Hsiang-tao* (*Guide Weekly*), the official Communist journal. The attack on Chao was published as a pamphlet in Hunan. Mao told Snow that he had first proposed a radical land policy in his "Analysis of Classes," and, after Ch'en refused to publish it, had published it in *Chung-kuo nung-min* (*Chinese Peasant*).[20] A much revised version of this work, now dated March 1926, introduces the first volume of HC.[21]

Actually, the first articles Mao published in *Chinese Peasant* on the analysis of classes in Chinese society appeared in January and February 1926.[22] The revised versions in HC bear little resemblance to the originals. Two deletions are of special significance. The first is a sweeping analogy: "The attitude of the various classes in China toward the national revolution is more or less identical with the attitude of the various classes of Western Europe toward the social revolution."[23] This position was much closer to Trotsky's than to either Lenin's or Stalin's, which may have been Ch'en Tu-hsiu's reason for refusing to publish the article. The second deletion of interest is Mao's enumeration of the five subdivisions of the lumpenproletariat: soldiers, bandits, robbers, beggars, and prostitutes. In the original article, Mao identifies the whole of the lumpenproletariat with peasants who have lost their land and handicraftsmen who have lost their livelihood. He holds that they can fight bravely and, if properly led, can become a revolutionary force. (In 1951 he added that they also tend to become destructive.)[24] The issue of the lumpenproletariat was becoming important in late 1925, as bandit forces in

Kwangtung became the objects of competition between the KMT, which sought to incorporate bandits into its own armies, and the Communists in the KMT Peasant Department, who sought to attach them to the peasant self-defense corps.[25] Since the KMT refused to issue weapons to the Peasant Department, the bandits were one of its few sources of arms. Moreover, the Communists hoped to capture leadership of the unemployed peasants in the bandit gangs, either by winning over bandit leaders or by inciting the ordinary bandits to overthrow their leaders and reorganize themselves into peasant self-defense corps under Communist control. In his article on peasant classes, Mao urged that bandits be allowed to join the peasant associations, which should in turn help them find employment.[26]

From the Marxist point of view, Mao's analysis of classes was full of errors. He divided Chinese society into upper, middle, and lower strata primarily on the basis of wealth and property. Thus he identified the big landlords (which Marxists identify as a feudal class) with the big urban bourgeoisie (which Marxists identify as a capitalist class). He thereby confused two distinct stages in the Marxist theory of historical development. Mao had yet to master the distinction between feudalism and capitalism. He saw the bourgeoisie simply as owners of property, and the proletariat as the propertyless. Therefore he put landlords in the same class with capitalists, and landless peasants in the same class with modern industrial workers. The only characteristic distinguishing soldiers, bandits, robbers, beggars, and prostitutes from all other persons who owned no property was that members of these groups, usually through no fault of their own, had lost access to respectable ways of earning a living.

While no trace of Mao's radical land policy proposals of this period remains in the 1951 version of this article, its January 1926 version concluded with a plea that especially evil and corrupt landlords, those who refused to lower rents and interest payments, be driven out of the countryside by the peasants.[27] The peasants of Hai-lu-feng were already doing this. The question Mao posed to the CCP and Ch'en Tu-hsiu was simple: should they support the radical actions of the peasants even if this increased the existing tension between Nationalists and Communists in the KMT? Actually, the Central Committee had already answered this question in the negative before Mao's articles appeared. In October 1925 an ad hoc peasant commission of the Central Committee had tentatively suggested that the time had come for the CCP to begin popularizing the idea of land confiscation. The Central Committee rejected this notion and, in a letter to the peasantry issued in late October, invited the peasants only to join peasant associations and form self-defense corps, for it felt the time had not yet come to urge the peasants to go beyond the limits of self-defense.[28] By this time Mao Tse-tung, the Kwangtung Provincial Committee, and the aroused peasants of Hai-lu-feng had all gone beyond these limits laid down by the Central Committee and its cautious Comintern advisers, who still hoped to continue the alliance with the KMT.

Chiang's Coup

When KMT unity appeared threatened by the growing militancy of the peasants' and workers' movements and the increased strength demonstrated by the Communists at the Second Congress of the KMT in January 1926, Chiang Kai-shek acted. In March 1926, on the pretext that the Communists and Wang Ching-wei had been planning a coup against him, he arrested most of the prominent Communists in Canton and placed the KMT's Russian advisers under house arrest. He excluded all Communists from responsible positions in the KMT party, government, and army, expelled Wang Ching-wei, halted the Hong Kong general strike, and demanded that the Northern Expedition begin immediately. He also sent off a telegram to Moscow respectfully requesting that certain Soviet advisers be recalled, including Kisanko, Rogachev, and V. V. Kuibyshev, a prominent member of the CPSU Central Control Commission who was then in Canton. Chiang also requested that Galen remain and that Borodin return to Canton from Outer Mongolia, where he had gone to persuade Feng Yü-hsiang to join forces with the KMT. Chiang's requests were granted: the Russians he disliked returned to the Soviet Union, and Borodin returned from Mongolia to acquiesce in his demand for Soviet support of the Northern Expedition. In the meantime, Wang Ching-wei and several members of the KMT left wing fled from Canton, and several of the more prominent members of the right wing arrived there from Shanghai. Members of the extreme right wing left Canton as part of Chiang's bargain with Borodin, but the Communists who had been expelled from office did not return. T'an P'ing-shan went to Moscow, and Chiang himself took over T'an's position as head of the Organization Department. Li Chih-lung left the Naval Bureau and went to Shanghai to work in the CCP Politburo. Chou En-lai left the Whampoa Academy to work with Li Lisan in the Shanghai labor movement; he was replaced by T'an Yen-k'ai, the Hunanese governor under whom Mao had received his position at First Normal. Lin Tsu-han and Lo Ch'i-yüan left the Peasant Department. Lo went to Hai-lu-feng to work with P'eng P'ai; Lin was replaced by Kan Nai-kuang, but soon reappeared as the chief political officer in Chiang's First Army.[29] Mao lost his position in the Propaganda Department to Ku Meng-yü (who characterized peasant activity as "a movement of vandals, scoundrels, and idle peasants"[30]), but managed to retain his position as principal of the Peasant Institute, although most other Communists holding positions of similar rank in the KMT had been dropped. Chiang may have retained Mao because he knew or suspected that Mao was not in agreement with other high-ranking Communists on the peasant question, but it is far more likely that Chiang felt he could not afford to alienate T'an Yen-k'ai and other Hunanese leaders of the KMT. The Northern Expedition was about to be launched into Hunan, and the rising military men in the KMT were Hunanese. Since Soviet agents were already on the lookout for an officer as able as Chiang who might also be more responsive to their directives, it was wise for Chiang to remain on good terms with as many powerful men in the Hunanese branch of the KMT as he could. Mao Tse-tung and Lin Tsu-han were among those he decided to favor.[d] Like the Communists, Chiang could play the game of driving wedges among temporary allies in order to gain time to broaden and consolidate the base of his own power in the party.

After Chiang's coup, the Kwangtung Communists took a more radical position than either their Soviet mentors or the CCP Central Committee in Shanghai. The Comintern advisers urged them to unite with the left wing of the KMT, neutralize the center, and hold on to the right wing as long as possible. However, the Kwangtung Provincial Committee (according to the Central Committee) believed that there was no longer an independent left in the KMT organization: the workers and peasants were the only true left, and the only alternatives were to unite with the right against the workers and peasants or unite with the workers and peasants against the right.[31] In inner-party circles Mao appears to have shared these views. If he did not fully share them, he frequently acted as a representative and spokesman for those who did. As the revolutionary armies marched northward, he became a partisan of T'ang Sheng-chih and opposed

[d] T'an Yen-k'ai's power in Chiang's entourage also may account for the reappearance of Hunanese Communists such as Lin Tsu-han in Chiang's First Army.

Chiang, as did almost every Communist from Hunan.[e] Stalin, however, did not drop Chiang until he turned on the CCP and wiped out the Shanghai labor movement the following April.

The Northern Expedition, which began in the summer of 1926, gave the Communists a new opportunity to expand their influence. The student agitators Mao had trained in Canton swarmed out into the countryside ahead of the advancing KMT troops and led the peasants' attacks against towns and cities. In Kwangtung, in Kiangsi, and especially in Hunan, the peasant movement exploded into a militant force. Peasant associations became de facto village governments and were soon so powerful that it was difficult for the newly established KMT provincial government to collect taxes. The leaders of the CPSU were disturbed by this turn of events, and in October Stalin dispatched a telegram ordering the CCP to restrain the peasant movement in order to avoid antagonizing the KMT generals in command of the Northern Expedition.[32] Mao was directly responsible for this disturbing development. In July, or possibly in March,[f] he had been summoned to Shanghai to become the head of the new CCP Peasant Department. Mao found no peasants in Shanghai (and also continued to find it difficult to work with Ch'en Tu-hsiu), so by August he was again in Hunan. There he directed the peasant movement for the next five months.

[e] In January, T'ang Sheng-chih had secretly agreed to join the Nationalists at the first auspicious moment. That moment came in March, when he forced his old superior, Chao Heng-t'i, out of office. Within the month Wu P'ei-fu came to Chao's rescue and drove T'ang's forces out of northern Hunan, backing them up against the Kwangtung border. (Clubb, p. 133.)

T'ang immediately asked the Nationalist armies in Kwangtung for assistance. He appeared to be allied with the left KMT and generally opposed to Chiang Kai-shek. At the beginning of the Northern Expedition the KMT's Russian advisers saw to it that T'ang received ample assistance, sometimes at Chiang's expense. (Wilbur and How, pp. 416–18.)

[f] Mao may have gone to Shanghai to take over the new CCP Peasant Department shortly before Chiang's March coup. Jerome Ch'en interprets Mao's interview with Snow in this way. (Jerome Ch'en, p. 102; cf. *Materials of Modern History* [55], I, Part 2, 136, and IV, Part 3, 346.) If this was the case, Mao returned to Canton before March 30, when he attended a meeting of the KMT Peasant Department. (*Chinese Peasant,* No. 5 [May 1, 1926], pp. 1–12.) All sources agree that Mao was principal of the Peasant Movement Training Institute during its sixth term, May 3 to October 26, 1926 (*Chinese Peasant,* No. 4 [April 1, 1926], p. 5), but he certainly was not in Canton continuously from March to October; he is reported to have been in Shanghai after the March 30 meeting, and he went to Hunan to take charge of the peasant movement there sometime in August or September. (Chang Tzu-sheng, "Chronicles of the Northern Expedition," *Eastern Miscellany,* August 10, August 25, and September 10, 1928, [4]; Mao Ssu-ch'eng [76], VIIIc, 105b–112b.)

When Ch'en Tu-hsiu received Stalin's October 26 telegram he summoned a Plenum of the Central Committee, which met in Hankow on December 13. That Plenum decided that the northern warlords could not be defeated by an army divided on class lines. It followed that Communist officers should not carry on their own propaganda in the Nationalist armies, peasants and workers in the armies should not be recruited into the CCP, peasant associations in the villages should not be armed, and the land problem should not be discussed.[33] It was at this time that Ch'en Tu-hsiu appointed Mao inspector of the Hunan peasant movement, and it is highly likely that Ch'en ordered Mao to restrain the peasantry—a mission Mao had no intention of carrying out. In a speech delivered to the Conference of Peasant Delegates in Ch'angsha on December 20, Mao declared that the peasant problem was the central issue in the national revolution. Until it was solved it would be impossible to defeat the imperialists and the warlords and develop Chinese trade and industry.[34] Immediately after this conference the Hunan peasant associations, under Mao's leadership, began to confiscate and redistribute land. In a number of hsien they continued doing this until the following May.[35] They also began to take over mission stations as administrative headquarters. In Ch'angsha hsien alone, six of the eight substations of one mission society were taken over in December 1926. The Wuhan government ordered the peasant association to return the substations to their owners in February, but the peasants seized them again in late March and early April, when foreigners were evacuated in the wake of the Nanking incident. The Provincial Peasant Union itself took over five residences belonging to the YMCA and the Theological Institute in Ch'angsha, and was not dispossessed of them until the night of May 21, when, after a pitched battle, its forces were driven out by the troops of Hsü K'o-hsiang.[36]

Hsiang-hsiang, the home of Ts'ai Ho-shen, was reputed to be one of the most radical districts in Hunan. In most places the peasants only took over empty buildings, and declared them to be the property of the Chinese people and subject to the "people's power."[g] But in Hsiang-hsiang missionaries were actually ordered out of their homes. In a single four-week period, the peasant association there executed some twenty persons under the authority of the "people's power." The peasant association, under the same guise, also organized the "People's Food" to commandeer hoarded rice before the

[g] At that time, Communist agitation for a general strike in Shanghai was conducted under the slogan of the "People's Power."

spring harvest. Most of it was distributed at low prices to peasants on the poor list. The excess rice was sold on the open market and the money ostensibly used to establish schools for poor peasants, but some of it was undoubtedly spent for weapons for the peasant self-defense corps. In some areas, the "People's Food" gave ceremonial feasts for the poor in clan temples. Since traditionally only the very old and persons with degrees had been allowed to eat in clan temples, this act symbolized a revolutionary attack on the authority of clan elders.[37]

A political report issued on January 8, 1927 (while Mao was still investigating the peasant movement in Hunan), indicated that the CCP Central Committee feared the repercussions of these events:

> In the provinces of Hunan, Hupeh, and Kiangsi, now occupied by the Northern Expeditionary Forces, the mass movement has entered the revolutionary path and revolutionary work has penetrated deeply into the villages.... Assassinations of local bullies and the bad gentry continue to occur without end. The current social movement of the people is much more far-reaching than during the Revolution of 1911 or the May Fourth Movement. ... A violent reaction would ensue should there be a military setback.[38]

Ch'en Tu-hsiu's great fear was that if the peasants pressed their demands too far, the all-class front against imperialism would split apart: the national and social revolutions would cease to support each other, the national armies would be defeated, and the conservative officers in the KMT would turn their guns against the workers and peasants. Russian history after 1905 would be replayed, and Stolypin's neckties would adorn the Chinese countryside. Events six months later justified Ch'en's fears, but as the new year dawned in 1927, Communists and Nationalists in the lower ranks were still bound together in the exhilaration of success.

As the Nationalist Army moved north, the Communists raced to control the growing mass movements in the newly occupied territory and the factions within the civilian KMT raced to control local governmental and party units.[h] Military men who disagreed with Chiang Kai-shek's policies or were his potential rivals began to work with

[h] The first revolutionary local governments were formed by coalitions of the peasant associations, the labor unions, and the local KMT committees. In many places Communists held a few positions on the KMT committees; they controlled the peasant associations and labor unions almost everywhere. Communists and their left-wing allies thus managed to control most hsien and city governments liberated by the Nationalist Armies until Chiang, Li Chi-shen, and finally T'ang Sheng-chih and the left KMT politicians of Wuhan turned on their Communist allies and "reorganized" the labor unions, dispersed the peasant associations, and appointed their own men to local governing committees.

the left KMT and the Communists to prevent Chiang from placing his supporters in key positions in either local or provincial party and military units. In Hunan and Hupeh, the CCP allied itself with T'ang Sheng-chih to keep Chiang's appointees out. The tacit alliance between T'ang, the Communists, and the left KMT soon turned Hunan into a stronghold of Communist power. Throughout the following year, however, the CCP's power was limited by T'ang's army, which continued to be relatively untouched by revolutionary agitation, for it had very few Communist officers. Further, the policies adopted by the CCP Central Committee limiting revolutionary agitation in the armies to KMT propaganda prevented the Communists from infiltrating and winning over sections of T'ang's army or converting its officers to Communism. In Kiangsi, Chiang seized control of the provincial government, but an alliance of local left KMT factions with the CCP managed to gain and hold control of many hsien and city governments. The result was a virtual civil war between provincial and local governments throughout most of the province. A similar situation prevailed in parts of Fukien, Chekiang, Anhwei, and Kiangsu. Meanwhile, in Kwangtung (the old revolutionary base), the departure of the revolutionary armies and propagandists for the front lines soon allowed local men led by Li Chi-shen, who had consistently stood for control of Canton by the Cantonese, to regain the power they had lost in 1925. In late 1926, Chiang Kai-shek established his military headquarters in Nanch'ang and the radical civilian leaders of the KMT moved their government from Canton to Wuhan.[i] Left-wing members of the old KMT Political Committee were at last in contact with the rapidly growing mass movements of the central provinces. The Wuhan labor unions demonstrated their power on January 3, 1927, when they occupied the British Concession in Hankow without provoking armed intervention by the gunboats stationed on the Yangtze.[39]

As the leaders of the right wing of the KMT quickly gathered around Chiang Kai-shek in Nanch'ang and those of the left around Borodin in Wuhan, each faction attempted to entice the other to its own headquarters for a plenary session of the KMT Central Executive Committee. But each was wary of the other's lair. On January 10 Chiang tried to break the deadlock by going to Wuhan in person to invite the CEC members there to a conference in Nanch'ang. Having

[i] Wuhan is the name for the great metropolitan area at the juncture of the Han, Hsiang, and Yangtze Rivers. It comprises three cities: Hanyang and Hankow on the north bank and Wuch'ang on the south.

received a cool reception from Borodin and the Wuhan radicals, he returned to Nanch'ang, convinced that Borodin had become his personal enemy. (He knew, however, that other Soviet advisers still favored him and that the Soviet Union wanted to continue its alliance with the KMT.) Chiang now felt that he must gain control of the mass movements before the continued success of the Northern Expedition could be ensured.[40]

Chiang made one of his first moves against the urban mass organizations in the newly occupied areas in February, when Ch'en Tsan-hsien, chairman of the labor union in Kanchow (a large city in southern Kiangsi), was murdered and his union driven underground. Then, on February 19, Chiang announced that the time had come to expel the Communists for they were no longer "true comrades." The KMT must be purified of all "disparate elements." It was at this time that Fang Chih-min, the Communist who had been in charge of KMT Party Headquarters for Kiangsi, was removed.[41] Chiang's attitude became more evident when the Shanghai General Labor Union launched an insurrection on February 22 in anticipation of the early arrival of Nationalist troops, who were then only some 25 miles south of the city. Chiang issued an order to suspend the advance for the time being, and Li Pao-chang, Chang Tso-lin's subordinate in command of the Shanghai garrison, put down the insurrection within three days. Several weeks later when he went over to the Nationalists, Li was rewarded with command of the Eighth Nationalist Army.[42]

On February 24, before the first Shanghai insurrection was suppressed, the Wuhan KMT convened a conference that called for a return of party power to the CEC, for the revival of the Military Committee, for the subordination of military officers to party direction, and for the participation of Communists in the CEC. The conference also called for a Plenum of the CEC on March 10 in Wuhan, urged Wang Ching-wei to return from his self-imposed exile in Europe, and condemned all reactionary elements in the party who were compromising with imperialists. As the date of the Plenum approached, Chiang denounced Borodin, proclaimed his continued support of the alliance with the Soviet Union, and denied that he was negotiating with representatives of either Chang Tso-lin or Japan.[43]

When the Plenum met in Wuhan on March 10, it voted to restore the regular party organs whose power Chiang had usurped after his March coup the year before, to reestablish the Military Committee under civilian control, to place the Commander-in-Chief of the Nationalist Army—Chiang—under CEC control, and to abolish the chairmanship of the CEC, a post also held by Chiang. Wang Ching-wei was elected chief of all major party organs.[44] As the Plenum in Wuhan was drawing to a close, Chiang's police raided the headquarters of the labor unions and the peasant, student, and women's organizations in Kiukiang and Nanch'ang. Communist and other left wing leaders were arrested and shot, and the KMT headquarters were dissolved pending reorganization. Similar incidents occurred in Anking on March 23, in Wuhu on March 24, and in Hangchow on March 30 and 31.[45]

When the Shanghai General Labor Union declared a general strike on March 21, the commander of the Nationalist army waiting outside the city refused to come to its assistance, apparently hoping the workers' strength would be sapped before he entered the city. He was mistaken—by nightfall of the following day the workers had driven out the last of Chang Tso-lin's troops, the Communists in the General Labor Union had organized a municipal government in which they had only minority representation, and the government had invited Chiang's Nationalist army into the city once again.[j] As local Communists were being arrested by Chiang's supporters, Voitinsky and the other Comintern advisers on the scene equivocated, stalling for time while urgently requesting new instructions from Moscow. When the new directives arrived, Voitinsky ordered the CCP to arouse the masses, to conduct a propaganda campaign against the right, and to welcome Chiang Kai-shek. The General Labor Union was ordered to hide its weapons in order to avoid a clash between Chiang and the workers.[46] (Presumably, the alternative course of action that the ECCI had rejected would have been to direct the Communists in the Shanghai municipal council to announce their support for the decisions of the March Plenum of the CEC in Wuhan and to arouse the workers to welcome Wang Ching-wei!)

Chiang arrived in Shanghai on March 26 and immediately began negotiating with the great Shanghai bankers, the Chinese Chamber of Commerce, the consuls of the Western powers, and the chiefs of the city's criminal gangs. Finally, on April 12, having made his bargain with the Chamber of Commerce and borrowed sufficient funds

[j] While the people of Shanghai waited for Chiang, Chang Tso-lin's police, with the permission of the foreign diplomatic corps, invaded the Russian Embassy in Peking and arrested Li Ta-chao and 19 other members of the CCP and KMT who were on the premises. (Degras, *Communist International,* II, 363–64.) This incident loosed a torrent of anti-Communist violence throughout the north.

from the banks, Chiang turned on his erstwhile allies. Early in the morning, members of the notorious Green and Red gangs, supported by Nationalist soldiers and the Shanghai police, invaded the workers' quarter, and also attacked KMT and labor union headquarters throughout the city. Taken completely by surprise, the workers' pickets were routed from almost all their positions within a few hours. Anyone even suspected of being a Communist or a leader of one of the mass organizations was summarily executed. The next day, when the CCP, following instructions from its Comintern advisers, brought the disarmed workers out on to the streets in a peaceful demonstration, hundreds were mowed down by Nationalist machine-gun fire.[47]

Chiang had demonstrated that he no longer needed the Communists, and the CCP in Shanghai had bitterly learned that compliance with directives from the ECCI could lead overnight to the destruction of a great proletarian movement.

Two days later, Chiang established a Nationalist government in Nanking in rivalry with the left KMT government in Wuhan. While the two governments competed for the allegiance of the Nationalist armies, the CCP desperately sought a closer alliance with the left KMT. To preserve their position and avoid alienating the generals and politicians in the left KMT, the Communists had to hold the mass movements in check, deny the economic demands of the workers and peasants in territory controlled by the Wuhan government (and refuse to arm them as well), and refrain from establishing soviets even in territory held by Chiang's armies. In this tragic dilemma, the CCP could not advance and it could not retreat. Its leaders were indecisive and its central apparatus almost ceased to function. Local party units had to act on their own initiative.

In areas controlled by KMT armies whose allegiance to Chiang or the left KMT was still unclear, Communist groups did begin to defend themselves. The greatest danger lay in Kwangtung, where the anti-Communist Li Chi-shen was in command. Though the Kwangtung CCP had been making preparations for a break since early spring, it had a long way to go. Local branches had been recruiting new members for the workers' pickets and the peasant self-defense corps, and had continued their desperate search for arms. (In some areas as much as 75 percent of the income of peasant associations had been appropriated for this purpose.[48]) But when Li struck on April 15, the Communists had not yet completed their underground organization. As a result, many in the city of Canton were arrested and executed, including Ch'en Tu-hsiu's son Ch'en Yen-nien, the party head in Canton. The party organs directing the peasant movement immediately organized underground special committees to take over if the open party apparatus were destroyed. One of the first of these —the Tung-chiang (East River) Special Committee—was organized in Hai-lu-feng, where the Communists also formed an underground military organization known as the Workers' and Peasants' Party Relief Army.[49] These organizations were the prototypes of the CCP special committees that began to function in most parts of China before the end of the year. None, however, were immediately organized in the territories controlled by the left KMT government in Wuhan. The Workers' and Peasants' Party Relief Army appears to have been an intermediate stage between the old peasant self-defense corps and the peasant insurrection corps created at the time of the Autumn Harvest Uprisings later in the year. While there is no clear proof, it is probable that the secret party organs in the underground army in Kwangtung were also the prototype of the Front Committees organized during the Nanch'ang Uprising in July, and in Mao's First Workers' and Peasants' Red Army. These secret special committees were in existence in Kwangtung by the end of April 1927. There is no evidence that Mao took part in their formation—he was then still engaged in organizing the peasants from his position within the left KMT.

The Moscow Line

In November-December 1926 the Seventh Plenum of the ECCI convened in Moscow to consider the Comintern's united front strategy in China. In the Chinese Commission at least four sets of theses on relations between the KMT armies and the peasant movement were proposed. In his speech to the Chinese Commission, Stalin attacked the proposals of all four of his China experts—Petrov, Mif, T'an P'ing-shan, and Rafes—all of whom except Petrov were in favor of encouraging the peasants to confiscate land owned by landlords immediately. Stalin believed that the peasant movement should not be developed to that point until the cities were firmly under the control of the revolutionary forces. Until the revolution triumphed in the cities the peasant movement should be kept in check. He acknowledged that the bourgeoisie would inevitably abandon the revolution, but in November 1926 he argued that since the Nationalist armies were still fighting the northern warlords they were still anti-imperialist. Therefore the economic interests of the Nationalist officers had to be protected: since many of the officers were of landlord families, the lands of those families should not be confiscated. Only the lands of officers in the armies of the reactionary militarists should be confiscated, and that measure should be taken only through the action of the KMT government, in which Nationalist army officers had a voice.[50] Until the revolutionary forces had a firm hold on the cities, the armed forces under Chiang Kai-shek were to be considered revolutionary armies fighting against counterrevolution. If the peasants rebelled at this point, the financial and political bulwarks of the KMT government and armies would be threatened.

According to Stalin, the revolutionary peasant committees were inadequate to the task of organizing the great hordes of Chinese peasants, dispersed as they were in their tens of thousands of villages. Only the proletariat—i.e., the party of the proletariat—could carry a radical agrarian policy through to its conclusion. On their own, the peasants would fail to do it.[51] Stalin's policy was adopted by the ECCI on the basis of this analysis. The Communists were ordered to enter the KMT government and influence the peasantry through the government and the revolutionary armies.

Three basic principles evolved at the Seventh Plenum governed Comintern policy toward the Chinese revolution until September 1927, when Stalin was forced to concede that dissolution of the alliance was inevitable. The first principle was that the Communists were not to provoke a split. The second principle was that peasant demands should be met; land should be redistributed as soon as possible. The third principle was that it was still too early to organize soviets. In Stalin's view soviets were an institution designed to bring a government down, and the government of the KMT merited support. Even though the first principle was supposedly primary, once the peasant movement actually grew powerful enough to take the government into its own hands, the first and second principles became contradictory. At that point the CCP leaders divided over the peasant question. The right camp favored continuing the alliance with the KMT even though this entailed sacrificing the interests of the peasants, while the left camp favored meeting the peasants' demands, including the confiscation and redistribution of land.

It was possible to put both principles into effect as long as the peasants were held in check in territory occupied by the KMT and land was redistributed only in territory still under the control of the warlords. But Mao's student agitators had done too good a job. By the winter of 1926 the peasants of Hunan, like their brothers in Kwangtung, were executing local rascals and oppressive gentry, including those collecting taxes to support the KMT armies. In the countryside the peasant unions became the sole organs of authority. As principal of the school for peasant agitators, as head of the CCP's Peasant Department, and as the CCP Politburo's responsible instructor to the Hunan provincial party, Mao was directly responsible for bringing about a situation that highlighted the inconsistency of the Comintern's two major policies regarding the peasant movement.

Mao Inspects the Peasant Movement in Hunan

Reminiscences recently published by some of Mao's old comrades have provided much new information about his activities in the first half of 1927, and especially have cast fresh light on the relation between Mao's practice and the words of his famous report on the peasant movement in Hunan.

Mao was sent to Hunan as inspector of the peasant movement when the Northern Expedition reached Wuhan (November 1926). He gathered information in the villages of Hunan for roughly five weeks, from January 4 to February 5, 1927. He gathered most of his data in Ch'angsha, Li-ling, Hsiang-t'an, Hung-shan, and Hsiang-hsiang, the five hsien in which the peasant movement was strongest, but he gathered reports of some kind from 57 of the 75 hsien in Hunan.[k] On the basis of this information he wrote his famous report to the KMT Peasant Department and the CCP Politburo, demanding that the left KMT lead the peasants in an unrestrained attack on the economic and political power of the landlords.

According to what he told Snow, Mao submitted his report to the Politburo in February and published it in March. *Guide Weekly*, the official organ of the CCP, printed parts of it during the March Plenum of the KMT Central Executive Committee in Wuhan.[52] Both the Politburo and the CEC Plenum rejected his suggestions. But Mao persisted, and in April proposed his radical solution of the land problem to the founding congress of the All-China Peasant Association.

[k] According to the first introduction to Mao's *Nung-ts'un tiao-ch'a (Rural Survey)* [88], hereafter cited as NTTC, the original draft of this survey and the notes on which it was based were lost on May 21, 1927, in the Hsü K'o-hsiang massacre. (Mao, NTTC, p. 1.) The tables of information on the 57 hsien were published in the Chinese editions of Mao's report. From these tables, not included in either HC or SW, it is easy to see that most of the organizers and leaders of the peasant movement were middle school students and primary school teachers. Many of the latter may have been students at Hunan First Normal when Mao was principal of its primary school. (Mao, *Report on an Investigation into the Peasant Movement in Hunan* [81], pp. 11–15.)

This congress was attended by a wide variety of political, military, and mass movement leaders, as well as by their Comintern advisers. Mao was supported by P'eng P'ai, the famous peasant leader from Hai-lu-feng; by Fang Chih-min, the leader of the peasant associations in Kiangsi province; and by two Russians (York and Volen, as Snow transliterates their names) who were apparently advisers to the KMT Peasant Department. Mao's proposal was adopted by the conference and again submitted to the CCP Politburo, which again rejected it. He was then appointed chairman of the All-China Peasant Association, and was given the distasteful task of suppressing the movement he had helped to build. He had already been removed from his position as head of the CCP Peasant Department, perhaps in December 1926. Mao also submitted his report to the Fifth Congress of the CCP, which took place from late April to early May, but Ch'en Tu-hsiu would not permit it to be discussed and it was omitted from the agenda of the Congress.

In July 1927, according to Mao's report to Snow, Ch'en Tu-hsiu removed him from his post as inspector of the peasant movement in Hunan and ordered him to Szechwan. But Mao persuaded Ch'en to rescind that order and instead send him to Hunan as secretary of the provincial party. Ten days later, Ch'en directed him to return to Wuhan, accusing him of organizing an uprising against T'ang Sheng-chih, the new militarist supporting the left KMT government in Wuhan.[53]

Although Mao's report to Snow probably relates his political views at the time correctly, his dates may be inaccurate. According to an account of these events published in a Communist journal one year later, Ch'en had ordered him to go to direct the peasant movement in Hunan while the Fifth Congress was still in session.[54] According to two reports published in the *Hankow People's Tribune* at the time, he had attended the first meetings of the Congress, but was then sent off to Honan (rather than Hunan) to organize the peasant movement in newly acquired territory there and did not return to Wuhan until after the Congress had adjourned.[55] Since these three reports corroborate each other's dates, I have concluded that Mao was not present during the last week of the Fifth Congress.

Being absent from the center of power until the end of May, he did not participate in the final decisions of the Fifth Congress—decisions that were shortly labeled opportunistic by the Comintern. Nor did he take part in any of the conferences of the Central Committee of the CCP or of the KMT government in the latter part of May.

It is of course possible that these stories in the official KMT press may have been written to conceal Mao's actual location and mission. If so, Mao concealed his true destination by starting for Honan, then returned to Wuhan and proceeded to his old haunts in Ch'angsha. It is also possible that Ch'en ordered him to go to Honan or Szechwan and that after publicly starting in the right direction he went on to Hunan, with or without Ch'en's permission.

At any rate, Mao did arrive in Ch'angsha in time to take part in planning the uprising against T'ang, an uprising that was precluded when the Nationalist division commander Hsia Tou-yin staged a revolt of his own. Taking advantage of the waning power of the Wuhan government, Hsia took Yochow, between Ch'angsha and Wuhan, thus cutting off communication between the two cities.[56] When Hsia's army began to drive northward toward Wuhan, the independent regiment led by the Communist Yeh T'ing that had been acting as praetorian guard to the left KMT government evacuated Wuhan and defeated Hsia's troops not far from the southern approaches to Wuch'ang. While Communist-led troops from Wuhan were coming to T'ang Sheng-chih's rescue the Communists in Ch'angsha could hardly rise against T'ang's local garrison. So the uprising planned by the Hunanese Communists was postponed until a more opportune moment should arise.

While Mao was in Ch'angsha, he also took part in the decisions of the Hunan Provincial Peasant Association to call for the confiscation of all land belonging to big landlords—this probably soon after the Fifth Congress had decided to confiscate only the land belonging to enemies of the revolution. The peasants answered the call with enthusiasm. T'ang Sheng-chih responded by issuing a secret order for Mao's arrest.[57] Somehow the Ch'angsha Communists got wind of T'ang's order, and on May 11 Mao, Kuo Liang, Hsia Hsi, and T'eng Tai-yüan fled together to Liu-yang, near the Kiangsi border. In the meantime, land redistribution continued in villages so close to Ch'angsha that the peasants measuring the fields could be seen from the city walls. T'ang's garrison commander in Ch'angsha, Hsü K'o-hsiang, infuriated by these confiscations, which he probably knew had been forbidden by the CCP's Fifth Congress, attacked the armed workers' pickets in Ch'angsha on May 21, destroyed the headquarters of the peasant unions, and declared his allegiance to Chiang Kai-shek. Lo Hsüeh-tsan, Mao's close friend and one of his first recruits into the CCP, was killed in the onslaught. On hearing the news, most of the Hunan Provincial Committee gathered around Mao in Liu-yang to organize a peasant uprising.[58]

While Hsü's troops swept out from Ch'angsha, killing and looting, the peasant self-defense corps were mobilized for a counterattack. According to Ts'ai Ho-shen, the Provincial Committee had actually begun to mobilize some 300,000 peasants for an attack on Ch'angsha on May 30. Li Wei-han, who had been sent from Hankow, furiously opposed the decision. Li argued that if the Communist-led peasants were to take Ch'angsha, "T'ang Sheng-chih will march on Wuhan and will overthrow the Nationalist government. . . . As long as the Wuhan government exists we must ask it to end [Hsü's] insurrection by lawful means."[59] After Li expressed this opinion, the committee agreed to cancel the uprising, but orders had already gone out and it was impossible to reach every peasant unit in time. According to M. N. Roy, more than 20,000 peasants were nearing the city gates of Ch'angsha when orders to retreat reached them from Communist headquarters in Hankow. As they turned their backs on the city, they were attacked by Hsü's troops and killed without mercy.[60] Mao, in the meantime, had returned to Hankow, arriving there about June.[61]

Although this reconstruction of events undoubtedly retains some inaccuracies, it seems clear that Mao was following a line far to the left of the Central Committee and the Comintern in the spring of 1927. He advocated confiscating land, and under his direction the peasants of Hunan did exactly that. He participated in planning one armed uprising and may have had a hand in directing another before he was recalled to Wuhan. It should be emphasized that much of what Mao did and said while serving as inspector of the Hunan peasant movement did not find its way into his published report. His March report did not advocate Communist leadership of the peasant movement, nor did it suggest that the land be confiscated, nationalized, and distributed among the peasants; it proposed only that the Peasant Department of the KMT lead the peasant movement and support whatever action the peasants were taking in the villages against evil landlords and bad gentry. In his May report to the Fifth Congress of the CCP, Mao had supported the proposal that all landed property be confiscated, but the Fifth Congress had decided to confiscate only the land of those opposed to the KMT. Mao and his followers supported confiscation of all land in Hunan.[62]

After the Hsü K'o-hsiang massacre, the coalition between the left KMT and the CCP began to dissolve. In his telegram of June 1, Stalin proposed to Borodin that a revolutionary court be set up, chaired by a trustworthy leader of the left KMT, to try reactionary officers and bring unreliable generals under control. Roy, the new Comintern adviser to the CCP, showed a copy of the telegram to Wang Ching-wei, the most prominent member of the left KMT. The alliance never recovered from that blunder.

In spite of the fact that immediately after this incident the left KMT began to disarm the Hankow labor and peasant unions, which formed the CCP's chief support in the Wuhan area, on June 11 the CCP made 11 proposals to the KMT left wing asking that together the two parties carry on the revolution and prepare to fight the Nanking government of Chiang Kai-shek. Even the Enlarged Plenum of the Central Committee of the CCP that convened on July 3 continued to take a conciliatory attitude. It was not until July 13 that, under great provocation, the CCP finally withdrew the Communist ministers from the Wuhan government. On July 15, the left KMT formally expelled all Communists. In late July Borodin and Galen were withdrawn as Soviet advisers to the KMT and were not replaced. Roy was replaced as Comintern representative to the CCP by Besso Lominadze, who was soon joined by Heinz Neumann. This turnover of Comintern advisers did not usher in a change of policy. The immediate aim of the CCP was to bring down Wang Ching-wei while continuing to work within the left KMT and exerting influence from below. According to Stalin, Wang had betrayed the revolution, but the masses in the left KMT had not done so.

Stalin had been deeply and publicly involved in the tactical direction of Chinese party policy since late 1924. During this period his leadership of the CPSU, as well as his China policy, was under continuous attack from the United Opposition (Trotsky, Zinoviev, and Kamenev). Stalin and Bukharin clung to the alliance with the KMT as the basic tenet of their China policy. In his concentration on overwhelming the opposition in the CPSU, Stalin closed his eyes to the coming debacle of the united front in China. Restrained by Stalin's orders, the leaders of the CCP were unable to prepare a strategic retreat before Chiang Kai-shek, and then Wang Ching-wei and other leaders of the left KMT, broke their alliance with the CCP and turned to slaughter their erstwhile comrades. Even in July 1927, when the leaders of the left KMT expelled the Communists from their government posts and ordered a purge to rid the left KMT of its Communist members, Moscow ordered CCP members to stay in the KMT army and party in order to influence its leaders from below.

Both before and after Moscow acknowledged the break with Chiang Kai-shek, the position that Mao and other Communist leaders of the KMT Peasant Department advocated pushed toward an open break between the CCP and the KMT. Before Chiang Kai-shek's attack on the workers of Shanghai, this radical peasant position had caused friction between Chiang and the left KMT. When the split between Chiang and the left KMT became final, Mao's position pressed the CCP toward a rupture with the left KMT in the Wuhan government. As the situation became more tense, old factions began to dissolve. Frustrated and fearful, the Politburo ceased to function as a unit. Even the most sober and cautious members of the Central Committee were ready for some mad adventure. In June and early July a coalition of dissident CCP leaders began to form. They had been ordered to cooperate first with Chiang Kai-shek while he was attacking labor unions in Shanghai, then with T'ang Sheng-chih while his subordinates were attacking labor and peasant organizations in Hunan, Hupeh, and Kiangsi, and finally with the left KMT while it was forcing Communists out of office. This cooperation had led to the destruction of their party cells and mass organizations in the cities, and to the massacre of workers and peasants in Shanghai, Ch'angsha, and Wuhan. It was clearly time for a new policy.

The Nanch'ang Uprising

By the middle of July 1927, the dissidents had formulated a plan to stage a putsch in Nanch'ang. According to Chang Kuo-t'ao, when Stalin received the news toward the end of the month he sent an order to the Central Committee in Wuhan to forestall the putsch. Chang personally conveyed this order from Wuhan to the Communists in Nanch'ang, but they were either unwilling or unable to follow Stalin's orders, and the putsch took place on August 1.[l] This date is now celebrated as the official founding day of the Red Army.

There are other sources, however, that disagree with Chang, and his interpretation cannot be accepted without qualification. In fact, the only points generally agreed on are that Stalin did send a telegram and that Chang, on the basis of his interpretation of its ambiguous message, attempted to stop the uprising and failed. Shortly thereafter, a long, tortuous debate began among CCP leaders over whether what had occurred at Nanch'ang had been a revolution, a

[l] This is my own conclusion drawn from the findings of Conrad Brandt, which in turn are based on interviews with Chang Kuo-t'ao. (Brandt, pp. 142–45.) The validity of this conclusion depends on Chang's reliability as an informant. His story is partially confirmed by reports of the uprising in *Central Newsletter* [46], October 30, 1927.

military putsch, an insurrection *(pao-tung)*, an incident *(shih-pien)*, or an uprising in a righteous cause *(ch'i-i)*. The last interpretation finally prevailed, but for at least four years official sources referred to the uprising simply as an incident or an insurrection. It was not sanctified as an uprising in a righteous cause and the founding day of the Red Army until 1932, after Li Li-san and Lominadze had fallen from power and Chou En-lai had replaced Mao as Commissar of the Chinese Red Army.

It is not easy to ascertain who participated in planning the uprising. Mao told Snow in 1936 that Ho Lung, Yeh T'ing, and Chu Teh were its leaders, and did not associate himself in any way with either its planning or its execution. In contrast, a year later Chu Teh claimed Mao had indeed taken part in a meeting held on the evening of July 18, 1927, in a small village near Nanch'ang, at which the uprising was first proposed and approved.[m] The Communists Chu listed as attending the meeting were T'an P'ing-shan and Su Chao-cheng, the former ministers of agriculture and labor in the Wuhan government; Chou En-lai and Li Li-san, the leaders of the Shanghai labor movement before the April 12 massacre; Mao Tse-tung and Fang Chih-min, the two chief organizers of the peasant movement in Hunan and Kiangsi; Yeh T'ing and Yeh Chien-ying, two army officers who had been close associates of Chou En-lai at Whampoa; Lin Tsu-han, who had been minister of finance in the revolutionary KMT government in Canton and then political commissar of the KMT army that had occupied Nanking; and Ho Lung (who had not yet actually joined the CCP), Chu Teh, and other officers in the KMT armies in Kiangsi. Of the men named, only Li Li-san and Chou En-lai were members of the acting Politburo or Secretariat at the time.[63]

According to Chu, the assembled Communists agreed to break with the KMT, arm the workers and peasants, and begin the agrarian revolution. The first action they planned was a military uprising in

[m] According to the story Chu told Nym Wales in the spring of 1937, Mao was not present in Nanch'ang before the uprising. (*Inside Red China*, p. 119.) According to the story Chu told Smedley several months later, Mao was present, although he and Chu did not have an opportunity to talk together. (Smedley, *Great Road*, pp. 199–201.) In this account I follow Chu's story to Smedley, which is more apt to be reliable, considering the close friendship between Chu and Smedley and her apparent promise that none of his disclosures would be published without his permission. Shortly before her death, Smedley asked that her notes be sent to Chu, through whose hands they presumably passed before they were published. (Confidential communication to me, May 1951.)

the Nanch'ang-Kiukiang area by the Fourth Army, against its commander, Huang Ch'i-hsiang. After the uprising, the army was to march to Canton and establish a new national revolutionary government there. A Front Committee, probably the first ever established by the Chinese Communists, was elected to direct the uprising. Its chairman was Liu Po-ch'eng and its vice-chairman Chou En-lai; among its members were Yeh Chien-ying, Li Li-san, Chang Kuo-t'ao, Yeh T'ing, Ho Lung, Chu Teh, T'an P'ing-shan, and Lin Tsu-han. Chu does not mention Mao, Fang Chih-min, Su Chao-cheng, or P'eng P'ai as members of this committee. These four men, he says, were assigned to undertake preparations elsewhere. Fang was to leave Nanch'ang before the uprising and prepare peasant organizations on the route of the march southward. Su was to alert the labor unions along the Yangtze. P'eng P'ai returned to Hai-lu-feng with Yeh T'ing's troops. (Chu claimed the Nanch'ang putsch was to signal a whole series of coordinated peasant uprisings in the rear of the armies of Chiang Kai-shek and Li Chi-shen.) Mao was to return to Wuhan, wait for the signal from Nanch'ang, and prepare to lead the Communists among the Whampoa military cadets in the Wuhan garrison southward into Hunan.[64]

Contemporary records do not mention Mao's presence at any of the meetings at which the uprising was planned. Perhaps, as his account to Snow suggests, Mao returned to Wuhan, went on to Szechwan, and returned to Wuhan again sometime after August 1. Or, like most well-known Communists, he may have been in hiding. In late July the broad swords of KMT executioners were littering Wuhan's streets with severed heads. Mao, with his genius for being elsewhere, disappeared.

The accounts of events leading up to the revolt published in the CCP *Central Newsletter* in November do not mention the July 18 meeting recorded by Chu Teh, although it is clear that the uprising had been discussed before the first meeting cited in the *Newsletter* account written by Li Li-san. According to Li, that meeting took place in Kiukiang on July 19, the day he and Teng Chung-hsia arrived there.[n] The Central Committee in Wuhan had just begun its preparations for the Autumn Harvest Uprisings, but had not yet adopted any policy on military revolts. When Li and Teng left

[n] If there are no omissions in Chu's and Li's lists of those attending the July 18 and July 19 conferences, respectively, no one attended both except conceivably Li himself. (Chu says Li attended the July 18 meeting, but Li does not mention it.) Mao could have attended the July 18 meeting and left directly afterward.

Wuhan, the Central Committee had not assigned them any responsibility to prepare for a military uprising. They learned that a revolt was being planned only after they arrived in Kiukiang. Upon hearing the news, they immediately went to the nearby resort area of Lu-shan to confer with Ch'ü Ch'iu-pai. (Ch'ü was probably accompanying Borodin, who had arrived in Lu-shan some days earlier to take a short rest before his arduous journey back to Moscow.) At that conference, held on July 19, those present decided to cast aside an earlier plan, which the meeting recorded by Chu Teh had probably supported, that involved depending on the Nationalist General Chang Fa-k'uei. Instead they agreed that the Communists in the armies must first stage an uprising on their own, and then, from a position of strength, compel Chang and Chu P'ei-te, the two leading KMT generals in Kiangsi, to unite with them against Chiang Kai-shek and T'ang Sheng-chih. The overall plan had four stages: to unite Ho Lung's 20th Army with Yeh T'ing's 11th Army, to revolt at Nanch'ang, to subjugate the other generals in the area, and then to establish a new government opposed to both Wuhan and Nanking. Unlike the Communists at the meeting Chu described, the July 19 conferees intended to remain in Nanch'ang rather than march to Canton after the revolt. No one present opposed this new plan, and Ch'ü set out for Wuhan to clear it with the Central Committee.[65] According to Chang T'ai-lei, when Ch'ü arrived in Wuhan on July 20 he found that the Central Committee already knew a revolt had been planned and had already determined its attitude toward Chang Fa-k'uei. The Committee members had agreed that if Chang associated himself with Wang Ching-wei, he would have to be overcome in Kiukiang, but that if he took an independent stand, the Communists in his army should support him until his army reached Hai-lu-feng. This decision, based on a report from the July 18 meeting, overruled the maneuver agreed upon by Ch'ü, Li, and Teng at the Lu-shan conference on July 19. Chou En-lai, who had brought the report of the earlier meeting to the Central Committee, had been appointed chairman of the Front Committee and sent back to Kiukiang to manage the affair.[66] The Central Committee continued to support the uprising from July 20 through July 25. The Comintern representative (perhaps Roy, perhaps Lominadze) also supported it and asked Borodin for the necessary funds.

When Borodin went to Lu-shan early in July, Roy and Galen remained in Wuhan.[67] Lominadze, the new Comintern representative, probably arrived sometime between July 15 and July 18, and took over Roy's position sometime before the 26th.[o] He lost no time in seeking someone on the temporary Politburo willing to condemn Ch'en Tu-hsiu for the CCP's alleged failure to carry out Comintern policy. Chang Kuo-t'ao, then the de facto leader of the Politburo, loyally insisted that all members of the Central Committee had shared in the decisions of the Fifth Congress that led to the split with the left KMT. While Lominadze widened his intrigue in an attempt to replace both Ch'en Tu-hsiu and Chang Kuo-t'ao, the Politburo continued to appeal to Borodin for funds. The Politburo also managed to convince at least two Russian advisers to go to Kiukiang to contact Borodin and to assist the Chinese comrades there in their attempt to confer with the remnants of the left KMT in Kiukiang and Nan-ch'ang.[68]

A telegram was sent to Moscow asking for approval of the proposed uprising. Stalin's reply arrived on July 26, and that evening Lominadze held a meeting of the Russian advisers and such Politburo and Secretariat members as could be summoned on short notice. According to the report Chang Kuo-t'ao wrote for the November Plenum, the Central Committee members present were Chang Kuo-t'ao, Chang T'ai-lei, Chou En-lai, Ch'ü Ch'iu-pai, and Li Wei-han (Lo Mai). Seven Russians were also present: Lominadze, Galen, an unidentified representative from the Youth International (possibly Pavel Mif), and four lesser advisers, Chi-kung (probably Zikon, alias Kumanine), Chia-chen (Volen?), Fan-k'o (unidentified), and Jo-k'o (York or Iolk).[p] Galen outlined the situation and proposed that the Communists split Chang Fa-k'uei's army from Chu P'ei-te's, and simultaneously split Chang's army from within. However, Lominadze an-

[o] According to Chang Kuo-t'ao, the new Comintern representative was present at the July 26 meeting of Russian advisers and important CCP members in Wuhan. Upon his arrival in Wuhan he had criticized a resolution on the KMT dated July 13 that had overemphasized the continuing role of Sun Yat-sen and his program. He had also criticized a resolution on the peasant movement that had called for the Autumn Harvest Uprisings and advocated rent reductions, but had not made land confiscation its central point. Confiscation of landlords' land became the main point of the agrarian policy included in the Program of Action adopted by the Central Standing Committee of the CCP on July 18, perhaps, although Chang does not say so, as a result of Lominadze's criticism. On the basis of this evidence (from Chang Kuo-t'ao's letter of November 8, 1927, to the Enlarged Conference of the Provisional Central Politburo) I conclude that Lominadze probably arrived sometime between July 15 and July 18. He may have taken over from Roy on or before July 18; he was certainly in command by July 26. (Wilbur, "The Ashes of Defeat," p. 47.)

[p] Borodin was probably still in Lu-shan or Kiukiang. Roy, who was still in Hankow, did not attend. "York" is Snow's spelling—the Russian is probably closer to Yolk or Iolk.

nounced that money was no longer available for the uprising. He had just received two telegrams from Moscow, he said. One directed him "not [to] permit Russian advisers under any circumstances to join the revolt." The other stated, "If the revolt has no hope of victory, it would be better not to start it, and the comrades in Chang Fa-k'uei's army should all withdraw and be sent to work among the peasants."[69] He suggested that Chang Kuo-t'ao should inform the comrades in Kiangsi. (With Chang out of the way, Lominadze evidently expected Ch'ü Ch'iu-pai to help him reorganize the central party organs and expel Ch'en Tu-hsiu.) Chang was convinced that Lominadze had supported the revolt until the telegrams arrived on July 26. He knew that Galen had supported it and helped plan it, but gathered from his speeches at the meeting that day that he had changed his mind. This was also Chou En-lai's impression. Chang then started for Nanch'ang to prevent the uprising. He was, however, accompanied by Chou En-lai, who was evidently unwilling to let the telegrams from Moscow determine the outcome and proposed only to take another look at the situation before coming to a final decision.[70]

The wording of the second telegram, of which we have only several sentences quoted in several Chinese translations, was much more ambiguous than Chang's interpretation of its intent. In the reports issued by the November Plenum of the Central Committee, which admitted that the uprising had been a failure, several participants gave their versions of the telegram and their interpretations of what it had meant. Chang T'ai-lei, who had been present at the July 26 meeting and had heard Lominadze speak, drew conclusions exactly opposite from those of Chang Kuo-t'ao. He believed that the Comintern had decided the uprising *should* take place, and that it was Chang Kuo-t'ao who thought otherwise.[71] Chang Kuo-t'ao's version of the message ("If the revolt has no hope of victory . . . it would be better not to start it") also differs from Li Li-san's, which reads: "If there were a guarantee of success the revolt could be started, but otherwise we must not take action."[72] After the rebellious army had finally been dispersed in eastern Kwangtung, the Central Committee, now made up in large part of those who had planned and led the uprising, gave its interpretation (or translation) of the relevant sentence: "If there is no chance *at all* of victory, it will be all right not to start the Nanch'ang Revolt."[73] This version, and particularly the crucial phrase *at all,* appears to have been devised to fit the interpretation of the directive that the Central Committee wished it had received. Whatever Stalin's intent, and whatever interpretation may have been placed upon his message, the Communists in Nanch'ang decided to go ahead with the revolt. Because news of the impending uprising had been leaked to Chu P'ei-te's headquarters by a Yunnanese officer in Ho Lung's army, the uprising occurred earlier than planned. The Communists who were still in the headquarters of Chang Fa-k'uei and Chu P'ei-te near Kiukiang could not be warned in time, and most of them were shot. But the troops of Yeh T'ing and Ho Lung occupied Nanch'ang without difficulty, and a new Revolutionary Committee of the KMT (which included Chang Fa-k'uei) was proclaimed that opposed the KMT of Chiang Kai-shek, Wang Ching-wei, and T'ang Sheng-chih. The people of Nanch'ang gave the rebels little or no support. Neither did the peasants along the line of march to Kwangtung: the rebels were treated like another warlord army. They failed to help the peasants in the Autumn Harvest Uprisings, and concentrated on taking urban centers. They captured Swatow in late September, but were driven out again within a few days. After that defeat the army began to disperse.

Aside from Ho Lung, who joined the CCP several weeks later, the Nanch'ang Uprising was entirely a Communist venture. After the decision to begin the uprising had been made on the spot, several of the Communist leaders in Kiangsi returned to Wuhan to report to the Central Committee. The Committee promptly informed Moscow that the uprising had occurred, but pretended it had been led not by the CCP but by the left KMT, and was therefore a move that the Comintern ought to support. Stalin supported it—he could hardly refuse public approval of a *fait accompli* his disciple Lominadze had been unable to prevent.

By August it had become obvious that the whole series of failures of Stalin's policy must be acknowledged as such and blamed on someone. If the authority of the Comintern was to be preserved at the time the fight with the Trotskyites was mounting to its climax, the Moscow leadership could not shoulder the responsibility for failure. At the August 7 Emergency Conference of the CCP, Ch'en Tu-hsiu and T'an P'ing-shan were held responsible for the failure of Stalin's policies in China. T'an P'ing-shan was found guilty of curbing the peasants, i.e., of performing the distasteful task of suppressing the peasant and labor associations in Ch'angsha that had been assigned to him in May. At the time he was condemned, T'an was the leading political commissar among the troops who had taken part in the Nanch'ang Uprising.[74] He accompanied the rebel armies south to Kwangtung and was expelled from the CCP three months later, at the November Plenum of the Central Committee. Shortly thereafter he emerged as a leader of the Third Party.[q] Ch'en was condemned for "right opportunist" errors. If he himself is to be believed, he had opposed the Moscow line laid down in the spring of 1927. He had trusted neither Chiang Kai-shek nor Wang Ching-wei, but after making his protest through official channels, as a disciplined Communist he had submitted to Comintern orders and imposed the Moscow line on the CCP. Only after he had been made the scapegoat for the failure of Stalin's policy did he openly object. He later published a letter to all party members protesting the Central Committee's adoption of the defense of the USSR as one of its policies. In that letter he had the temerity to attribute the policies followed by the CCP in 1927 directly to Stalin. In November 1929, Li Li-san expelled him from the party as a Trotskyite.[75]

From the Emergency Conference to the November Plenum (August 7 to November 15, 1927)

Immediately after the August 7 Emergency Conference, which deposed Ch'en Tu-hsiu and made Ch'ü Ch'iu-pai leader of the party, Mao returned to Hunan to organize the Autumn Harvest Uprisings. The program he announced called for confiscation of all land of great, middle, and small landlords (but not for the nationalization of the land), the creation of a workers' and peasants' army, complete sever-

[q] The leaders of the Third Party accepted the so-called "Three Great Policies" of Sun Yat-sen, to wit: the Chinese government should adopt a pro-Soviet policy, the coalition between the KMT and the CCP should be continued, and the government should support the growth of labor unions and adopt radical land reform policies. (Linebarger, pp. 178–79.)

They differed from the Communists mainly in refusing to subordinate their party to the whims of the Comintern. They stood for national independence as well as for socialism. When Yenan was open to foreign visitors between 1936 and 1939, Communists interviewed there frequently mentioned the Third Party as the chief enemy of the early soviets in Hupeh, Fukien, and Szechwan. But in Hunan and Kiangsi the chief internal enemy was alleged to be the Anti-Bolshevik Corps. This suggests that the Third Party may have had strong support in Kiangsi and Hunan and that some of the members of the Maoist faction who emerged triumphant from the inner-party struggles in those two provinces were in sympathy with the brand of independent socialism advocated by the members of the Third Party. There is some support for this thesis: the Maoist faction advocated collaboration with the Third Party during the Fukien revolt in 1933, and several of the calls for a united front from below issued between 1931 and 1935 were channeled through Mme. Sun Yat-sen, who had close associations with the Third Party. Moreover, several of the surviving leaders of the Third Party, including T'an P'ing-shan, became members of the People's Government after 1949.

From NANCH'ANG to CHING-KANG-SHAN
August 1927 – April 1928

HUPEH
ANHWEI
KIANGSI
FUKIEN
HUNAN
KWANGTUNG

Hankow
Wuch'ang
Kiukiang
Nanch'ang
P'ing-kiang
Ch'angsha
Liu-yang
Hsiang-t'an
Chu-chou
Hsiang-hsiang
Li-ling
P'ing-hsiang
Heng-yang
Lei-yang
Sui-ch'uan
Hsing-kuo
Ning-tu
Yu-tu
Jui-ching
T'ing-chow
Shang-hang
Amoy
Swatow
Canton
Hai-feng
Lu-feng
Hong Kong

31°
29°
27°
25°
23°N
113°E
115°
117°

ROUTE OF THE YEH-HO ARMY
CHU TEH'S ROUTE
MAO'S ROUTE
SOVIET DISTRICTS
REPORTED UPRISINGS

MILES
0 50 100 150

ance of all ties between the CCP and KMT organizations in Hunan, and the immediate organization of soviet governments. In a letter to the Central Committee dated August 20, he wrote:

[3.] A certain comrade has come to Hunan announcing that a new instruction from the International proposes the immediate establishment of soviets of workers, peasants, and soldiers in China. On hearing this, I jumped for joy. Objectively, China has long since reached 1917, but formerly everyone held the opinion that we were in 1905. This has been an extremely great error. Soviets of workers, peasants, and soldiers are wholly adapted to the objective situation, and we must immediately and resolutely establish the political power of the workers, peasants, and soldiers in the four provinces of Kwangtung, Hunan, Hupeh, and Kiangsi. As soon as established, this political power should moreover rapidly achieve victory in the whole country. We expect that the Central Committee will without a doubt accept the instruction of the International, and we will moreover apply it in Hunan.

This new instruction of the International influences my view of the Kuomintang. In the period of soviets of workers, peasants, and soldiers, we should no longer use the flag of the Kuomintang. We must raise high the flag of the Communist Party to oppose the flag of the Kuomintang raised by Chiang [Kai-shek], T'ang [Sheng-chih], Feng [Yü-hsiang], Yen [Hsi-shan], and the other militarists. The Kuomintang flag has already become the flag of the militarists. Only the flag of the Communist Party is the people's flag. I was not very well aware of this when I was in Hupeh. These last few days, since I have come to Hunan and seen what T'ang Sheng-chih's [Kuomintang] Party Bureau is like, and what the people's attitude toward it is, I have decided that we really cannot use the Kuomintang flag, and that if we do, we will only be defeated again. Formerly, we did not actively seize the leadership of the Kuomintang, and let Wang [Ching-wei], Chiang, T'ang, and the others lead it. Now we should let them keep this flag, which is already nothing but a black flag, and we must immediately and resolutely raise the red flag. As for the petty bourgeoisie, let them rally entirely under the leadership of the red flag; objectively, they are certainly entirely under the leadership of the red flag.

4. *The Land Question.* This time, in the course of investigations of the peasantry in Ch'ing-t'ai (Ch'angsha hsien), where I went myself, and Shaoshan (Hsiang-t'an hsien), from which five people came to the provincial capital, I have come to understand that the Hunanese peasants definitely want a complete solution of the land question. Yesterday, I talked with some peasant comrades from the country, and on the basis of conclusions drawn from their opinions, I propose some guidelines for the land question, of which the most important are:

(1) Confiscate all land, including that of small landowners and peasant proprietors, make it all collective property, and distribute it fairly to all those in the village who want land. . . .[76]

The Central Committee reproved him for his errors ten days later and demanded that he conform to its line. He did not, and the tactics he proposed in this letter, including his call for soviets, formed the essential elements of his line during the Autumn Harvest Uprisings.

In early September, Mao was busily organizing a new peasant attack on Ch'angsha. He was secretary of the Front Committee directing preparations for the attack; the commander of his little army was Lu Te-ming. The army consisted of four regiments: the first made up of Whampoa cadets and others who had deserted from the KMT forces in Wuch'ang; the second of miners from An-yüan and P'ing-hsiang, and a few peasants from Liu-yang; the third entirely of peasants from Liu-yang, commanded by Mao himself; and the fourth of deserters from the division of Hsia Tou-yin, the Nationalist commander who had rebelled against Wuhan in May.[77] The aim of the uprising was to take Ch'angsha. The first regiment was to approach the city from the north, the second and third to attack it from the east, and the fourth to take P'ing-hsiang and prevent KMT troops from moving in from Kiangsi. According to a report in the CCP *Central Newsletter* of September 30, they met with initial success:

> From September 8 to 12, the first few days of the Uprising, we were winning. The amount of arms and ammunition in our hands more than doubled. At P'ing-hsiang our peasant army had 700 to 1,300 rifles, and at An-yüan about 2,100. Thousands of peasants came with their spears and swords to join us. All the important towns in eastern Hunan—P'ing-hsiang, Liu-yang, Liling, and Chüchow—fell into our hands. On September 13, Ch'angsha was in a state of panic.[78]

Mao expected the workers of Ch'angsha to rise and assist the peasants in capturing the city—they did not. Then came the debacle. The deserters from Hsia's division in the fourth regiment attacked the deserters from Wuch'ang in the first regiment. The peasants and workers of An-yüan and Liu-yang in the second regiment were surrounded by KMT forces and almost annihilated. Mao's third regiment ran into an ambush; Mao himself was detained for a time but was able to buy his freedom before being recognized. When the uprising had collapsed, Mao reorganized the remnants of the four regiments into the First Regiment of the First Division of the Peasants' and Workers' Red Army and retreated southward toward the Chingkang Mountains.[79]

In recent years there has been a hot debate over whether Mao's call for soviets did or did not precede Stalin's.[80] In 1936, Mao still believed that in proposing rural soviets he had run ahead of Stalin's and the Comintern's directives to the Central Committee of the CCP. By late July 1927, Stalin had recommended adopting "the slogan of soviets," but he had not yet indicated that this was a call for immediate action. On July 25, *Pravda* declared "the slogan of soviets is correct now."[81] This did not imply that members of the CCP were immediately to organize soviets. Under the prevailing system of democratic centralism, such orders had to be issued through the Chinese Central Committee. And the Central Committee in turn had to await instructions from the Comintern before issuing the call. In fact, the August 7 Emergency Conference, convened 13 days after this *Pravda* editorial appeared, did not issue a call for soviets.[82] The editorial was, in short, only a call for a slogan, not a call to organize soviets immediately. Not until September 27 did Stalin unequivocally sanction the actual organization of soviets.[83]

Did Stalin call for rural soviets only, urban soviets only, or both? Was he already making his distinction between uprisings that were supported by armed troops and uprisings that were not?[84] We cannot be sure. We do know that in October and November Stalin began to call for urban soviets, urging the Politburo to instigate an uprising in Canton.[85] In 1959, Chang Kuo-t'ao testified that he could not remember any specific calls for rural soviets before the November Plenum, which approved the call to organize soviets and expelled Mao from all his party posts.[86]

According to his own account, Mao called for and attempted to organize rural soviets in Hunan during the Autumn Harvest Uprisings, which began on September 8 and disintegrated ten days later.[87] Moreover, he formulated his intention to organize soviets before the uprisings began. It was not until September 30 that *Pravda* proclaimed, "The propaganda slogan of soviets must now become a slogan of action."[88] This *Pravda* article was a reprint of the speech Stalin had delivered three days earlier. Thus Mao's first attempt to organize soviets, as well as his plan to do so, predates Stalin's call to organize them. Did Stalin refer to rural soviets on September 27? This seems unlikely, for throughout October and November he was urging the Chinese Politburo to organize at least one soviet in a large city.

Mao's interviews with Snow may conceal more than they reveal about his role in the Autumn Harvest Uprisings. In these interviews Mao treated the Nanch'ang and the Autumn Harvest Uprisings as separate, uncoordinated incidents. While he had in fact been planning the uprising since early August, he reported that he became the chairman of the party Front Committee of the "First Division of the First Peasants' and Workers' Army" only after he had succeeded in organizing the Hanyang miners and the peasant guards of the five hsien near Ch'angsha, in mid-September. He does not trace the uprisings in Hunan back to Nanch'ang. In contrast, a year later Chu Teh spoke of Mao's uprisings in Hunan as part of a coordinated effort by the same dissident Communists who also planned the Nanch'ang Uprising.[89]

There is some parallel between Mao's Autumn Harvest Uprisings in Hunan and the Nanch'ang revolt in that Front Committees were organized in both cases. There are also differences. The slogans adopted by the Nanch'ang putschists included "Begin the agrarian revolution" and "Arm the people." The Nanch'ang Front Committee certainly intended to overthrow the existing government from below, but did not plan to use troops to confiscate landlords' estates or support peasant uprisings: "Such actions were left to cadres of the people's organizations and of our Party."[90] It failed completely to coordinate workers' and peasants' revolts with the movements of the army. In Hunan and Kiangsi, by contrast, both Mao and Fang Chih-min attempted to arm the peasants, and both called for the beginning of the agrarian revolution. Mao did use military force to incite peasant uprisings, following a policy not yet adopted by the Central Committee. He also attempted to use both the peasants and his troops to capture Ch'angsha, the major urban center in Hunan, thus prefiguring the Li Li-san line of 1930.

While rebelling troops were used in both Nanch'ang and Hunan, the planned coordination between the two risings Chu's account suggests probably did not exist. The Autumn Harvest Uprisings were first planned by the Central Committee in June or early July, long before the movements of the KMT armies created the opportunity for a revolt at Nanch'ang. Mao's use of the army was condemned at the time. He was supposed to lead a peasant rising, but he had been ordered neither to take Ch'angsha nor to organize peasant soviets. In 1936 Mao advanced the claim that he alone had called for soviets during the Autumn Harvest Uprisings.[91] In calling for soviets as he marched his little band south into Hunan, Mao differed from the Front Committee organized at Nanch'ang.

However, in addition to Mao's soviet, a peasant soviet government was created by P'eng P'ai in Hai-lu-feng, although it was not labeled as such until November 18, after Stalin had called for soviets.[92] In their slogans and actions the leaders of the Nanch'ang Uprising (Chou En-lai, Li Li-san, Chang Kuo-t'ao, Chu Teh, and T'an P'ing-shan) were far to the right of the leaders of the Autumn Harvest Uprisings

(Mao, Fang Chih-min, and P'eng P'ai). In the latter group, P'eng and the Hai-lu-feng soviet stood far to the left. Mao had previously agreed with the left policy of P'eng P'ai, but had moved toward the right before the uprisings took place. When Comintern policy lurched to an extreme left position in November 1927, the line Mao had pursued during the uprisings was repudiated as too far to the right. Whether Mao had issued his first call for soviets before or after the Comintern may not have been deemed important by the November Plenum. Rather, he was criticized for not having burned and killed enough, and for having adopted too moderate a policy toward the petty bourgeoisie in the cities and the small and middle landlords in the countryside.[93] He was also rebuked for relying too heavily on his army, for contacting bandits rather than peasants, and for failing to rely on the peasants as the main force in the agrarian revolution. Li Li-san argued that a revolt by the military was not a revolutionary uprising—a genuine revolutionary uprising had to be a spontaneous insurrection by the people themselves.[94] Ch'ü Ch'iu-pai agreed: "A purely peasant uprising without the leadership and help of the proletariat cannot achieve conclusive victories."[95]

Under the guidance of Stalin's protégé Heinz Neumann, the November Plenum turned to the problem of supplying a rigorous political discipline in order to create a party capable of dealing with the continuing upsurge of the revolution. After striking out at many of the old leaders of the CCP, and at most of the leaders of the Nanch'ang Uprising, the Central Committee Resolution on Political Discipline condemned Mao and his comrades in Hunan for their subversion of the Central Committee's plans for the general peasant uprising in Hunan, Hupeh, Kiangsi, and Kwangtung:

> After the August incident this year [the CCP] publicly announced its withdrawal from the National Government, and decided that its previous policy of compromise with the leaders of the petty bourgeoisie must be abandoned and that it must resolutely lead the masses of the workers and peasants to rise in armed insurrection. The Conference of August 7 pointed out in greater detail that our Party, having previously committed errors of opportunism, from now on should without the slightest hesitation rely on the strength of the masses to thoroughly execute the program of the agrarian revolution and should decisively lead the peasants of the four provinces of Hunan, Hupeh, Kiangsi, and Kwangtung to rise at the time of the autumn harvest, thus carrying out the struggle of the agrarian revolution.
>
> At this time there should not have been the slightest hesitation in pursuing our policy. However, in the course of the insurrection in the various provinces the leading organs of our Party and the responsible comrades committed many serious mistakes in violation of the strategy....

The Hunan Provincial Committee was cited as one of the party organs that had committed mistakes:

In guiding the uprising of the peasants the Hunan Provincial Committee violated the strategy of the Central Committee even more seriously [than the Kwangtung Provincial Committee]. The Central Committee had pointed out repeatedly that the insurrection in Hunan should rely chiefly on the peasant masses, and it openly reprimanded Comrade P'eng Kung-ta, the Secretary of the Provincial Committee, for having committed the mistake of military opportunism. It asked the Provincial Committee to rectify this mistake and rely on the peasant masses as the main force in the uprising, and to make practical preparations in accordance with the Central Committee's plan for insurrection in Hunan and Hupeh. At that time, after the argument had gone back and forth, and although in the end Comrade Kung-ta reluctantly agreed, the Provincial Committee, in directing the uprising, still did not rectify its old mistake of military opportunism.

(1) Kung-ta violated the Central Committee's instruction and regarded the uprising as a purely military operation. He made contact only with bandits and troops of various political hues, without getting the broad peasant masses to rise. Consequently, at the beginning of the uprising only the workers of An-yüan bravely participated in the struggle; the peasant masses of the different regions did not participate at all.

(2) In areas of insurrection there was no agrarian revolution and no [setting up of] political power. Hence the peasants thought the Communist Party only wanted to make trouble, and the Provincial Committee even doubted whether the peasants wanted land. Instead [the Committee] launched the slogan of an eight-hour day.

(3) In areas through which the Peasants' and Workers' Army passed the policy of butchering the local bullies and the bad gentry was not carried out. Hence the peasants regarded it as a "guest army" on the move. Because of these mistakes in guidance and their problematic results, the peasant insurrection in Hunan was a failure of purely military opportunism.

Finally the Central Committee announced the punishment of Mao and his comrades:

The Enlarged Conference of the Provisional Politburo of the Central Committee decides that the above-listed Party organs, which carried out the policy wrongly, and the responsible comrades be punished as follows.... The Provincial Committeemen, P'eng Kung-ta, Mao Tse-tung, Yi Li-jung, and Hsia Ming-han, shall be deprived of their membership on the Hunan Provincial Committee. Comrade P'eng Kung-ta shall be deprived of his alternate membership in the Central Politburo and placed on probation in the Party for one year. The Central Committee sent Comrade Mao Tse-tung to Hunan after the August 7 Emergency Conference as Special Commissioner to reorganize the Provincial Committee and carry out the Autumn Harvest Uprising policy of the Central Committee. He was in fact the core of the Hunan Provincial Committee. Therefore Comrade Mao should shoulder the most serious responsibility for the mistakes made by the Hunan Provincial Committee. He shall be dismissed from his position as alternate member of the Provisional Politburo of the Central Committee. . . .[96]

Mao was allowed to remain a party member—possibly on probation—but he lost all his official positions. All the actions he took and all the theses he proposed while in the Ching-kang Mountains were developed under these conditions. He was to remain in this limbo until the Central Committee rehabilitated him in June 1928, news of which did not reach him until November of that year. His boldness, creativity, and originality first became clearly manifest while his position in the party was extremely tenuous.

CHAPTER IV

Mao's Struggle in the Ching-kang Mountains 1927–28

Mao's independent political, military, and organizational lines were developed in the course of a prolonged struggle against the extreme left line adopted by the Central Committee Plenum of November 1927—the Plenum that expelled him from the Central Committee, the Hunan Provincial Committee, and the Front Committee. The history of Mao's resistance to directives from higher party organs throughout the year following this Plenum is obscure, but at least part of it can be reconstructed from several extant versions of the party struggle in the Ching-kang Mountains. The story of his life that Mao related to Edgar Snow in 1936 contains the earliest of these. Chu Teh's interviews with Agnes Smedley a year later reveal additional, sometimes conflicting details. Still more information is available in Mao's "Report of the Ching-kang-shan Front Committee to the Central Committee," which was first published in December 1947,[a] and a land law dated December 1928 is available in NTTC *(Rural Survey)*. The only eyewitness account from a hostile source is that of Kung Ch'u, a commander who deserted from the Red Army during the Long March. Kung came to Ching-kang-shan with Chu Teh's troops in April and left for another assignment before the end of the summer. His autobiography, *The Red Army and I,* includes the most detailed account available of the first conference of party organizations in the Hunan-Kiangsi border area (the First Mao-ping Conference) as well as a land law dated May 1928 and attributed to Mao.

These sources make it clear that the notion that Mao was undisputed czar of Ching-kang-shan is incorrect. In order to get his policies accepted by other Communist leaders in the border area he had to struggle constantly against opposition from the Southern Hunan Special Party Committee and the Hunan Provincial Party Committee, which acted as agents for the Politburo. He continually objected

[a] This report was republished in abridged form in HC under the title "The Struggle in the Ching-kang Mountains."

to directives that if carried out would have decimated the Red Army and wiped out the soviet base. His political line was much more moderate than that laid down by the party's leaders at the November Plenum.

Mao's Military Opportunism

When he raised the slogan of soviets during the Autumn Harvest Uprisings, Mao took the first step in the development of a line of his own deviating from that of the Central Committee. The most important political organ he created during these uprisings was a Soldiers' Soviet. He also abolished the KMT system of political directors in his army, and his Front Committee took over its functions.[1] Under the guidance of the Front Committee, the Soldiers' Soviet eliminated differential pay and rations for soldiers and officers, and instituted a completely egalitarian system controlled by the ordinary soldiers.

Until Chu Teh arrived with his troops, Mao had no competent Communist officers in his army, so he used the Soldiers' Soviets to draft reluctant non-Communist officers. In this way he forced Yü Sha-t'ou, a commander of the garrison troops in Wuhan, to take command of the army on the march to the Ching-kang Mountains. However, by the time the army reached Ning-k'ou, near the base of the mountains, Yü had deserted to the KMT, and Mao was forced to reorganize his troops. Cheng Hao, who was pressed into Yü's place, also deserted to the KMT at the first opportune moment. These desertions of experienced military officers probably forced Mao into his famous alliance with Wang Tso and Yüan Wen-ts'ai, the two bandit chiefs who had ruled Ching-kang-shan before Mao's troops arrived.[2]

When Mao set up his first independent government in the border area, in Ch'a-ling (Tsalin), he created two organs of political power—a representative Council of Workers', Peasants', and Soldiers' Deputies, and an executive organ, the People's Council. Mao did not explicitly identify this soviet government with its Russian progenitor. As a name for the representative organ he used *kung-nung-ping tai-piao hui* (Council of Workers', Peasants', and Soldiers' Deputies) rather than *su-wei-ai,* the transliteration of the Russian term "soviet." The Hunan Provincial Committee later reproved him for this oversight. It also assumed that in organizing an executive organ called "The People's Council" *(jen-min wei-yüan-hui)* he had created village councils similar to those that the Fifth Congress of the CCP had advocated in May 1927, before the break with the KMT. Those councils were to have supervised the rural economic system, but not to have attempted to seize political power.[3] It is highly likely that Mao did not know that the Comintern had called for a final break with the KMT before he set up the Ch'a-ling soviet. Ignoring this, the Hunan Provincial Committee interpreted Mao's creation of a "People's Council" in Ch'a-ling as an act of willful disobedience to the new left line and an indication of his continuing rightist proclivities, as well as a continuation of his tendency to underestimate the revolutionary quality of the unarmed peasantry. In fact, Mao admits to having followed very moderate class policies in Ch'a-ling. He attempted neither to confiscate nor to redistribute land there, although he did lead a number of guerrilla uprisings against the landed gentry in neighboring hsien.[4] However, these uprisings were carried out by his army in order to obtain food and weapons. Few local peasants in the neighboring hsien cooperated with him. On the whole they were cold and reserved, treating his troops as a "guest army."

Mao did not learn of the November Plenum's action against him until Ho T'ing-ying, representing the Southern Hunan Special Party Committee, arrived at his base of operations in March 1928. Ho deprived Mao of all his power, abolished his Front Committee, and distributed its functions to two new committees. A Divisional Party Committee with Ho as secretary took charge of all party organizations in the Red Army; a separate local committee took control of the civilian party personnel working in the border areas. Mao was denied a position on either committee. Ho assigned him the post of mere troop commander. Shortly after this minor revolution, according to Mao's own account, he was "invited" to work in southern Hunan by the Special Party Committee there.[5] The new Divisional Party Committee abolished the Soldiers' Soviets in the army and created a Political Commissariat in their place, while the local party committee abolished the People's Councils and created soviet organs, called *su-wei-ai,* in which soldiers did not take part.[6] This reorganization provided for little or no direct consultation between leaders of the local soviets and the Red Army.

Mao writes that he carried out his moderate policies from November through February. When he was deposed by Ho he was criticized for leaning too far to the right, for failing to "turn the petty bourgeoisie into proletarians and then force them into the revolution," and for not using the slogan "All factories to the workers."[7] All these slogans appear in the resolutions of the November Plenum, and all were proclaimed by the leaders of the Canton Commune. After Mao was dispatched to southern Hunan he became more rigorous about confiscating the property of merchants in cities and in assessing "contributions" from rich peasants and landlords, but he still failed to satisfy the Special Party Committee's appetite for burning and butchery.[8] The demands of the Southern Hunan Special Committee reflected the policies of the November Plenum.

Chu Teh and the Southern Hunan Special Party Committee

The date the Committee was first established has not been determined, but we do know that it was reorganized after the CCP's turn to the extreme left at the November Plenum. Chu Teh may have participated in the conference at which it was reorganized. In 1937 he reported to Agnes Smedley that he had sent out a call for a special conference of party delegates from southern Hunan and northern Kwangtung early in November 1927. The conference was held in Kuei-tung, Hunan, in the Ching-kang Mountains, from November 26 to 29. Its purpose was to plan for peasant uprisings in southern Hunan, which were to be spearheaded by the troops of Chu's revolutionary army. Mao was invited to come to the conference in person or to send a representative.[9] He may have sent his brother, Mao Tse-t'an.[10]

By the time the conference was held, Chu's army had absorbed troops from the Fourth Army, which had been defeated at Swatow; peasant troops from the Hai-lu-feng soviet area; troops of the Wuhan garrison who had served under Mao in the Autumn Harvest Uprisings but had since lost contact with him; the Communist labor organizers and some of the miners from Ta-yü, Kiangsi; and small groups of peasant organizers from Kwangtung, southern Kiangsi, and southern Hunan.[11] Thus a cross section of revolutionary activists in South China was represented at this conference.

After the Kuei-tung Conference, agitators spread out through southern Hunan and northern Kwangtung to prepare for the peasant uprisings, which had been scheduled for mid-December. According to Chu Teh, on the last day of the conference, after having sent two hundred Wuhan garrison troops back to Mao in Ch'a-ling to help him maintain his soviet government, he received a message from the Kwangtung Provincial Committee ordering him to march immediately to Canton.[12] Stalin had ordered a workers' insurrection and the proclamation of a soviet there, evidently hoping an insurrection would lend credence to his theory that the revolutionary tide was rising in China and would thereby serve to justify his China policies to the Fifteenth Congress of the CPSU.[13] After receiving this urgent call from the Kwangtung Committee, Chu began to move toward Canton. But as his troops left Kuei-tung, the peasants of southern Hunan rose, attacked their landlords, and sent to him for help. Instead of rushing all his troops to Canton, Chu sent small groups in all directions to help the peasants. As a result, by the time the main body of his army had crossed the Kwangtung border the Canton commune had collapsed. In late December, the peasant uprisings began as planned at the Kuei-tung Conference.[14] These uprisings became known as the Southern Hunan Uprisings of January 1928.[15] According to Chu's account, they actually began early enough in December—perhaps even before the Canton Commune was proclaimed—to prevent his troops from reaching Canton in time to assist with the hopeless putsch.

Kung Ch'u's story of Chu Teh's maneuvers in this period may be more accurate. According to Kung, Chu received a letter from Fan Shih-sheng in the early fall of 1927, while Chu was still in Shanghang, Fukien. Fan was a Yunnanese and an old friend of Chu's, and was then the commander of the Sixteenth Nationalist Army occupying the North River District in Kwangtung. He sorely needed more troops to control his district, so he wrote Chu that if Yeh T'ing's army was victorious in its attempt to gain control of eastern Kwangtung, he would join it, but that if it was defeated, Chu could come and surrender to him. Chu kept the letter secret, and when Yeh's army was defeated he retreated into southern Kiangsi. His army still flew the KMT flag, lived off the land, preyed on small merchants, and made no attempt to agitate among the peasants. By mid-November, with food and ammunition in short supply and the people hostile, Chu called Ch'en Yi and Wang Erh-jo, his chief political officers, and told them of Fan's offer. The three comrades agreed that they should temporarily surrender to Fan and then contact the Kwangtung Provincial Party Committee for further orders. They wrote Fan that they would be willing to surrender to him if he would permit Chu to retain command of his troops and political officers, would prohibit his political officers from interfering with political education in Chu's army, and would send Chu's army a month's supply of food and ammunition.[16]

Fan agreed to these terms, and Chu's tired army began to move toward Shao-kuan, Kwangtung, Fan's headquarters. While en route, Chu received a message from the Kwangtung Provincial Committee ordering him to march at once to Canton to assist in the uprising there. Chu discussed this order with Ch'en Yi and Wang Erh-jo, but they decided to keep their agreement with Fan. They surrendered to him in Shao-kuan on December 19, by which time the Canton Commune had collapsed.[17]

Chu's position as Fan's subordinate was extremely precarious because Fan had acted independently of his superiors in Nanking in negotiating Chu's surrender. On learning of it, Nanking disapproved of the arrangement. Early in January 1928, Fan wrote Chu again, warning him to rebel because Fan had been ordered to arrest him. Again Chu met with his political officers. They decided to rebel and march north into Hunan, where the remnants of P'eng P'ai's peasant army were located. At this conference Kung Ch'u, who had been working in Chu's political department, introduced Hu Shao-hai, a left KMT member in sympathy with the CCP, who was accepted as a replacement for the military commanders who had deserted or been killed in the long march from Nanch'ang. Before the end of the first week in January, Chu's army was in southern Hunan. Party secretaries in the major hsien were in contact with him before the middle of the month, and on January 22 his army took I-chang. On the following day, Chu reorganized his army. The KMT flag was ceremoniously lowered for the last time, and the hammer and sickle was raised. Chu's troops became the Fourth Red Army, divided into two regiments: the 28th, with Wang Erh-jo as commander and Ch'en Yi as party delegate, and the 29th, with Hu Shao-hai, the left KMT man, as commander and Kung Ch'u as party delegate.[18] Then, with the assistance of the Southern Hunan Special Party Committee, the Southern Hunan Uprisings were launched. After the major hsien cities of southern Hunan fell, Chu's troops were ordered to attack Ch'angsha. They were driven back, lost all the territory they had gained in Hunan, and withdrew eastward into the Ching-kang Mountains.

In Kung's account there is no mention of any contact with Mao's troops before Chu's army arrived in I-chang. There is no conference at Kuei-tung, and no orders concerning uprisings in southern Hunan until sometime in January. Chu's move to Hunan was occasioned by Fan's letter, not by instructions from the Central Committee.

Chu Teh's story of the Kuei-tung Conference is probably a fabrication intended to conceal the fact that he had refused to go to Canton when he could have done so. No peasant risings prevented him. No previous agreement with another Communist organ comparable in rank to the Kwangtung Provincial Committee excused his disobedience. This conclusion is partially confirmed by a letter the Central Committee sent to Chu Teh sometime between November 15 and November 30, 1927. That letter warned Chu against following Mao into the dangerous deviation of relying on existing rebellious military forces, and thereby neglecting to lead armed forces formed spontaneously by the masses. It also warned him against leading his army into a reactionary army and then using his forces to suppress mass uprisings while maneuvering within the reactionary camp. That tactic had failed at Nanch'ang and was not to be repeated. While Chu may not have received this letter personally, the Central Committee did publish it on November 30, and it was undoubtedly circulating in northern Kwangtung when he decided to join Fan's army.[19] Neither Mao nor Chu mentions any active cooperation between their two armies before the messenger from the Southern Hunan Special Committee arrived in March to abolish Mao's Front Committee. Evidently Mao had his hands too full establishing the Ch'a-ling soviet and then coping with the bandit troops he recruited to be of much assistance in the Southern Hunan Uprisings.

The uprisings continued until March 1928. The policies the Southern Hunan Special Committee urged on Mao at that time were in line with the orders of the November Plenum. Under the committee's direction the peasants did burn and kill; they also confiscated the property of the merchants in the cities and took large requisitions from the holdings of the rich peasants and landlords. These policies tended to fall in line with the inclinations of the bulk of Chu Teh's army at the time. After the defeat of the troops of Yeh T'ing and Ho Lung at Swatow, Communist officers who disapproved of the abrupt turn to the left had deserted Chu, while at the same time men who supported the new radical line had joined him. Among the latter were some of P'eng P'ai's peasant troops from Hai-lu-feng. Several of the hsien capitals in southern Hunan that rose first in December 1927 and January 1928 had been occupied by P'eng's troops in May 1927, after an unsuccessful peasant uprising against the right KMT in Canton. Wu Chen-min, for example, had occupied Ling-hsien in June. After retreating from there in July, his troops circled around in southern Hunan and Kiangsi, avoiding attack, until they joined forces with Chu's army in November.[20]

By January 1928, then, most of Chu Teh's troops probably favored the extreme left line of the November Plenum. Mao was more moderate, and more daring as well. The line he followed from November to March was directly contrary to that of his immediate superiors and of the highest party authority in China.

The Ninth Plenum of the ECCI (February 1928)

When the messenger from the Southern Hunan Special Committee arrived at Mao's headquarters in March, the policy he forced on Mao's soviet had already been officially changed. On February 25, the Ninth Enlarged Plenum of the ECCI had passed a resolution that criticized the November Plenum for its "leftist putschism" and laid down the basic features of the line adopted at the Sixth Congress of the CCP in August and September.[b] Stalin played an active role in formulating the theses on China that were presented to the Ninth Plenum of the ECCI. Neumann and Lominadze, along with Li Li-san and other CCP members, arrived from China in late January. Together with these men and his other colleagues and subordinates in the Comintern, Stalin worked out an explanation of events in China after the collapse of the united front that was consistent with the failure of the Canton Commune and with his new line on the third period of capitalist crisis. In the background was the new drive against the kulaks that he had ordered in an effort to speed the collection of grain in Siberia.

A committee composed of Stalin, Bukharin, Li Li-san, and Ho Meng-hsiung presented the resolution on China to the Ninth Plenum. This resolution enumerated a whole series of blunders for which the local leaders of the CCP and the "direct leaders who are politically responsible to the Communist International (Comrade N. [Neumann] and others)"[21] were accountable. Preparation among the workers and peasants had been inadequate, the enemy troops had not been sufficiently subverted, there had been a faulty appraisal of the loyalties of workers in non-Communist unions, strikes had been badly organized, members of the Canton soviet had been appointed

[b] The resolution enunciating this line was drafted by Stalin, Bukharin, Li Li-san, and Ho Meng-hsiung. (North, *Moscow*, p. 120; Eto, Part 2, p. 179.) Bukharin helped formulate the theses because in February 1928 Stalin had not yet split with the right wing. Li Li-san probably superseded Ch'ü Ch'iu-pai, who was criticized at this Plenum. Li and Ho remained rival leaders of the left and right wings of the CCP until the Third Plenum of the Central Committee, in September 1930. After the Sixth Congress of the Comintern, in July 1928, Li's major opponent was Mao, but before the two could come into direct conflict, Mao had to settle his differences with both the Southern Hunan Special Committee and the Hunan Provincial Committee.

rather than elected, and in general the entire affair had been ineptly planned. A revolutionary uprising, the resolution proclaimed, must be an uprising of the masses, not a putsch. "To play with insurrection instead of organizing a mass uprising of the workers and peasants is a sure way of losing the revolution."[22]

Nevertheless, the Canton Commune was hailed as a new beginning of the Chinese revolution. Stalin began to speak of the revolution as though it were an encroaching sea: the first wave had passed, and for the moment the revolution lay in a "trough between two waves," but both the workers' and peasants' movements were on their way to another "mighty upsurge." In this situation the greatest danger to the party, the vanguard of the workers' and peasants' movements, was that it might run too far ahead of the masses. It was essential that the CCP devote its energies to winning over the masses and integrating the scattered guerrilla actions of the peasantry into the coming "new upsurge of the revolutionary wave" in the great centers of the urban proletariat. A single, national Red Army must be organized out of all the separate guerrilla detachments so that the CCP could carry out its leading task, the agrarian revolution.[23] Only after a nationwide armed insurrection could the agrarian revolution be carried to completion.

In this resolution, accepted unanimously by the Ninth Plenum, Stalin asserted that his policy had been correct and that armed urban insurrections were to constitute the main form of struggle in the immediate future. Violence and illegality—but organized violence, and carefully prepared illegality—characterized Stalin's program for China, paralleling his emergency measures for grain collection. The Communists were to unite the small guerrilla units existing in South China into a Red Army and carry out the agrarian revolution. There had been too much unorganized action since November. Now, in the trough between waves, the CCP was to stop "playing with insurrections" and thoroughly organize its cadres everywhere for the coming uprising of workers and peasants.[24] But the next great revolutionary wave had to take place under the leadership of the proletariat. Rural uprisings on a massive scale, similar to those of the winter of 1927, must be avoided until the proletariat was ready to take the lead. To do otherwise would be to play with insurrections, to split up the party's forces and allow them to be smashed in separate detachments.

A more complete analysis of the Chinese situation was worked out in the crowded months between the Ninth Plenum and the Sixth

Congress of the Comintern, during which the new program for the CCP was coordinated with that of other parties in colonial countries.

The Retreat to Ching-kang-shan

Combining the stories of Mao and Chu leads to the conclusion that they followed divergent policies before March 1928. Chu had followed the directives of the Central Committee in August and again in November 1927. Mao, however, had taken up his independent line shortly after the August 7 Conference. By the time he was expelled from the Central Committee he had formed Soldiers' Soviets and People's Councils. He had advocated soviets before the Central Committee and the Comintern officially approved of the slogan calling for them. When he set up his soviet at Ch'a-ling, he did not know that the Comintern had already called for the establishment of an urban soviet in China. In fact, as late as 1936 he did not seem to realize that Stalin had adopted this line shortly before the establishment of the Ch'a-ling soviet.[25]

Mao was also in opposition on the peasant issue: during the Autumn Harvest Uprisings he had armed all the peasants, making no class distinctions among them. Even before the November Plenum, he had decided that the policy of terrorizing everyone except the workers and the very poor peasants was not expedient for the party when it needed broad support. So as the Central Committee adopted a leftward policy, Mao veered to the right. He followed a rather lenient policy toward the rich peasants and small landlords from November until March, when he found himself deposed and his Front Committee simply abolished by the Southern Hunan Special Committee (of which Chu Teh may have been a leading member, since he was commander of the Red Army in southern Hunan at the time).

If my reconstruction of the history of Mao's first winter in the Ching-kang Mountains is correct, Chu Teh and the leaders of the troops with him were in contact with Ho T'ing-ying, and thereby knew that Mao had lost all his party posts before Mao himself did. After informing Mao of his deposition, Ho ordered him to take some of the troops from Ch'a-ling and go to southern Hunan to assist Chu in the last phase of the peasant uprising. So there were still considerable political differences between Chu and Mao when they met in late April and retreated with their armies to Mao-ping, in Ning-kang hsien, Kiangsi.[26]

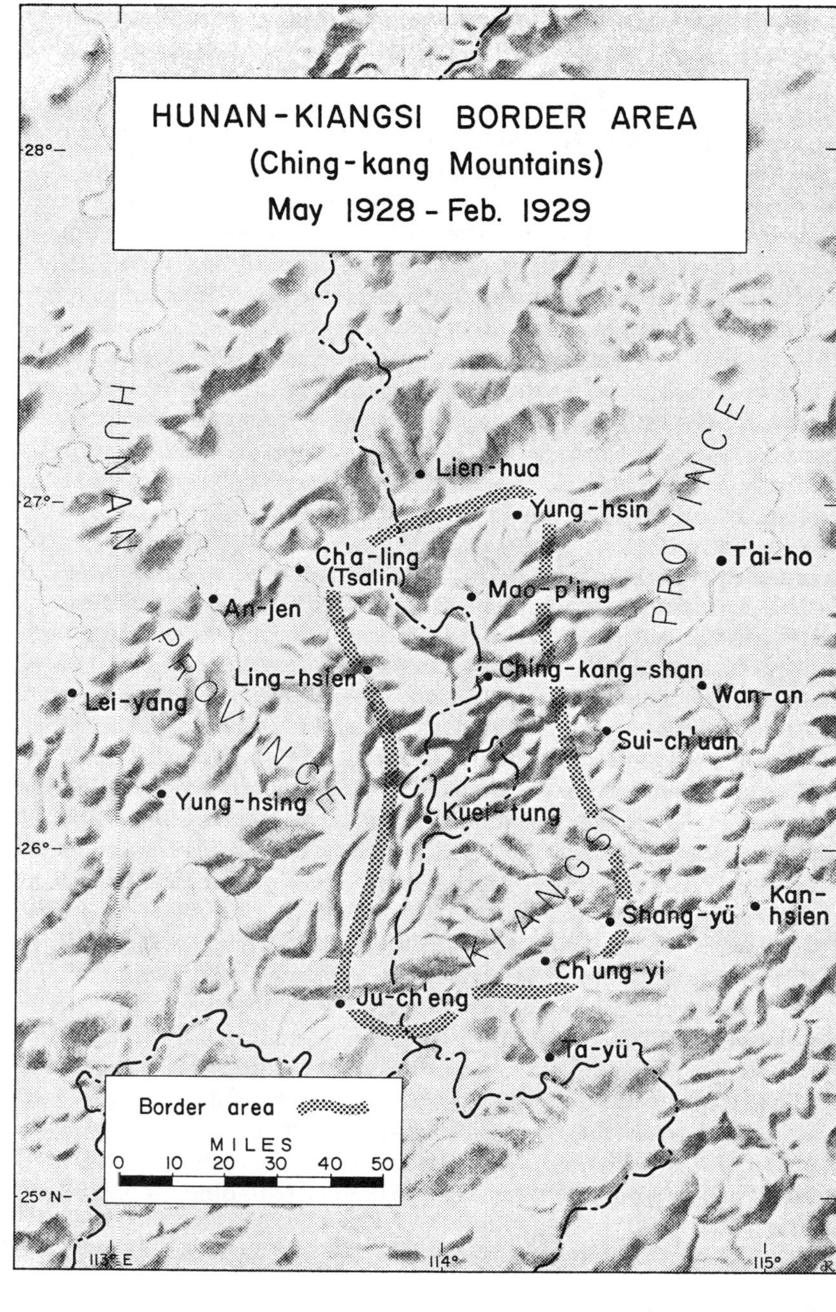
HUNAN-KIANGSI BORDER AREA
(Ching-kang Mountains)
May 1928 - Feb. 1929
HUNAN PROVINCE
KIANGSI PROVINCE
Lien-hua
Yung-hsin
Ch'a-ling
(Tsalin)
T'ai-ho
An-jen
Mao-p'ing
Ling-hsien
Ching-kang-shan
Wan-an
Lei-yang
Sui-ch'uan
Yung-hsing
Kuei-tung
Kan-
hsien
Shang-yü
Ch'ung-yi
Ju-ch'eng
Ta-yü
Border area
MILES
0 10 20 30 40 50
28°
27°
26°
25° N
113° E
114°
115°

The First Mao-ping Conference

The two armies led by Mao and Chu withdrew to Mao-ping and revived the soviet regime in the Ching-kang Mountain area. Mao and Chu were the dominant figures at the first congress of party organizations in the border area, held on May 20. This congress set up the First Ching-kang-shan Special Committee, which was composed of twenty-three members, with Mao as its secretary.[27] Ho T'ing-ying's Divisional Party Committee was probably abolished at this time, if it had not disappeared earlier. If a committee had been appointed to take charge of local party organizations when Mao's Front Committee was dissolved in March, it was probably either eliminated or absorbed into the First Special Committee. The Special Committee revived the local soviet governments, which had collapsed after Mao's troops left the Ching-kang Mountain base in March. An Army-Party Committee was also elected at Mao-ping. It abolished the system of political directors in Chu's army and established Soldiers' Soviets instead. In his November report to the Central Committee, Mao defended this change on the grounds that the old political departments were a bad influence. Harking back to the charge of military adventurism that had been made against him at the November Plenum, he held that the Soldiers' Soviets would serve to weaken militarist tendencies: "When the political departments existed, the soldiers believed that political work was to be done only by the few persons in the political department. All others had only the duty of fighting. After the political departments were abolished everyone both fought and did political work. This broke the precedent of simple military-mindedness."[28]

From May until early in July, the Chu-Mao coalition was relatively free from interference by higher party agencies. The alliance these two leaders formed at the First Mao-ping Conference survived all subsequent attacks by Li Li-san and the Returned Students. The policies they worked out at their very first conference concerning the strategy of the Red Army, soviet bases, and agrarian policy form the essential core of the Maoist line. Chu Teh, Lin Piao, Ch'en Yi, Hsiao K'e, Wang Cheng, Ch'en Kuang, Chou Hsing, Teng Fa, Ho Ch'ang-kung, Ch'en Po-chün, Chang Wen-ping, T'an Chen-lin, and T'an P'ing, all of whom remained Mao's firm supporters and reached the upper echelons of the Red Army by 1945, and some of whom were elected members of the Central Committee at the Seventh Congress in that year, were present at this seminal conference. They were all aware at the time that Mao, the man whose policies they were adopting, was not in good standing and might well be expelled from the party if his line varied too greatly from that of the new Central Committee, which was soon to be elected at the Sixth Party Congress in Moscow. As Chu Teh has testified, this conference proved to be "the most important party conference after the counterrevolution began."[29]

At the First Mao-ping Conference Mao singled out five basic characteristics of China's revolutionary war that he believed must govern the strategy and tactics of the party.

1. China was a semicolonial country. Its political development was uneven. It had relatively few workers, who were concentrated in the great industrial cities on the coast, under the guns of the imperialists. Modern cities coexisted with a backward, semifeudal countryside teeming with hundreds of millions of peasants.

2. China was large; it had abundant resources for revolution. The southern provinces had passed through a great revolution in the course of which the seeds of future revolutions had been sown. Moreover, a workers' and peasants' Red Army had been created.

3. The counterrevolutionary forces were strong. Politically organized in the KMT, they now controlled the country and were recognized by imperialist powers. Therefore they could organize huge armies, and secure weapons to slaughter the people and surround and attack the small, scattered Red Armies.

4. The revolutionary forces were weak. The Red Armies existed only in poor, backward, mountainous areas. They had no consolidated bases. They were dependent on the enemy, either through raiding or through illicit trading, for all of their supplies. This factor, Mao held, should be the major determinant of strategy and tactics.

5. Finally, the peasants were ready to revolt and redistribute the land if given the opportunity. The opportunity could arise if the revolutionary army directed by the Communist party offered them protection. In turn, the revolutionary army could exist and withstand the offensive campaigns of the counterrevolutionaries if—and only if—it were amply supported by the peasants.[30]

On the basis of Mao's analysis, Chu Teh and his associates advanced their ideas of the tactics appropriate for a small, weak Red Army faced by a powerful enemy:

> Enemy advances, we retreat.
> Enemy halts and encamps, we harass.
> Enemy seeks to avoid battle, we attack.
> Enemy retreats, we pursue.[31]

The Conference also adopted the famous "three disciplines" and "eight additional rules" to govern the conduct of the soldiers of the Red Army. These were designed to gain and hold the trust of the people.[c]

The conferees further decided that the six-hsien area in the Ching-kang Mountains should first be consolidated as a revolutionary base and then gradually expanded into the surrounding provinces in a series of waves. In the revolutionary base all land was to be confiscated without compensation and distributed to the peasants, who were to be armed, organized, and trained to defend their new possessions. Chu and Mao agreed that enemy prisoners should be treated generously and absorbed into the Red Army whenever possible. Mao's policy of moderation toward the intermediate classes—small merchants and middle and rich peasants—was adopted. Free trade with the KMT areas was allowed and even encouraged.[32] These decisions of the First Mao-ping Conference governed the strategy and tactics of the CCP and the Red Army in the Ching-kang Mountain base from May until early July, when delegates from the Hunan Provincial Committee arrived with new orders.

Mao's Conflict with the Hunan Provincial Committee: The Three Letters

According to Mao's November report to the Central Committee, the first of three letters from the Hunan Provincial Committee was delivered in late June. Yüan Te-sheng, who brought it, at least approved of the Front Committee's plan to establish a soviet regime in the six-hsien area. He disapproved of practically everything else.

Early in July two more messengers, Tu Hsiu-ching and Yang K'ai-ming, delivered another letter from the Hunan Provincial Committee to the effect that the army at the base should advance immediately into southern Hunan. Only two hundred rifles were to be left to defend the base itself. When Tu and Yang arrived, a special conference of the Army-Party Committee (Ch'en Yi as secretary), the Special Party Committee (Mao as secretary), and the Yung-hsin Hsien Party Committee (probably Wan Hsi-hsien as secretary) met and decided to disobey the orders from the Hunan Provincial Committee. Tu and Yang remained. Using their influence over the peasants who had fled

[c] These were rules regarding the behavior of the army in the villages. They were designed to prevent the soldiers from antagonizing the population. See Mao Tse-tung, *Selected Works of Mao Tse-tung*, vol. IV [84], 155–56.

to the base from southern Hunan in March, they persuaded the 29th Regiment of the Red Army to march to Chen-hsien. The Army-Party Committee then directed the main body of troops to follow them. Mao was left behind with the Yung-hsin Hsien Committee.[33]

Mao's tactics at the joint conference were probably too clever. The conference had been held in Yung-hsin, Kiangsi. Although the votes of the Yung-hsin Hsien Committee probably gave him the majority he needed to reject the orders of the Hunan Provincial Committee, the majority of the Army-Party Committee may have voted against him. From Mao's confused report of the incident, one may gather that the decision of the Army-Party Committee to follow the orders of the Hunan Provincial Committee was taken after the joint conference broke up. Mao and Wan Hsi-hsien remained in Yung-hsin after the joint conference and were therefore not present when Tu and Yang brought pressure to bear on the 29th Regiment and the Army-Party Committee.[34]

Wang K'ai-ming held another ace, which he soon played. He had been appointed secretary of the Special Committee of the Border Area by the Hunan Provincial Committee, and had arrived in Yung-hsin with his credentials in order. Mao had held that position before Yang arrived. Evidently after the joint conference in Yung-hsin broke up, Yang's authority was recognized by the Army-Party Committee. He then became "acting secretary" of the First Special Committee, either by displacing Mao or by creating a rival Special Committee. According to Mao, Yang remained "acting secretary" from July until September. It was under Yang's direction that almost the whole of the Red Army marched into southern Hunan and more than half of its men were lost. While Chu Teh's army was in southern Hunan, the Hunan Provincial Committee ordered the abolition of the Soldiers' Soviets and the creation of a regular Political Commissariat. Although many soldiers opposed this move, Chu bowed to superior party authority and carried out his orders. The immediate result was the desertion of the 29th Regiment and the complete failure of the southern Hunan campaign. Mao labels this episode the "August fiasco." After the army returned to the border area, the Soldiers' Soviets were reestablished and the Political Commissariat again abolished.[35]

Ten days after the second letter arrived, Yüan Te-sheng, the first messenger, returned bearing a third letter. By this time Mao had probably lost his position as secretary of the First Special Committee. The third letter, he writes, cursed him bitterly and demanded that the Red Army should immediately set out for eastern Hunan; it warned that this policy was correct and must be followed without delay.[36] Mao pointed out to Snow that at the time he received the letter such a policy was pure adventurism. By this time the 29th Regiment had probably already left for southern Hunan.[37] The orders from the Hunan Provincial Committee not only led to the "August fiasco," but also caused the Red Army to miss an opportunity to link up with P'eng Teh-huai's new Red Army in P'ing-kiang, a hsien in northeastern Hunan in which Communists had organized strong miners' unions.

Mao evidently favored a movement to the north into Kiangsi, but only for reconnaissance. In July, P'eng Teh-huai had led an uprising among the KMT troops attacking the Ching-kang-shan base from the north. This led to a minor civil war among KMT forces, providing an opportunity to enlarge the Communist base. But, Mao writes, almost the whole of the Red Army had left the base in late July, in accordance with instructions from the Hunan Provincial Committee, leaving him with too few troops to take advantage of the split among the KMT forces in Kiangsi. Only a small vanguard could be sent to join P'eng's forces, for the KMT armies on the Hunan front were not fighting among themselves at the time. To have sent a large force to either eastern or southern Hunan would have exposed the base to an attack it could not have withstood.[38] When Mao wrote his critique in November, the advance to southern Hunan had already proved disastrous. The Red Army had fought at Chen-hsien only to be defeated; it had taken Kuei-tung only to lose it. Finally, in late August, Mao's forces marched to assist the main body of the Red Army and helped to suppress a mutiny in its ranks. These adventurous military actions aroused the KMT in both Hunan and Kiangsi: in September it launched a tight blockade of the small mountain base.[39]

Mao Purges His Opponents

In June, when Mao still controlled the First Special Committee, open recruitment in all six hsien increased the number of party members in the base area to more than 10,000. After Yang took over the Special Committee and Chu Teh's army left the base, the KMT invaded the entire area. The new party members then became turncoats and led the *min-t'uan* (private forces of the landlords) to arrest many of their comrades. In early September, after the main Red Army returned, Mao and his cohorts carried out a drastic purge of the party, dissolved the party organization in the two hsien in which the greatest number of turncoats had been recruited, and ordered a complete reregistration of all party members in the base. At the same time an underground party organization was created with a structure parallel to that of the visible party. This underground organization, the first in the border region, controlled all the visible operations of the party.[40] The September purge was the first major party purge in the base area. It enabled Mao and his adherents to create a loyal and disciplined party unit out of the scattered remnants of the party inherited after the collapse of the first united front with the KMT. According to Mao, careerists, adventurists, and opportunists were the main targets of this purge.[41]

The Ching-kang-shan party organization was in a peculiar position. The area it controlled included six hsien, three in Hunan and three in Kiangsi. In ordinary times the hsien party organizations would have been subject to the authority of their respective provincial committees, and it is quite evident that the Hunan Provincial Committee claimed jurisdiction over Mao and the soviets in Hunan. Mao attempted to reject the claim and sent out feelers to the party organizations in Kiangsi. He contacted the Wan-an and Ki-an hsien organizations, but he does not mention any contact with the Kiangsi Provincial Committee.[42] He probably knew that the Kiangsi Provincial Committee was not operating in the southwestern part of the province. Its leader, Fang Chih-min, had led his troops to northeastern Kiangsi in August 1927. He was having quite as difficult a time with hsien party leaders in that area as the leaders of the Hunan Provincial Committee were having with Mao. A delegation from Wan-an did manage to reach Ching-kang-shan before the blockade closed in on the mountains in September. Thus when the Second Mao-ping Conference opened in October, representatives of the Hunan Provincial Committee as well as delegates from at least one hsien in Kiangsi outside the base area were present.[43] Their presence ensured that viewpoints different from those of Mao and Chu would be well represented.

The Leaders of the Hunan and Kiangsi Provincial Committees

Fang Chih-min was secretary of the Kiangsi party in 1926 and 1927. He probably continued in that office in 1928. He did not leave the area to go to Moscow for the Sixth Congress, at which he was elected to the Central Committee, but remained in Kiangsi until 1935, when he was captured and killed by the KMT.[44] There is no evidence that Mao's relations with Fang were antagonistic. In January 1930, Mao claimed that Fang agreed with the policies he and Chu had worked out in Ching-kang-shan.[45]

The exact opposite appears to have been the case in regard to Mao's relations with the man who became secretary of the Hunan Provincial Committee in the summer of 1928. The first secretary to hold the post in 1928 disappeared or was killed before the end of the summer, and Kung Ch'u was summoned from Ching-kang-shan to take his place. Kung left Ching-kang-shan in August, but was unable to reach the Provincial Committee's headquarters in Ch'angsha and so was sent on another mission. Another man, probably Jen Cho-hsüan, was appointed secretary instead, and held office until 1930.[d]

The accusations the first secretary of the Hunan Provincial Committee had brought against Mao did not become less useful to Mao's enemies after the secretary's disappearance or death. Li Li-san later made use of them, condemning Mao for his supposed alliance with lumpenproletarians and bandits, his conservatism, his "localism of peasant consciousness" (parochialism), and his "guerrillaism infected by the viewpoint of the lumpenproletariat."[46] This seems proof enough that the Comintern leadership approved the November Plenum's condemnation of Mao; that these epithets were not the secretary's own devious inventions, but rather expressed authoritative disapproval of Mao's policies and fears for his ideological soundness.

The Sixth Congress of the Comintern, July–September 1928

The new Stalinist line of the Ninth Plenum of the ECCI was amplified at the Sixth Congress of the Comintern; its application to China was spelled out at the Sixth Congress of the CCP, held concurrently in Moscow. The line adopted at the Comintern Congress declared that the capitalist world was at the end of its stable phase and entering an epoch in which its internal contradictions would cause wars, revolution, and the ultimate disintegration of the capitalist system. In order to take full advantage of the coming high revolutionary tide, the Communist parties must radicalize the proletariat and bring it directly under their control. Alliances with leaders of the social democratic parties were no longer in order. Social democrats were worse than the bourgeoisie; they were the very worst traitors to their class.[47]

In highly developed countries, where capitalists were the main enemy, the revolution would lead directly to the dictatorship of the proletariat. But in semicolonial countries, of which China was one,

[d] Kung was ordered to go to a tiny soviet district in southwest Kwangsi near the Indo-Chinese border. (Kung [63], pp. 157–60.) Jen Cho-hsüan (Yeh Ch'ing), like Mao, was a founding member of the CCP. In 1922 he had reorganized the Chinese Youth Corps in France, ridding it of anarchists. Jen spent much of his time between 1921 and 1925 in France and Moscow, then returned to China to become a leader of the Chinese Communist Youth Corps in Kwangtung.

native capitalists were not the main target—the primary objective was the elimination of feudalism and foreign imperialism. In such countries the revolution would lead to a dictatorship of the proletariat *and* the peasantry. The CCP was instructed to break all connections with the bourgeoisie, build up independent leadership of the proletariat, and ally itself with the peasantry. Independent leadership of the proletariat was to be achieved through strikes, demonstrations, dissemination of revolutionary propaganda among members of unions controlled by the bourgeoisie, and the creation of Communist-controlled unions among unorganized workers. The CCP was to become the party of the proletariat rather than a two-class party. Therefore the peasants were not to be recruited into the party; Communists were to reach them by working through and with committees and unions of peasants. When the revolutionary situation warranted, the CCP should establish revolutionary action committees to coordinate workers' and peasants' organizations. Ultimately, in the period of mass uprisings, soviets of workers' and peasants' deputies were to be elected.[48]

Finally, the long-run defense of the Communist movement required that in the coming upheaval all Communist parties must work to protect the interests of the USSR.

The Sixth Congress of the CCP, July–September 1928

There are no verbatim reports available of the proceedings of the Sixth Congress of the CCP. There is no complete list of delegates, and there are few accounts of what happened at the Congress. Putting together the stories of Li Ang (who did not attend) and Chang Kuo-t'ao (who did), I have drawn up the following account of the factional groups in the Chinese delegation and their relations to the new cleavage between Stalin and Bukharin.

The Chinese delegates were highly factionalized in spite of the fact that known supporters of Ch'en Tu-hsiu were not allowed to attend. Supporters of the United Opposition among the Chinese students in Moscow at Sun Yat-sen University were also excluded. The factions in the Chinese delegation, however, did not divide along the same lines as did the supporters of Zinoviev, Trotsky, and Stalin in the European parties. According to Ch'ü Ch'iu-pai, the fundamental division of opinion at the Sixth Congress was between the leftists, who believed that in spite of the CCP's defeat in 1927 the revolutionary tide would soon rise again, and the rightists, who feared that it had subsided for an indefinite period.[49] On this issue the leftists were in basic agreement with Stalin's new line, while the rightists were in agreement with Bukharin and the Trotskyites. Trotsky held that the reactionary forces in China were still very powerful, and characterized by stability, while the revolutionary forces were extremely weak and had an unstable base of support. Bukharin's interpretation of the forces in action during the "third period" was similar to Trotsky's.

According to a recent account by Chang Kuo-t'ao, the left wing was led by Li Li-san, Chou En-lai, and Ch'ü Ch'iu-pai, and the right wing by Chang Kuo-t'ao, Ts'ai Ho-shen, and Hsiang Ying. The Chinese delegates were so evenly divided that Pavel Mif (Stalin's agent in the China section of the Comintern's Far Eastern Bureau) was able to pick the semi-literate Shanghai worker Hsiang Chung-fa as a compromise candidate for secretary-general of the CCP. Because the conflict between the two wings of the party was so intense, the wording of several passages in the resolutions of the Sixth Congress was ambiguous, based on uneasy compromises. According to Chang Kuo-t'ao, Mif had a great deal to do with the day-to-day proceedings of the Congress.[50] There is no record of any former Comintern representatives to the CCP attending. Nor is there any record that Stalin himself either attended the Congress or personally intervened in the drafting of its resolutions. Mif and Bukharin, the latter now in silent opposition to Stalin's new left turn, jointly worked out a line to which Stalin did not publicly object at the time. The new struggle between Stalin and Bukharin in the CPSU Politburo had not yet been publicly disclosed to the Chinese comrades, but they were as aware as others in Moscow of the still concealed conflicts.

The Sixth Congress of the CCP mirrored the general statements of its sister congress, tempered by Bukharin's still considerable influence and by the fact that the CCP had been almost totally obliterated. The revolutionary tide was to rise in China, but caution forbade a policy assuming the new wave would come in the near future. The CCP was not at the time in a position to stage uprisings—all uprisings after the Canton Commune debacle had been adventurist. The Nanch'ang, Autumn Harvest, and Canton uprisings, however, had not been adventurist. They had failed because the leaders had not correctly estimated either the extent of the failure of the revolution in July 1927 or the strength of the imperialist and reactionary forces at the time of the rebellions.[51] The uprisings had been foredoomed by an overemphasis on the peasant movement, to the neglect of the urban workers. "The direction of [party] work should have been resolutely shifted from direct armed insurrection on a large scale to better day-to-day organization and mobilization of the masses."[52] The activities of Chu and Mao—the Southern Hunan Uprisings as well as the premature establishment of soviets on Ching-kang-shan—clearly fell under this rebuke.

As head of the Comintern, Bukharin had overall supervision of the proceedings of the Congress. In spite of his duties elsewhere, he found time to reprimand Ch'ü, Chou, Chang, Li, and Hsiang Chung-fa.[e] He reprimanded all the leaders of the left wing and only one of the leaders of the right. All reported reprimands of the leftists were for the failure of the Canton and Nanch'ang uprisings. Chang was reprimanded for "opportunism."

The Ninth Plenum had directed that guerrilla units in the countryside should be linked together for organization into a national army; the Sixth Congress shifted the emphasis to regaining control of the workers' movement in the cities.[53] The organization of a nationwide Red Army could be completed only on the eve of a nationwide insurrection, and the agrarian revolution could be carried to completion only after the insurrection. As long as the revolutionary waters were relatively calm, the main task of the party was to win over the masses and bring the workers' movement abreast of the peasant movement. The failures of the CCP after July 1927 were in part laid to the fact that the upsurges of the workers' and peasants' movements had not coincided. While the peasant movement was still forging ahead of the workers' movement it was necessary for the party to concentrate its energies and its best cadres in the cities. Especially in those provinces where the revolution might first be victorious it was necessary for the workers' movement to lead the peasants. Before the new upsurge, the party was to strengthen discipline in both its central and provincial organs, as well as its local cells. When the new revolutionary wave broke, the CCP was to call for simultaneous armed uprisings in the countryside and in the urban centers. When the likelihood of victory in one or several provinces was assured, a workers' and peasants' democratic dictatorship should be created. This government should take the soviet form under the hegemony of the proletariat. The significant phrase "hegemony of the proletariat" did not appear in the resolutions of the Ninth Plenum of the ECCI; it was not added to the formula until the CCP's Sixth Congress.[54]

[e] No reprimands to others present at the congress have been recorded. See North, *Moscow*, p. 128. North's information is based on Li Ang [66], chap. 6. Though Li started for the congress, he was suspected of anti-Stalinist proclivities and sent back to China after reaching Irkutsk.

Politically the new formula meant that both workers and peasants would be represented in the soviets, but that the CCP would be the sole party in the state. From the economic point of view it meant that the peasant movement could not overcome the entrenched power of the feudal classes in the villages without the help of the proletariat. The reasons for this were simple. The agrarian revolution could not be completed without assistance from some urban class. In colonial countries, and also in semicolonial countries such as China, the bourgeoisie was oppressed by both feudalism and imperialism and was therefore too weak to lead the agrarian revolution against feudalism. Only the proletariat was potentially strong enough and progressive enough to assist the peasants in their war on the landlords.

As the strongest Communist party in Asia, the CCP was enjoined to model itself on the German Communist Party, which played a similar role in Europe. Li Li-san was to follow the pattern for armed insurrection laid down in Heinz Neumann's manual, which described the tactics used in urban insurrections from the Paris Commune to the Canton Commune. It is likely that from late 1928 through 1930 the CCP received its instructions through the Comintern bureau in Berlin.[f] It is also possible that Li Li-san may have been instructed to follow the same tactics Neumann used in late 1928 in breaking up the bloc of Stalinists and Bukharinites in the German party to prevent any unification of Chinese factions in opposition to the new left line emanating from Moscow.

At the conclusion of the Sixth Party Congress a new Politburo was elected (see Table 2). The left extremists, having been reproved for Stalin's errors, won control of the party. All but one of the men Bukharin reprimanded for their left putschist activities during the uprisings of late 1927 were included in the new Politburo. Hsiang Chung-fa, the new secretary-general; Li Li-san, head of the Propaganda Department; Chou En-lai, head of the Orgburo; P'eng P'ai, head of the Peasant Department; Ch'ü Ch'iu-pai, the new Comintern representative—all were left-wingers. The sympathies of Liu Shao-ch'i, head of the Labor Department, and Hu Wen-chiang, head of the Military Department, are not known for this period, but both men probably inclined toward the left. This, at any rate, was the belief of

[f] In the absence of diplomatic relations between China and the Soviet Union from 1928 until 1932, Soviet interests in China were represented by the German government. Communication with the CCP via Germany may have been swifter in that period than by the difficult routes through North China or Japan, though it seems likely that Soviet diplomats and trade representatives in Japan also acted as Comintern agents at least part of the time.

TABLE 2

CCP Politburo Elected at the Sixth Congress

Name	*Post*	*Political Leaning*
Hsiang Chung-fa	Secretary General	Left (?)
Chou En-lai	Organization Bureau	Left
Li Li-san	Propaganda Bureau	Left
Hu Wen-chiang	Military Bureau	?
Liu Shao-ch'i	Labor Bureau	?
P'eng P'ai	Peasant Bureau	Left
Ch'ü Ch'iu-pai	CCP Representative to the Comintern	Left
Chang Kuo-t'ao	?	Right
Ts'ai Ho-shen	?	Right

NOTE: With the exception of the data on Ts'ai Ho-shen, this is from Brandt, Schwartz, and Fairbank, pp. 24–25. The item on Ts'ai is from North, *Elites*, p. 111.

Comintern officials, grounded on the fact that each had previously worked under Li or Chou.

In the year following the Sixth Congress the CCP Politburo had a mandate to guard against the "right danger," which in China meant predominantly the influence of Ch'en Tu-hsiu, not of Bukharin. However, Stalin already had warned against the right danger in the Comintern, and shortly after the Congress he launched his major attacks on the new right opposition in the CPSU Politburo.

Mao's Assessment of the Sixth Congress of the CCP

In 1945 Mao condemned the Sixth Congress for its lack of foresight on the issue of how soon the revolution would be consummated. The delegates, he said, had overlooked "the protractedness of the democratic revolution."[55] However, Mao did agree with their judgment that the immediate task of the party "consisted not in launching attacks or organizing insurrection, but in winning over the masses."[56] Mao also agreed with the Congress's analysis of Chinese society, and with its ten-point program (a general statement of things to be accomplished during the democratic stage of the revolution).[57] He also agreed with its statement that the revolution was developing unevenly and that in midsummer 1928 the political situation was relatively quiescent.[58]

By 1945 Mao had identified three defects or mistakes in the work of the Sixth Congress. The first and most important was its failure to make a correct assessment of the vacillating character of the intermediate classes, and, as a result, its failure to devise policies to take full advantage of the contradictions existing in the reactionary camp.[59] Because the delegates to the Congress failed to comprehend class alignments, on their return to China they opposed the correct theses and policies on the relation between the agrarian revolution and the land revolution that Mao had advocated as early as the spring of 1927. The main point of these theses was that "the peasants' fight for land is the basic feature of the anti-imperialist and anti-feudal struggle in China.... The Chinese bourgeois-democratic revolution is in essence a peasant revolution; the basic task of the Chinese proletariat in the bourgeois-democratic revolution is therefore to give leadership to the peasants' struggle."[60] These theses, Mao implies, were opposed by the August 7 Emergency Conference, by the November Plenum, which expelled him from the Central Committee, and by the Sixth Congress of the CCP. Opposition to these theses in the Central Committee of the CCP, sanctioned by the Comintern, laid the basis for continued attacks on him after the conclusion of the Congress. The new Politburo also opposed the thesis Mao presented in April 1929, which declared that the Chinese bourgeois-democratic revolution would fail only if the peasants were deprived of proletarian leadership, but it would never be impaired by the overwhelming peasant majority in the Chinese revolutionary forces.[61] Later the Politburo also opposed the thesis he presented in defense of his land law of February 1930, the essence of which was that small landlords should not be deprived of the means of making a living, since the revolution, while weak, could not afford to alienate the vacillating intermediate classes.[62] Mao writes that he first proposed this thesis in the conferences held in Ching-kang-shan from October to December 1928.[63] He indicates that these correct theses were opposed by Li Li-san and the Returned Students on the basis of the defective resolutions of the Sixth Party Congress.

In his critique of the way in which the Li Li-sanists interpreted the line of the Sixth Congress, Mao attacked their tactics for dealing with the bourgeoisie. The left line in all periods, he states, "invariably stood for a fight against the bourgeoisie as a whole, even the upper stratum of the petty bourgeoisie."[64] Moreover, in the period of the third left line (January 1931–January 1935) the Politburo under Wang Ming and Po Ku placed as much stress on the struggle against Chinese capitalists (including the rich peasants) as on that against landlords and imperialists, and so narrowed the base of peasant support for the revolution that the Red Army was forced to evacuate the old soviet base in the south.[65]

The errors in estimating the alignment of class forces made at the Sixth Party Congress, and the Politburo's failure to make sound judgments of changing class alignments (their ebb and flow), resulted in the party's failure to utilize correctly "every fissure in the camp of the opponents" and its own "ability to find allies."[66] Before 1931 the outstanding intermediate political group was the Third Party. Between 1931 and 1935 the main opportunity for cooperation with a political group opposed to the KMT occurred during the Fukien revolt of 1933. In neither case did the Politburo sanction cooperation or alliance. Not everything Mao condemns in the estimate of the situation by the Sixth Party Congress can be found in its resolutions. The judgment of the Politburo on the ebb and flow of class alignments was determined, especially after Stalin's ruthless attack on all rightists in the first half of 1929, by a strictly Stalinist interpretation of these resolutions. In 1945 Mao admitted that his opposition to Li's left line originated in the middle of 1929.[67] Thus it coincides with the completion of the first known exchange of letters between the new Politburo and the Front Committee, with the expulsion of Bukharin from the chairmanship of the Presidium of the ECCI, and with the rise of the ultra-leftist interpretation of the resolutions of the Sixth Party Congress. Bukharin's fall does not, of course, enter into Mao's public account of his controversy with the left extremists. In fact, in his account he denies to the Comintern or its agents any effective role in China after the Sixth Congress of 1928: his attack is on the leaders of the CCP. It would seem that the CCP Politburo acted independently after that date.

The Conferences in Ching-kang-shan, October–November 1928

The KMT blockade of Ching-kang-shan that began in September 1928 did not completely isolate the base. A messenger from the Ki-an Hsien Committee brought the news of Mao's reappointment as secretary of the Front Committee on November 2, and P'eng Teh-huai's army broke through the blockade in December.[g] The messages brought on November 2 included no information about the Sixth

[g] This information has been omitted from the 1951 HC, but can be found in HC (*hsü-pien*), p. 53. Li Wen-ling was probably the messenger who brought the letter from Ki-an to the base, since a Red Army brigade under his command entered the base on November 2. See Mao, HC (*hsü-pien*) [87], pp. 60–61.

Congress of the CCP. Mao had been reappointed by the Central Committee before the Congress convened—he certainly was aware that his position might have once again been undermined at the Congress itself.

One of the purposes of the September purge was probably to give the Maoist faction a majority at the conferences scheduled for October and November. In the course of the purge, Yang K'ai-ming was removed from his position as acting secretary of the First Special Committee and replaced by T'an Chen-lin.[h] The second congress of party organizations in the border area, the Second Mao-ping Conference, was called soon afterward. It convened on October 14. On the last day of the Conference, a nineteen-member Second Special Committee was elected. T'an Chen-lin became secretary, and Ch'en Cheng-jen became his deputy. The membership list of the new Special Committee throws some light on the balance of forces in the party organization after the September purge. Mao was on the committee, ranking fifteenth in a list of nineteen. Everyone outranked him except Wan Hsi-hsien, his supporter at the joint conference in July; Wang Tso, one of the two bandit chiefs with whom he had formed an alliance when he first fled to the Ching-kang Mountains; and Yang K'ai-ming and Ho T'ing-ying, the two instructors from the Hunan Provincial Committee.

T'an, though chairman, appeared to have little following of his own. He was someone's front man, quite possibly Mao's—his later career points in that direction. But it is possible that he was chosen by a military clique not yet quite convinced that Mao was their ideal political leader. Chu Teh was the first military man to recognize the necessity of subordinating the army to political direction. At the First Mao-ping Conference he had found in Mao the political mentor he could trust and follow for the rest of his life.[i] The other military men in Ching-kang-shan probably did not realize quite so soon that without leadership by the civilian political center the military leaders might degenerate into ordinary warlords with a veneer of radicalism, and their troops into bandits. The names of Chu Teh and Ch'en Yi stand out on the list of members of the Second Special Committee, but additional military men were surely represented among the obscure persons on the list. At the Second Mao-ping Congress, ac-

[h] Mao writes that "Yang fell ill and T'an Chen-lin took his place." (SW, I, 97.)
[i] Smedley, *Great Road*, pp. 226–27. This is also Schwartz's thesis in *Chinese Communism*, p. 173.

cording to HC, Mao presented his exposition of the party's situation at the time and his proposals for its tasks in the future, after which the Congress adopted his resolution titled "Political Problems and the Tasks of the Border Area Party Organization." But this does not mean that he was already a dominant figure in party councils, for he does not claim to have been a member of the Standing Committee elected from among the members of the Second Special Committee.[68]

The letter Mao received from the Central Committee on November 2 was dated June 4. It reappointed him secretary of the previously abolished Front Committee, which he then reorganized on November 6. According to his report, the reorganized committee was made up of five members with himself as secretary, Chu Teh ranking second, and T'an Chen-lin ranking third. All three were members of the Second Special Committee. The other two members were Sung Ch'iao-sheng, one of the first Communist labor organizers in the mines of Hunan and Kiangsi,[69] and Mao K'e-wen, a peasant comrade. Neither of the two had been elected to the Special Committee. Together with these four men, Mao took over the direction of the Second Special Committee. The Front Committee, he reports, took charge of the local party, thereby usurping the role assigned to the Standing Committee elected by the Second Special Committee.[70] The right of Mao's new Front Committee to make policy was severely limited. According to the directive of the Central Committee, it was to be subject to the Hunan Provincial Committee when it was in Hunan and to the Kiangsi Provincial Committee when it was in Kiangsi.

The Sixth General Assembly of the Red Army was held on November 14, about a week after the Front Committee was reorganized. The same letter from the Central Committee that authorized reorganization of the Front Committee also demanded the abolition of Soldiers' Soviets and the immediate establishment of a Political Commissariat —a repetition of instructions previously sent through the Southern Hunan Special Committee and the Hunan Provincial Committee. Under Mao's leadership, the Sixth General Assembly of the Red Army refused both to abolish Soldiers' Soviets and to organize a separate political department. Mao defended his system of army-party organization by asserting that there were too few political workers. Those sent by the Central Committee, he explained, could just as well be utilized in the Soldiers' Soviets.[71]

At this meeting a new Army-Party Committee of 23 members was elected, of whom five men became the Standing Committee. Chu Teh, who was more favorable to Mao, replaced Ch'en Yi as chairman of the Standing Committee.[72] By this process the Front Committee subordinated the Army-Party Committee to itself, and Mao established his supremacy among the army and party men in Ching-kang-shan. Under a strict system of democratic centralism, Mao's position was secure as long as two men on his Front Committee voted with him. In addition to a secretariat, four departments were organized under the control of the Front Committee: propaganda, organization, trade union, and military. As long as Mao and Chu remained in the Ching-kang Mountains, the Front Committee was in charge of the local party organs. The Special Committee was retained, however, so that the Front Committee could travel with the army.[73]

After the experience of the summer's fighting, most of the men gathered on the mountains reaffirmed the policies laid down by the First Mao-ping Conference. Their basic problem was military: to hold the base. In adverse circumstances they were to struggle resolutely against the enemy, and preserve discipline in defeat; in favorable circumstances to advance gradually "in a series of waves," not by leaps over enemy territory. The strategic plan of the army was to concentrate Communist forces when the enemy could be successfully attacked, but never to allow their own phalanx to be broken into small contingents that could be separately crushed.[74] As long as they were small and weak, they favored a mountainous base difficult for the enemy to attack with large concentrations of troops. The conference recognized that political tasks also required the army's attention, particularly the need to develop in the base a civilian party organization, deepen the agrarian revolution, and train a local militia so the peasants could defend their economic gains after the redistribution of land.

The problem of the party leaders was twofold: to control the military and subordinate military to political strategy, and to win over the masses who lived in the bases and strengthen their loyalty to the soviet government. The system of Soldiers' Soviets was designed to create a close bond between soldiers and their officers and also, by involving every soldier in political education, to instill in the army a strong political loyalty to the Red regime. Effective implementation of a correct policy on the agrarian revolution would not only win the support of the peasants in the bases; it would gain the support of peasants on the fringes of the soviet area, who would then assist the Red Army in its travels through their territory.

Solution of the Agrarian and Peasant Problem

During their first year in the Ching-kang Mountains there was too much fighting both with the enemy and within the party to permit the Communists to work out a realistic solution to the problem of land redistribution. Nevertheless, several party units had the opportunity to carry out at least one land reform. Such experiences led to a reevaluation of agrarian and peasant policies. When the major portion of the Red Army left the base in August the loyalty of the various classes of peasants to the revolutionary forces was severely tested. In Mao's judgment after the event, the agrarian policies of the first year had been too radical. Because the party had attacked the small landlords and rich peasants unremittingly, these classes had "incited the reactionary troops to set fire to large numbers of houses of revolutionary peasants."[75] In Mao's judgment the poor peasants were isolated in Nationalist areas by counterrevolutionary power and weakened in Red areas by CCP policy. Mao believed the solution to this problem lay in a more lenient policy toward the intermediate classes, who in the villages he defined as small landlords and rich peasants.[76] The major political task of the party, as long as it controlled only a small and weak base, was to win the support of these classes. Here we have the wellspring of Mao's "rich peasant line."

In the small areas actually occupied by the Red Armies in 1927–29, soviets were created and land redistributed. Whenever the Red Army was driven out by KMT troops the land was returned to its original owners and the soviets either disappeared entirely or went underground. Only a very few, small, scattered areas remained in Communist hands continuously throughout that period. Ch'a-ling, where Mao had proclaimed his first soviet, was held tenuously, and only from November 1927 until early spring 1928. The party operated more or less continuously only in the mountainous areas in Ning-kang and Yung-hsin hsien.[77] In these three areas in which the party held control for some time, Mao's moderate agrarian policies were applied.

To the west of the base area, in the village of Sha-tien, Kuei-tung hsien, land was redistributed twice: once in March, according to one formula, and again in August, according to another. Both formulas followed the radical policies of the Central Committee. KMT troops took over after each redistribution and returned the land to the landlords.[78] To the east of Ching-kang-shan, the Wan-an Communists established a soviet that for a short time in 1928 claimed jurisdiction over 100,000 peasants. This soviet issued slogans demanding the division of landlord-owned acreage among the peasants, as well as the confiscation of retail stores, small factories, and industries, but it probably distributed no land.[79]

In at least one area the party experimented with collectivization. Wang Shou-tao, secretary of the Special Committee of the Hunan-Hupeh-Kiangsi Border District, reports that in the spring and summer of 1928:

> The collective system of cultivation was experimented with in Liu-yang and P'ing-kiang, but nobody knew how to begin the land revolution, having had no experience. Later on we received instructions from the party, after the Sixth Congress [of the Comintern]. The collectivization experiment had no good results. We attempted to consolidate all farms and share work among the peasants, dividing crops at harvest. The peasants did not respond well to this. Their demand was for land of their own which each family could cultivate for itself. The party recognized this and altered its policy. . . . The division of land then began, and development was accelerated. In 1929 the "Soviet Government of the Hunan-Hupeh-Kiangsi Border District" was established, and I was a member of the committee, being then twenty-two years old.[j]

The experiment in collectivization in P'ing-kiang and Liu-yang is important to our story because it was from this area that P'eng Teh-huai led his troops to the Ching-kang Mountain base in mid-December. In bringing with him men who had experience in collectivization, P'eng disturbed the delicate balance in favor of the moderate policies of Mao and Chu.

A document titled "Confiscate All Land, Set Up Soviets!" issued by the Central Committee sometime between February and June 1928 had been included with its letter of November 2. The document called for the confiscation of all land. Ownership was to remain in the hands of the soviet government with the peasants retaining only use-rights, and all sale of land was prohibited.[k] This Central Committee directive laid the basis for a new struggle against Mao's moderate agrarian policy. After long discussion among the comrades in Ching-kang-shan, Mao drew up his December 1928 land law, which incorporated the Central Committee directive.

The law is printed, with an annotation, in NTTC. In the absence

[j] Wang Shou-tao, interview with Nym Wales, *Red Dust*, pp. 78–79. The addition in brackets identifying the Sixth Congress as that of the Comintern was made by Wales. However, Wang was surely referring to the Sixth Congress of the CCP, held concurrently and also in Moscow.

[k] Mao, HC (*hsü-pien*), p. 54. Both provisions were later features of the Li Li-san line.

of another English translation of this, the earliest known land law written over Mao's signature, I have translated it in full, with Mao's annotation.

LAND LAW

December 1928, on Ching-kang-shan

I

All land shall be confiscated and shall become the property of the soviet government. Three methods shall be used in dividing the land:

A. Division among the peasants, each cultivating his share independently.

B. Division among the peasants for collective cultivation.

C. Distribution to the soviet government for the organization of model farms (to be cultivated under the supervision of the soviet government).

Of these three methods, the first shall be primary. Under special circumstances, and when the soviet government has the strength, the second or third method shall be initiated and used.

II

After the soviet government has confiscated and divided the land, all sale of land shall be prohibited.

III

After the land has been divided, all persons except the old, the young, the sick, those who have no strength to work, and those who hold responsible public positions shall be compelled to work.

IV

Criteria that shall be used in redistributing the land:

A. According to the number of persons in each family: men and women, old and young, shall each receive an equal share.

B. According to ability to work: those able to work shall receive twice as much as those unable to work.

Of the two criteria above, the first shall be primary. Under special local circumstances the second criterion may be used. Reasons for using the first criterion are:

1. If the old and the young receive smaller shares of land before the government has completed its preparations for caring for them, it will be impossible for them to maintain life.
2. Dividing the land according to the number of persons in each family is a more simple and convenient method.
3. The number of families in which there are neither old nor young is very small. Also, if the old and young who are unable to work in the fields do not receive an equal portion, before the land has been divided the government must set aside an appropriate amount of land for public welfare institutions to be responsible for their care.

V

Standard geographical or political units within which the land is to be divided:

A. The village as the unit.
B. Several villages as the unit (e.g., Hsiao-chiang-ch'ü in Yung-hsin).
C. The *ch'ü* [the political and administrative subdistrict] as the unit.

Of these three, the first shall be primary. Under special circumstances either the second or third criterion may be used.

VI

Regulations for dividing mountains and forested lands:

A. In dividing tea mountains and kindling mountains, the same method as that used in dividing rice fields shall be followed. The village should be taken as a unit. Within that unit there should be equal division. Once the redistribution has been completed, each person shall have the use of those areas that have been distributed to him.
B. Bamboo mountains and mountains with large trees shall become the property of the soviet government. However, after receiving permission from the soviet government the peasants may have the use of the bamboo or wood. For permission to use less than fifty units [i.e., trees] of either bamboo or wood, the village soviet government shall grant permission. For permits to use [more than fifty and] less than a hundred units, permission must be received from the ch'ü soviet government. For the use of more than a hundred units, permission must be received from the hsien soviet government.
C. Only the hsien soviet government shall sell bamboo or wood outside the hsien. Money from these transactions shall be used to support the higher levels of the soviet government.

VII

Regulation for the collection of land taxes:

A. According to the circumstances of production, the land tax shall be assessed at three levels: (1) fifteen per cent, (2) ten per cent, (3) five per cent.

   Of these three levels, the first shall be primary. Under special circumstances, and after permission has been received from the higher levels of the soviet government, the second or third level of taxation may be applied.
B. If there are natural disasters or other special circumstances, and if permission from the higher levels of the soviet government has been received, no land tax shall be collected.
C. The land tax shall be collected by the hsien soviet government. The moneys received from this tax shall be allocated by the higher levels of the soviet government.

VIII

Handicraftsmen working in the villages or *hsiang* [townships], if willing to participate in the division of land, shall receive one half as much as full-time peasants.

IX

Officers and soldiers of the Red Army and the Red Vanguards, and responsible workers in the government and other public organs, shall receive a share in the division of land equal to that of the peasants. The soviet government shall employ persons to work their land for them.

Mao's annotation to this early land law was without question added later, probably either in 1937 or in 1941. It reads as follows:

This land law was enacted in the winter of 1928 in Ching-kang-shan (soviet of the Hunan-Kiangsi Border District). It was our conclusion after one full year of experience in the land struggle, from the winter of 1927 to the winter of 1928. Before that period no one had any experience. There were several mistakes in this land law. First, all land was to be confiscated. Only the land of the landlord class should have been confiscated. Second, the ownership of land remained in the government. It should have been returned to the peasants. The peasants were granted only the right of use. Third, the sale of land was prohibited. All of these were errors in principle; later all were corrected. As for collective cultivation and the use of the criterion of labor power in the distribution of land, the law stated that these were not to be the primary methods. Private cultivation and the criterion of equal distribution according to the total number of persons were to be the primary methods. At the time, although those who wanted to follow the first methods [redistribution according to labor power and collective cultivation] had found them unsatisfactory, the comrades who continued to advocate their use were not few. Therefore the law was written in this way.[l] It was changed afterward, and only the latter methods [equal distribution and private cultivation] were to be used. The provision that persons were to be hired to cultivate the land allotted to Red Army men was later changed to read that peasants should be mobilized to cultivate it for them.[80]

The provisions of the law containing what Mao described as errors in principle were changed four months later to comply with a directive issued by the Central Committee after the Sixth Congress. According to Mao's record, the Central Committee also proposed that a person with ability to work should receive twice as much land as one without, while his own position (which had been attacked at the Sixth Party Congress as an "illusion of petty-bourgeois socialism") was that land should be distributed to old and young, male and female, each receiving an equal share.[81]

[l] Mao implies here that many of the comrades from P'ing-kiang and Liu-yang who had attempted to make collective cultivation work were dissatisfied with the system (and knew that the peasants objected to it). There were, nonetheless, a number of comrades, including some who had only a theoretical knowledge of collective cultivation, who continued to advocate this system, so the law did not entirely prohibit it. The models for these collectives were probably the communes that had appeared in Soviet Russia during the period of War Communism. Stalin's model of collective farms had not yet been invented.

Mao does not concede that this conflict involved principle. At issue, of course, is the definition of principle. Mao suggests that formulas for determining how much land each person should receive were a matter of tactics, which local party units should have the right to modify. However, the Central Committee and the Comintern—for this directive on agrarian policy was undoubtedly written in Moscow—held that these formulas were essential elements of the line, and that no mere local committee could modify them. The issue at stake, then, was Mao's willingness to obey Comintern instructions and implement Central Committee directives.

Mao argued against the policy of "complete confiscation and thorough redistribution" at the Second Mao-ping Conference because this policy brought both the landed gentry and the intermediate classes under attack and caused the poor peasantry to become an isolated force.[82] Nevertheless, that policy was written into his December land law. On this issue, at least, Mao and Chu appear to have submitted to the Central Committee's directive and altered the moderate agrarian policies for which they had previously achieved a majority.

Collectivization and equal distribution of land probably were the main issues rehashed in December after the arrival of P'eng Teh-huai. P'eng himself may not have disagreed with Mao and Chu (in spite of the rumors to that effect rampant in the early Kiangsi period), but it is quite likely that some of the men in his army did. While the decision to leave Ching-kang-shan in January 1929 was precipitated by a shortage of food, the decisions on who should leave and who should stay were probably influenced by individual positions taken in the December debates over agrarian policy. Once Mao and Chu left the base with their own supporters, their policies again took on the more moderate tone characteristic of Mao's report to the Central Committee on the Second Mao-ping Conference.

Summary

This review of the history of Mao's year in the Ching-kang Mountains indicates that he developed his moderate policies on the agrarian problem and on the treatment of intermediate classes soon after the failure of the Autumn Harvest Uprisings. He was unable to convince everyone at the two Mao-ping Conferences of the correctness of these policies—they were even unacceptable to many of the Communists gathered in the base itself. This may have been because of Mao's tenuous position in the party. That he had been deposed from his position on the first Front Committee was no secret; Chu Teh and others learned of it from their connections in the Southern Hunan Special Committee. Mao's power was nearly as shaky as his official position. Even though his Front Committee was revived under another name in May, he could not maintain control over it in the face of the challenge from the Hunan Provincial Committee in June and July. Only after the military policy advocated by the Provincial Committee had ended in failure was Mao able to purge the party and begin to build a machine loyal to himself. His conflict with the Provincial Committee was probably a factor in the choice of Kiangsi as the Red Army's field of operations after the descent from Chingkang-shan, in spite of the fact that the areas for expansion chosen by the Second Mao-ping Conference had been Hunan and Hupeh. The fact that Chu had many contacts in the KMT army in Kiangsi was also a major determinant.

The policies pursued by the CCP after the August 7 Emergency Conference were first drawn up at the secret meetings outside Nanch'ang in late July 1927. Stalin, who had refused to condone the Nanch'ang Uprising before it occurred, seemingly gave his approval after the fact. However, he probably did not trust the men who had voted to carry it out against his direct orders. Everyone who had planned armed uprisings before Stalin's reversal on Nanch'ang certainly stood under the dark cloud of his disapproval. At the November Plenum of the CCP almost all the leaders of the Nanch'ang and Autumn Harvest Uprisings were reprimanded. When Mao was expelled from all his party offices for undervaluing the leadership of the proletariat in the agrarian revolution, he was particularly criticized for the failure of the Autumn Harvest Uprisings. The Central Committee attributed this to his "military opportunism"—his reliance on the army rather than on the people themselves—as a result of which he had prematurely created Soldiers' Soviets.

When Stalin moved to the left after December 1927, Mao moved to the right. Fundamentally, Mao's moderation was a pragmatic response to the difficult situation in which the small guerrilla units in South China found themselves. His awareness of the wider horizons of the world Communist movement probably had little or no effect on his tactics, nor did the shifting alignments in the CPSU have much influence on the policies he worked out and recommended to the CCP Central Committee at the Mao-ping Conferences. With Stalin's shift to the left, the old moderate leaders of the peasant movement in the CCP began to lose their hold on positions of importance in the party. They were initially replaced by cadres drawn from the student leadership of the labor movement and from the extremely radical leaders of the Hai-lu-feng soviet. When the Sixth Congress of the CCP met, Li Li-san and Hsiang Chung-fa were selected as the new leaders of the party.

In the years following, the major conflict between Mao and the Li Li-san Politburo centered on the issues of peasant and proletarian consciousness. Li, a labor leader, represented the proletariat in the party, while Mao stood for peasant consciousness. Li viewed Mao's emphasis on egalitarian distribution of land and equality between soldiers and officers as characteristic of peasant consciousness. When he returned to China in the fall of 1928, Li was well prepared to point out the errors of Mao's military and agrarian policies. Mao had been reappointed secretary of the Front Committee, but Li intended to subordinate that committee to the Politburo, through regular party channels. In his view Mao's appointment was probably on condition of good behavior.

In the Ching-kang Mountains Mao had begun to work out his independent military, organizational, and political lines in opposition to higher party organs. Those who agreed with him formed the nucleus of the faction that would continue to support him in his prolonged conflict with Li Li-san and the Returned Students.

CHAPTER V

The Leftward Turn in the Comintern

Until the left KMT expelled the Communists in July 1927, Stalin consistently supported the CCP-KMT united front from above and within, which entailed dual membership of all Chinese Communists in the CCP and KMT as well as participation of CCP members in the governing organs of the KMT party, army, and government.[a] In 1927, in a last massive assault on Stalin's growing power, Trotsky, Zinoviev, and their followers (the United Opposition) concentrated their attack on Stalin's policy toward the KMT. Throughout the spring of 1927, Trotsky argued that Chinese soviets should be organized immediately. Stalin and the majority of the CPSU Politburo refused to countenance the suggestion. By July the opposition withdrew the demand, for by that time the revolution had already been defeated as a result of Stalin's bungling. Without soviets to rely on, the tactics of the united front from above and within had exposed the workers' movement to disaster and the CCP to defeat and decimation. No clearer illustration could be found, the opposition argued, of Stalin's erroneous Menshevik trust in the bourgeoisie.

Stalin picked up the soviet slogan soon after Trotsky dropped it. By November he was urging the immediate formation of urban soviets in China. Heinz Neumann organized the Canton Commune in mid-December on Stalin's direct orders, and carried it through in the face of serious misgivings on the part of CCP leaders in Canton. It was Stalin's last desperate attempt to demonstrate the wisdom of his

[a] The united front is always part of a Communist party's tactical arsenal. In right-wing periods, a party may ally itself with leaders of Social Democratic parties against capitalists, thus forming a united front from *above*. In left-wing periods it may ally itself directly with the workers against Social Democratic leaders, in an attempt to achieve control of the entire workers' movement. This would be a united front from *below*. The united front with the KMT was unique: by joining the KMT and officially holding membership in both parties—even subordinating themselves to the KMT leadership during crucial periods—the Communists formed a united front from *within*.

strategic direction of the Chinese revolution from 1925 to 1927. But the Canton Commune was a fiasco—it existed less than three days. In its aftermath the KMT literally wiped out the CCP's Canton branch, which had been one of the most powerful and best organized of its urban units.

However, events in China could not shake Stalin from his position of power. At the 15th Congress of the CPSU (in December 1927), the Congress at which Trotsky and the United Opposition were permanently overcome, Stalin had the audacity to hail this fiasco as the successful product of his correct guidance of Chinese policy. Attempting to vindicate his belated demand for soviets in China, he opined that the era of capitalist stabilization was coming to a close and that a "third period" was about to begin in which capitalism would face an ever-deepening crisis. Communist parties everywhere must prepare to take advantage of the tides of revolution rising all over the world, but because the crisis in the capitalist world increased the danger of military attack on the Soviet Union, they must also be prepared to defend it, the bastion of world revolution.

When this argument was first advanced in December 1927, it was purely a theoretical justification of Stalin's strategic direction of the Chinese revolution. No signs of crisis had yet appeared in the capitalist world. Nonetheless, the new thesis immediately drew the support of the majority of the CPSU Central Committee, a majority composed of the Stalinist center and the Bukharinist right wing. That coalition had consistently formed the majority in the CPSU Politburo since the rupture of the Zinoviev-Kamenev-Stalin Troika in 1925.

Once the United Opposition had been overcome, Stalin could afford to adopt many of its policies. In January 1928, he tentatively repudiated the New Economic Policy (NEP), which had been adopted in 1921 to increase production, particularly of food, and to maintain the economic and political bonds between town and country in the USSR. He thereby rent the former majority in the Politburo and drove the right wing into opposition. In this struggle, the primary issue was the peasant question.

Stalin's Leftward Turn in Internal Affairs

Stalin's sudden departure from the NEP probably resulted more from a necessity of the moment than from a deliberate plan of long standing. His apparatus had to devise a way to meet a sudden crisis in grain procurement. By 1927 the amount of grain on the market had fallen to half the prewar level, and during that year there was another precipitate fall. By January 1928 grain on the market stood at three-eighths the prewar level.

Food for the cities was in short supply, and no grain was available for exports, which were urgently needed to pay for the machinery required for the relatively modest industrial construction projects approved by the October 1927 Plenum of the CPSU.

Stalin and his *apparatchiks* reacted to the new crisis in characteristic fashion. With his staunch supporter Molotov, Stalin set out for the grain-growing regions of western Siberia, where he ordered "emergency measures." He invoked the clause of the criminal code providing for the confiscation of the land holdings of speculators, and revived the committees of the poor that in the era of War Communism (1918–21) had supported the Red Armies and the factory workers by forcefully requisitioning "surplus" grain from the villages. Members of the new committees were promised one-fourth of all grain confiscated from individuals exposed by their investigations.

On his return to Moscow, Stalin launched an attack against the local party and soviet officials who opposed his emergency measures, accusing them of disregarding the needs of the village poor and of protecting the kulaks and grain speculators. On February 13, while the Ninth Plenum of the ECCI was in session, Stalin delivered a slashing attack against those who opposed him.[1] The Commissariat of Agriculture became a hunting ground for scapegoats. The commissar himself, A. P. Smirnov, was dismissed from his post on March 6 and accused of "peasant deviations." In April Stalin informed the Central Committee that a thorough purge of the grain-collecting agencies had already been completed, and that "obviously corrupt elements, who do not recognize classes in the villages and do not want to 'quarrel' with the kulak"[2] had been eliminated. At its April Plenum the Central Committee announced that in order to obtain grain in adequate quantities the state had begun an intensive drive against the kulaks, and that a program was immediately being undertaken to transform individual peasant farms into collectives.[3]

Stalin's emergency measures had instantly aroused opposition in the Politburo. The members of the emerging right opposition—Rykov, Tomsky, and Kalinin—opposed his drastic measures in Siberia, his order to drop Smirnov, and his purge of the grain-collecting agencies, but they were not powerful enough to deter him. In July Trotsky referred to the rightist faction as Rykovist, not linking Bukharin's name with it at all. In fact, as late as May, Bukharin had failed to make any firm commitment to members of the pro-peasant or Rykovist faction. At first he greeted the new policy of collectivization as "a cultural revolution" in the countryside. A few weeks later (in June) he changed his mind and privately attacked Stalin as the real source of Trotskyite peril in the Politburo.[4] By that time the mutual recrimination in the Politburo and Central Committee had become so bitter that it was obvious Stalin intended to eliminate all who supported the former NEP line on grounds of genuine conviction. Bukharin felt threatened by Stalin's intrigues and secretly went to consult with Kamenev, one of the leaders of the left opposition he had helped to depose the previous year. He recognized at last that Stalin was an "unprincipled intriguer" who would change his theories "according to whom he needs to get rid of at any given moment."[5]

At the July Plenum of the Central Committee, held while the Sixth Comintern Congress was in session, Bukharin presented his objections to Stalin's extraordinary measures in Siberia. Exploitation of peasants through taxation of their productive capacity he deemed correct, but not so the criminal and semi-criminal "excesses" to which they had been subjected.[6] To him Stalin appeared to regard violence as an end in itself. Replying to these attacks, Stalin coolly identified opposition to the ruthlessness of his methods of accelerating collectivization with opposition to the goal of collectivism itself. In Communist theory collectivization is a historically progressive step that should bind the socialist towns and the peasant countryside together at a new and higher level. According to Stalin, by resisting his emergency measures the pro-peasant faction was maintaining and developing capitalist relations in the countryside, a policy that would ultimately increase antagonism between town and country. Stalin, on the other hand, was planning on overcoming the contradictions between the proletariat and the peasantry through collectivization, which would establish a new bond between the two great classes. All who opposed his policies he termed "not Marxists or Leninists, but peasant philosophers, looking backward instead of forward."[7]

Although he had thrown down the gauntlet in the Politburo, Stalin's first public moves were cautious. Throughout 1928 he warned of the right danger but neglected to identify anyone in the Politburo as a rightist. In November, he could still obtain the support of the right wing to unseat three highly placed members of the Moscow branch of the party and replace them with his own supporters. At the Eighth Trade Union Congress in November and December, Tomsky's grip on the trade union apparatus was undermined by the election of five Stalinists to the Trade Union Council. At the joint meeting of the Politburo and the Presidium of the Central Control Commission that was held in early February 1929, Stalin broadened his attack against Bukharin, Rykov, and Tomsky. Trotsky had just been deported, and the Trotskyites had just published the records of Bukharin's secret talks with Kamenev the previous summer. This provided the issue. Called before the joint session to account for his unprincipled factional behavior, Bukharin refused to retract his errors. At a later session of the same joint meeting (on February 9) the three leaders of the right presented their platform denouncing the Stalinists for "military-feudal exploitation" of the peasantry, for "dissolving the Comintern," for "propagating bureaucracy," and for eliminating all democratic practices within the party. A majority of those present in turn condemned the trio for advocating the preservation of a free market economy and a reduction in the tempo of industrialization. Only after the right presented its platform were certain unnamed rightists condemned in *Pravda* for breaking with Leninism.[8]

The rightist objections to Stalin's new course were based on Bukharin's theory of economic equilibrium, which held that the essential element in planning was the determination of the conditions for maintaining a dynamic equilibrium between all spheres of production. Super-industrialization, Bukharin asserted, would precipitate breakdowns in the economy, thus causing shortages, and would ultimately retard the economy's speed of development. The greatest sustained rate of industrial development, he argued, could be obtained only on the basis of a rapidly expanding agriculture. Each sector of the economy must receive back a part of its profits as well as its cost of production. If any sector failed to receive back at least a part of its own profits the whole economy would fall into disequilibrium, stagnation, and decline. Long-continued deprivation of the agricultural sector would slow the development of industry, break the bond between peasants and workers, lead the party into a reactionary system of "military-feudal exploitation" of both peasants and workers, increase the powers of the bureaucracy, and lead to the degeneration of the Soviet state. Overwhelming the rightist leaders with disciplined majorities at the April Plenum of the Central Committee, the Stalinists declared that Bukharin's theory of economic equilibrium was a screen for political attacks on the party's leaders, and that all laws of equilibrium were "class alien" non-Marxist notions, i.e., notions that did not take class struggle into account.[9] In order to condemn Bukharin's economic theories on the broadest possible ground, Stalin interfered for the first time in the philosophical controversy between two Marxist schools, the mechanists and the dialecticians. In 1929 Bukharin was the most popular exponent of mechanist views, while A. M. Deborin and A. S. Martynov (two former Mensheviks) were the leaders of the dialecticians. The mechanists emphasized the continuity of development from lower to higher forms, and the links between all levels of phenomena. The dialecticians, on the other hand, stressed discontinuities between higher and lower forms and processes, and dwelt upon the idea of a dialectical leap that separated various orders of lawfulness.

The dialecticians provided the theoretical basis for Stalin's attack on Bukharin's theory of equilibrium. Stalin found the notion of the dialectical leap most useful in his attack on the political line Bukharin deduced from his economic theory. In objecting to accelerated industrialization, Bukharin had stressed the necessity of continuity of development and the dependence of higher social orders on less developed forms. He had stressed, in other words, continuity in economic development from the capitalist system to the new social order. Thus he called for objectivity and balance in state planning. The Stalinists emphasized the independent role of human consciousness, the notion that willful purposive activity could overcome the old deterministically ordered capitalist system and replace it by a higher social order. The leap from the old to the new would be determined not by nature but by men.[10]

Stalin made clear the political import of Bukharin's philosophical views in his speech to the April Plenum of the Central Committee. In that speech he charged that the Bukharinist faction did not understand the class changes taking place in the Soviet Union, that they did not understand that the class struggle must be intensified in the period of transition to a completely socialist economy. As a result, they did not realize that the kulaks had become a class enemy. They did not understand that on the collective farms a new, consciously created bond was developing between the workers and peasants. While Bukharin was certainly a theoretician, Stalin said, he could not be called a *Marxist* theoretician: his views on the state were befouled by anarchism, and he had never really understood the Leninist theory of the transition period, the theory of the dictatorship of the proletariat.

At the Second Congress of the Marxist-Leninist Institute of Science, held in April 1929, mechanism was denounced as a philosophical movement blatantly inconsistent with the fundamental principles of Marxist-Leninist philosophy. The dialectical school of Marxist thought that was led by Deborin was declared to be orthodox for all loyal Communists. The dialectical philosophers were given control over the philosophical section of the State Printing House, the appointments to all important philosophical posts in the Soviet Union, and all relevant publications.[b]

Stalin held that Bukharin was not only a bad theorist, but an unprincipled, devious intriguer as well. While Bukharin had accused the party's leadership of deviating toward Trotskyism, he himself was secretly trying to form a bloc with the Trotskyites. Moreover, the objections that he and Rykov had made to Stalin's emergency grain measures on the grounds of principle could only be based on bourgeois-liberal sentiments; they were not Marxist. The rightists, Stalin argued, now had a line of their own, contrary to that of the Leninist majority. This right deviation, as well as all conciliatory tendencies toward it, must be fought—by ideological persuasion if possible, by organizational weapons if necessary.[11]

Such was the substance of Stalin's speech to the April Plenum. At the time Stalin charged that Bukharin's ideas were a perversion of Marxism, everyone was fully aware that the philosophical views of the right wing had been well within the pale of orthodoxy until the moment he made his speech, that Stalinist *apparatchiks* did not control the schools and universities of the Soviet Union, and that the dialecticians, while opposed to the philosophical views of the mechanists, were not Stalinists. The very fact that Stalin had charged that one school of philosophy was unorthodox and had linked it with a category of political deviation inevitably aroused resistance in new

[b] As events were soon to reveal, even the dialecticians were not Stalinists. Deborin, together with Y. Sten, N. Karev, and others among his students, had previously belonged to a minority faction among the philosophers whose ambitions Stalin used in his struggle against the right wing. (Wetter, pp. 132–36; Daniels, pp. 361–62.) Within a year Stalin was to censure the Deborinist school as menshevizing idealists whose philosophical views were all too closely associated with those Trotsky espoused. (Wetter, pp. 154–74.)

This was almost inevitable, for Sten had sided with Trotsky in Trotsky's clash with Stalin over soviets in China in the spring of 1927. Sometime in 1930 or 1931, Sten and Karev were demoted for opposing Stalin's war on the kulaks. Martynov, who like Deborin had been a Menshevik, had at one time propounded the thesis that there would be a peaceful transition in China to the dictatorship of the proletariat "without decisive collisions and acute conflicts with the existing government [of KMT China], without a second revolution." In the great debate in the spring and summer of 1927, Trotsky and Zinoviev had endeavored to place the responsibility for this thesis on Bukharin and Stalin. (Stalin, *On China*, p. 106.)

quarters. Stalin's own *apparatchiks* were not able to take over the main philosophic posts and entrench his brand of undisguised class partisanship (*partiinost*) in all Soviet philosophy until January 1931.[12]

Tomsky, Rykov, and Bukharin eventually lost their positions of power, but the process covered a three-year period. The attack on Bukharin did not lead immediately to a purge of all comrades with right-wing views in the Political Secretariat of the Comintern or the Central Committees of non-Russian parties. Stalin needed time to replace the older cadres with men loyal to himself. In the spring of 1929 his major problem was the consolidation of control over the apparatus of the Soviet state. Its international appendages were important, but few of his men could be spared from the more immediate task at home.

The Purge of the Right Opposition

Throughout the first half of 1929 the Comintern apparatus in Moscow was racked with a purge of rightists and Trotskyites, in a prelude to the removal of Bukharin from his position as chairman of the ECCI on July 3.[13] Before Bukharin's public disgrace the right opposition in the CPSU had stressed the continued danger of Trotskyism, while the old left opposition split up. Some leftists continued to support Zinoviev and Kamenev, while others gave their support to Stalin's new left line. After Bukharin's public disgrace, the Stalinist majority in the CPSU Central Committee continued to struggle on two fronts. On the one hand, they stressed that the right deviation was now the main danger, and on the other, they accused the followers of Bukharin, Trotsky, Zinoviev, and Kamenev of forming an unprincipled alliance against the correct leadership of the party. This new turn in the struggle had immediate repercussions in the ongoing purge of the Comintern.

After the purge of Bukharin, Stalin became the dominant figure in the Comintern. This great change was signaled on Stalin's fiftieth birthday in December 1929, when the unremitting adulation of Stalin began. After that date, no other individual in the Comintern acquired a position of prestige similar to that previously held by Zinoviev and Bukharin—which is to say that no one was ever again to seriously rival Stalin's leadership of the party.[c]

[c] Replacements for the Comintern officials who fell in the purge were almost all Stalin's men. Molotov, who stepped into Bukharin's shoes as chairman of the ECCI, remained one of the most powerful men in the Comintern until he was elevated to the chairmanship of the Soviet Council of People's Commissars after the

Factional Alignments of Representatives to the CCP

Galen, Borodin, and Voitinsky

After the collapse of the united front with the KMT, all of the advisers associated with that fiasco were recalled. Galen, Borodin, and Voitinsky had all been sent to China while Lenin was alive and Zinoviev still chairman of the Comintern. All were replaced during the purge of the United Opposition.

After the capitulation of Zinoviev and some of his supporters, and their subsequent readmission to the CPSU on a probationary basis in June 1928, Galen, Voitinsky, and Borodin reappeared to play minor roles in the public life of the Soviet Union. However, they were never again allowed to take part in the formation or execution of Comintern policy or to act as Comintern representatives in China. Their fate in the great purges depended on their ability to disassociate themselves from all opposition groups. Galen succumbed in 1938. Borodin probably survived to die a natural death. Voitinsky's fate is obscure. His name appeared frequently in Soviet sources until 1938, after which, except for one instance in 1947, he was never again mentioned.[d]

Lominadze-Syrtsov attempt to oust Stalin was defeated in December 1930. The other chief figures to emerge from the purge of the rightists were Dmitrii Manuilsky, chief of the Secretariat and a major Comintern spokesman until 1943; A. Lozovsky, head of the Red International of Trade Unions; Otto Kuusinen, head of the Comintern Far Eastern Department, who survived both Stalin and de-Stalinization to become the chief theoretical exponent of Khrushchevism; and Osip Piatnitsky, chief of the Orgburo until 1937. All except Piatnitsky proved themselves reliable Stalinists by surviving the purges. (McKenzie, p. 30.) Pavel Mif and L. Magyar were the most powerful men in the Eastern Department until the great purges. (Nollau, p. 136.) Earl Browder, a Bukharin-Lozovsky appointee who had been political secretary of the Far Eastern Bureau in Shanghai since 1927, began to falter in late 1929, but his influence probably was not eradicated until Mif was sent to China in May 1930. Browder's place was taken by Gerhard Eisler and Paul Ruegg (Hilaire Noelens), both Stalin's appointees. Li Li-san probably began to develop his own line partly because of Browder's dismissal. (Nollau, p. 142.)

[d] Borodin became editor of the English-language *Moscow Daily News* in 1930, and continued in that position until his death in 1953. (Eudin and North, p. 458, Isaacs, p. 276*n*.) Galen was commander of the Soviet Union's Far Eastern Special Army from August 1929 until 1938, when he was purged. (Eudin and North, p. 457.) After a period in obscurity, Voitinsky became head of the Department of Public Affairs of the Institute of World Economics and Politics in the Communist Academy, first vice-president of the USSR Council of the Institute of Pacific Relations, and editor of *Tikhii Okean,* the journal of the USSR Institute of Pacific Relations. He lost his exclusive editorship in October 1937, when the journal was

From 1927 to 1935 the Chinese Communists who had found favor with Voitinsky, Borodin, and Galen, the men who had risen most rapidly in the party hierarchy from 1924 to 1927, were suspect. Ch'en Tu-hsiu, who had been selected as leader of the CCP by Voitinsky, was expelled, as was T'an P'ing-shan, who had also risen under Voitinsky's and Borodin's auspices. Chang Kuo-t'ao, one of Voitinsky's recruits into the party, long-time manager of the Orgburo, and the leader of those who did not want Ch'en purged for the failure of the united front policy, was soon labeled a rightist. None of the officers of the CCP fraction at the Second KMT Congress (January 1926) held a Politburo post between 1928 and 1935.[e] Of all the old cadres who had risen to the Central Committee before the Fifth Party Congress, Chou En-lai alone has since remained on the Politburo continuously. Chou's outstanding competence as a diplomat may account for his ability to stay in office, but even he was subject to frequent reprimands at least through 1931.

Pavel Mif

By 1927 Pavel Mif was the rising star who was soon to take his place as Stalin's leading China expert. He had worked in the administration of Sun Yat-sen University since its founding in 1924. After a visit to China, he had served as one of the experts who formulated theses

---

placed under a joint editorial board made up of himself, Mif, and Varga. The journal ceased publication in June 1938, at which point both Voitinsky and Mif disappeared.

Varga, however, not only survived, but continued as chairman of the Institute of World Economics and Politics until it was abolished in 1946 (probably as a direct result of the controversy between Varga and Voznesenskii over changes in capitalist economy resulting from World War II). Varga survived again, but Voznesenskii was dismissed from the Central Committee at some time in 1949, shortly after Zhdanov's death. However, Varga's authority as an economist was not revived by the purge of Voznesenskii. In Stalin's pamphlet *Economic Problems of Socialism in the USSR,* published immediately before the 19th Congress of the CPSU, Stalin sided with Varga's opponents. In the course of the attack on Varga, Voitinsky's short pamphlet *Kitai i velikie derzhavy* (*China and the Great Powers,* Moscow, 1947, cited in McLane, p. 291) was republished. Thus the Chinese debacle of 1927 remained an issue in controversies over world economics and world politics in 1945–53. (Eudin and North, p. 464; McLane, p. 102; Columbia University Russian Institute, pp. 58–59; Schapiro, pp. 532–34.)

[e] The officers were T'an P'ing-shan, Chang Kuo-t'ao, Kao Yü-han, Yün Tai-ying, Mao Tse-tung, Lin Tsu-han, Wu Yü-chang, Yang Pao-an, Han Lin-fu, Hsia Hsi, and Yü Shu-te. This group, directly supervised by Borodin, Voitinsky, and Ch'en Tu-hsiu, met daily to discuss the problems of the Congress, including persons to be supported for election. See Wang Wei-lien, "Election of the CEC at the Second Congress," *Materials of Modern History* [55], I, 94–95.

on the Chinese revolution for the Seventh Plenum of the ECCI (November 22–December 16, 1926), theses that Stalin considered defective. Mif had proposed the immediate formation of peasant (but not urban) soviets, thus advocating a line far to the left of that adopted by the Plenum. His role in early 1927 is obscure. According to one source, he was sent to Wuhan, with Wang Ming as his interpreter, in the spring of 1927. He may have carried one of the special messages Stalin dispatched to the CCP at that time. Po Ku, one of Mif's protégés from Sun Yat-sen University, who had accompanied him from Moscow, was elected to the CCP Central Committee at the Fifth Congress in May. Po became a member of the Politburo on July 13, when Chang Kuo-t'ao reorganized it after the downfall of Ch'en Tu-hsiu. However, Po lost the post less than a month later, at the August Seventh Conference. This fact suggests conflict between Mif and Lominadze, whom Stalin sent to replace Roy and Borodin in late July.[14]

By November Mif was back in Moscow and had taken over Karl Radek's position as rector of Sun Yat-sen University. In the test of strength between the Stalinist apparatus and its opposition in the demonstrations on the tenth anniversary of the October Revolution, most of the student body at Sun Yat-sen University marched for the opposition. Mif was able to muster only a few students to demonstrate for Stalin. These were the 28 Bolsheviks, the Returned Students who, under Mif's direction, took over the CCP's Central Committee at the Fourth Plenum, in January 1931. By that time Mif had become the dominant figure in the Far Eastern Bureau of the Comintern. Before his position could be secured, however, it was necessary that Roy, Lominadze, and Neumann, the other Comintern representatives Stalin had sent to China in 1927, be discredited.

M. N. Roy

Roy's fall was relatively easy to accomplish, for he had powerful rivals, and both his associates and his theories were suspect. Borodin had met him in Mexico City and recruited him into the Communist party in 1919, and had recommended him to Lenin as the man most capable of founding a Mexican Communist party. On the strength of this recommendation, Roy was appointed Mexican delegate to the Second Congress of the Comintern. At this Congress, despite his disagreement with Lenin over the formulation of Communist strategy in colonial areas, he was selected to organize a Communist party in India. Roy chose to establish his party through an Indian Bureau in

Berlin. There he clashed with a group of Indian nationalists led by Virindranath Chattopadhyaya, the lover of Agnes Smedley, who attempted to form a rival Indian Communist party, and sought Lenin's recognition for it at the Third Congress of the Comintern. But with the help of Radek Roy managed to retain recognition as the official leader of the Communist Party of India (CPI). Chattopadhyaya continued to intrigue against him and by 1925 had formed links with Indian members of the Communist Party of Great Britain. By late 1926, Roy's rivals were organizing conferences in Europe without his approval and the British party was sending its own emissaries to India to take over his organization. Roy's mission to China may have been masterminded by his rivals for control of the Indian party. As the British party's emissaries left for India, the Comintern sent Roy on his mission to China. While Roy was in China, a delegation of Indian Communists in Moscow charged that he had been exaggerating the size of the Communist apparatus in India and misappropriating Comintern funds. Roy left Hankow for Moscow on August 8, 1927, one day after the August 7 Emergency Conference that Lominadze had led. On his arrival in Moscow he learned of Stalin's new struggle against the United Opposition and of the charges brought against him by the new Indian delegation.[15]

Previously Roy and Trotsky had both opposed the KMT alliance, and had resisted the Stalinist-Bukharinist strategy based on the support of the bourgeois nationalists in colonial and semicolonial areas —i.e., in China and India. Roy felt that his position was now vindicated. Nevertheless, he sided with Stalin and placed the entire blame for the failure of the united front with the KMT on the leaders of the CCP.[16] Since this was the course Roy chose, the Chinese Communists could not be blamed for attacking any new theses he might propose. Despite Roy's tactical alliance with Stalin, his association with Borodin in Mexico and China, his arguments with Lenin at the Second Congress, his basic agreement with Trotsky on the nature of the bourgeoisie in colonial areas, and his association with Radek in Berlin all made him vulnerable to attack. When the Ninth Plenum of the ECCI opened in February 1928, Roy was still a member in good standing of the ECCI's Presidium, and he believed that both Stalin and Bukharin were his personal friends. Nevertheless, when he became ill he encountered difficulties in obtaining medical care. Apparently frightened, he fled to Berlin under an assumed name while the Plenum was still in session.[17] Although he had consistently offered public support for the Comintern line on the united front with the bourgeoisie in colonial countries, he had objected to it within the closed circles of the Comintern. His independence could not be accommodated in Moscow's increasingly monolithic atmosphere.

Before fleeing Moscow, Roy had prepared a set of theses that could have been used to justify the extension of Stalin's new left line to the colonies. In what was later called the "decolonization thesis," Roy held that the national bourgeoisie in the colonies had by that time developed a sufficiently broad economic base of their own to make them willing to ally themselves with the imperialist powers against emergent class enemies within their own countries.[18] The tactical imperative suggested by Roy's theses was that all alliances with bourgeois parties must be avoided, and that Communists must oppose all political groups sponsored or controlled by the bourgeoisie. This tactical line was adopted at the Sixth Congress of the Comintern even though Roy's decolonization thesis itself was rejected. By July 1928 it also became clear that the Russians had joined the British in wanting to abolish the Indian Workers' and Peasants' Party, the legal front of the CPI, on the grounds that no party could represent two classes. Roy was unwilling to give up the CPI's only legal front organization. Roy's direct influence on Comintern policy had ended in February 1928, at the Ninth Plenum. Yet even though he fled Moscow before the Sixth Comintern Congress and refused to support its new line, his articles continued to be published in *Inprecor* until February 1929, when Bukharin was removed as editor of *Pravda*.

One of the main reasons Roy's career was terminated may well have been that his most consistent supporters in the Berlin Indian Bureau were from the right wings of the Indian, German, and Russian parties. It is possible that he was also involved in an intrigue of Bukharin and the German Communist leaders Heinrich Brandler and August Thalheimer to weaken the power of Heinz Neumann and Ernst Thälmann, Stalin's agents in the German party.[19] When Bukharin and Roy were expelled at the Tenth Plenum of the ECCI (July 1929), Roy was labeled a right-wing opportunist, "the comrade of Gandhi, or at least the comrade of Brandler and Thalheimer."[20]

Indirectly, Roy's enemies provided the Chu-Mao faction with one of their most valuable propagandists. In 1928 Agnes Smedley arrived in China as a correspondent of *Frankfurter Zeitung*. Following the policy worked out at the February 1927 Brussels Conference of Oppressed Nationalities, she assisted in organizing the League of Left-Wing Writers and at the same time began to gather material for her famous books on the Chinese Communists. Through Smedley and others like her, the Chu-Mao faction found a voice to communicate its point of view to the non-Communist left wing in China.

Mao's judgment of these foreign advisers is curiously non-political. In 1936 he said that he regarded Roy as a fool, Borodin as a blunderer, and Ch'en Tu-hsiu, their agent, as "an unconscious traitor."[21]

Besso Lominadze and Heinz Neumann

Lominadze and Neumann, both Stalin's men, were the Comintern representatives to the CCP between July and December 1927. Lominadze appeared first. His primary mission was to make a last attempt to find some remnants of KMT left-wing leadership still willing and able to allow a Communist fraction to operate within the KMT. After the Nanch'ang Uprising occurred, he may have assisted Ch'ü Ch'iu-pai to conceal the fact that the uprising was a purely Communist affair.[22]

Over the opposition of Chang Kuo-t'ao, Lominadze chose Ch'ü to be the new leader of the CCP before the August 7 Emergency Conference.[23] Since Ch'ü, Hsiang Chung-fa, and Li Wei-han were the only full members of the Politburo who attended the Conference, and since Lominadze presumably called only on those whose support he was sure of, we can tentatively identify these men as the Chinese comrades who were closest to him.[f] We can similarly identify the men who were probably opposed to his policies as being those who had been the firmest supporters of the Nanch'ang Uprising, together with those who were eliminated from the ruling clique at the August 7 Conference: Chang T'ai-lei, Po Ku, P'eng P'ai, Su Chao-cheng, and possibly Chang Kuo-t'ao.[24] In the absence of a quorum of either the Central Committee or the Politburo, the August 7 Emergency Conference was actually illegal. But Lominadze was willing to condone this breach of Communist legality in order to secure a new CCP leadership that would embrace Stalin's policies. He assuredly would not have taken this drastic measure unless he was confident of Stalin's support.

[f] Li Ang [66], p. 21. Chang Kuo-t'ao reports five Central Committee members present at the August 7 Conference, but he himself was not there. Li Ang was. (Brandt, p. 214*n101*.)

Ch'ü later claimed that 12 members of the Central Committee attended. According to his report, the Conference took place in Nanch'ang, not Wuhan. If it did take place in Nanch'ang, a quorum could have attended, for enough Central Committee members to have formed a quorum of that body were there. (Brandt, pp. 150, 214–15.)

A conflict over some unknown issue of policy or personnel quite probably divided Mif and Lominadze after the latter arrived in China. It is indicative that Mif's protégé Po Ku, who had been elected to the Politburo when it was reorganized in July, was eliminated from it at the August 7 Conference, which Lominadze directed. A conflict between the two Russians might very well explain why Ch'ü Ch'iu-pai gave conflicting accounts, none correct, of the location of the Conference and the number of people present at it. It might also account for the fact that Lominadze did nothing to dispel the rumor that he was in some way related to Stalin.[g]

Relative or not, Lominadze did have Stalin's confidence. In the spring of 1927 he had been appointed secretary of the Communist Youth International to succeed Vuyovich, who was a Zinovievite.[25] In December 1927, Lominadze became a full member of the CPSU Central Committee. As the secretary of the Communist Youth International, he had a voice in Comintern affairs until December 1930, when he was expelled from the Central Committee in the course of the Lominadze-Syrtsov affair, which coincided with Li Li-san's trial before the Comintern Presidium. The CCP faction led by Ho Meng-hsiung and Lo Chang-lung, which was at that time advocating an Emergency Conference rather than a regular Plenum to reorganize the CCP, was probably operating under Lominadze's influence. At any rate, it was advocating the method he used to reorganize the party in August 1927—and all of its members certainly were opposed to Mif and his 28 Bolsheviks.

Thus until late 1930 Lominadze was probably one of Mif's rivals for Stalin's ear. When he was dropped from the Central Committee, the policy of urban insurrections was abandoned in favor of organizing a provisional central soviet government in those rural areas under the sway of the Red Army. While there is not enough evidence to permit the conclusion that Mif supported the latter policy, his advocacy of peasant soviets in 1926 points toward that possibility.

Before Lominadze returned to Moscow in November 1927, Stalin dispatched a young German named Heinz Neumann to South China to assist and cajole the CCP into organizing an urban uprising in time for the 15th Party Congress of the CPSU. Neumann had had experience in organizing workers' insurrections in Hamburg in 1923–24, and the technical arrangements for the Canton Uprising were

[g] This rumor was evidently unfounded, although Franz Borkenau asserts that Lominadze was Stalin's brother-in-law. However, no evidence has been discovered that supports Borkenau's assertion. (Brandt, p. 214*n96*; Borkenau, *World Communism*, p. 28.)

basically his work. After the collapse of the Canton Commune, he was recalled to Moscow, accompanied or followed by Li Li-san, Chou En-lai, Ch'ü Ch'iu-pai, and other Communists who had managed to escape the "White terror" in Canton and other Chinese cities: Teng Chung-hsia, Huang P'ing (who had been foreign affairs commissar of the commune), Yeh T'ing, Yeh Chien-ying, and Ho Meng-hsiung.

When these survivors of the first armed insurrections began to trickle into Moscow in early 1928, Stalin personally took Neumann and Lominadze to task. As in the previous July, he refused to take any responsibility for the failure of the program he had initiated, but held the miscalculation of the comrades on the spot responsible for the failure of the uprising.[26] Even though Neumann was reproved for his tactical errors, he remained in favor for several years, and his treatise on armed insurrections became the standard work on the subject. In 1929 he became one of the dominant figures in the German party. Paralleling Li Li-san in China and Barbé in France, he guided the German party along an extreme leftist course until the purge of 1931 transferred power to the hands of a more moderate group. The evidence available suggests that from early 1929 to early 1931 Stalin used the leaders of the Communist Youth International to guide all major Communist parties outside the Soviet Union along this course, the course he himself took after the expulsion of Bukharin.

At the Sixth Congress of the CCP, in the summer of 1928, the left extremists were reproved for their tactical errors, but nevertheless won control of the party. Ch'ü Ch'iu-pai, who had never been a good organizer, was replaced by Li Li-san, Chou En-lai, and Hsiang Chung-fa, who jointly ruled the party until they were unseated by Mif and his protégés late in 1930. One cannot say whether any of the left extremists in the CCP had special ties to Neumann, for it is impossible to separate out those linked to Neumann but not to Lominadze, or vice versa. But the leftists among the leaders of the CCP and the Chinese Communist Youth Corps can be identified as those who held positions in the Politburo after the August 7 Conference and were also reelected at the Sixth Congress—Chou En-lai, Ch'ü Ch'iu-pai, Hsiang Chung-fa, and Li Li-san[27]—together with those who held similar positions in the Youth Corps: Chang T'ai-lei (killed in December 1927), Jen Pi-shih, Kuan Shang-yin, Yüan Ping-hui, Wang Yung-sheng, and Hu Chin-hao.[h]

[h] Wales, *Inside Red China*, pp. 98–99, tentative list. The last three were never important figures—all of them disappeared during the Li Li-san period or shortly thereafter.

By 1930, Stalin's left turn had begun to produce factional groups with similar characteristics in both metropolitan and colonial countries, and the Comintern was taking on the character of an incomposite monolith. Borkenau suggests that Comintern secretary Manuilsky purged the true believers in left extremism in the first half of 1930, replacing them with political opportunists who would willingly change their line at any time it should be required of them.[28] In the latter part of 1930 and the first half of 1931, Li Li-san, Lominadze, Neumann, and Barbé, all left extremists, fell one after the other.

At the Fourth Plenum of the CCP, in January 1931, Mif and the 28 Bolsheviks unseated the left extremists. The new ruling clique drove many of the old leftists' supporters out of the party, but after a decent interval it revived some of the characteristic features of the Li Li-san left line. The main difference between the new and the old ruling cliques was that the power of the new clique was not based on indigenous Chinese factions, but on Comintern support.

Although Mao undoubtedly met Roy, Mif, and Lominadze while they were in China, no one has ever suggested that he associated himself with the Stalinist faction in the 1920's.

Purge of the Chinese Delegation to the Comintern

After Bukharin's disgrace in July 1929, Ch'ü Ch'iu-pai and Chang Kuo-t'ao, the leaders of the left and right factions, respectively, in the Chinese delegation to the Comintern, had united their forces in opposition to the educational policies of Mif, who had recently become president of Sun Yat-sen University and director of the party unit in that institution. Thereby they were able to muster a majority of the Chinese delegation. While the two disagreed on many issues, they were united in opposition to the growing power of Mif and his young protégés, Wang Ming, Po Ku, Shen Tse-min, and others. This open alliance between the right and left leaders in the CCP delegation to the Comintern laid them open to the same sort of accusation that the Stalinists were then employing against the right and left oppositions in the CPSU: they had formed an unprincipled factional alliance against the correct leadership of the party in Sun Yat-sen University and against the central apparatus of the Comintern.

Both Ch'ü and Chang were disgraced in the ensuing struggle. Ch'ü was removed from his post as representative of the Chinese party in the Comintern; Mif instructed Li Li-san to send Chou En-lai to Moscow to replace him. Chang went on leave.[29] Other members of the delegation were also reprimanded. After Chou En-lai's arrival in the spring of 1930, the delegation was reorganized: Teng Chung-hsia and Yü Fei were removed. They were sent back to China, with Ch'ü and Chou, in August 1930. If the CCP delegation was not reorganized again later in the year, the men who replaced Ch'ü, Teng, and Yü were Chou En-lai, Ts'ai Ho-shen (who had come to Moscow several months earlier because of his disagreements with Li Li-san over agrarian policy), and Huang P'ing, a survivor of the Canton Commune. Although Chou returned to Shanghai with Ch'ü, Teng, and Yü before the Third Plenum of the CCP, Ts'ai and Huang continued to serve at least until December 1930, when both appeared to testify in the trial of Li Li-san.

Conclusion

Stalin's condemnation of the pro-peasant faction in the CPSU held definite implications for the internal politics of the CCP. It is obvious that the accusations raised against A. P. Smirnov and the Rykovist faction in the CPSU Politburo laid the basis for Li Li-san's charge (later echoed by Wang Ming) that Mao was a representative of "peasant consciousness" in the CCP. Implicit in this charge is the related one that Mao did not have proper Communist respect for the accomplishments of the CPSU in building socialism in one country, inasmuch as the use of state power first to restrict the kulaks' economic power and then to eliminate them as a class was an essential element of the Stalinist technique for building socialism. And it is true that in his HC Mao fails entirely to mention either the defense of socialism in one country or the methods Stalin used in collectivization. It is almost certain, however, that when Li first raised the charge that Mao was a representative of peasant consciousness, no connection with the theoretical shortcomings of Bukharin was intended or implied. In elaborating their charges against Mao and his views on the peasantry, members of the CCP Politburo were unable to link the charge of "peasant consciousness" with the theoretical errors attributed to Bukharin until August 1929, when Stalin publicly announced that Bukharin had associated himself with the Smirnov-Rykov defense of the peasantry. Li Li-san was able to attack Mao as a representative of "idealism" and "peasant consciousness" before the public denunciation of the Russian right opposition, but he was never in a position to take advantage of Stalin's attacks on the right deviation in the Soviet Union to charge Mao with sympathy toward the *rich* peasants, or with the attendant sin of right opportunism. Indeed, Stalin's attacks on Bukharin's pro-kulak views were echoed in China not in attacks by the Central Committee on Mao and his Front Committee but in attacks by the Comintern on the leadership of Li Li-san himself. As a party unit still subordinate to provincial party organs, Mao's Front Committee was not directly threatened. So Li's charge that Mao represented peasant consciousness implied that Mao was an idealist of the Russian Social Revolutionary type, not that he was a Bukharinist or a Trotskyite.

The downfall of the right opposition in the CPSU, the struggle for collectivization and the elimination of the kulaks, and the imposition of a new, rigid, doctrinaire philosophical orthodoxy were all aspects of the consolidation of the absolute power of the Stalinist faction in the CPSU. Stalin's polemics against the right opposition in the CPSU furnished the standard epithets used in all later struggles against the right opposition in the Comintern. All the accusations Wang Ming and Po Ku later brought against Mao were used by Stalin at this time. When the 28 Bolsheviks rose to power in the CCP they not only extended the domination of the Stalinist faction into the CCP, but were also the bearers of the new philosophical orthodoxy and the doctrine of *partiinost*. Under their regime, Mao's ideas on the peasant question, which Li had attacked as "idealistic," were transformed into a "rich peasant line."

CHAPTER VI

Conflict Between Mao and Li Li-san, 1928–29

The first tasks facing the members of the new Politburo when they returned to China in September 1928 were to contact the scattered surviving members of the CCP, inform them of the new line adopted by the Comintern, get them to accept it, and start preparing for urban insurrections.

It was at about this time that the Chu-Mao forces were holding their Second Mao-ping Conference in the Ching-kang Mountains, working out their basic strategy of maintaining small rural bases in the mountains with guerrilla forces supported by a large part of the peasantry. This strategy, as Mao recognized, implied leniency toward the rich peasants and small landlords, the intermediate classes. Meanwhile, the new Politburo turned its attention to preparing armed insurrections in the larger cities. The fears Stalin had expressed in the spring of 1928 about the development of "peasant consciousness" in the CPSU were echoed in the first letters the CCP Politburo addressed to the party in October and November.

Given the fundamental differences between these strategies, conflict was inevitable. In the exchange of letters between the Central Committee and the Front Committee in early 1929, Mao and Li disagreed over military strategy, agrarian bases, location of the future soviet regime, and land redistribution. Although the Comintern line veered sharply to the left in the spring of 1929, the Comintern did not hold Mao responsible for following a rich peasant line, since he was presumably attempting to follow the confused and ambiguous directives of the Central Committee.

Li's Attack on "Peasant Consciousness"

When Li returned to China in October 1928, almost all party cells in China's cities had been destroyed. Those that remained were "pulverized and isolated." By November, there was hardly one solid industrial cell in the whole of China.[1] Throughout 1929 the main object of the Li Li-san regime was to recapture the leadership of the working class. Work in the villages was not to be ignored, but the main duties of party members lay in China's great industrial cities—Shanghai, Wuhan, Nanking, Tientsin, Dairen, Harbin, and Canton. In a report on the Sixth Congress dated October 1928, Li wrote: "The Congress recognized that there is a danger that the base of our party may shift from the working class to the peasantry and that we must make every effort to restore the party's working-class base."[2] Later in the same month, in a letter addressed to all party members, he wrote:

As a result of the particular development of the struggle in the countryside during the past year, and the fact that peasants now constitute 70 to 80 percent of our party membership, the *peasant mentality* is now reflected in our party.... The Communist Party acknowledges that the peasantry is an ally of the revolution. At the same time, [the party] recognizes that the peasantry is petty-bourgeois and cannot have correct ideas regarding socialism, that *its conservatism* is particularly strong, and that it lacks organizational ability. Only a proletarian mentality can lead us onto the correct revolutionary road. Unless we proceed to correct the dangers involved in this peasant mentality, it may lead to a complete destruction of the revolution and of the Party.[3]

Thus Li began his attack on "peasant consciousness" immediately after his return to China. He may have intended party members to guess that his assault on "peasant consciousness" in his letter of October 1928 was directed against Mao. In RSQHP Mao, presumably referring to this letter, says that Li accused him personally of representing "localism and conservatism of peasant mentality" in the CCP.[4]

Leading the Fourth Red Army, Chu and Mao descended from the Ching-kang Mountain base on January 4, 1929. Early in March, after a short and costly battle at Ta-po-ti, they reached Tung-ku in southeastern Kiangsi, where they were greeted by Li Wen-ling, the former Whampoa cadet who had brought the news of Mao's reinstatement as head of the Front Committee to Ching-kang-shan in November 1928, and who now led several small bands of partisans in the area around Ki-an. Li Wen-ling was later to become one of the more prominent victims of the Chu-Mao purge of Li Li-sanists in the aftermath of the Fu-t'ien incident of December 1930, but in March 1929 that conflict still lay in the future. After resting their troops for a few days, Chu and Mao continued to march eastward. In a few weeks they took Ting-chow (now known as Changting), a large city on the western border of Fukien province.[5] From this base Chu and Mao began to extend the authority of their Front Committee over all party and army units in the small soviet districts already existing in several counties in southeastern Kiangsi, northeastern Kwangtung, and southwestern Fukien.[6]

Many of the comrades Chu and Mao met on their march from Ching-kang-shan to Ting-chow (January–March, 1929) may already have seen several letters from the new Politburo. The October letter addressed to all party members had probably arrived in some of the districts through which Chu and Mao passed before the Front Committee received the first letter addressed specifically to Mao. If leaders of the guerrilla bands on the Kiangsi-Fukien border interpreted Li's attack on "peasant consciousness" as a personal attack against Mao—and the long-standing enmity between the two was widely known in higher party circles—it is likely that when Chu and Mao set up their First Red Army Headquarters at Ting-chow, some of the local party leaders resisting the authority of Mao's Front Committee realized that they had Politburo support.

The February Letter to the Front Committee

Communications between Shanghai and the small soviet bases in South China were irregular throughout the whole soviet period, from 1927 to 1935. A number of messengers from Shanghai were arrested or killed by the KMT army or police as they crossed the lines from Nationalist to Communist territory. There is no authenticated record of any letter from the Central Committee elected at the Sixth Party Congress having reached Ching-kang-shan before the Fourth Red Army left in January 1929.[a]

Soon after Mao and Chu descended from Ching-kang-shan they sent a messenger to Shanghai with reports on the conferences held in the autumn of 1928.[b] The first letter from the new Politburo probably had not yet arrived, and it must have been awaited with no little anxiety, for Mao's political career depended on whether or not the Sixth Congress had elected a Politburo that would look with favor on his military and political tactics.

Together Mao and Chu have given three different accounts of the arrival of the first letter from the new Central Committee. In 1936

[a] Two statements in Mao's revised HC seem to contradict this, but they refer to a letter written before the Sixth Congress met. (Mao, SW, I, 91; HC, I, 73; Snow, RSOC, p. 171.)

[b] Neither Mao in his interview with Snow nor Chu in his interview with Smedley stated when the reports were sent.

Mao told Snow that it arrived in the winter of 1928.[7] In 1937 Chu more precisely reported to Smedley that it reached them after they captured Ting-chow in March 1929.[8] This letter, Chu reported, brought instructions from the new Politburo and related the decisions of the Sixth Congress. The first letter from the Central Committee to Mao and the Front Committee mentioned in HC is dated February 9, 1929. This may be the letter to which both men referred in their interviews with Snow and Smedley.[c]

No copy of the Central Committee's February letter to the Front Committee is available. Mao quotes from his April 5 reply to it in his "Letter to Comrade Lin Piao" (January 5, 1930), but no contemporary copy of this letter is available either. The version in the revised HC is distorted and incomplete; for instance, the word "subjectivism" is substituted for "idealism," in line with the terminology adopted after the first party rectification movement.[9] The two main points covered in the February letter were the new Politburo's estimate of the situation at the time, i.e., that "a revolutionary upsurge will arise soon,"[10] and its strategic plan for the movements of the Red Army. According to the view of the Front Committee, the ideas set forth in the Central Committee's letter were incorrect. The Front Committee's own ideas were set forth in Mao's reply, dated April 5.[11]

According to those excerpts of his reply to the February letter that Mao chose to quote in his "Letter to Lin Piao," the Politburo also made several demands or requests of the Front Committee with which Mao and Chu simply refused to comply. They were enjoined to disperse the Red Army into small guerrilla bands, leave the ranks, and come to Shanghai. Rural uprisings were to be delayed until the party rebuilt its strength in the cities.[12] Moreover, the immediate creation of small hsien-sized soviets was discouraged. For these demands or requests the Politburo could claim the backing of the Sixth Congress of the CCP, as expressed in its Political Resolution.

If the published excerpts from Mao's reply are faithful to the original, his allegation in 1936 that he approved of the policies laid down by the Sixth Congress is simply untrue. He was opposed to its mili-

[c] The annotators of HC testify that Mao received a letter dated February 9. (HC, I, 110*n6*. This note does not appear in SW.) Mao's phrase "the winter of 1928" need not be interpreted as meaning before January 1, 1929, but before the Chinese New Year. Mao uses both the western and the Chinese calendar in his writing (e.g., NTTC, pp. 9, 16, 17), and if the phrase "winter of 1928" refers to the Chinese calendar, the letter could have been received any time before the Chinese New Year in the spring of 1929. According to Chu Teh, the Red Army took Jui-ching (shortly before it captured Ting-chow) in time to finish the Chinese New Year feast prepared for the KMT officers there. (Smedley, *Great Road,* pp. 237–38.)

tary strategy from the moment he first received a communication from the new Politburo, a communication in effect written by Li Li-san. In RSQHP, Mao writes that his disagreement with Li began in the summer of 1929, which would mean *after* Li had received Mao's April 5 letter and in turn sent Mao his reply.

Mao's reply probably was written after he and Chu had consulted with P'eng Teh-huai, and P'eng may have supported the views stated therein. Chu's statements substantiate this. Chu told Smedley that shortly after the messenger with the February letter arrived from Shanghai another messenger arrived from P'eng, who had been driven out of the Ching-kang-shan base soon after Chu and Mao had left it. Upon learning which direction they had taken, he had followed them across southern Kiangsi as far as Jui-ching. Mao and Chu immediately returned there to confer with him on military strategy. At this Jui-ching meeting, Smedley writes: "The reports and decisions brought by the messenger from Shanghai were studied and discussed, but Chu dismissed this aspect of the conference with the terse and grim remark: 'We accepted the decisions and began carrying them out.' "[13] However, Chu's account of the Front Committee's military and political moves during the next two years clearly indicates that they did not in fact carry out all of the Politburo's directives, and that they objected to the Politburo's urban orientation.

Disagreements Between Mao and Li Li-san

In the spring of 1929 the Maoist faction and the Li Li-sanists were divided on at least four issues. First, on the "estimate of the situation": Mao believed that the revolutionary tide would rise soon, while Li was allegedly pessimistic about such a possibility. Second, on guerrilla tactics: Mao believed that the Red Army should be somewhat centralized under the general direction of the Front Committee, while Li advocated dispersal of the troops into small, autonomous guerrilla units. Third, on agrarian bases: Mao believed that they were necessary and important, while Li objected to "premature" creation of peasant soviets. Fourth, on tactics to be used to solve the agrarian and peasant problems: Mao favored immediate land redistribution in the soviet bases, while Li wanted to postpone redistribution until a later time.

Li's Estimate of the Situation

Estimates of the situation, in Communist jargon, are judgments of whether or not the historical moment has arrived when society is ripe for revolutionary action. These historical moments are determined by the development of acute crises in the economic and political order, and by the prevailing disposition of the masses. In making their estimations Communists normally discuss two categories of factors, objective and subjective. Objective factors are all economic and political developments beyond the control of the party. Subjective factors concern the strengths and weaknesses of the party's organization, the attitude of party members, and the ability of the party to organize and control the disposition of the masses through propaganda and agitation. All Communists acknowledge that factors within both categories develop unevenly.

In evaluating the factors contributing to a revolutionary situation Communists may be optimistic or pessimistic—they may underestimate or overestimate the length of time before the historically correct revolutionary moment will arrive. In the Leninist view, which rejected the original Marxist thesis that the proletariat will make its own revolution, it was possible for the revolutionary moment to arrive and find the party completely unprepared. The chief tasks of party leaders, therefore, are organization, propaganda, and agitation, to prepare for the arrival of opportune revolutionary moments. In 1929, the coming revolutionary moment was visualized as the point at which the CCP could successfully organize a nationwide armed insurrection of workers and peasants that would lead immediately to the creation of a workers' and peasants' dictatorship. The insurrection might begin in the villages, but clearly it had to be carried to the cities, to become a proletarian-led uprising.

In the spring of 1929 the right wing of the CCP did not believe that the revolutionary moment would arrive for many years. In this they agreed with Trotsky. The Li Li-sanist left wing, in agreement with the Comintern, believed that the revolutionary moment would arrive very soon. All factions acknowledged, however, that the time of the nationwide armed insurrection had not yet come. All agreed that the situation was developing unevenly. In 1929 the peasants of South China were in a revolutionary mood, but the urban masses were not. Li's pessimism followed from the Politburo's inability to overcome the passivity of urban cadres who saw no use in political demonstrations and political strikes, its inability to inculcate some of its official enthusiasm into the urban party sections, and its ineffectualness in changing the temper of the urban masses through agitation and by organizing Red trade unions and Red insurrection corps in the cities.

On February 9, the day Li sent his letter to Mao, the Chinese Politburo received an ambiguous Comintern directive warning against any precipitate action in anticipation of the new revolutionary wave, but at the same time warning against failure to perceive the first signs of revival of the revolutionary forces. It stressed the need to watch and prepare for an upsurge among the urban masses, but did not mention the agrarian problem.[14]

This Comintern letter was probably the most immediate cause of Li's pessimism about whether an organized Red Army in the countryside could have a significant revolutionary role. There were no signs of the "general new rising tide" when Li sent the February letter, certainly none in the cities. Peasant uprisings were not to be interpreted as such—they were too sporadic and isolated. Few were under the control and leadership of the urban proletariat or the new Politburo. The uprisings sponsored by the Chu-Mao Red Army were premature. They had been premature in 1928 and continued to be premature throughout 1929. In addition, Li thought, they represented a completely incorrect emphasis on the importance of the peasant movement—a danger that the party might shift entirely away from its urban base and so be prey to all sorts of peasant deviations.

In February 1929, after five months of work, the party-sponsored labor organizations in the cities showed little sign of revival. There were no signs of spontaneous revolutionary activity. KMT "yellow" unions were adequately meeting the economic demands of the workers, so Li's Red unions had little success in winning support. Peasant revolutionary forces in the villages under CCP control were still very weak, but they were nevertheless stronger and better organized than any Red union or party cell Li had been able to rebuild in the cities. The move of the Chu-Mao forces from the Hunan-Kiangsi border to the Kiangsi-Fukien border threatened Li with the possibility that the peasant movement would rise to its next crest before the workers' movement had revived and therefore be doomed to failure. The resolutions of the Sixth Congress had pointed out that agrarian revolution could not succeed without the assistance and leadership of the proletariat. The growth of the peasant movement had to be retarded if the new revolutionary tide was to reach its peak simultaneously among the workers and the peasants. A workers' and peasants' soviet dictatorship could be set up in one or more provinces only if the uneven development of the workers' and peasant movements could be leveled out in those areas in which the revolution was most likely to reach fruition early.[15] Thus Li had a mandate from both the Sixth

Congress of the CCP and the Comintern itself to retard the formation of a united Red Army and soviets in the countryside. This he translated into a mandate to curb the influence of Mao Tse-tung, whom he must have regarded as a personal rival for power in the CCP.

In Mao's January 1930 "Letter to Lin Piao," he argued that Li's February letter had been too pessimistic, so he had suggested in his reply that the phrase "a revolutionary wave will arise soon" meant that it could arise within a year. But Mao could not agree that the revolution depended for its success on the party's bringing its workers' organizations abreast of the peasantry. To this notion he opposed his own view: "The revolution in semicolonial China will fail only if the peasant struggle does not have the leadership of the workers, but in no case will it be disadvantageous to the revolution itself if the development of the peasant struggle goes beyond the influence of the workers."[16] In semicolonial countries where the struggle against feudalism (the agrarian revolution) and the struggle against imperialism (the national revolution) were combined, the workers' struggle against capitalists could and should take second place to the struggle for a position of leadership in the revolutionary movement as a whole.

It appears that at the same time Li informed Mao and his comrades that Mao was again partially rehabilitated, Li tried to make sure that Mao would be unable to consolidate his power in the army and party. Li's February letter directing Mao and Chu to leave the ranks suggests that he was maneuvering to bring them under his control by shifting the headquarters for directing guerrilla activities from Front Committee headquarters in Kiangsi to the military section of the Central Committee in Shanghai. Had Chu and Mao obeyed Li's instructions, he could have sent his own men to run the headquarters of the Fourth Red Army and implement his policy from there. Without an institution like the central headquarters on the scene, cooperation between the dispersed guerrilla bands in the border districts of Kiangsi, Fukien, Hunan, and Kwangtung would have been impossible.

Li's concept of the function of guerrilla bands also caused friction between Mao and the Politburo. In 1929 the guerrillas of greatest value to the Politburo were those who confiscated the largest amount of portable wealth. Small dispersed bands could gather money from landlords and merchants in the countryside and small towns to support the party's work in the cities. It was in this way that Lenin had used partisans after the failure of the 1905 Revolution in Russia, and it was in this way that Li expected to use Mao and Chu. When he requested them to leave the ranks of the army and come to Shanghai for consultation, he presumably expected them to bring money. But Mao took an entirely different view of the function of guerrilla warfare. While the army was weak and small, he wrote, leaders were needed in the ranks; also, it must be kept together most of the time. It could be dispersed only for short operations in a small radius.[17] A relatively large army under firm leadership was necessary if Mao's plan of taking Kiangsi province within a year was to be accomplished. The fact that the party center needed money did not justify turning the troops of the Red Army into common bandits.

In his letter of April 5, Mao opposed the guerrilla tactics advocated by the Politburo. Not only did he refuse to disperse his army as directed, he took over additional local partisan units in Kiangsi and Fukien and subordinated them to his newly created First Red Army Headquarters. Because it was still small, he argued, the Red Army should maintain its sound guerrilla character: local units must remain independent in tactical matters. In the conditions under which it operated, the Red Army should not be brought under a rigidly centralized command and it should not be forced into banditry. Mao and Chu refused to leave the ranks. Mao wrote that a disciplined, competent, strong, and politically united Red Army could be created only if the leaders stayed in the ranks and conducted a resolute political and military struggle.

According to Mao's later explanation, the Politburo underestimated the party's organized strength in the villages and incorrectly predicted that war would not break out between the left KMT and the forces of Chiang Kai-shek surrounding the tiny soviet districts.[18] Thus Li's estimate of the situation was unduly pessimistic. Had Mao and Chu left the ranks and followed Li's orders, history might have borne out his pessimism.

Chu Teh commented that the February letter described the Chinese Trotskyites as accusing Mao and himself of having "retreated to isolated mountains in the interior to engage in military adventurism and banditry instead of returning to the industrial cities to lead the struggle of the proletariat and urban petty-bourgeoisie for the completion of the democratic revolution. . . . As for Mao and myself and the troops which we commanded—we had no intention of laying down our guns and offering our necks to the Kuomintang butchers."[19] When Li Li-san received Mao's courteous refusal to come to Shanghai, he repeated and embroidered some of these same epithets. Mao and Chu stayed on their mountaintops and held onto their guns. In this initial dispute over Mao's concept of the "sound guerrilla character" of the Red Army and Li's tactic of scattering the Red forces throughout enemy territory we find the beginnings of many later controversies between the Maoists and the 28 Bolsheviks over guerrilla tactics and guerrillaism.

We do not know whether or not Chu disclosed the contents of the February letter accurately, but we do know that his representation does not accurately describe the attitude of the Chinese Trotskyites at the time. In early 1929, the small band of Chinese Trotskyites still consisted mainly of students who had been expelled from Moscow's Sun Yat-sen University in late 1927 and had returned to China soon after. These students believed that Mao had been in agreement more often with Trotsky than with Stalin in the years from 1925 to 1927. They knew that he had been expelled from the Central Committee at the November Plenum—about the same time they had been expelled from Sun Yat-sen University—and they presumed it had been for the same reason. They also knew that the Comintern still frowned on Mao's activities. So they approved of Mao's partisan warfare against the KMT and wished to ally themselves with him to work in his guerrilla units. At the same time, they distrusted Li Li-san and Chu Teh equally, believing that both men were opportunists flexible enough to suit Stalin's purposes. Chu may, then, have been relaying a correct account of the Trotskyites' attitude toward himself and Li, but not of their attitude toward Mao.[20]

Stalin's attitude toward Mao's guerrilla warfare in China may have stemmed from his own experience in the Caucasus in 1905–7. In those years the Bolshevik faction was desperately short of funds, so Lenin, who believed that the revolution had not yet spent its force, organized fighting squads of Bolshevik guerrillas to raid banks and government treasuries. These Robin Hood escapades, typically indistinguishable from simple robbery, were especially numerous and successful in Transcaucasia, where Stalin organized the raids and arranged for smuggling the loot abroad to Lenin. Trotsky, along with the Mensheviks and finally a portion of the Bolshevik faction as well, condemned the raids. Lenin's view was ambivalent. For him this kind of guerrilla warfare was auxiliary to the "regular army" of the whole Russian people in insurrection. However, he admitted that without a general rising guerrilla raids were hopeless adventures that could only demoralize the party. Once the Bolshevik coffers were refilled, he too opposed expropriations. Social revolutionaries might hope to overthrow bourgeois governments by guerrilla warfare alone, but the Bolsheviks, as true Marxists, knew that guerrilla raids were only one technique, and never the decisive one, in great popular revolts. Because of Lenin's doubts, Stalin's part in the expropriations was never considered respectable enough to be included in the Stalinist legend. Following Lenin, Stalin was perfectly ready to condemn partisan activity that had no visible connection with any mass revolt, but since he had himself been involved in directing guerrilla activities that Lenin had sponsored and Trotsky opposed, he was unwilling to condemn guerrillaism under all circumstances. The Comintern's official line in 1929 was that the revolutionary tide was rising in China. But since the great popular revolt had not yet broken out, the question was whether or not Mao was correct in his belief that guerrilla raids could set off a great popular uprising. Li Li-san, according to the Maoist record, was pessimistic. The Comintern condemned guerrilla activities that had no connection with mass uprisings—a sound Leninist position—and remained suspicious of Mao's guerrilla tactics and his association with bandits.[21]

The Location of the New Soviet Regime

The place in which political power in the form of soviets should first be established was also a point of contention between Mao and Li. Li anticipated creating an urban soviet after a period of preparation and agitation. We do not know which city Li proposed for the new political center in his February letter, but it is possible that at that time he favored Canton. The evidence for this hypothesis is admittedly almost entirely negative. First, Mao stated that the Politburo had sent out a circular suggesting that war between Chiang Kai-shek and the Kwangsi warlords might not break out.[22] The Kwangsi warlords at the time held Hankow and territory extending eastward along both sides of the Yangtze river into Kiangsi. They also had troops in Kwangsi and Peiping. Until they were weakened by war, Wuhan, their power center, was an unlikely candidate for the new soviet capital, and we may be fairly certain that Li did not favor it as such when the February letter was sent. Second, in his April reply Mao argued against a proposal to set up political power in Hunan and Kwangtung, indicating that Li may have suggested the capital of Kwangtung, Canton.

In his April 5 letter to the Central Committee Mao also argued against dispatching the Red Armies to Hunan. The enemy forces were strong there, he wrote, and "because of the party's adventurist mistake [in the preceding summer] we have lost almost all our mass following outside as well as inside the Party."[23] It is worth noting that the secretary of the Hunan Provincial Committee at this time was probably the same man who had directed the attack on Mao and Chu after the Second Mao-ping Conference. As late as January 1930, Mao was still berating the Hunan Provincial Committee for its misjudgments of the stability of the KMT regime in Hunan during 1928 and 1929.[24] From Mao's reply to the February letter, I gather that Li had ordered Mao and Chu to divide up their forces and send them back to Hunan and Kwangtung. Li probably wanted them to assist in reviving the Hai-lu-feng soviet in eastern Kwangtung—it was rumored that he had sent P'eng P'ai back to the East River District for that purpose in early 1929.[25]

Mao proposed instead that the Red Army concentrate on Kiangsi, attempt to take the entire province within one year, and try to take western Fukien and western Chekiang as well. While he admitted that he was not clear on the state of the party's organizations and following in Kiangsi (its "subjective conditions" in Communist jargon), he argued that objective conditions in Kiangsi were more favorable than in either Hunan or Kwangtung. Because the province as a whole was poorer than Hunan or Kwangtung, there was less money available to the provincial treasury from local merchants and foreign imperialists to finance the fight against Communist troops. There were also fewer *min-t'uan* (private troops under the control of local landlords), and the Kiangsi Provincial Government had no locally raised army of its own. The KMT occupying troops had few local connections or interests to defend.[26] In fact, many of their officers were from Yünnan and had at one time been friends and admirers of Chu Teh.

In his "November 1928 Report to the Central Committee," Mao had proposed that the Ching-kang-shan base be consolidated and expanded until it formed a long thin line between Kiangsi and Hunan, running from the Kwangtung border in the south to the Hupeh border in the north.[27] But by April 1929 he had changed his mind about which area in South China had the greatest potentialities for the immediate establishment and consolidation of a revolutionary base. In his April letter he proposed to create two bases: a central base to be located on the Fukien-Kiangsi border and a subsidiary base on the Hunan-Kiangsi border. Under favorable circumstances both bases could be expanded to meet in the center of Kiangsi. This strategy would place the Communist base between the forces of Chiang Kai-shek in the lower Yangtze valley and those of the Kwangsi warlords in Hupeh and Hunan. When the two KMT cliques began to fight, the Red Armies would be able to expand the base rapidly, not only toward the center of Kiangsi, but possibly also eastward toward the coast, opening a way to the sea and undermining Chiang's defense line in Chekiang and Fukien. Mao's strategy suggests that at the time he was attempting to differentiate among the cliques within the KMT and take every possible advantage of splits between them.[28] Li Li-san sent off the February letter after he himself had been reprimanded by the Comintern for doing just that.

In his January 1930 comment, Mao admits that his judgment that Kiangsi could be taken within a year had smacked of impetuosity. He is very careful, however, not to suggest that he had ever proposed aligning the Red Armies with either Chiang or the Kwangsi warlords when they were at war. He had consistently held that the Red Armies could contend with both. By January 1930 the Comintern had forbidden alliance with any faction in the KMT.

Agrarian Bases and Peasant Soviets

Li and Mao also disagreed over the means to be used in preparing for a general insurrection, whether in Kiangsi or in all China. Mao thought the uneven development of the revolution could be turned to advantage in devising strategy and tactics. That the peasant movement was stronger than the workers' movement should be exploited, he argued, by developing the Red Army and the party in the villages. Mao wished to centralize the strategic direction of peasant guerrilla bands under his Front Committee and use the Red Army to assist the peasants to redistribute the land and organize soviet governments. Having won the allegiance of the peasants, the Red Army could expand and move from the mountains to the valleys, taking first the small market towns and then the larger hsien capitals. It could attack counterrevolutionary forces where they were weakest, destroy their armies—the major means of maintaining the political power of the landlord class—surround the cities with a revolutionary countryside, and bring the imperialists to their knees by extinguishing the feudal remnants in the villages.

With his urban, worker-centered strategy, Li could not but disagree with Mao and label his strategy a manifestation of the "localism and conservatism of peasant consciousness." "Localism" implied that Mao took no account of the situation in China as a whole, or of factors in the world situation that the CCP should exploit. The uneven development of Chinese revolutionary forces should be remedied, Li maintained, by leading the workers, not by allowing premature putschism in the countryside to destroy the party's tenuous hold on the peasantry. Mao did not want to wait for the workers' movement to rise before setting up small (hsien-sized) soviet districts in the countryside. He believed that taking some hsien capitals would stimulate peasant revolt in surrounding territories. As he put it, a well-placed spark could start a prairie fire.

The Agrarian Problem

Although there is no record that the February letter from the Central Committee contained directives on the agrarian question, it is likely that either the letter itself or one of the circulars accompanying it did, for in April Mao rewrote the Ching-kang-shan land law to bring its provisions into accord with the decisions of the Sixth Party Congress.

Mao returned to the base at Hsing-kuo and Tung-ku immediately after the Jui-ching Conference. If his account to Snow was accurate, Huang Kung-lüeh accompanied him and took over command of the partisan troops in the area from Li Wen-ling and Tuan Liang-pi.[d] By the end of April both hsien had fallen before the onslaught of

[d] Tuan Liang-pi, like Li Wen-ling, was a former Whampoa cadet. Both had participated in the Nanch'ang Uprising, then deserted from the Yeh-Ho army on its march south to recruit a guerrilla band from the villages near their family homes in Hsing-kuo and Tung-ku. They cooperated with Mao's troops in the recapture of the Ching-kang-shan base in September–October 1928. Then, according to reports from Maoist sources, their partisan bands established soviet governments in the villages surrounding the Li and Tuan family estates. These little soviets reduced rents and burned mortgages but did not redistribute the land. After Li and Tuan were displaced by Huang Kung-lüeh, they left the base at Hsing-kuo and Tung-ku and moved to southwest Kiangsi, where they secretly joined a faction opposed to Mao. They may have been among the delegates to the Conference of Delegates from the Soviet Areas held in Shanghai in late May 1930. Returning to Kiangsi after that Conference, they took part in establishing a Provincial Action Committee that tried to subordinate to itself the Front Committees in the Red Army and competed with the Maoists for leadership of the assault on Nanch'ang and Kiukiang in the summer of 1930. Mao allegedly continued to trust Li and Tuan until November, when he arrested them for being associated with the KMT's Anti-Bolshevik Corps (the A-B Corps) and imprisoned them at Fu-t'ien. They were released from prison by a detachment of partisans from their old base in Hsing-kuo. The following year they were recaptured and executed by the Maoist faction as agents of the A-B Corps. Mao's charges against these two men may be false, but they are lent credence by the fact that during this period Tuan Hsi-p'eng, a relative of Tuan Liang-pi, headed the KMT's A-B Corps in Kiangsi. (Smedley, *Great Road,* pp. 239–43, 255, 280–82; Snow, RSOC, pp. 150, 170–79, 182; Hsiao, pp. 98–113; Li Ang, *Red Stage,* English translation, see [66], Chap. 14; Schwartz, *Chinese Communism,* pp. 175–78.)

Mao's troops, and sometime in the same month he promulgated the Hsing-kuo land law.[29]

In the Hsing-kuo land law the provision of the Ching-kang-shan law stating that "all land shall be confiscated and shall become the property of the soviet government" was altered, in line with the decisions of the Sixth Congress, to read "all public land and all the land of the landlord class shall be confiscated and shall become the property of the soviet government."[30] Mao wrote in his later annotations that this was the only alteration in principle.[31] However, three other changes were made:

1. The provision for collective cultivation was eliminated, as well as the provision looking forward to the establishment of model farms by the soviet government.
2. The provision that the peasants should be compelled to work after the land had been confiscated and divided among them was omitted.
3. The provisions forbidding the sale of all land after division were changed. The Hsing-kuo law forbade only the sale of land that had been confiscated and redistributed; in other words, it applied only to lands formerly held by public institutions and the lands of the landlord class. Land that had not been confiscated and redistributed could be bought and sold.[32]

All other provisions remained the same.

Neither the December 1928 Ching-kang-shan law nor the April 1929 Hsing-kuo law was published before 1941, when Mao annotated both of them. In these annotations he does not mention that his "correction in principle" was due to a decision of the Sixth Party Congress, nor does he attribute any changes in the Hsing-kuo law to orders from the Politburo, decisions of the Sixth Congress, or Comintern directives.[33] Instead he wrote: "In these two land laws, one can observe the development of our understanding of the struggle for land."[34] The Hsing-kuo law, he wrote, remained in effect until 1930, in other words, until the February 7 Conference passed a new land law, which Mao himself had worked out.

There is no evidence that Li issued any directives on how to divide the land in his February letter, nor is there any evidence of disagreement between Mao and the Politburo over specific provisions of the Hsing-kuo law during 1929. Perhaps at the time it appeared to be of only passing significance, for within a month Mao's troops retreated from the base in Hsing-kuo and Tung-ku and entered western Fukien, and until January 1930 he concentrated his efforts on building soviet governments in the area surrounding the small mountain base at Ku-t'ien in Shang-hang hsien, Fukien. Mao probably implemented the Hsing-kuo law in the Fukien soviets, but no documents dealing with Fukien soviet land laws in this period are available.

When Mao and Chu returned to Hsing-kuo the following year, they applied the land law of the February 7 Conference.

By that time they had so aroused the hostility of the local Li Lisanists that an open break occurred between the party units led by Mao and his Front Committee and those dominated by the Li Lisanists. After the May 1930 Conference of Delegates from the Soviet Areas, Mao's opponents in the southern Kiangsi base broke away, held their own "Second Plenum," and passed a Li Li-san–sponsored land law reviving the provisions of the December 1928 statute, which forbade the sale of land and directed total collectivization. We may surmise that some of the men opposed to Mao in 1930 had objected to his agrarian line at the Second Mao-ping Conference on Ching-kang-shan, and had probably also opposed the Hsing-kuo law, which embodied Mao's program.

Li Wen-ling and Tuan Liang-pi probably made their peace with the Central Committee after Mao imposed Huang Kung-lüeh as the commander of the guerrilla bands they had organized. Their membership in the Whampoa cadet faction, of which Chou En-lai was the leader, probably inclined them toward the military policies of the new Politburo, whose military committee was then dominated by Chou and the Whampoa cadet faction. Mao probably antagonized other Communist military officers when he attempted to replace them with military officers loyal to himself, and to bring the guerrilla forces they controlled under the authority of his Front Committee. According to available evidence, Mao's reorganization continued sporadically throughout 1929 and 1930.

Mao's Reorganization of the Red Armies

When the extent of the disagreements between Mao and the Politburo became clear, a contest over the control of party organizations in the Red Armies and the village soviets was inevitable. According to Mao's version of developments in these areas, he prepared for that conflict even before Li replied to his letter of April 5. Early in 1929, he told Snow, he had reorganized the small bands of guerrillas led by Li Wen-ling and Li Su-chu in Tung-ku and Hsing-kuo hsien into the Third Red Army, which was placed under the command of Huang Kung-lüeh,[35] with Chu Yi as its political commissar. The partisans of western Fukien (who had established their first soviets early in 1928) he reorganized into the 12th Red Army. These guerrillas had been led by Chang Ting-chen, Teng Tzu-hui, and Hu Pei-teh. Shortly after Mao's arrival they were placed under the command of Wu

Chung-hao, a Whampoa cadet who had played a part in Mao's Autumn Harvest Uprisings. After Wu was killed, Lo P'ing-hui, a recent Communist convert who had led a mutiny among the KMT troops in Ki-an in July 1929, became commander of the newly created 12th Army, while T'ai Tsung-ling became its political commissar.[36] In June 1930 Mao and Chu organized the First Army Corps Headquarters, with Chu Teh as the military commander and Mao the political commissar. One section of the troops they had led from Chingkang-shan was placed under the command of Lin Piao and continued to bear the old name of the Fourth Red Army. This army remained the core of Mao's and Chu's power in the military structure. It not only fought the enemy; its officers and political commissars were sent into the newly created Third and 12th Armies to bring them under the command of the First Army Corps Headquarters staff. When this military reorganization was completed, Mao and Chu had about 10,000 men at their disposal.[37]

Chu Teh's story is not entirely consistent with Mao's, for he does not mention Front Committee efforts to control the other armies *until* June 1930. According to Chu, he and Mao separated in the late spring of 1929, immediately after the Jui-ching Conference. Mao returned to Hsing-kuo and Tung-ku, where he organized a soviet government, while Chu attacked and captured Ning-tu. Then they united their forces, marched eastward past Ting-chow, and captured Lung-yen, in Fukien. There the Fourth Army again split in two. Mao remained behind in Fukien while Chu campaigned throughout the summer in southern Kiangsi and southeastern Fukien. From early September until December 1929 Mao was dangerously ill and remained in the town of Ku-t'ien, high in the Fukien mountains. Chu continued to campaign in Fukien, Kiangsi, and northern Kwangtung until December, when he fought his way back to Ku-t'ien.[38]

The two were together for less than two months in 1929, after the first capture of Ting-chow. Chu records only three short periods in the entire year during which he and Mao met and consulted. Under these circumstances, control by Mao's Front Committee over other partisan bands must have been tenuous indeed, resting mainly on the persuasive abilities of the men Mao sent in to take over command. Chu does not mention any attempt of his own to send in men to reinforce or control local guerrilla bands in Fukien, Kwangtung, or southern Kiangsi, except for one instance during the October campaign in the East River District in Kwangtung, when he left some of his troops behind to reinforce the East River guerrillas. All officers and political commissars Chu mentions—Liu An-kung, Dr. Nelson Fu, and Lin Piao—stayed with the Fourth Army.[e]

Mao does not claim that P'eng Teh-huai's Fifth Army, which continued guerrilla operations on the Hunan-Kiangsi border after the Jui-ching Conference, was placed under the jurisdiction of the First Army Corps or the Front Committee. The troops of Ho Lung and Hsü Hai-t'ang, in western Hunan and northeastern Hupeh, respectively, were too far away to be subordinated effectively to Mao's headquarters. In northeastern Kiangsi, Fang Chih-min and his troops also continued to operate independently. A group of partisans in the East River districts in Kwangtung, led by Ku Ta-chen and made up of men who had fled after the KMT reoccupied the Hai-lu-feng soviet area, did establish contact with Chu and Mao sometime during 1929. Later this group formed the cadres of the 11th Red Army, which continued to carry on partisan warfare in the same areas into 1949. Another group of partisans, led by P'eng Kuei, operated in the East River districts from 1929 until after 1931, when P'eng was assassinated. There is no record, however, that they formed any connection with the Chu-Mao headquarters, and it is probable that by the middle of 1930 they were under the control of Li Li-san's Politburo, in direct obedience to the Tung-chiang (East River) Special Committee.[39] It is most likely that some of the Red partisan bands operating in South China were in contact with Li's new Politburo before Mao and Chu received their first communication from Shanghai. Li may have reached the bands in southeastern Kiangsi even before Mao and Chu arrived there with their troops.

From 1929 to 1934, the core of the resistance to Mao and his Front Committee in the soviet districts of Kiangsi and Fukien consisted of the men who had been displaced in the military reorganization Mao began in the spring of 1929. By 1931 the Maoists were claiming that their enemies in Kiangsi were associated with the A-B Corps. In Fukien their enemies were accused of being Social Democrats. Li Wenling was cited as a leader of the A-B Corps and his following in Hsing-kuo and Tung-ku was wiped out. In Fukien, Hu Pei-teh was tried as

[e] Fu and Lin had been on Ching-kang-shan. Liu was a recent arrival from Europe who had joined the Fourth Army before August 1929. He had been one of the messengers from Shanghai, perhaps the one who had carried the first letter, earlier that year. There is a puzzle concerning this man—Chu Teh praised him, but Mao, in his interview with Snow, condemned as a Trotskyite intellectual a man with a very similar name: Liu En-kung. The two could well be the same man, for Snow's transliteration of Chinese names is occasionally faulty. (Smedley, *Great Road,* pp. 261–62, 265–66; Snow, RSOC, p. 174. See below, p. 179.)

one of the leaders of the Social Democrats. He disappeared before October 1931. After Li Li-san fell from power in late 1930, most of Mao's opponents were also accused of following the Li Li-san line. If in 1929 and early 1930 they had supported the line of the Central Committee against any contrary suggestions on tactics advanced by Mao, there may be some truth in Mao's later charge that they were Li Li-sanists during the period in which Li was de facto secretary of the CCP. Mao, however, resisted Li's strategy and tactics from the moment the two began to correspond. The seeds of the conflict between Mao and local soviet leaders and military commanders in southeastern Kiangsi were planted in the spring of 1929.

The Comintern Letter on the Peasant Question (June 1929)

Until the recent discovery and publication of many Communist documents captured by KMT troops between 1930 and 1934, the view most widely accepted in the West was that the lines of Li Li-san and the Comintern coincided until the Red Army was defeated at Ch'angsha in September 1930. After that dramatic failure Li did take the blame for Moscow's mistaken evaluation of the Chinese situation.[40] However, on the basis of the new evidence provided by these documents it is necessary to revise the old view of the events of this period (February 1929 to September 1930).

Under the impact of Stalin's drive to exterminate the kulaks as a class, the ECCI reformulated its views on the peasant question in early 1929. The "Letter of the ECCI to the CC, CCP on the Peasant Question" dated June 7, 1929, was written to correct right-wing views that had found their way into the Resolutions of the Sixth Party Congress.[41] This letter was allegedly written to correct errors made by Li Li-san and Ts'ai Ho-shen in their letters from the Central Committee to Mao's Front Committee. The Central Committee's letters to Mao in the spring of 1929 advocated a rich peasant line. According to the ECCI, the confused formulations in these letters could be traced back to disputes between Li and Ts'ai at the Sixth Party Congress. As leader of the Politburo, Li was held responsible for the formulation of tactics to be used in dealing with the rich peasants in soviet areas.

An Earlier Interpretation of the Letter

This letter is of extraordinary importance in interpreting Comintern evaluations of Mao and his peasant movement in 1929, for it is the first letter from the Comintern, so far discovered, in which Mao is mentioned by name. Charles McLane, who cites one of the references to Mao in this letter in his excellent book *Soviet Policy and the Chinese Communists: 1931–1946,* characterizes the ECCI's attitude toward Mao as "distinctly uncomplimentary," and interprets the reference as a sharp criticism of Mao's position on the rich peasants or kulaks.[42] Using another translation of the same letter, I have reached the conclusion that the criticism cited by McLane was not directed against Mao, but against Li Li-san and Ts'ai Ho-shen, for compromising their differences on this issue and for sending Mao directives that simultaneously expressed both left and right views. Since this letter marks a turning point in the history of the CCP's attitude toward the rich peasants, I shall quote from it extensively.

The Substance of the Letter

Basing their directives firmly on the position that no new revolutionary wave had yet appeared in China, the Comintern authorities wrote:

> It is not necessary to begin the peasant movement with calls for carrying out an agrarian revolution, with a guerrilla war and uprisings. On the contrary, the current situation in China dictates to the Party the task of using the particular and small conflicts, of fanning them up, of widening the day-to-day struggle of the basic masses against any and all kinds of exploitation and elevating it to a higher political level. [We must direct our efforts to] the struggles against collection of tax-levies, against militarist war, and against tailism and oversplitting, the struggle to improve the labor conditions of the tenant farmers, and especially the struggle for reducing or for non-payment of taxes. All this must be the intermediate link, by grasping which the Party will be able to rouse the millions of the masses, consolidate its influence, and advance to a new upsurge in the peasant movement.[f]

In spite of the fact that no revolutionary wave was yet in sight, the Comintern did not recommend an alliance with the whole of the peasantry against landlords and militarists but stressed that the party must struggle vigorously against the kulaks even in those areas where kulaks worked their own land.

[f] Mif, pp. 236–37. "Tailism" was the tactical and strategic error of following the masses rather than leading them. I am not sure of the meaning of "oversplitting," but I suspect that it may have been the error of dividing the population into a great many classes and strata, as Mao did. If this is the case, by dividing Chinese society into more classes than Marxist analysis perceives in a capitalist society the oversplitters—and Mao—were wrongly asserting that Chinese society had not yet become predominantly capitalistic, that it had not yet passed out of the feudal stage. The point is important, for if Chinese society were still feudal the rich peasants were counterrevolutionary, whereas if it had entered into a capitalistic stage the rich peasants had become progressive.

The tactics recommended by us must be applied not only to the kulak who is a semi-landlord, but also to the less widespread type of kulaks in China who work their own land. As to them, the Party must not restrain the class struggle of the peasant masses. It must not in any way subordinate its activity to the position held by this type of kulak in the liberation movement. It must not limit its activity by making concessions to the kulaks, even if they would participate in the anti-tax levy and anti-militarist movement. The Party must not change its general line on the kulaks. It must fight them for the leadership [of the revolution] through the peasant masses and not give them an opportunity to use the masses in their own interests.[43]

In this "restatement" the line of the Sixth Party Congress was abandoned as the Comintern moved to the left. The Political Resolution of the Sixth Congress had stated: "Alliance with the petty bourgeoisie and the rich peasants against all reactionary forces (is necessary), but it is also necessary to lead the laboring people against all exploiters."[44] To be correct, according to this resolution, the party needed to induce the owner-peasants to join the struggle to confiscate landlords' land, as well as the struggle against taxation by warlords. At the same time, it had to avoid "too great concessions" to the rich peasants.[45]

By June 1929 any concession to the kulaks was forbidden, for they had gone over to the counterrevolutionary camp. It was evident by then that the class struggle had developed rapidly, and that the struggle against rich peasants had to be carried on simultaneously with the struggle against warlords, landlords, and gentry.[46] Having shifted its line, the Comintern censured the CCP's Central Committee for its adherence to the previous line of alliance with rich peasants, citing the Central Committee's expression of this point of view in a number of resolutions, documents, and letters:

Such a point of view was shared by individual comrades—and this is important—but in a whole host of resolutions and documents of the Central Committee we encounter this type of interpretation of the tactics of the party on the matter of the alliance with the kulaks.

Let us take a case in point, the "Letter from the CC to Comrade Mao Tse-tung," in which we read: "Following the general tactical objective (struggle with the landlord class), it is necessary to conclude an alliance with the rich peasants; it would be wrong if we began deliberately to fan up the struggle with the rich peasant-kulaks . . ."

Or in another place, "Nevertheless the party must not abandon the class struggle of the poor peasantry against the kulaks and the rich peasants just because 'our general tactical line requires an alliance with the rich peasants.' "[47]

Then the letter reproves Ts'ai Ho-shen and Li Li-san for continuing to make the same mistakes they made at the Sixth Party Congress.

> Instead of rectifying the confused formulation of the Resolution of the Sixth Congress, the comrades [Ts'ai Ho-shen and Li Li-san] deepened their error, attempting theoretically to justify the alliance of the proletariat with the kulak (making, for example, a parallel between the stage of our bloc and that of the national industrial bourgeoisie).[48]

Considering the whole of this letter on the peasant question in the light of the debate then raging within the CCP Central Committee, it is evident that the aim of this Comintern letter was not to comment on the policy Mao advocated (a policy the Comintern may not yet have been aware of) but to change the tactics of the Central Committee. The alliance with the bourgeoisie—including the rich peasants—was now to be abandoned. Rather than being designed to set off an attack against Mao, this letter was instead one of the first volleys in the Comintern's attack on Li Li-san.

CHAPTER VII

The Struggle in Shanghai, June–November 1929

The Second Plenum of the CCP Central Committee, held in Shanghai in June 1929, confirmed the leadership of Li Li-san, Chou En-lai, and Hsiang Chung-fa, the new triumvirate that dominated the Politburo. Officially optimistic, because the Sixth Party Congress had determined that the Chinese revolution would soon reach the stage of mass uprisings, the men who gathered for the Plenum knew nonetheless that the party had made little real progress in the past year. The Red trade unions had been able to win over very few urban workers from the KMT-sponsored "yellow" unions. The Red Army was only beginning to expand its guerrilla activities. Furthermore, small opposition groups within the CCP were forming in all the major urban centers. The great majority of students returning from Sun Yat-sen University, for example, counted themselves Trotskyites. Ch'en Tu-hsiu, the deposed party leader, still wielded great influence, and was soon to contact the Trotskyites returning from Moscow. Prominent leaders of the Red unions had resisted Li's directive to expose members of the weak Red unions in public demonstrations such as the one the Politburo had organized in Shanghai on May Day. When Li, Chou, and Hsiang agreed on a policy, they usually found Ts'ai Ho-shen, Lo Chang-lung, and Ho Meng-hsiung lined up against them in the Politburo.

When the Second Plenum met, Earl Browder, a Bukharin appointee, was still political secretary of the Comintern's Far Eastern Bureau and head of the Pan-Pacific Trade Union Secretariat (PPTUS) in Shanghai. Otto Kuusinen was in charge of the Far Eastern Department of the Comintern Secretariat, assisted by L. Magyar and Pavel Mif.[1] Trotsky was already in exile in Prinkipo. Stalin had carried his struggle against the right opposition into the Comintern apparatus in Europe, but Bukharin had not yet been removed from his position in the ECCI. With the shift to the left, the Profintern was reviving; a new agency, the Seamen's and Port Workers' International (ISH), had just been established. Its headquarters in Hamburg included a Chinese section that competed for personnel with the PPTUS, which was soon forced to neglect union organization in the interior cities of China and place major emphasis on the organization of seamen.[2] Although the Far Eastern Bureau may not have been officially subordinated to the West European Bureau located in Berlin, it had for some time received its instructions and funds from that source. Now Browder found that his PPTUS was also losing its relatively autonomous status and falling under the control of an apparatus based in Germany. Browder could not have relished the change, and his attitude may have influenced some Chinese union leaders.

Li Li-san's difficulties with Comintern agencies began at this time. His initial difficulties were probably not attributable to any failures on his part, but rather to the leftward swing in the Comintern and the accompanying policy changes in the agencies through which it exercised control over the CCP. The general swing to the left was evident to everyone, but since no one knew how far the Comintern would move, or when another reversal might take place, it is not surprising that the Plenum chose to allow its position on a number of issues to remain unclear.

In spite of the fact that the rich peasant question was one of the major issues dividing the right opposition from the Stalinists, the Second Plenum of the CCP took an ambiguous stand even on it. The resolutions of the Second Plenum emphasized the anti-imperialist movement and accorded relatively little attention to the Red Army and the rural soviets. The Plenum did, however, reject at least one of Mao's proposals on these subjects. In the ten months between the Sixth Congress and the Second Plenum, the new Politburo had not been able to achieve anything approaching centralized control over the scattered, sporadic guerrilla activities of party units in South China. It was essential for the revolution's success that this condition be altered and centralized leadership and control imposed. To this end the Second Plenum set down 15 major tasks facing the party leadership.

The Resolutions of the Second Plenum

The Primacy of the Anti-Imperialist Movement

The first problem was the anti-imperialist struggle. Only after the imperialists had been driven out and China united would it be possible to successfully consummate the agrarian revolution. Although the anti-imperialist struggle and the agrarian revolution were inseparable tasks, the Plenum nevertheless declared: "This does not mean . . . that there is no independent anti-imperialist movement outside the agrarian revolution."[3] The anti-imperialist struggle in China had to be coordinated with the international movement opposing a new world war and supporting the Soviet Union. In the struggle against the KMT and the warlords the CCP was to pursue a defeatist line, i.e., to spread demoralizing propaganda among the Nationalist soldiers.[a]

All Communist parties adopted the line of supporting the Soviet Union in 1929, regardless of its effect on their strength and prestige. In China the policy resulting from this line took on a peculiarly antinational cast, for the KMT and the Soviet Union were then engaged in a dispute over the Chinese Eastern Railroad, and the CCP threw in its lot with the Soviet Union. When the Second Plenum met in June, both Nanking and Moscow were preparing for war. The Comintern demanded that the CCP adopt the slogan "Protect the Soviet Union." Li Li-san urged the adoption of the slogan, with all of its anti-national, anti-Chinese implications, and the majority of the Plenum supported him.[4] Communist officers in KMT and warlord armies who had managed to keep their party affiliation secret were directed to carry on defeatist propaganda among the troops they commanded. While the defeat of the Manchurian troops by the Soviet armies cannot be attributed to such tactics, at least one uprising of KMT troops (the Ki-an Uprising in July 1929) probably resulted from an abortive attempt to carry out this kind of subversion. The propagandists were discovered by loyal KMT officers, and had to precipitate an uprising to save their party organization and themselves.[5]

The anti-imperialist movement continued to take precedence over the agrarian revolution throughout 1929. Even in the areas in North China and Manchuria where the peasantry might easily have been roused to revolutionary action because of a famine, the peasant struggle was subordinated to the main anti-imperialist strategy prescribed by the Comintern.[6]

The Soviet Movement

The primacy of the anti-imperialist struggle had practical implications of immediate importance to the soviet districts in South China.

[a] Brandt, Schwartz, and Fairbank, p. 171. The translators of the "Resolutions and Spirit of the Second Plenum" have added the word "not" to the key sentence on the party line ("Our general line is [not?] to adopt a principle of defeatism"), commenting, "the text seems erroneous here in omitting a negative." I have omitted the negative, which does not occur in the original text.

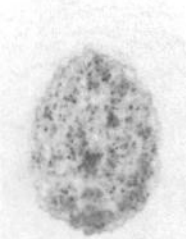

The focus of the party's activities shifted from South to North China. Fewer men could be allocated for political missions to existent soviet areas; military resources were retained in the Soviet Union or sent to North China rather than to Red Army units in the south. Hsieh Chüeh-tsai and Liu Po-ch'eng, for instance, were sent to work in Manchuria.[7]

Perhaps Communists attending the Second Plenum had some inkling of what was to come, for among the 15 great tasks they set for themselves, reinforcement of leadership of the agrarian revolution ranked below the struggles against the imperialists, the gentry, the compradores, the capitalists, the KMT, and the warlords. Leadership of the peasant movement ranked eighth on their list; direction of guerrilla warfare, expansion of the soviet areas, and centralization of control over the Red Army ranked even lower.[8]

The Agrarian Question

The Second Plenum's line on the agrarian question was ambivalent. The agrarian revolution was to be strengthened in the sense that the party was to work for peasant support. It could not be completed until after the victory of the general political revolution, but this did not imply that no agitation should begin prior to a nationwide uprising, only that the peasants should not be incited to armed insurrection before the workers were ready to take the lead.[9] However, the Plenum found cause for pessimism in the beginnings of the next revolutionary upsurge it perceived in the peasant struggles in South China. The renewal of class warfare in the villages before the urban workers showed signs of spontaneous activities was sufficient cause, for if the party was unable to iron out the uneven pace of revolutionary developments in the countryside and the cities, it would fail in its next revolutionary insurrection. The Plenum viewed the activities of the guerrillas and the Red Army in South China with mixed feelings—it wanted the countryside in the mood to join the insurrection when it came, but it feared the peasants might initiate a premature uprising doomed to defeat. In the Plenum's warning against premature armed insurrection we find anew the pessimistic attitude Mao noted in the Politburo's February letter to the Front Committee.[10]

Critique of Politburo Directives to the Front Committee

The Central Committee proposed to give more positive leadership in order to prevent premature leftist adventures. "Putschism and im-

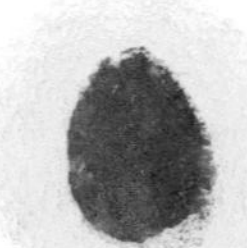

patience," it declared, "must all be liquidated by the Party to correct the Party's alienation from the masses."[11] To "win over the masses and hasten the upsurge of the revolutionary tide,"[12] it was necessary for the Central Committee to improve communications and especially to strengthen the committee on the peasantry led by P'eng P'ai. In his report on the meeting held on Ching-kang-shan in the fall of 1928, which the Plenum undoubtedly considered, Mao had noted that the masses were cold and reserved.[13] The Plenum responded that more guidance from the center would enable the Red Army to overcome its separation from the masses. The fault lay less with the Central Committee's direction than with the putschist disposition of the guerrilla units and the extreme democratic tendencies of the Red Army leaders. The Plenum acknowledged that the Politburo had not given leadership to the agrarian revolution but nevertheless affirmed that the policies of the Sixth Congress had been correctly applied and that the party had made some progress in consolidating its position. The resolutions noted that the Central Committee had been slow to react to political changes, and as a result some of its interpretations of the policies of the Sixth Congress had been too mechanical or too exaggerated, leading some members of the Central Committee to develop incorrect political ideas. Since the only directives of the Committee to which the Plenum gave its wholehearted approval were the detailed directives on the May Day and May 30th demonstrations in the cities, we must assume that mechanical and exaggerated interpretations were to be found in directives to the Front Committee and other party units in rural areas.[14]

The directives of which the Plenum was most critical were those dealing with peasant and agrarian questions and with the tactics of the Red Army and guerrilla units. There had been a "lack of positive direction" from the Committee over party units working in these movements. It had not been able to coordinate the various movements and had devoted too little attention to anti-imperialism in directives to rural workers. Directives to the Red Army, guerrillas, and party units in soviet areas were also defective in not calling for better coordination with party organizations in Wuhan and Canton.[15]

Rejection of Mao's April Proposals

The Politburo had received Mao's April letter before the Plenum met. Although he was not reproved by name for his disagreement with the tactics the Politburo had proposed to the Front Committee,

one of the counterproposals he offered in his April letter—that the Red Army should concentrate its efforts in Kiangsi—was specifically rejected. Urban areas were to remain the center of party work. The peasant movement should not be allowed to run ahead of the urban movement in South China; Wuhan and Canton were to continue to be the key districts. The Plenum evaded the question of whether the Red Army forces should be concentrated or dispersed, declaring that this matter was to be determined by objective circumstances in each situation.[16]

The Politburo's directives on the line to be taken toward the rich peasants are not available, nor are Mao's counterproposals (if he made any). But the available documentary evidence indicates that Mao's approach to the rich peasants differed from that of the Central Committee. Mao had written land redistribution laws in December 1928 and again in April 1929. Li Li-san, on the other hand, did not sponsor a land law until immediately before the Conference of Delegates from the Soviet Areas in May 1930.[17] The resolutions of the Second Plenum stressed the organization of unions of poor peasants and hired farmhands, not mentioning land reform. In line with the decisions of the Sixth Congress, Li Li-san evidently argued that land redistribution could not be successfully completed until after the general political revolution.[18] Mao's practice of redistributing land in areas temporarily held by the Red Army was not specifically approved by the Second Plenum. In June 1929 the confiscation of landlords' land was still a major slogan of the agrarian revolution, but it was not yet considered time to turn from agitation to action. To put any program of land redistribution into effect immediately would only bring the time nearer when the rich peasants would defect from the revolutionary movement. If they were to defect before the revolutionary tide could rise in urban areas, the revolutionary movement would inevitably be isolated and defeated, not only in the countryside but in the cities as well. The party must at all costs direct its activities toward overcoming the general unevenness in the development of revolutionary forces. It was, therefore, "still a mistake to oppose rich peasants unconditionally."[19] Here are the seeds of Li's rich peasant line—a justification of an alliance between the rich peasants and the proletariat, a rational ground for not breaking the alliance with the peasantry as a whole by premature actions. This line is Li's own. It is contrary to several statements in the Comintern directive on the peasant question he received shortly after the Second Plenum—for example, the statement that the party must fight

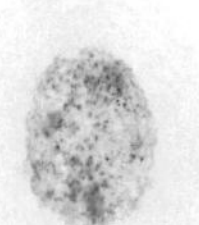

the rich peasants through the peasant masses and not give the rich peasants "an opportunity to use the masses in their own interests."[20] The alliance of the proletariat with the rich peasants could no longer be justified after this directive was received. According to Mao's later account, he, like the Comintern, opposed Li's line on the peasant question after the Second Plenum.[21] On the basis of the evidence presented here, I conclude that in June of 1929 Mao disagreed with Li's position because it was still too far to the right, giving too much latitude to the interests of the rich peasants.

For his part, Li opposed Mao because he considered the actions of Mao's Red Army units premature. When Mao's Front Committee drew up the April 1929 land law and began to redistribute land in the areas controlled by its armies, it was running too far ahead of the Chinese masses. The implementation of the land reforms should wait, as Li was waiting, for signs that the revolutionary high tide in urban areas was imminent. Mao's "guerrillaism"—his call for immediate uprisings on the basis of the peasant movement alone—was also premature. This facet of the Second Plenum's line found some support in the June directive from the Comintern.[22]

On the basis of this somewhat sketchy evidence, I conclude that disagreement on the peasant question between Li Li-san and the Political Secretariat of the Comintern dates from Li's interpretation of the June Comintern directive on the peasant question, an interpretation he worked out in debates with Ts'ai Ho-shen and other leaders of the right wing of the CCP. The Comintern's next letter on the peasant question was not precipitated by any act or proposal of Mao's, but by disagreements between Li and Ts'ai. According to Chang Kuo-t'ao, after the receipt of the June Comintern directive, Ts'ai published an article expressing his views on the peasant question. Li condemned Ts'ai's position, and an appeal was made to Moscow to settle their dispute. The Secretariat endorsed Ts'ai's interpretation.[23] Of course Li had to submit to the Comintern's judgment, and in August 1929 the Central Committee passed a resolution accepting the directives.[24] But, according to Chang Kuo-t'ao, Li was never again on good terms with Moscow after this episode. He banished Ts'ai to Moscow; in doing so he sent an able man to represent his opposition in the central apparatus of the Comintern and helped precipitate his own downfall a year later—Ts'ai testified against Li at his trial in 1930. Ts'ai's presence in Moscow may incidentally have given a voice to Mao and his Front Committee against attacks launched by Li or his supporters.

In this clouded history of the political relations between Li, Mao, and Ts'ai, and in their differing interpretations of the correct tactical line toward the rich peasants, we find an explanation of Li's failure to continue his attacks on Mao's peasant line by using the new ammunition provided by Stalin in his attack on the right opposition. After June 1929, Li's enemies in Moscow and Shanghai were prepared to use his interpretation of Comintern directives on the peasant question against him. His directive to Mao's Front Committee had been condemned. In formulating new directives to the Front Committee, Li could be sure that his political enemies were watching for the first opportunity to attack his political orthodoxy once again.

When Mao placed the origins of the left features of the Li Li-san line in the summer of 1929, he carefully avoided mentioning all the points in dispute between himself and Li and between Li and Moscow at that time. The central issue, the issue that Mao completely obscures in RSQHP and in the "Letter to Comrade Lin Piao," was the shift in the Comintern line on the rich peasants precipitated by Stalin's attacks on the right opposition and by the letters on the agrarian question from the CCP Politburo to his Front Committee.

After the Second Plenum: The Attack on the Trotskyites

The CCP Politburo did not undertake any major purge before the Second Plenum, which called for a resolute fight against both the right and left deviations.[b] Neither was stressed as the main danger. Equivocation on this issue was natural: Ch'en Tu-hsiu, the right opportunist of 1927 who would soon join the Trotskyites, was still a member of the CCP, and Bukharin, Stalin's helpmate in formulating the charges against Ch'en Tu-hsiu, and now a rightist, had not yet been publicly censured.

The Second Plenum's resolution on this subject warned that it was necessary to guard against the party's tendency to tolerate divisive factions that could destroy it. The rightists did not yet constitute a dangerous faction, but the CCP was to purge itself of the remnants of opportunism and liquidationism (the deviation of advocating

[b] Purges before the Second Plenum were minor indeed. Two members of the Shun-chih Committee in Hopeh were expelled from the Central Committee after the failure of an uprising at Shun-chih planned for October 1927. Although without constitutional grounds, this act was retroactively approved by the Second Plenum. The Plenum also approved the dissolution of the Kiangsu Provincial Executive Committee of the CCP in September 1927 because its members planned an unauthorized coup to occupy the headquarters of the General Labor Federation in Shanghai. (Brandt, Schwartz, and Fairbank, pp. 168, 488.)

dissolution of the party's secret organizations), while carefully avoiding the dangers of "putschism and impatience." Factional opposition was to be eliminated by "ideological argument and organizational discipline." Only leaders and active elements in the opposition were to be purged from the party.[25]

Two developments in the summer of 1929 opened the way for Li Li-san's first major purge of the CCP. The first was the dispute between the Nanking government and the USSR over their respective rights in the Chinese Eastern Railroad.[26] This dispute came to a head on November 16, 1929, when Soviet troops, accompanied by some Chinese Red Army units that had been training in the Soviet Union, crossed the border into China. As tension increased, Li Li-san issued the slogan "Protect the Soviet Union." Ch'en Tu-hsiu immediately objected. In an "Open Letter" to all party members he criticized the new slogan, arguing that it would strengthen the hand of reaction. After all, the Soviet Union's interest in the railroad was of the old imperialist order, and one of the main tasks of the party was to struggle against all types of imperialism. Under the circumstances, Ch'en argued, the slogan "Protect the Soviet Union" might easily be misunderstood—it might make the CCP appear anti-Chinese. He suggested instead the slogan "Oppose the Kuomintang's mistaken policy." Emphasize the errors of the KMT, he argued, not the protection of a foreign state.[27]

Ch'en's letter immediately provoked an angry retort from the Central Committee. Ch'en held his ground and issued a rebuttal stating his major disagreements with the party line and attacking the high-handed manner in which Li Li-san conducted CCP business. Having breached party discipline, Ch'en soon gathered a faction of old party leaders who had fallen from power in 1927 and a few young Trotskyite students who had recently returned from Sun Yat-sen University. Soon he became the most powerful potential leader in all opposition factions in the Kiangsu Provincial Committee.

Hard on the heels of the first interchange between Ch'en and the Central Committee came Bukharin's expulsion from the ECCI. Under the slogan of the "struggle on two fronts," with right opportunism as the main danger, the new coalition in the Comintern struck out at Bukharin's supporters in the central Comintern apparatus and its national sections. All Trotskyite remnants were cleared out at the same time.

Li's attack on Ch'en fitted into the new pattern. Ch'en was still a leader of the right wing in June, but by the end of 1929 he had adopted Trotsky's current line on the Chinese situation. After his "Open Letter" students from Sun Yat-sen University kept him informed on the major features of Trotsky's analysis. On November 15, 1929, one day before Soviet military units crossed the Manchurian border, Ch'en was expelled from the CCP as a Trotskyite and a liquidationist. Four of his closest associates—P'eng Shu-chih, Wang Tse-chieh, Ma Yü-fu, and Ts'ai Chen-te—were expelled from the Kiangsu Provincial Committee at the same time.[28] The removal of members of the old right wing from leading positions in the party increased the relative weight of Li's faction in the Central Committee, shifted the balance of forces in provincial committees to the left, and soon caused the new right-wingers, led by Ho Meng-hsiung, Lo Chang-lung, and other members of the Kiangsu Provincial Committee, to oppose the leftward shift in party strategy.

Ch'en continued his agitation from outside the party. Even beyond the pale he continued to exert considerable influence. In December he issued a manifesto titled "A Statement of Our Views," which stoutly attacked the current line of the Comintern and espoused many of Trotsky's theoretical views. In this manifesto Ch'en, like Trotsky, asserted that Chinese society was completely under the rule of capitalism, not feudalism. The free sale and purchase of land, he argued, was incompatible with feudal relations. Therefore, the revolutionary government must take the form of a "dictatorship of the proletariat." Stalin's formula of the "dictatorship of workers and peasants" did not accord with the objective situation in China. The KMT was simply a party of the bourgeoisie. Although both landlords and capitalists were members, the contradictions between them were contradictions between capitalists, not contradictions between representatives of two social orders in historically antagonistic stages of development. Therefore the Comintern could not expect that the KMT would soon collapse, torn apart by irreconcilable contradictions. It would not. China was entering a period of protracted counterrevolutionary stability. The Comintern's notion that a new revolutionary high tide was imminent was based on completely wrongheaded premises. To demand that the CCP engage in political strikes and prepare for armed uprisings at that time was the purest kind of revolutionary adventurism and putschism. The immediate tasks of the party should be to assist the workers in their daily economic struggles. Because the party could influence, organize, and lead the masses best under a democratic regime, it should immediately call for a democratically elected national assembly and a constitutional government. Finally, Ch'en echoed Trotsky's demands for more inner-party democracy. Erroneous lines could not be corrected quickly unless dissident views could be expressed to the whole party.[29]

In the face of Ch'en's decision to follow Trotsky's line so openly, one would expect that the Comintern would have immediately confirmed the resolution expelling him from the CCP. In fact, it did not. Instead, in a telegram dated February 8, 1930, the Comintern invited him to come to Moscow to participate in a discussion of his expulsion. On February 17, Ch'en restated his position in a long letter to the Comintern, firmly siding with Trotsky on the issues in the Stalin-Trotsky debate of 1927. Stalin, he wrote, had followed a right opportunist policy throughout the first half of 1927 and a putschist policy throughout the era of Ch'ü Ch'iu-pai's leadership. The current Comintern line was a continuation of the same opportunism. He reaffirmed his views, cited above, on appropriate policy for the CCP.[30] The Comintern later confirmed his expulsion.

Soon after the Second Plenum the Central Committee had undoubtedly sent letters to all party bureaus summoning resistance to Ch'en Tu-hsiu's "liquidationism," condemning open discussion in the party as extreme democratization, and making support of the slogan "Protect the Soviet Union" the criterion for determining loyalty to Li Li-san. The Central Committee sent such a letter to Mao's Front Committee sometime in September. This September letter, which also urged a general attack on non-proletarian ideologies in the Red Army, was sent before Ch'en and the Chinese Trotskyites had openly joined forces and before Ch'en had proclaimed his agreement with them. If my interpretation of the records is correct, Mao was not really open to the charge of "liquidationism." He was certainly not one of Ch'en's adherents in 1929. His assessment of the importance of the peasant movement was the exact opposite of Ch'en's before Ch'en became a Trotskyite.[c] From the viewpoint of Li Li-san and Chou En-lai, however, Mao's underestimation of the proletariat and overestimation of mountaintop soviets might have resulted in a premature insurrection and the subsequent liquidation of the party's urban base. At least in the eyes of the Central Committee, he was vulnerable on this issue.

According to Mao's RSQHP, Li's left line originated in mid-1929. On the all-important labor issue, he moved to the left with the Com-

[c] Paradoxically, Ch'en began to support Mao's guerrilla warfare after he became a Trotskyite, even though Trotsky himself never understood or supported it.

intern apparatus. On the peasant question and on the question of organizing the Red Army, he dragged his feet. The difference between the positions of Li and Mao widened after the Second Plenum. Li could and did insist on iron discipline and absolute obedience in action after his power was confirmed by the Plenum. He considered Trotskyism, rightism, and Mao's peasant consciousness non-proletarian ideologies to be purged from the party. Under the conditions prevailing in the Comintern at the time, all deviations were related and their exponents were unprincipled intriguers. In the interests of the Soviet Union, the Comintern was pushing the CCP toward a situation in which it would again be destroyed, to be reconstructed as Stalin wished. The basic position taken by the Central Committee toward the Maoists and other factions in the Red Army after the Second Plenum was stated in the letter sent to Mao in September. His *Ku-t'ien Resolutions* were drafted in response to that letter.

CHAPTER VIII

The Ku-t'ien Conference

In December 1929, Mao drafted the resolutions he presented to the Ninth (and last) Conference of Party Delegates from the Fourth Red Army, the Ku-t'ien Conference, which met the following January. At Ku-t'ien Mao finally agreed to reduce the powers of the Soldiers' Soviets and institute a regular Political Commissariat in the Fourth Red Army. Mao had resisted these changes a year before, but he now had several good reasons for making them. The Central Committee was becoming more insistent. Moreover, the Soldiers' Soviets could be used by rival factions to undermine the authority of his Front Committee. The resolutions Mao prepared for this Conference were not published until the first party rectification movement, in 1944, when they were used to illustrate and propagate Mao's correct organizational line.[a]

The Central Committee's Directive to the Conference (September 1929)

In these resolutions, Mao claimed that his approach to the problem of purging and reorganizing the Red Army was based on the spirit of a directive the Central Committee sent the Front Committee in September 1929, calling for the elimination of all non-proletarian ideas from the party organizations in the Fourth Army and for the immediate establishment of a Political Commissariat in its headquarters.[b] No copy of this directive is available, but it was probably based on the Second Plenum's declaration that the party was "still infected with

[a] The published versions of the resolutions are not called "draft" resolutions, but since they are dated December 1929, before Smedley's date for the opening of the Conference (January 1, 1930), I am treating them as such. (Smedley, *Great Road*, p. 267.)

[b] Mao, SW, I, 105; HC, I, 87. Since the Politburo had publicly accepted the Comintern's June directive on the peasant question, it is possible that the September letter also dealt with the most recent amendments of the Sixth Congress's line on the rich peasants in the soviet areas.

non-proletarian sentiment, particularly the tendency toward cliques and sectarianism which can easily be utilized by the international oppositionists to split the Chinese Party." The Plenum's recommendations had continued:

> The Plenum deems it not only necessary for the Party to apply correctly the political line, but also to call for an enforcement of iron discipline within the Party. A resolute fight must be waged by the whole Party against various incorrect deviations. *Incorrect ideas on organizational problems must be resolutely opposed.* And the activities of the oppositionists within the Party must be eliminated by ideological argument and organizational discipline, and their leaders and active elements must be purged from the Party.[1]

Sent after Bukharin's fall had been publicly announced but before the Comintern had perceived the beginnings of a new revolutionary wave, the September letter undoubtedly called for a general purge of opposition elements in the Red Army. It probably also called for the immediate establishment of a regular Political Commissariat and for limiting the autonomy of Soldiers' Soviets.[2] Since Mao's death was reported to the Central Committee at about this time, the September letter may have been predicated on the assumption that he was dead and that it would therefore be easier for the Politburo to control the Red Army. The Central Committee was misinformed. Mao was sufficiently alive to call the conference of party workers in the Fourth Red Army to meet at Ku-t'ien. During the month of December, while still recovering from his illness and resting at Ku-t'ien (a market town high in the mountains of Shang-hang hsien, Fukien), he drafted his resolutions for the conference. By January 1, Chu Teh and the main body of the Fourth Red Army had fought their way to Ku-t'ien, and the obscure but historic conference convened.

According to all later accounts, the Ku-t'ien Conference was a key event in the development of Maoist strategy and the expansion of the Maoists' power. Agreements were reached at Ku-t'ien that allowed the Front Committee to consolidate its control over the entire Fourth Red Army. Organizational plans for provincial soviet government organs were drawn up as well. The resolutions Mao prepared for the Conference set forth the basic essentials of his organizational strategy, to which he has adhered consistently up to the present time.[3]

Varying Accounts of the Conference and of Mao's Draft Resolutions

In spite of the avowed importance of this Conference in materials published after 1936, it is not mentioned at all in contemporary sources. Official accounts of its proceedings are vague, and those that appeared in 1936–37 contradict those that have appeared since 1945. There is no record that Mao's resolutions were ever made generally available to party members in any form until the first party rectification movement. Three versions were published between 1944 and 1951. Four sections of what in the full version is the first chapter appeared in 1944 in *Cheng-feng wen-hsien* (the *Party Rectification Papers*).[c] The full version itself first appeared in January 1944, in a special edition used in the rectification movement for party cadres in the liberation armies. This version was reprinted several times between 1944 and 1949. When Mao's HC appeared in 1951, only the first chapter was included, and that in a completely rewritten form.[4] No other work in HC—at least none for which earlier versions are available for comparison—has been so thoroughly revised as this one chapter.

The mystery that surrounded the Ku-t'ien Conference before 1936, the differing accounts Mao and Chu have given of its main events, and the fact that its resolutions were rewritten before publication in HC call for some kind of explanation. The obscurity before 1936 is easily explained, since Mao did not begin to tell his story to the world until after his triumph at the Tsun-yi Conference. Different emphasis on the importance of the Conference can be explained by Mao's alliances and struggles with other factions in the CCP. For instance, in his interviews with Snow in 1936, Mao did not mention any conflict with Li Li-sanists at the Conference. Nor did Chu Teh in his interviews with Smedley in 1937. According to Snow's account, at Ku-t'ien the Maoist faction won a decisive victory, got rid of the Trotskyite influence, consolidated the Front Committee's control of the Fourth Red Army, and laid the basis for the establishment of higher soviet organs.[5] According to RSQHP, Mao had begun to disagree with Li Li-san in the summer of 1929.[6] Robert Payne's biography of Mao supports this story, relating that Mao and Chu found few supporters for their program at Ku-t'ien, and that whereas Trotskyites may have been eliminated, the struggle with the Li Li-sanists was well under way by the time the Conference convened. According to Payne, Mao and Chu were unable to command majority support for their theses on the rural center of the soviet regime. All but a few of the field commanders and political commissars in the Fourth Red Army continued to

[c] Shanghai: Liberation Press, 1949, [12]—henceforth referred to as CFWH. Boyd Compton has compared the 1950 Chinese text of CFWH with two earlier editions. (Compton, pp. x, 239–45.) The *Ku-t'ien Resolutions* were not included in the papers published after the 1942 party rectification movement. See *Collection of Important Documents from the Beginning of the Resistance War to the Present* [24a].

support the Li Li-san line on the importance of urban bases for almost a year after the Conference.[7] These differences between the 1936–37 and post-1945 versions of the Ku-t'ien Conference are easily explained by the fact that in 1936 and 1937 Mao was working in close alliance with a number of former Li Li-sanists and did not want to say anything derogatory about Li, whereas by the time Payne interviewed Mao and his intimates in 1947 a new conflict with Li Li-san had begun.

Other than the two partial versions of the draft resolutions that were published before the Seventh Congress, nothing Mao wrote during the winter of 1929–30 appeared until 1947, when the "Letter to Comrade Lin Piao" appeared in a supplement to the 1947 edition of HC. Strangely enough, Mao did not mention the Conference at all in this letter, although he did discuss the theses of his resolutions. He claimed the support of Chu Teh, Fang Chih-min, Ho Lung, and Li Wen-ling for his line on the revolutionary character of the Chinese peasantry, on the creation of soviet bases, and on the military strategy and tactics the Front Committee had been advocating since the First Mao-ping Conference in May 1928.[8] He did not discuss the organizational strategy designed to strengthen the Front Committee's control over the Fourth Red Army. Unlike the 1936–37 version of the Conference, this letter does not stress the conflict with the Trotskyites, but, like Payne's account, it takes up the questions of military strategy on which Mao claims to have disagreed with Li Li-san after the first exchange of letters between the Front Committee and the Politburo. The republication of this letter in the 1951 edition of HC also points to a growing conflict with Li Li-san.[d]

The revision of the draft resolutions in HC can also be laid to Mao's shifting factional alliances. The first two versions had been published when the main objects of Mao's attack were Wang Ming and Po Ku, when Mao was struggling against the interpretation of "deviations" Wang had laid down in his pamphlet *The Two Lines*. During the first party rectification movement Mao substituted his own interpretation of deviations for Wang's. So much of Wang's pamphlet was devoted to condemning Li Li-san's deviations that it was natural for Mao, in revising Wang's analysis, to reevaluate Li's political program and substitute his own judgment for Wang's. By 1945, Mao judged the line of the 28 Bolsheviks much more harshly than the Li Li-san line. He stressed the fundamental correctness of his own organizational line as originally elaborated in his *Ku-t'ien Resolutions*. Liu

[d] The 1951 version of the letter omits the names of Ho Lung and Li Wen-ling from the list of men who supported him. Mao, SW, I, 112; HC, I, 102.

Shao-ch'i echoed these sentiments in his speech to the Seventh Congress.[9] By referring for the origin of his line to a set of resolutions written in opposition to Li Li-san, Mao showed that he had not been associated with Li Li-san in all the errors of which Wang Ming found Li guilty. Mao's revision of Wang's analysis of deviations in the party had made Li's position far less heinous. Had Li accepted Mao's revision, it could have opened the way for a reconciliation between Mao and Li after Li returned to China in 1945.

At Li's trial before the ECCI in December 1930, his line was adjudged to be "semi-Trotskyite," a view Wang Ming later elaborated in *The Two Lines.* RSQHP states that the source of all three left lines lay in the "subjectivism" of Chinese party leaders, by which it means specifically their blind attempts to follow the Russian model for revolution, ignoring the different development of Chinese society. Mao never attributes any direct influence to the CPSU or its factions. The resolution containing this analysis remained secret until 1953, when it appeared in the third volume of HC.[e]

RSQHP may once have contained a reference to Li Li-san's "semi-Trotskyism" that was eliminated from the 1951 HC. One such reference, to "semi-Trotskyite Li Li-sanism," was eliminated from the HC version of Mao's concluding speech to the National Conference of the CCP in May 1937. Publicly, Mao's line on Li's deviations continued to agree with Wang's and the Comintern's analysis until 1951, when the altered version of the first chapter of the draft resolutions was published in HC and the terminology Mao worked out during the first party rectification movement was adopted. Then Mao accused Li of being a subjectivist.

In the version of Marxism-Leninism developed after Stalin's in-

[e] "Subjectivism" in this context refers generally to the rejection of the theory that history is governed by objective laws—laws that men can understand only by testing their ideas in practice and modifying them in accordance with the results of such tests. Through this process, subjective ideas can come to reflect objective truth. However, Marxists hold that in all class societies men's ideas are class-bound and therefore cannot reflect absolute truth. Russian Marxists argue that in our era socialism is the progressive form of society, and that the subjective interests and ideas of the proletariat coincide with the objective laws of history. Proletarian philosophy, therefore, is objective partial truth for our era. The Maoists, following the same line, argue that new democracy was the most progressive form of society for China from the 1920's to the early 1950's. The thought of Mao Tse-tung coincided with the objective development of Chinese society and therefore became the objective partial truth for China in that era. Those Chinese Marxists who adhered strictly to the partial one-sided theories of the Russians—which, given the Marxist notion of the class-bound nature of all thought, could not reflect absolute and universal truth—were subjectivist. Only Marxists living in a classless society can understand the universal laws governing all history. Until that stage of history is achieved, all theory must prove its truth in revolutionary practice.

cursions into the field of philosophy in 1929, Trotsky's philosophical views were condemned as "idealist." This epithet was used to account for the fact that Trotsky favored a greater degree of inner-party democracy than Stalin was willing to tolerate.[10] Since Li Li-san's political errors were "semi-Trotskyite," as Wang termed them, it followed that Li was philosophically a "semi-idealist." He justified his political judgments with theories characteristic of Trotsky's idealism, but his theories were only semi-idealist because he never developed them into an integrated world view. Such was the line Wang Ming and the Comintern took on Li's errors throughout the 1930's.

The 1944–49 texts of *Ku-t'ien Resolutions* attack the alleged Trotskyites in the Fourth Red Army as "idealists." The 1945 RSQHP and the version of the resolutions in the 1951 HC removed the stigma of "semi-Trotskyism" from Li Li-san's line by changing the term "idealism" (*wei-hsin-kuan-nien*) to "subjectivism" (*chu-kuan-chu-i*).[11] This alteration constituted an open challenge to the whole Comintern line between 1927 and 1935. By this tactic Mao identified two old enemies, Wang and Li, as exponents of the "second and third left lines," disassociated himself from all left lines, and reaffirmed the uniqueness of his views and the creativity of his thought. Altering the term "idealism" would also have obscured two points that Li may have brought up in his letter to the Front Committee in September 1929. He had probably charged Mao with peasant consciousness again, and had perhaps suggested that Mao now agreed with Trotsky. Mao's change in terminology suggested three related notions. First, opposition factions in the Russian party had been dangerous sources of deviations in the CCP before Mao took over; second, Mao's reorganization of the party at Ku-t'ien had prevented such factions, Russian or otherwise, from gaining any influence in the Fourth Red Army; and third, Moscow's repeated assertion between 1928 and 1935 that right deviations were the main danger should never have been applied to the Chinese party. The problems of the Chinese party were unique, and successful solutions of them required a set of analytic terms different from those employed by the Communist movement as a whole.

To the cadres of the CCP who had studied the abridged version of the resolutions in the party rectification papers and the longer version issued for cadres in the army, the revision of language in the HC rendition was one of the first signals that Mao had decided not to accept orthodox Communist definitions and terminology in conducting his disputes with old opponents in the CCP. If either Wang or Li had received any backing from Stalin after their return to China (in 1937 and 1945, respectively), the change also suggests that by 1951 Mao was able and willing to conduct the dispute between Peking and Moscow on his own terms.

There are two possible reasons why the terminological changes were not publicly made until 1951. First, the dispute over Maoism continued to rage in the highest CCP circles even after the Seventh Congress. Opposition to Mao increased after Li's return from Moscow in late 1945. Mao did not overcome that threat to his power until after the decisive victories of the Communist armies in 1948–49. After the People's Republic was established, Mao's power over the CCP was firm enough so that a covert dispute between Moscow and Peking could be suggested to Chinese cadres studying documents on Chinese party history.

The second possibility stems from the fact that at the time the resolutions were drafted Mao was in opposition to the Li Li-san Politburo's policies on military strategy and party organization. Corollary to these issues was the problem of the degree and type of control over CCP policy that the Comintern or Stalin's agents in it (or both) were attempting to exercise. But was Mao opposing Li and his followers, or was he in disagreement with the policies advocated by Pavel Mif? Actually, both are possible. Conflicts between Li and the staff of the Comintern's Far Eastern Department had developed over the content of the Politburo's February 1929 letter to the Front Committee. Li's point of view was condemned and Ts'ai Ho-shen's upheld by the ECCI's July letter on the peasant question. In spite of Li's efforts to conform to the Comintern line, new disagreements developed between himself and the Far Eastern Department in the second half of 1929 and the first half of 1930, disagreements that culminated in the Li Li-san line in China and the expulsion of Ch'ü Ch'iu-pai from his position as leader of the Chinese delegation to the Comintern in Moscow. Both events can be attributed to the rise of Stalinists, Russian and Chinese, in the Comintern's Far Eastern Department, and the attempt of these new men to impose a tighter system of bureaucratic controls over the CCP Politburo. In this conflict both Li and Mao may have been on the side of the old cadres in the Chinese delegation to the Comintern. So it is possible that the organizational strategy Mao worked out in his draft resolutions, while officially a means of resisting the influence of sundry deviations in the army, may actually have been a basic factor in the ability of the Front Committee to resist Li Li-san's line in the summer of 1930, and later in Mao's resistance to the 28 Bolsheviks' attempt to take over all the important political posts in the soviet areas. If so, the organizational line Mao worked out to implement his political line not only was used against the CCP Politburo from 1930 to 1935, but was also used to frustrate the Comintern in its endeavor to bring the CCP and the Red Army more firmly under its direction. It is hardly something Mao could have admitted before his power and authority were securely established.

The Purpose of the Conference

The conference at Ku-t'ien may have been called and planned before the September letter arrived from Shanghai. Chu Teh states that conferences were held at least once a year and this one was the ninth conference of party representatives in the Fourth Army in slightly more than three years. The delegates had some real problems to settle, with or without the September letter. Evidently Mao and Chu intended to persuade the party leaders and military commanders in the Fourth Army to replace the system of party representatives in the army with a Political Commissariat and to limit the powers of both the Council of Soldiers' Deputies and the Soldiers' Soviets. They used this struggle for greater centralization of authority to combat those opposed to their views. The Central Committee's September letter, which had attacked the leaders of the Fourth Army as idealists, probably gave Mao and Chu the opportunity to attach the potent epithet of Troskyite to their opponents in the army. According to Mao's interview with Snow in 1936, "idealism" was not among the faults of the Red Army at the time of the Conference. The army was then characterized, he said, by guerrillaism, by lack of discipline and organization, and by remnants of old-fashioned militarism, such as officers beating the common soldiers and discriminating among them on the basis of personal feelings.[12] In other words, the Fourth Red Army had all the defects of the Russian army in 1917–18, when it too had been thoroughly disorganized by the creation of Soldiers' Soviets. The problem Mao faced was similar to Trotsky's when he became commissar of war. Like Trotsky, Mao needed to introduce strict central controls enforced by disciplinary measures. In order to hold the army together, he was attempting to overcome the weaknesses inherent in the extremely decentralized soviet system by introducing through the Political Commissariat a higher type of "ideological" leadership. Mao was finally willing to acknowledge the necessity of a political commissariat—but he intended to keep it under the Front Committee's control. He claimed that "a Trotskyist faction in the party and military leadership" had used the Soldiers' Soviets "to undermine the strength of the movement." This faction, Mao said, "bitterly attacked our program and everything we advocated. Experience having shown their errors, they were eliminated from responsible positions and after the Fukien Conference lost their influence."[13]

Mao identified only one member of this faction to Snow. Since this man, the army commander Liu En-kung, was undoubtedly one of the officers Li Li-san had sent to southern Fukien to exert control in the name of the Politburo, the mention of his name in 1936 probably was an indirect attack on Li. A year later, Chu Teh told Smedley that one of his greatest losses had been "regimental commander Liu Ankung, one of the most brilliant and highly educated Red Army commanders," who had been killed in battle in October 1929.[f] By the time Chu made this statement, the Russian purges were in full swing. Chu probably did not want to do anything to endanger the life of Li Lisan, who was then in Moscow, and denouncing one of Li's former agents as a Trotskyite could have done so.

The available versions of Mao's draft resolutions do not name any particular person as the object of attack. However, they clearly reveal that he intended to purge the party cells in the Fourth Red Army, reorganize party structure in the army, increase his personal control over both party and military men, and then use the new Political Commissariat to bring the unruly Soldiers' Soviets under control. In the process he could eliminate "Trotskyites" and "opportunists," i.e., opponents of all types, and turn the Fourth Red Army into the strongest, most highly disciplined unit of all the Red Armies, a model for others to follow. With the army again firmly under control, he could use it to influence and guide the work of civilian soviet leaders and party cells working in southern Fukien and southern Kiangsi.

Continuous battle, many casualties among both officers and men, and constant recruitment for almost a year made the Fourth Army of January 1930 a very different army from the one that had descended from Ching-kang-shan in January 1929. The party control system Mao's Front Committee had organized after the Second Mao-

[f] The difference between Snow's *En* and Smedley's *An* may arise from different systems of transliteration. In any case, there are enough similarities in the two accounts to tentatively identify An-kung and En-kung as one and the same. Mao refers to him as an army commander, Chu as a regimental commander. Mao's description of the Trotskyites' intent "to destroy the Red Army by leading it into difficult positions in battles with the enemy" suggests that the circumstances of Liu's death may well have been as Chu reported them. According to Chu, in late October 1929 he lost a battle to the 19th Route Army, which, as Smedley puts it, "hurled against him its three full divisions, armed to the teeth." Liu was among those killed in this encounter. (Smedley, *Great Road*, p. 266; Snow, RSOC, p. 174.)

ping Conference had been weakened by division of the army into guerrilla columns. Moreover, Mao's illness had prevented him from firmly controlling even old party representatives committed to his ideas. According to Mao's draft resolutions, which I paraphrase here, the party organization in the army was characterized by extreme laxness by the end of 1929. Since the descent from Ching-kang-shan, the requirements for admitting officers into the party had deviated significantly from previously established norms. (Mao does not indicate whether these norms were those he had established at the Second Mao-ping Conference or those established by the Politburo.) Even in the absence of directives from the Central Committee, a purge was desirable. Admission standards had to be more rigorously enforced in the future.[14]

On Ching-kang-shan, cadres and ordinary soldiers were all mixed in the same cells; but when the Ku-t'ien Conference met, the officers were organized in a single cell that excluded common soldiers. (When, where, and at whose instigation the change was made Mao does not say.) The mixed cells were to be reintroduced. A drive for new party members was to begin after the purge, drawing new members from the ranks of common soldiers. Cells for officers only were to be broken up. Mao's resolutions called for a party branch in every company and a cell in every platoon. Before that goal was achieved, as a temporary measure, cells might be set up in each column. Existing party groups might be divided up and their members sent into each platoon in a systematic manner. Eventually enough common soldiers were to be recruited so that every platoon would have a cell. As Mao had written in his resolutions for the Second Mao-ping Conference, at least a quarter of the men in the Red Army should be party members. Noncombatants and supporting troops were not to be entirely excluded from party membership.[15] Ordinary workers and intellectuals as well as officers and common soldiers were to be mixed in the same cells. Appropriate methods of dividing work in each cell among members of unequal ability had to be devised.

Since the descent from Ching-kang-shan, many persons had been casually admitted into the party simply because they were officers. As a result of such conditions, party directives frequently did not reach the soldiers' cells, and no meetings were held to explain and interpret directives that did filter down. Meetings for informing, propagandizing, and educating ordinary party members had become very infrequent.[16] Mao wanted a politically oriented army that could and would instill Communist ideals as it marched through the countryside. He did not wish to become an ordinary warlord. He had no desire to control territory for its own sake.

Because of the heavy losses that the army had suffered, not infrequently a person responsible for important work had no one to report to, and no one to check on his work. When mistakes were made nothing was done for a long time, if ever, and no discipline was administered. In this atmosphere, even those who were directly responsible to a superior did their best to evade discipline for their errors. A more comprehensive and equitable system of responsibility had to be worked out if party discipline in the army was not to break down entirely.[17]

Mao's Proposals for Reorganizing Party Units

In his resolutions Mao criticized the central bureaus in Shanghai for failing to maintain close relations with the lower ranks of the party. The party center, he wrote, rarely replied to reports made by lower-ranking members. Because the center lacked an activist attitude toward its work, its direction of the lower ranks was deficient; directives received were neither detailed nor thorough. This was especially true of directives dealing with practical work such as leading an army unit in guerrilla warfare. Because directives dealing with guerrilla warfare lacked detail, there were still several army units for which not even skeletal plans had been formulated.[18] Workers sent by the Politburo to direct work in the Fourth Army, for whom party officials at the capital gave their bond, frequently knew nothing about the practical work of the organizations to which they were sent. They usually devoted themselves strictly to party activities. Neither political nor military problems would appear on the agenda of party meetings they directed until a decision had been made by the Politburo. As a result, party bureaus in the Red Army allowed army officers to make tactical decisions on purely military grounds and important political factors were neglected.[19] To remedy this disgraceful situation, Mao proposed to purge all those:

> Who have mistaken political attitudes;
> Who just want to eat well and live high;
> Who smoke opium and gamble;
> Who merely wish to get rich on foreign money;
> Who commit crimes frequently and refuse to reform.[20]

In his categories of potential purgees, Mao did not mention any specific deviationist groups or their leaders; "mistaken political attitudes" were left undefined. The attack on those who wished to live high is obviously a sally against those who advocated capturing a large city, as well as against those who wished to leave the rural areas and engage in urban work. Gamblers could not be tolerated among those who handled party funds, and opium addicts were suspect for the same reason. Although it is barely possible that some men were joining the CCP in the hope that Russian money would be available to them, as it had been before the breakdown of the united front, it is more likely that Mao's reference to those who wished to get rich on foreign money was directed against intellectuals who wanted to get an overseas education and were eager to leave the ranks of the army to go to Moscow. Since the Central Committee's September letter was written immediately before the Soviet Army invaded northern Manchuria, it may well have contained a request for volunteers to train and study in the Soviet Union. If so, it would appear that Mao was entirely opposed to this move and attacked those who, for whatever reason, wished to comply.

Mao's Conditions for Party Membership

Mao proposed that after the purge was completed only persons who met the following five conditions should be admitted as party candidates:

> They must demonstrate no incorrectness in political viewpoints (including class consciousness).
> They must be completely honest.
> They must have the spirit of sacrifice and the ability to work actively.
> They must have no desire to get rich on foreign gold.
> They must not smoke opium or gamble.[21]

Since the great majority of new party members were to be drawn from the ranks of the army, it is obvious that Mao did not intend that they should possess the class consciousness of the proletariat, for the army was generally made up of peasants. Genuine workers were few and far between in the mountains of Fukien and Kiangsi, so the correct political viewpoints could only refer to desire for revolutionary change. To justify this recruitment policy, Mao must have invoked the extraordinary revolutionary quality of the Chinese peasantry, for which he was later condemned by the 28 Bolsheviks.

The procedures Mao suggested at Ku-t'ien for inducting new members were not the standard procedures set forth in the Party Constitution adopted by the Sixth Congress, nor were the eligibility requirements Mao set up for new members mentioned in that document. According to the Constitution, candidates' eligibility was to be determined by class membership and recommendation by party members, in the following manner.

> Factory laborers: to be recommended by one party member and approved by one branch of a production party organ [i.e., one in a factory].
>
> Peasants, handicraftsmen, intellectuals, and public functionaries of the lower grades: to be recommended by two party members.
>
> High public functionaries: to be recommended by three party members.[22]

No provision was made for the admission of persons drawn from the landlord class or the bourgeoisie.

Mao, however, made no distinctions at all between classes in his list of qualifications for membership. He proposed no general rule excluding gentry, bourgeoisie, rich peasants, or other classes, nor did he propose that members drawn from enemy classes be sponsored by more than one party member. In Mao's regulations one sponsor was sufficient. Of course, most of the members introduced in organs under his control must have been drawn from the peasants or the small handicraftsmen.[23]

Mao proposed that the sponsor examine the candidate's qualifications before introducing him. A representative of the party branch was also to investigate the candidate before enlisting him, and then report on whether or not he met the conditions for membership. On enrollment, the sponsor was to guarantee the new member's trustworthiness. The sponsor gave the new member a detailed account of the life of the party and the operation of the cell he had joined, including its secret work, and explained to him those aspects of party life a member must conceal from all non-members. The sponsor remained the guarantor in both Mao's regulations and the Constitution.[24]

Mao made no special provision for the entry of former members of other parties, nor did he specifically forbid it. All were evidently to be admitted on an equal footing and to assume full rights as party members as soon as the party branch completed the investigation of their qualifications. The Constitution, on the other hand, required the recommendation of three party members of more than three years' standing before a former member of another party could be admitted to the CCP. Such a candidate could become a full CCP member only with the approval of the Provincial Party Committee. If he had been an officer, or had held any special status in the party from which he came, his membership in the CCP required the sanction of the Central Committee itself.

According to the Constitution, a party member had to agree to accept the regulations, constitutions, and resolutions of the Comintern and the higher organs of the CCP, as well as to pay dues on a regular basis. In the 1944 version of *Ku-t'ien Resolutions* there is no indication that Mao was aware of these requirements (as surely he must have been) and no reference to the Comintern, except for the derogatory remark about those seeking foreign gold.[25]

Mao also attacked the problem of inner-party education and propaganda in his resolutions. At each level, he wrote, party organs must do more to lead practical work than make decisions—they must also carry out their responsibility of educating party members. This was to be done in a systematic manner. Each higher party organ was to determine the study materials to be used by the branches and cells under its control, work out an agenda for study for each meeting, set the time of the meeting, and check on what was actually done. Detailed reports were to be made to the higher organs, which were to discuss them thoroughly and reply to them. If possible, the higher organs were to send representatives to meetings of the lower branches and cells.[26] Excuses by the higher organs pointing to shortages of workers, insufficient time for their own tasks, etc., were not to be tolerated. Such excuses concealed passivity and slackness in the upper ranks of the party; behind them the upper strata in fact neglected their own work.[27] In this Mao was surely pointing an accusing finger at the Politburo, upbraiding it for its attitude toward the Red Army and the rural soviets.

Mao's Proposals on the Relationship Between Military Officers and Political Commissars

In the final chapter of the draft resolutions, Mao worked out a plan for relations between the political and military commands in the Fourth Red Army, and between the army and the local soviet authorities in the period of transition, when higher organs of the soviet governments were being established. The following is a free translation of this last chapter.

1. Under the direction of the Front Committee, the military command and the political commissariat shall participate jointly and equally in directing matters of significance to the whole army before the higher-level local soviets are set up.

2. Relations between the Red Army and the masses.

a. The organs of the military command and the political commissariats shall act equally and jointly in all affairs of concern to the whole army, such as the promulgation of political policies.

b. All mass work preparatory to setting up governments in areas where local soviets have not yet been organized (such as propagandizing and organizing the masses, creating local organs of political power, confiscations, judgments, appeals for subscriptions to support departing troops, devising other ways and means of raising money, and aiding famine and flood victims) shall be entirely under the jurisdiction of the political organs in the army.

c. In places where local soviets already exist, the Red Army must allow them to administer all their business independently, in order to create confidence on the part of the masses in their own political power. Only where the organs of local political power are not yet strong shall it be permissible for the political commissariat to work jointly with the local soviet organs, and even then only on matters relating directly to both the local organs and the political commissariat.

d. To aid in the creation and expansion of local armed guards is the responsibility of the political commissariat of the Red Army, and training them in time of peace and directing them in battle the responsibility of army headquarters. Nevertheless, orders to local Red Guards shall be given through the channels of local political organs whenever possible.

3. Within the army, the military and political systems must have independent lines of administration and control of their personnel. In affairs in which both systems have related interests, such as joint mobilization of personnel and joint propagation of news, the method of equal participation in signing and issuing proclamations shall be employed.

4. In giving directives to the agencies of another system, formal contact must be made with the highest-ranking officer on the spot, and the directives shall then be sent down by him through regular channels. Both the military and political departments shall jointly and equally employ the principle of obedience according to rank in the administration of military discipline (both ceremonial and punitive). No member of one department should be allowed to plead that the two departments were autonomous as an excuse for disrespect or failure to obey orders emanating from the other.

5. On general administrative arrangements regarding food, lodging, health facilities, fighting schedules, etc., the political department must submit to the direction of military headquarters. [In other words, the new political commissars were not to demand better food, housing, etc., than that available to their opposite numbers in the military chain of command. They were not to forage for themselves or set up a separate system of requisitioning for the needs of the political departments.] In this area, the sole authority of the military officers must be enforced. But in the realm of political discipline and mass work, the military system must submit to the direction of the political department.

6. Decisions regarding fund-raising, as well as the use and dispersal of all funds for political purposes, shall be under the direction of the political departments, but overhead expenses for the political departments shall be remitted by the appropriate military departments. Moneys for the use of party organs should be distributed by the political commissars.

7. All strictly military orders should be countersigned by the political commissars without objections. All orders for which the political organs are solely responsible require no military countersignatures.[28]

Mao's definition of the power of the political commissars in the army limited the rights of purely military men to participate in making the political policies of the army. It effectively terminated the power of the Soldiers' Soviets to control food, fuel, and lodging arrangements. Control over administration of these arrangements passed into the hands of the military officers, a provision designed to check any tendency on the part of the political commissars toward assertion of special privilege. Mao's resolutions also introduced a strict disciplinary code, the elements of which are not spelled out in *Ku-t'ien Resolutions.* This code, designed to prevent ordinary soldiers and purely military officers from entering into independent relations with local soviet governments, required that the soldiers and officers work through the political organs of the army. Military training and the direction of local armed units in actual battle were the only exceptions allowed to this rule.

Both the military command and the political department of the Fourth Red Army were subject to the direction of the Front Committee, where the two chains of command joined. The Front Committee was also the chief party organ in the army, and all lower party organs were directly subordinate to it.[29] If the party delegates from the Soldiers' Soviets who attended the Ku-t'ien Conference had agreed to adopt Mao's proposals, they would have conferred on him the power to subject all political and military actions, both inside and outside the army, to his control. If he had achieved such support for his proposals, in the following months he could have used the Fourth Red Army delegates to the conferences called to form higher soviet governments as a single bloc, voting for the policies previously worked out by the Front Committee. The reports of the Ku-t'ien Conference published after 1945, however, suggest that he did not achieve a majority for his policies at Ku-t'ien even among the soldiers' delegates. According to Robert Payne's account, Mao's field commanders overruled him at Ku-t'ien. They were convinced that the small abandoned villages of Kiangsi would never support an army and that the Red Army must prepare to march to some large city in the industrial heart of China. Following the Li Li-san line, they rejected Mao's view that the army could be built up in the rural areas, to spread over a period of time from the villages to the large cities. This, after all, was one of the ideas condemned in the Central Committee's resolution of 1929. If Payne's account is correct, not even a majority of the men officially subject to Mao's Front Committee supported his resolutions. When the army set out for Kiangsi toward the end of January, its delegates were not prepared to vote as a unified bloc at the provincial party conferences that were soon to convene.

Many were willing to vote against Mao, to throw in their lot with Li Li-san and the Politburo.

There are three possible reasons why so many disagreed with Mao. First and most important, he was opposed to the proletarian line of the Central Committee. Second, he was reiterating ideas condemned in 1927. Third, if all his organizational resolutions had been accepted, as chairman of the Front Committee he would have had the right to transfer political commissars who did not follow the new regulations. He could also have limited the power of the new commissars by the simple expedient of appointing persons other than political commissars as secretaries of the party cells. If the commissars still proved cantankerous, he could have given them especially dangerous assignments. Payne's story—that Li Li-san's supporters in the Fourth Army refused to accept Mao's proposals and continued to struggle against them for almost a year after the Ku-t'ien Conference—is probably correct. Mao's own story of the Conference may also be correct, aside from his omission of the conflict with Li's supporters. Some of his proposals were accepted, and some of the delegates from the Soldiers' Soviets supported those that were not. In the future, they would also support his effort to limit the power of the newly appointed political commissars. After the Conference, the controversy between Li and Mao was to take a new form. Henceforth it was to be played out in a power contest between two political agencies in the Red Army—the Front Committee and the Political Commissariat.

Conclusion

Existing records lend support to Mao's statement that he began to oppose the left aspects of Li Li-san's line in the middle of 1929. With the first exchange of letters between Mao's Front Committee and the new Central Committee, Li attacked the theses on the Chinese revolution Mao had worked out on Ching-kang-shan in the year after he was removed from the Central Committee.

In the spring of 1929 the Comintern line veered to the left, and in June it directed the CCP to embrace an anti-rich-peasant line. This shift was generated not by any new analysis of class relations in China, but by Stalin's drive to collectivize agriculture and eliminate the kulaks from the economic life of the USSR. The shift did not involve a condemnation of Mao's rich peasant line. Li Li-san was held responsible for those sections of the resolutions of the Sixth Party Congress that had called for an alliance with the rich peasants, and also for sending directives to Mao requiring that he maintain such an alliance. After this initial challenge, which he could not have foreseen, difficulties between Li and the Comintern became more and more frequent.

In 1928–29, while Stalin was consolidating his control over the CPSU, Mao was building his political machine in the soviet bases in South China and refining the political, military, and organizational strategies he and Chu had worked out on Ching-kang-shan. There is no evidence that Mao ever acknowledged his political errors during this period. On the contrary, he continued to develop the military line for which he was expelled from the Central Committee in November 1927, adding to it his new theses on land revolution and soviet bases. Since his theses were opposed by the Central Committee, he rarely lacked opponents in the soviet districts and the Red Armies. His own power was bound up with his Front Committee. If the Central Committee had succeeded in separating him from that organ, his power might have been broken. So throughout 1929 he was careful not to leave the seat of his power, even to go to Shanghai to consult with the Central Committee. Li Li-san would not extend the authority of Mao's Front Committee, but owing to the success of the political and military strategy Mao and Chu employed, the Fourth Red Army had become the largest and best disciplined Red Army in China before the end of 1929.

At Ku-t'ien, Mao compounded the military deviations for which he had been condemned in 1927. He refused to concede control of the Fourth Red Army to provincial party organs, and he refused to accept recommendations, or orders, from the military bureau of the Central Committee. He devised the *Ku-t'ien Resolutions* in order to curb the growing authority of Politburo appointees to the new Political Commissariat. He could not have retained his influence without the support of military officers such as Chu Teh and Li Wen-ling. His power in the Front Committee still rested largely on his willingness to support their military tactics in the face of the military bureau's attempts to alter them.

By the end of 1929 Mao was convinced that the Red Army could be used as a major instrument of the revolution by establishing soviet governments and inciting the peasants to rise against their landlords and redistribute the land. On his return to Kiangsi in January 1930, he believed that his plan would enable the Communists to win all Kiangsi before the end of the year. If this proved true, his power in the party would inevitably be increased, and his deviations vindicated by success.

CHAPTER IX

Mao's Agrarian Policy in 1930

The year 1930 was crucial in the history of the world Communist movement. In that year, men who were steadfast Stalinists took over many of the non-Soviet Communist parties. The Chinese party was no exception. Before the year was up, Li Li-san, Ch'ü Ch'iu-pai, and Chou En-lai had fallen from power and been replaced by the students of Pavel Mif, the 28 Bolsheviks. Mif drove Ch'ü from his position as CCP representative to the Comintern and called Chou En-lai to Moscow to take his place. Then Mif set out for China to entrap Li Li-san. The trap was not sprung without a struggle, but by the end of the year Li Li-san was in Moscow standing trial for his errors while Mif's protégés were making their final assault on Chou and Ch'ü, the only men on Li Li-san's Politburo who still had power enough to be dangerous.

In a subtle way the assault on Li Li-san's power began in October 1929, when the ECCI, claiming to see a rising revolutionary wave in China, directed the CCP to prepare the masses for a general insurrection leading to a dictatorship of the proletariat and peasantry. Li responded in the early months of 1930 by planning the part each major party unit was to play in the coming uprisings, and by drawing up a general political program, including provisional labor and land laws to be proclaimed by the future soviet government. Both his plans for the insurrection and his political program were based on the ECCI instructions, which had noted the increasingly important activities of the peasants and the Red Army, but had stressed that these remained only side currents in the general revolutionary wave. Li was directed to continue to give particular attention to the workers' movement. The party must lead the spontaneous activities of the labor movement from economic struggle into political action before the revolutionary wave reached its crest. On February 25, 1930, the CCP and the Chinese National Labor Federation jointly issued a call for a National Conference of Delegates from the Soviet Areas to discuss the political program of the future soviet government. The Labor Federation's co-sponsorship of the Conference emphasized the primary role the proletariat would play in the insurrection and the government.[1]

All the basic points in Li's political program were published in the Comintern journal on April 9, which indicates that the Comintern had not yet perceived anything unorthodox in Li's political judgment.[2] At the last possible moment before the Conference, Li decided to call in the Red Army to assist the workers. He directed the individual armies to collect all arms in the soviet areas and begin assembling for a general assault on the cities of Central China. The directives were sent after Chou went to Moscow; Li alone was responsible for them. The First National Conference of Delegates was held in late May. Li's political program, including the labor and land laws, was officially adopted.[3]

Mif was in Shanghai as the Comintern representative to the CCP when the Conference met. Some of the 28 Bolsheviks were also present, and with Mif they disapproved of Li's high-handed methods of conducting meetings and also of some of the resolutions he presented. Ho Meng-hsiung and his faction in the Labor Federation, men who had probably been closely associated with the recently deposed Browder, also opposed Li's resolutions. But they were divided among themselves into pro- and anti-Browder factions. Moreover, they distrusted Mif because he had been in favor of peasant soviets in 1926 and had never concerned himself with labor organizations. As a result of these divisions, Li's opponents could not unite against him, so he was able to carry the day and continue his preparations for an assault on the major cities of Central China.

Hopes for the success of that assault were raised by the outbreak of a war between Chiang Kai-shek's government and a coalition between the northern generals Feng Yü-hsiang and Yen Hsi-shan. Chiang was rapidly withdrawing his troops from South and Central China. The cities of Kiangsi, Hupeh, and Hunan were denuded of troops. For the first time since 1927, the Communist armies in Central China were as large as or larger than those of the Nationalists. On June 11, when preparations were complete and the Red Armies already in motion, Li had the Politburo pass a resolution calling for an attempt to take "one or several provinces," thereby inspiring the masses to rise throughout China. Li asserted that the world revolution would first break out in China and then spread until it engulfed the whole world. Preliminary success in one or more Chinese provinces would thus precipitate a direct revolutionary situation on a world scale. Wuhan, the industrial center of China, held the key to a nationwide revolution. The workers were the decisive factor in the revolutionary situation. Red Army assaults on the cities, insurrections in the KMT armies, and peasant uprisings could aid the workers, but could never replace them.[4] These were the essential elements of the "Li Li-san line."

Envisioning the approaching upheaval on this vast scale, Li argued that although the revolution would begin as an agrarian insurrection led by workers, i.e., a national and democratic revolution, upon success it would immediately pass into a socialist revolution. The main fear he expressed was that the right wing of the party might remain passive and let the great opportunity go by. No left deviation came under attack. In the June 11 resolution Li specifically singled out and condemned a number of Maoist notions. He pointed out that "some people" had perceived the unevenness of revolutionary development but had overlooked the unusual acuteness of the workers' struggle. This had led them to overestimate the peasant movement and look askance at the workers.[5] He further said that the guerrilla concept prevalent in the Red Army favored attacking but not occupying cities. Those who held it believed, contrary to the party line, that soviets should not yet be organized in the cities.[6] Wang Ming, Po Ku, Chang Wen-t'ien (Lo Fu), and Shen Tse-min opposed this resolution, supported by Mif. On this point they were joined by Ho Meng-hsiung and his followers in the Labor Federation.

Li, who probably realized that his future in the party depended on the success of his venture, ordered his colleagues not to talk to Mif. He then removed, reprimanded, or expelled most of Mif's students. Ho and his adherents were simultaneously removed from their committee assignments in the CCP and the Labor Federation and replaced with Li's own men. Although these moves gave Li complete control of the central organs, the men he had displaced soon made themselves heard in the local committees to which they were sent. Mif certainly was displeased by these developments, for Li had effectively isolated him from contacts with his supporters in the CCP.

In order to force his line on a generally reluctant party, Li formed a closely knit factional group to direct the assault on the cities. Since he could not get enough support for his line from many leaders of the various party organizations and affiliates, Li dissolved the party units, the youth corps, and the trade unions and formed action committees headed by the leaders who had agreed to follow his line. In early August, after P'eng Teh-huai's Red Army had captured and then been driven out of Ch'angsha, Li appointed a General Action Committee to direct the urban uprisings. But Mif was adamantly opposed to this move, and he was still the Comintern representative. As a result Li fell under an attack he could not withstand, and the party organizations, youth corps, and trade unions were officially revived when the Third Plenum met in September. Action committees nevertheless continued to function in many places until early 1931, when Comintern orders to terminate the Li Li-san line reached the outlying party sections.[a]

Professor Benjamin Schwartz holds that the concept of an incorrect "Li Li-san line" was invented in Moscow when the Red Army proved unable to seize and hold the cities of Central China in the summer of 1930. He notes that the Comintern's Resolution of July 23, an analysis of the revolutionary situation in China, agreed with Li on most points. Hsiao Tso-liang, on the other hand, holds that Li's line diverged from that of Stalin and the Comintern throughout the summer of 1930, that the Resolution of July 23 expressed the Comintern's disagreement with Li's line, and that the Comintern sent Ch'ü Ch'iu-pai and others back to overthrow Li in August, while he was still planning his second assault on Ch'angsha and Hankow. It is my view that there were probably two factions in the Comintern, one in favor of armed uprisings and the other more cautious. That the Resolution of July 23 agreed with Li on some points and disagreed on others was probably the product of compromise. That the men sent to overthrow Li actually favored some of the things he was attempting seems to indicate that neither faction had succeeded in gaining Stalin's favor before Li's successors left Moscow, and that Li's policies had not yet been totally rejected. The issue was at last resolved in December, when Lominadze, Li's staunchest supporter in the Comintern, circulated a petition among the members of the

[a] Minutes of the Enlarged Politburo Meeting, November 22, 1930, [22], in BIC; Hsiao, pp. 93–94. According to the account Chu Teh gave Wales in 1937, Red Army units had no radios until late August 1930, and were even then unable to use them for lack of operators. Radio communication was established between the units of the Red Army for the first time in May 1931. One may infer from this that at least until that date neither the Red Army nor the outlying party sections had radio communication with the Central Committee. In this period changes of line in the soviet areas date from the arrival of orders rather than from the date the Central Committee shifted its line in Shanghai. Messengers from Shanghai took from one to three months to go from Shanghai to the mountains of Fukien and southern Kiangsi. (Wales, *Inside Red China*, pp. 250–53.)

CPSU Central Committee requesting Stalin's removal. Lominadze was stripped of power soon afterward, and without his support the policy set down in Li's Resolution of June 11 became the "Li Li-san line."

On April 26, Li had set up a General Front Committee to direct the Third, Fourth, and Fifth Red Armies.[7] Mao and Chu dominated this Committee and used it to fight the Kiangsi Provincial Action Committee throughout the latter half of 1930. The Action Committee was dominated by former members of the Southwest Kiangsi Special Committee, which had been opposing Mao's line on rural bases since 1928. Conflict between the two committees grew so intense that the Kiangsi party split. In November Mao arrested many members of the Kiangsi Provincial Action Committee. They were released by anti-Maoists in the Third Army during the Fu-t'ien incident in December, after which the two Communist factions waged civil war until the middle of 1931.

The records of this intraparty conflict in Kiangsi are confusing, to say the least. Mao was opposing Li's Central Committee, the Kiangsi Action Committee was supporting it, and all the while Li was under attack by Mif. However, there is no evidence that Mao and Mif coordinated their efforts to oust Li. The comrades who replaced Li continued to resist Mif's directives until he received Moscow's official support in December. Then and only then was he able to place his protégés in control of the party.

The letter reconstituting the party probably did not reach Kiangsi until January 1931. Before then, Mao had had to assume that the Kiangsi Action Committee had the support of the Central Committee, so he could hardly have attacked the Action Committee as an anti-party group. Conveniently, he discovered that it was made up of Nationalist *agents provocateurs,* members of the Anti-Bolshevik Corps. After Li fell, Mao discovered that he had been wrong—the Committee's members had been Li Li-sanists all along. The 28 Bolsheviks agreed that they had been Li Li-sanists, all right, but questioned whether they had also been KMT agents. And what about Mao? Had he been correct in his methods of opposing Li all through 1930, or was he only a two-faced double-dealer, interested solely in power for himself? According to Mao, Wang Ming criticized him as a "narrow empiricist."[8] Wang based his indictment on the record of Mao's investigations and actions during 1930, a record to which we shall now turn.

The February 7 Conference

On February 7, 1930, a party conference attended by delegates from the Southwest Kiangsi Special Committee and the Fourth, Fifth, and Sixth Red Armies (commanded by Chu Teh, P'eng Teh-huai, and Huang Kung-lüeh, respectively) convened in southern Kiangsi.[9] According to Mao, it was at this conference that his controversial land law was adopted.[b] Although the law was actually applied for only two short periods in 1930 (February to July) and 1931, the principles of land distribution it set forth were disputed between Mao and Wang until the first party rectification movement. The dispute turned not on actual applications of the law, but on whether or not Mao had deviated from the party line when he first advocated the principles embodied in the law. Wang Ming flatly asserted that he had. Mao admitted in 1945 that he had been opposing Li Li-san when he advanced the law, but asserted that in the context of local and national conditions it had been correct policy.

In his interviews with Snow, Mao said that he had prepared for the February 7 Conference at the Ku-t'ien Conference. He must have prepared well, for he was better received in February. His own army gave him considerable support, and a majority of the soldiers' delegates from the Fifth and Sixth Red Armies probably sided with him as well.[10] It is unlikely, however, that the delegates from the Fifth and Sixth Armies supported Mao's resolutions unanimously. At that time Mao exercised no general authority over all the Red Armies in Kiangsi. The jurisdiction of his Front Committee was still confined to the Fourth Red Army, for the General Front Committee had not yet been created. Both Mao and Chu report that most of the party members in Kiangsi supported the Li Li-san line throughout 1930, and that some of Li's most ardent supporters were to be found among the political commissars in the Third Red Army, which was at this time incorporated into Mao's Fourth Army.[11]

Mao has also related that in the course of the debate on land policy at this Conference the leaders of the Southwest Kiangsi Special Committee led a struggle against his "opportunism," opposing redistribution of land. In Mao's words, after "the struggle against 'opportunism' led by those opposed to redistribution" was overcome, a majority of those still present at the Conference decided to carry out land reforms immediately, hasten the formation of local soviets, and establish a Kiangsi provincial soviet government.[12]

[b] See Appendix D for a complete translation of the February 7 Land Law.

Disputed Sections of the February 7 Land Law

Two principles embodied in the February 7 land law were Mao's unique contribution: "Take from those who have much to help those who have little," and "Take from those who have fertile land to help those who have poor land." These principles, as well as Mao's interpretation of the principle of equal distribution to mean equal shares to everyone—"men and women, old and young"—were condemned as a rich peasant line by the 28 Bolsheviks at the First Party Congress of the Central Soviet Area, held in November 1931.[13] Before that Congress condemned his land redistribution policy, Mao argued that the February 7 law followed an anti-rich-peasant line. He maintained that it was the Li Li-san land law—which left the rich peasants in possession of all the land they could cultivate and confiscated only the land they leased out—that really represented the rich peasant line. Of course, Mao did not admit that the rich peasant line pursued by Li's adherents in Kiangsi was attributable to Li until after Li had fallen from power.[14]

In opposing Li Li-san's land policy, Mao took a step to the left, in the direction of current Soviet policy. But he did not go far enough to satisfy the 28 Bolsheviks. He did not confiscate all the land of the rich peasants, nor did he allot them land inferior to that allotted the poor and middle peasants. Both these policies were put forward by the 28 Bolsheviks in a land law adopted at the First All-China Congress of Soviets, also held in November 1931.[15] Before 1930 the Comintern had supported equal distribution in some form. It supported the disputed principles in Mao's February 7 law on only one occasion, in a directive dated July 1931. It reversed its position before November.[16]

The principle of equal distribution had been laid down in the third section of the "Resolution on the Peasant Problem" adopted by the Sixth Congress of the CCP. According to Mao, the Central Committee never interpreted the principle in the same way he did. The Committee interpreted it not as equal shares for everyone, but only for those able to work in the fields full time. The very young, the very old, and the infirm were excluded.[17]

The Comintern's July 1931 letter to the CCP stated that "in redistributing land, one should take into account not only whether the land is large or small but also whether it is fat or lean."[18] This statement undoubtedly supports the provision in Mao's February law for classifying land into several grades before redistribution. It does not necessarily mean that the CCP should have incorporated Mao's two principles into the land laws they were planning for the future soviet government. In fact, these principles never appear again in the land laws of the Chinese soviet republic.

The conflict between the Maoists and the Southwest Kiangsi leaders dates back at least to 1928, and its roots could probably be traced to the intraparty conflicts over Mao's agrarian policy in 1927. The original leaders of the Southwest Kiangsi Special Committee have not been positively identified, but several of them may have served in the Ki-an and Wan-an soviets, to the east of Ching-kang-shan. Ki-an hsien in the Wan-an soviet bordered on Yung-hsin, one of the six hsien in the Ching-kang-shan soviet. According to HC, Mao maintained few contacts with these soviets. Their leaders refused to cooperate with or extend aid to the troops on Ching-kang-shan, even when it was feasible to do so.[19]

In 1928 the political program of the Wan-an soviet included confiscation of all industry, large and small. According to his own record, Mao never supported confiscation of shops and small factories. While in the Ching-kang Mountains his aim was to win over the petty bourgeoisie, both in small towns and in the countryside.[20] He probably clashed with the leaders of the Wan-an soviet over this issue, as well as over tactics toward the rich peasants, throughout 1928. In the jargon of the time, Mao's tactics were representative of peasant consciousness, while those of the Wan-an leaders stood squarely on the proletarian line. A jurisdictional dispute between the Communists on Ching-kang-shan and the leaders of the Wan-an soviet may have developed in May and June 1928, when the Ching-kang base expanded until it included small fringe areas in Ki-an and An-fu hsien in Kiangsi.[21] These old conflicts undoubtedly added heat to the disputes at the February 7 Conference.

General Principles of Land Distribution

Disagreements over land policy between Mao and the Central Committee, and correlatively between Mao and the Southwest Kiangsi leaders, can be traced back to the Sixth Congress of the CCP and the Second Mao-ping Conference. The principles to be applied in redistributing land were debated at the Sixth Congress. Immediately afterward the new Politburo formulated directives to local soviet leaders based on these principles. In October 1928, Mao and his colleagues in the Ching-kang Mountains debated the same problem at the Second Mao-ping Conference. If the version of events published in HC is correct, Mao's distinctive line on equal distribution dates from the latter Conference. Throughout the Li Li-san period, Mao's views on this problem differed from those of the Politburo, which were supported by the Southwest Kiangsi leadership.

The Sixth Congress had adopted the line that equal distribution was purely a transitional measure. The party could support equal distribution under special circumstances, but must criticize its general application. The principle of equal distribution itself was denounced as a false concept, an illusion of petty-bourgeois socialism characteristic of the *narodniks*. Equal distribution, the line went, does not in itself go beyond the limits of the capitalist system, and genuine equality is impossible under capitalism. On the other hand, the Congress approved equal distribution of land under appropriate circumstances—in areas where unemployed and poor peasants were very numerous—but only if a majority of the peasants supported the move. Equal distribution was not to be forcibly applied where middle peasants and small landlords constituted the majority, for it would "decidedly contravene the interests of the numerous middle peasants."[22]

The formulations of the Sixth Congress caused the Communists in Ching-kang-shan and southwestern Kiangsi to raise a number of factual questions. In which areas in China were unemployed and poor peasants in the majority? Were Ching-kang-shan and southwestern Kiangsi among them? Did the majority of the poor peasants in the soviet areas support equal distribution? Granted that the answers to the last two questions were affirmative, how should the equal shares be allotted? On the basis of a share for everyone, or on the basis of ability to work? If the latter, should the labor power of those able to work be calculated in units of able-bodied men or their equivalent, or in terms of existing productive power, including tools, farm implements, and draft animals?

According to Mao, all three criteria were proposed at the Second Mao-ping Conference. The Central Committee had decided before October 1928 that ability to work should be the criterion. Mao advocated equal shares to all, regardless of class or ability to work. Rich peasants in Ching-kang-shan, dissatisfied with both procedures, suggested that both labor power and capital should be taken into account.[23] On the basis of the Central Committee's line, Mao's proposal was rejected. The conferees decided to allot twice as much land to persons with ability to work as to those without, as proposed by the Central Committee. According to HC, this decision of the Second

Mao-ping Conference was never implemented. Land was actually apportioned according to the number of persons in each family until 1930. The method suggested by the rich peasants was discussed at Mao-ping, but the matter was referred to the Central Committee and conclusions deferred until a later meeting.[24]

The land laws of December 1928 and March 1929 were the next development in the conflict between Mao, his local opponents, and the Central Committee. In both land laws Mao's interpretation of "equal distribution" as equal shares for all was adopted as the principal criterion for apportionment. Division on the basis of labor power, as the Central Committee directed, was adopted as a secondary method to be applied only under special circumstances.[25] Productive power, the criterion offered by the rich peasants, was not included in either land law. There is no reason to believe that the Central Committee altered its criteria for land distribution between October 1928 and the Conference of Delegates from the Soviet Areas in May 1930. These criteria were apparently not affected by the Comintern directive on the peasant problem dated June 1929. No distinctive land law has been attributed to the Southwest Kiangsi leaders, so it is most likely that during this period they followed the Central Committee's program and used ability to work as the main criterion for apportioning land. Mao and his Front Committee, on the other hand, used the system of equal shares for all from March 1929, when the Hsing-kuo law was promulgated, until the February 7 Conference. No evidence has been uncovered to suggest that Mao wrote or sponsored any new land law or any revision of the Hsing-kuo law during this period.

In 1929 conflict between the Front Committee and the Southwest Kiangsi leaders had little chance to develop, for they were rarely in contact. Neither group distributed much land in that year (NTTC records only three places in Kiangsi where land was distributed in 1929), so neither developed elaborate rules or administrative techniques. Under these circumstances, Mao was willing to concede secondary status to the plan embodied in the Central Committee directive. By February 1930, however, the conflict between Mao and the Politburo was out in the open. The Southwest Kiangsi group wholeheartedly resisted encroachments by Mao's Front Committee on their local sphere of power. As tension grew, Mao refused to concede even secondary status to the criterion of ability to work. The February 7 land law contains one and only one criterion for land redistribution —equal shares for all.[26]

According to contemporary sources, Mao's opposition at the Conference was divided into two factions. One was led by Chiang Han-po, a member of the Southwest Kiangsi Special Committee who supposedly denounced any redistribution of land as a petty-bourgeois device consolidating the institution of private ownership of land.[c] Chiang was expelled from the Conference, but the majority of the Special Committee continued to oppose Mao's particular formula. Opposition to Mao's policies was not unanimous among the Southwest Kiangsi leaders, however. Two Kiangsi leaders, Tseng Shan and Liu Shih-chi, probably supported Mao at the Conference, if they attended it.[27] Tseng Shan was well known as Mao's man at the time. He was Mao's candidate for chairman of the Kiangsi soviet government in November 1930, and his later career indicates that he probably supported Mao in February.[28] Liu Shih-chi was expelled from the Second Plenum of the Kiangsi Provincial Action Committee in July 1930, for continuing to support the February 7 land law even after the Li Li-san land law promulgated by the May Conference of Delegates from the Soviet Areas was adopted by the Second Plenum.[29]

No complete attendance list of the February 7 Conference is available, but it probably included most of the local leaders who continued to oppose Mao's land policies throughout 1930: Tuan Liang-pi, Li Wen-ling (also known as Li Po-fang and Li Wen-lin), Hsieh Han-ch'ang, Chin Wan-pang, Ts'ung Yün-chung, Wen Tse-tung, Yang Ch'eng-fu, and Chiang Han-po.[30] Since the local party leaders were almost sure they had the backing of the Politburo in their resistance to the Maoist faction, they appealed the decisions of the Conference to the Central Committee. According to contemporary sources two members of the Southwest Kiangsi Special Committee, Tuan Liang-pi and Li Wen-ling, went to Shanghai to present the Committee's case to the Politburo and seek its support.[31] They had probably attended the Conference of Delegates from the Soviet Areas in May 1930.

While Tuan Liang-pi and Li Wen-ling were seeking help from the Politburo, their comrades in southern Kiangsi did what they could to prevent the Maoists from carrying out the first land redistribution under the provisions of the February 7 law. In June the Politburo ordered all the Red Armies to leave the area to attack Ch'angsha and Nanch'ang. In July, with the Third and Fifth Armies on their way to Ch'angsha and the Fourth Army marching northward to Nanch'ang,

[c] Hsiao, p. 106. According to NTTC, by November 1930 he had changed his position. He still opposed Mao's method of dividing land equally among all persons, but advocated division according to labor power. (Mao, NTTC, pp. 84–85.)

the Southwest Kiangsi leaders held the Second Plenum of the Kiangsi Provincial Action Committee. They repudiated the land policies of the February 7 Conference, adopted the Li Li-san land law, and expelled Liu Shih-chi for opposing it.[32] The following month, while most of the Maoists were still outside the area, they began to redistribute land in accordance with the provisions of the Li Li-san land law. In some areas where land had been redistributed according to the February law, it is highly probable that local peasant partisans resisted the second redistribution and attempted to defend the portions of land they had received in the first distribution. Indeed, Chu reports that before leaving the area he had organized and armed three small armies of local peasants, leaving them orders "to remain where they were as defenders of their native soil."[33] In NTTC Mao identifies Ch'en Yi, Ma Ming, and Ch'en Cheng-jen as the three most important Maoists who remained in southern Kiangsi in July and August.[34] Ch'en Yi was the political commissar of the 22nd Red Army. Ch'en Cheng-jen was the chairman of the Kiangsi provincial soviet government set up at the February 7 Conference. Ma Ming's official role is not recorded in NTTC.

Land Redistribution Under the February 7 Law

Under the February law, land was to be redistributed in a series of steps, achieving a greater degree of equality in the yield of land holdings at each step. Equal shares to all was the goal of the complete process.[35]

The first step was to confiscate all land and capital belonging to landlords, as well as all public and clan property. Then, taking the hsiang as a unit, the amount of land each person should receive was to be calculated by dividing the amount of rice harvested from all land in the hsiang by its total population. After redistribution was complete, each person in the hsiang should own irrigated land yielding 11 piculs of rice per year.[d] Rice lands confiscated from landlords were to be apportioned first, but identical procedures were to be applied in dividing all resources: public lands, tea plantations, bamboo groves, tung oil groves, mulberry trees, large trees for lumber, small trees for kindling, fish ponds, abandoned fields and houses, and stores of grain confiscated from landlord families.[36]

[d] Mao, NTTC, p. 83. A picul is a Chinese dry measure that varies from place to place, but is approximately equivalent to 133 pounds. The figure of 11 piculs per person per year was arrived at by dividing the estimated total rice yield of Kiangsi by its estimated total population.

The second step was to determine which villages in the hsiang had rice lands whose yields deviated from the average calculated for the hsiang as a whole. Wherever possible, fields were to be transferred from the richer villages to the poorer ones. If this proved impractical, people were to be moved from the poorer to the richer villages. After this step the confiscated rice lands were to be divided among the poorer peasants. Considerable inequalities would no doubt continue to exist between rich and poor peasants in every village, but at least everyone would have been informed of the yield he might get under a perfectly equitable division.[37]

The third step was to "take from those who have much to help those who have little." The amount of land apportioned to the poor from property confiscated from landlords rarely sufficed to create even approximate equality at harvest time. Land was therefore to be taken from the rich peasants and some of the middle peasants and distributed among the poor and landless. Usually the rich peasants agreed to surrender only some of their poorer land, so that even after this step the poor peasants would possess land yielding a smaller harvest than that of the rich peasants.[38] Dissatisfied, the poor peasants would support the next step in the struggle for greater equality, which was to take from those who had rich land to help those who had poor land. Land was to be classified into three grades, and every family was to be allotted some of each. This step was at the expense of the rich and middle peasants, who usually owned the more fertile lands.

While no compensation was to be paid for land, Mao agreed that some should be made for work that had been done in seeding, fertilizing, plowing, and cultivating a crop already growing when fields were distributed. According to NTTC, the previous owner either was paid for his labor or continued in possession until the harvest, in which case the new owner received a predetermined share of the crop.[39]

Mao announced that small landlords and dependents of landlords could participate in the division on the same basis as all others. Handicraftsmen, vagabonds, Red soldiers, government employees, the unemployed of neighboring towns, village peasants temporarily working elsewhere—all were entitled to equal shares. Only landlords who had fled to White areas or who possessed large amounts of capital were excluded.[40]

Rich peasants often objected to the participation of some or all of these groups; Mao admitted that even the upper strata of poor peasants were adversely affected by this policy. He argued, however, that the great mass of the lower strata—poor peasants, handicraftsmen, and tenants—supported the proposal, and even the upper strata of the poor peasants found the end results sufficiently attractive to dampen their opposition.[41]

According to Mao's figures, only one-fourth of the population of southern Kiangsi was able to work in the rice fields full time. Another three-eighths were able to work in the fields half the time, while the remaining three-eighths were unable to work at all. Families without able-bodied workers varied from five to twenty percent of the population, depending on whether or not the women had bound feet. These families were made up of widows, orphans, the aged, and persons engaged in revolutionary work.[42] Since the soviet governments did not have the means to provide for such families, Mao reasoned, their members should receive equal shares of land, which they could rent out. Only the rich and middle peasants owned sufficient tools and draft animals to work additional land, and they were not to be allowed to excuse themselves from their duty of cultivating the fields of the helpless. If a peasant capable of it refused to rent land from the helpless, the township government was to calculate the amount of additional land he could cultivate and force him to do so. Paying rent by dividing the harvest was forbidden. Only "iron rent"—a constant figure not to be reduced because of natural disasters—was allowed. The government was to set minimum rental fees in order to prevent exploitation by the tenant. Only in this way could the owner be guaranteed a constant source of income, while economic forces compelled the tenant to cultivate and fertilize the lands he rented as often and as well as those he owned.[43]

The key provisions in this land law, "take from those who have much to help those who have little" and "take from those who have fertile land to help those who have poor land," demanded that good land be taken from middle peasants and given to poor peasants and that some poor land worked by poor peasants be taken to piece out shares for vagabonds and strangers. If Mao had not allotted land to those without ability to work, between five and twenty percent of the families would have received no land (or no additional land), and the middle peasants and upper strata of poor peasants would have lost nothing at all. On the whole, the provisions on renting land from those unable to work benefited the new tenants, who in the main were rich and middle peasants. Although the rich peasants may have been neutralized and isolated by the class struggle, this provision enabled them to continue to be rich peasants. Mao's argument that they might need to be forced to rent the land of those unable to work was almost certainly specious. The middle and poor peasants, possessing little capital, would no doubt have found the provisions for "iron rent" onerous.

The land distribution policy embodied in the February 7 land law was designed to obtain the broadest possible support for the Red Army while it enlarged the soviet area in the Kiangsi countryside and prepared for a province-wide insurrection. This policy was attacked at the time by Li Li-san's Politburo, by the Southwest Kiangsi Special Party Committee, and by the Kiangsi Action Committee as yet another example of localism and peasant conservatism. A year later the 28 Bolsheviks held up the law as an example of Mao's rich peasant line. Mao's agrarian policy was more radical than Li Li-san's, but more lenient toward the rich peasants and small landlords than that of the 28 Bolsheviks.

Other Actions of the February 7 Conference

After the debate on land policy, the conferees elected members of the new provisional soviet government of Kiangsi. Like many other facts in the local history of the CCP in this period, the balance between factions in the new provincial government is unknown. Its members were probably drawn from both the Front Committee and the Southwest Kiangsi Committee. According to Po Ku, the chairman was Ch'en Cheng-jen, a relatively minor figure, a member of Mao's Second Special Committee, an intellectual. Mao, as we have seen, rated him as a more important member of the Maoist faction. In the early 1950's Ch'en became party secretary for Kiangsi province and deputy director of rural work.[44] Other Maoists likely to have been elected were Ma Ming, Ch'en Yi (now Foreign Minister), and Wang Huai.[45] Which members of the Southwest Kiangsi Special Committee were elected to this government has not been recorded, but several of the Committee's members worked in the new provisional government throughout 1930. These men continuously opposed Mao's land policies. They were the men who attempted to enforce the Li Li-san land law and even to reverse the initial stages of Mao's land reforms after the Conference of Delegates from the Soviet Areas.

CHAPTER X

The General Front Committee

In 1930 Mao built up his personal power by taking command of the new General Front Committee and pyramiding Red Army command structures until most of the Red Armies in South China were subordinate to it. From these posts he was able to defy orders from the Central Committee, call off the second attack on Ch'angsha, and bring the Li Li-san line to an abrupt end. The great majority of Mao's opponents were concentrated in the new political commissariats and in the soviets of southwestern Kiangsi. Their support of the Central Committee and Mao's continued defiance of it led to a split in the Kiangsi party, then to armed conflict between the two factions in the Fu-t'ien incident. Backed by the Third Plenum of the Central Committee, the Maoists took control of the new party bureau for the soviet areas in January 1931. Mao's triumph was short-lived—in the same month the 28 Bolsheviks gained control of the Politburo and deposed the comrades who had dominated the Third Plenum.

Consolidation of Mao's Power in the Red Armies

The Red Armies underwent at least three major reorganizations in the course of 1930, each one increasing Mao's power. The first was the result of a conference of the leaders of the Fourth Red Army, the Fifth Red Army, and the soon-to-be-reorganized Third Red Army, near Ki-an, Kiangsi, early in February. The Fourth Red Army had descended from the mountainous Fukien border early in January and marched into southern Kiangsi. At the same time, the Fifth Army under P'eng Teh-huai and Huang Kung-lüeh had come down from P'ing-kiang on the Hunan-Kiangsi border and provisionally united with Lo P'ing-hui and his partisans in the T'ai-ho district of Ki-an. A month later Chu and Mao arrived, whereupon the conference was held and the armies were reorganized.[1] All those who had attended the February 7 Conference attended this one too, except possibly the members of the Southwest Kiangsi Special Committee.

At this conference Mao attempted to implement the military and organizational policy worked out at the Ku-t'ien Conference as the first step in a general offensive against central Kiangsi. Chu reported almost a decade later that in 1929 the Central Committee had ordered Mao and himself to engage in partisan warfare in western Fukien, southern Kiangsi, and the East River District in Kwangtung.[2] The Ku-t'ien Conference decided instead to concentrate on Kiangsi, rejecting the Central Committee's policy as overly pessimistic. Mao, supported by Chu Teh, Fang Chih-min, and Li Wen-ling (Li Po-fang), decided to take steps to consolidate his power, create a stable military base, systematically build up soviets, and intensify the struggle for land reform. He planned to follow up by expanding the armed forces, organizing first hsiang and then hsien militia (the Red Guards) and then a local Red Army from which the most able troops could be incorporated into a regular Red Army.[3] In the "Letter to Comrade Lin Piao," Mao contended that in this way the political power of the soviets could be expanded and gradually move outward from the central stronghold in a series of waves. He repeated his thesis that the CCP's most potent weapon in the coming revolution would be the Red Army, recruited from a peasantry whose allegiance had been secured in the course of a genuine land revolution.[4]

In this letter, written before the conference, Mao did not claim support from anyone in P'eng Teh-huai's Fifth Army. However, at the conference he gave Huang Kung-lüeh, who had been working with P'eng in the Fifth Army, the command of a new Third Army, which was made up of some troops of the old Fourth (Chu-Mao) Army, the partisans from Tung-ku and Hsing-kuo commanded by Li Wen-ling and Li Su-chu, and the former *min-t'uan* troops of Lo P'ing-hui who had revolted in the Ki-an Uprising in August 1929.[5] According to interviews recorded in 1937, this was the point at which Chu Teh took personal command of the Third and Fourth Armies. These armies marched together to Hsing-kuo hsien, and from there, early in June, to Ting-chow in Fukien.[6] P'eng remained in control of the Fifth Army, but Mao and Chu probably commanded twice as many men.[a] Moreover, they had taken at least one of P'eng's best commanders, which in itself is sufficient reason for the frequent rumors of conflict between Mao and P'eng in this period.[7] The fact that Huang Kung-lüeh and Lo P'ing-hui (who had long admired Chu) had been withdrawn from P'eng's army is significant in the

[a] Wales states that in August 1930 there were 20,000 men in the Chu-Mao army and 10,000 in P'eng's. (Wales, *Inside Red China*, p. 250.)

power struggle between the Red Armies. Able military commanders were in great demand, and by depriving P'eng of a few good ones Mao and Chu were able to maintain the relative superiority of their Fourth Army. P'eng's Fifth Army remained the second largest Red Army in South China.

There is no evidence that this reorganization and transfer of commanders was ordered by the Central Committee. Li Li-san would hardly have favored Mao in a military reorganization if he could possibly have conferred power on someone else. By the end of April, however, Li had devised a new plan to establish more centralized control over the Red Armies, i.e., to put control into his own hands.

Creation of the General Front Committee

Two letters the Central Committee sent Mao in April 1930 reveal that sometime between April 3 and April 26 the Politburo decided to organize a General Front Committee to take charge of an insurrection in Hunan, Hupeh, and Kiangsi. The decision was Li's, for by this time Chou En-lai had gone to Moscow and Li was in complete control. The first letter, dated April 3, was addressed to the Front Committee of the Fourth Army. The second letter, dated April 26, was also addressed to the Front Committee of the Fourth Army, but was to be transmitted to "the General Front Committee of the Third, Fourth, and Fifth Armies." Li's distrust of Mao and his strategy is openly expressed in both letters.[8]

In the first letter Li outlined the essential theoretical elements of his line. Throughout China, he said, the general revolutionary wave was rising. The workers', peasants', and soldiers' struggles were approaching a more even development. In order to win in "one or several provinces," the party must immediately organize massive political strikes, stage local uprisings, and incite numerous mutinies among government troops. Preliminary success would immediately precipitate a revolutionary situation that would lead to nationwide victory. The immediate task of the Red Armies was to march on the key cities of the three central provinces (Hunan, Hupeh, and Kiangsi), with Wuhan as the center. Li explicitly rejected the strategy of creating an independent local regime in the mountainous border areas of Kwangtung, Fukien, and Kiangsi—a strategy he specifically attributed to Mao and Chu, and which they had indeed been following throughout the previous year. He labeled their strategy erroneous, conservative, and defeatist. The notion that Kiangsi could be taken, Li wrote, was not impractical, but it must be realized within the framework of initial victory in all three central provinces. Any plans Mao might have to utilize all the Red Armies to take Kiangsi alone must be abandoned, for the Third and Fifth Armies were to leave Kiangsi and move into central Hunan and Hupeh. A plan the Kwangtung Committee had put forth—that the uprisings should occur first in Kwangtung, Kiangsi, and Fukien—was not in itself erroneous, but the Fourth Army was not to march south to assist in this task because that would divert its strength from the party's central mission. Having rejected the Maoist strategy of setting up independent local soviet regimes in the mountains, Li went on to accuse the Fourth Army leaders of recruiting men into their army much too slowly. He traced their neglect of the army to their practice of arming and organizing the peasants into village Red Guards rather than recruiting them into the army itself. This, said Li, was another manifestation of Mao's conservatism. In conclusion, the letter commanded Mao to come to Shanghai to attend the Conference of Delegates from the Soviet Areas.[9]

On March 29 and again on April 5, five days before and two days after this letter was written, Li published articles in *Red Flag* in which he rejected three notions: that the labor movement still lagged behind the peasants, that the cities should be encircled by the countryside, and that the Red Army could take the cities by its own efforts.[b] Li's opposition to Mao's strategy had thereby been made public by the time he dispatched his instructions to Mao personally.

The second letter to Mao was shorter and its tone was more urgent than the first. Li simply explained that the party center was considering a major change in the responsibility of the Red Army, which by now had become the main force in determining the outcome of the revolution. Again he urged Mao to come to Shanghai. Li was evidently ready to consider using the army to take the cities even though the party might fail to involve the workers in a general strike and an insurrection first. But if the whole of the Red Army was to be thrown against the cities, those of its leaders who stood for conserving men and arms had to be removed. This assuredly motivated Li's renewed pressure on Mao to come to Shanghai. Li even suggested a number of arrangements to replace Mao during his absence. Chu Teh, for instance, was to take charge of all Communist armies in Kiangsi. He was also named the chief commander on the new General Front Committee.

[b] These points were stressed again in an article appearing on May 24. (Schwartz, *Chinese Communism*, pp. 138–39; North, *Moscow*, pp. 133–34.)

The letter of April 26 is the earliest document I have discovered that mentions the General Front Committee. Evidently the Politburo worked out the plan for establishing it sometime after April 3. That this letter was addressed to the Front Committee of the Fourth Army but was to be transmitted to the new General Front Committee, and that in it Li urgently requested Mao to come to Shanghai, would seem to indicate either that Mao was not appointed to the new Committee at all, or that his position was intended to be purely honorific.

According to Li's new line, the General Front Committee was to gather up all weapons, organize the peasant partisans into regular army detachments, evacuate the local soviets in the mountainous borderlands (leaving the villages undefended), and throw all its strength into one massive assault on the cities of Central China.[10] This new line was entirely contrary to the one Mao had worked out in his *Ku-t'ien Resolutions* the previous December. He was clearly the major opponent of the new line in the soviet areas. His removal was necessary if the Fourth Army, the center of his political machine, was to wholeheartedly obey the new orders. In Mao's absence military commanders and political officers selected or favored by Li Li-san might be able to dominate the General Front Committee, implementing the new policy without facing much active resistance. If Mao had gone to Shanghai immediately as Li requested, he probably would have found it difficult to return, and his political machine in the Fourth Army could well have disintegrated.

On the basis of existing evidence it seems unlikely that Mao went to Shanghai in the spring or summer of 1930.[11] The April letters made it obvious that the main reason Li wanted him in Shanghai was to remove him from Kiangsi. Consultation would clearly have been futile, since Li had already made up his mind. The exact date on which the April 26 letter arrived in the soviet area is unknown, but Chu Teh reported that a letter with similar contents arrived in Ting-chow sometime in June. Chu specifically mentions Mao's presence in the soviet areas on June 19, June 22, July 29, September 13, and September 30. According to Chu, Mao participated in the reorganization of peasant armies in southern Kiangsi in June and July. Then, after the failure to take Nanch'ang, he marched with First Army Corps Headquarters to the Hunan-Kiangsi border, where he was on hand to receive new orders from Li Li-san sometime in mid-August.[12] Since a trip from the soviet areas to Shanghai and back usually took two months or more, it is almost impossible for Mao to have gone to Shanghai in the summer of 1930.

Mao Develops a Tendency Toward "Extreme Democratization"

Pressures on Mao must have been very great in May 1930. According to the most recent Chinese edition of his works, sometime during that month he wrote a polemic against Central Committee inspectors who criticized mistakes and errors of local party cadres the moment they arrived in a province. He turned in fury against lazy local guerrilla leaders who agreed with the inspectors. They had not investigated actual conditions, he wrote, and had no grasp of local history. "If you have not made an investigation of a particular problem, your right to speak thereon is suspended."[c] It was shameful and reprehensible for Communist party members to indulge themselves in such empty, irresponsible talk:

> Undesirable!
> Undesirable!
> Stress investigations!
> Oppose irresponsible talk![18]

Many comrades, he wrote, believed that anything in "the book" (a reprint of the resolutions of the Sixth Party Congress) was right, treating it as a source of immutable strategic formulae that alone could lead the party to victory. This was essentially a conservative notion, he declared, one that appealed especially to those who sat lazily in their offices and drew up plans on the basis of the resolutions without once sticking their noses out the door to see if the masses were still there. In order to formulate correct strategy, Mao argued, one must go to the masses, participate in their struggles, and make practical investigations. Directives from the party's central organs were idealistic if swallowed whole—following them would result in adventurism unless they were flexibly applied by men who had made practical investigations and knew which parts to salvage and which to discard. "When we say that a directive issued by a higher leadership organ is accurate," he wrote,

> this is not simply because the directive comes from the higher organ, but because the contents of the directive are compatible with, and required by, the objective and subjective conditions of the struggle. Blind enforcement [of directives] without discussion and observation of practical conditions is an erroneous, formalist attitude built on the naïve "higher level" con-

---

[c] This quotation is the focal point of the Second Preface to NTTC, which first appeared in print in 1941. (Mao, NTTC, pp. 4–5.)

cept. . . . Blind, superficial, and inflexible enforcement of a directive from a higher level is not its true implementation, but is actually resistance to such implementation, or the most ingenious way of subverting it.[14]

Mao clearly opposed enforcing directives from the Central Committee unless he believed they were appropriate. If he believed a directive would result in alienating the masses or conceding unnecessary victories to the enemy, he would argue against accepting it. If a majority of the local committee overruled him, Mao would go along —protesting at every step and grasping the first opportunity to reopen the issue.

Mao had carried out many investigations in the previous years and had worked out a method he believed could give party leaders an accurate picture of class relations in a particular area. With this knowledge, he believed correct strategy was relatively simple to devise. Although his method of investigation probably gave him insights into local conditions, his division of the people into classes was far from Marxist—he discerned *thirteen* important social classes.[d] In each locality it was necessary to determine which classes were most powerful, which the major revolutionary force, which could be won over to the revolution, and which must be immediately attacked.

Mao would go into a village and call a meeting of anywhere from three to twenty persons who had a thorough knowledge of local conditions. He came to the meeting with an outline prepared and orally queried each of the participants, many of whom were illiterate. If some point remained unclear after the first round of questions, further probing would stimulate a debate that usually would reveal what he wanted to know. Mao insisted that *everyone* engaged in administering policy should undertake similar investigations. Reliance on written reports was in his opinion completely inadequate. He believed every investigator must himself record the questions and answers, as well as evaluate the evidence. To delegate the job of summarizing and analyzing the data recorded was to neglect the most important phase of the investigation.[15] Officers who did so, he said, were plainly lazy and ineffectual—too lazy to apply Marxism. Mao maintained that Marxist theory was correct not because Marx was a sage

[d] The industrial proletariat, handicraft workers, tenant peasants, poor peasants, urban poor, lumpenproletariat, handicraftsmen, small merchants, middle peasants, rich peasants, landlords, mercantile bourgeoisie, and industrial bourgeoisie. With the exception of the industrial proletariat and bourgeoisie, all could be found in the soviet areas. Mao had also mentioned these 13 classes in his 1926 "Analysis of Classes." His understanding of the Marxist differentiation between classes originating in feudal and in capitalist modes of production was not yet developed. (*Selections from the Works of Mao Tse-tung* [83], I, pp. 22–23.)

like Confucius, but because it was possible to verify his theories in the practice of the revolution. Marxist formulae, like party resolutions and Central Committee directives, must be tested and modified before they can be applied. May 1930 is the first time Mao used this argument. Though he later elaborated it in explaining how military commanders ought to think before planning a campaign, and still later it became the core of his epistemological theory, when he first used the argument it was primarily a justification for refusing to implement directives from Li Li-san's Politburo, a critique of the methods of analysis then prevalent in the CCP, and a reasoned response to the Politburo's demand for absolute, immediate compliance with its orders. Mao had, in fact, concocted a Marxist justification for disobedience to superior party organs. If Li Li-san had had time to examine Mao's argument before he fell from power, he would surely have denounced its "extreme democratization." He might well have turned Mao's sentiments upside down:

> Extreme democratization!
> Undesirable! Undesirable!
> Stress party unity!
> Oppose irresponsible criticism of higher party organs!

Li Li-san's Reorganization of the Red Armies (June 1930)

By June 1930, Mao and Chu were back in Ting-chow, Fukien, waiting for party leaders to come over from Kiangsi for another conference. A messenger from Shanghai reached them there, bringing two directives from the Central Committee calling for a complete reorganization of all the Red Armies to bring them under a centralized command. According to Chu Teh, he was to be commander-in-chief and Mao was to be chief party representative in the army.[16] The Red Armies were directed to leave the rural areas and capture the great industrial cities of Central China. In outlining this new strategy, Li again specifically rejected the Maoist tactic of encircling the cities with the countryside. Chu quoted Li as writing: "by such tactics our hair will be white before the revolution is victorious."[17] These directives may be the letters of April 3 and April 26 discussed above. If so, Chu's account is partially false. If the first letter he described was in fact the April 26 letter establishing the General Front Committee, Mao was not made the chief party representative in the armies, but was called to Shanghai. Of course it is possible that the letter Chu describes is not the April 26 letter but one sent on a later date. If this is the case, Li appointed Mao to the new General Front Committee sometime between April 26 and early June, with the intention of forcing him to carry out policies he believed to be premature, adventurist, and, from the purely military point of view, suicidal. Chu Teh, and perhaps a few other military commanders, agreed with Mao. In 1936 Mao stated to Snow:

> The Li Li-san line dominated the Party then, outside soviet areas, and was sufficiently influential to force acceptance, to some extent, in the Red Army, against the judgment of its field command. . . . Li Li-san overestimated both the military strength of the Red Army at that time and the revolutionary factors in the national political scene. He believed that the revolution was nearing success and would shortly have power over the entire country. This belief was encouraged by the long and exhausting civil war then proceeding between Feng Yü-hsiang and Chiang Kai-shek, which made the outlook seem highly favorable to Li Li-san. But in the opinion of the Red Army the enemy was making preparations for a great drive against the soviets as soon as the civil war was concluded, and it was no time for possibly disastrous putschism and adventures. This estimate proved to be entirely correct.[18]

This estimate also proved to be a self-fulfilling prophecy. The dilatory, begrudging manner in which Mao and Chu responded to the new orders from the Central Committee effectively prevented the implementation of the Li Li-san line and helped to bring it to an abrupt conclusion before the end of the year.

TABLE 3

Armies Reorganized in June 1930

Army	*Commander*	*Political Commissar*
First Army Corps	Chu Teh	Mao Tse-tung
Third Army	Huang Kung-lüeh	Chu Yi
Fourth Army	Lin Piao	?
Twelfth Army	Lo P'ing-hui	T'ai Tsung-ling
Twentieth Army	Liu T'ieh-ch'ao	?
Twenty-first Army	?	?
Thirty-fifth Army	?	?
Tenth Army	Fang Chih-min	Shao Shih-p'ing
Second Army Corps	Ho Lung	Yün Tai-ying*
Sixth Army	Tuan Te-ch'ang	?
Third Army Corps	P'eng Teh-huai	T'eng Tai-yüan
Eighth Army	Chang Yün-yi	Teng Hsiao-p'ing
Fourth Army Corps	K'uang Chi-hsün	?

NOTE: All data from Snow, RSOC, pp. 177–79, 182, and Jerome Ch'en, pp. 156–57, except for that on the Fourth Army Corps, which is from Wales, *Red Dust*, p. 155. The Fourth Army Corps was not organized until December 1930.

* Yün was already in prison in Nanking in June 1930.

Chu explained to Smedley that he and Mao were skeptical about the whole new strategy, and especially about incorporating all armed forces into the army, leaving the countryside without defense. Chu admitted, however, that they were virtually isolated in their position. "Apart from Mao and myself," he said, "there was very little opposition to the Li Li-san line. We had no choice but to accept it."[19] In accordance with the Central Committee directive, the First Army Corps was set up as a general headquarters in command of the Third, Fourth, Twelfth, Twentieth, Twenty-first, and Thirty-fifth Armies (see Table 3). The Third Army remained under the command of Huang Kung-lüeh, while the Fourth Army was taken over by Lin Piao. Wu Chung-hao probably remained in command of the regular army units in Fukien, which were reorganized into the Twelfth Army.[e] The Twentieth, Twenty-first, and Thirty-fifth Armies, organized for the first time, were made up of small bands of peasant partisans. Contrary to the orders of the Central Committee, Mao commanded these armies to remain where they were and defend the soviet bases.[20]

Neither P'eng Teh-huai's Fifth Army nor the Eighth Army on the Hunan-Kiangsi border was brought under the control of First Army Corps Headquarters at this time. The jurisdiction of the General Front Committee extended only over the armies on the Kiangsi-Fukien border. Chu claims that the nucleus of the Revolutionary Military Council was organized at the Ting-chow Conference. Officially composed of the commanders and political commissars in all the Red Armies, it did not in fact begin to function until later. For some time after it was established, its only contact with the Red Armies outside the jurisdiction of First Army Headquarters was by messenger.[21]

Most officers and almost all party men in the armies were willing to follow the Central Committee's line even though Mao and Chu opposed it. This is reflected in the names Mao and Chu chose to remember in their interviews with Snow, Smedley, and Wales in 1936 and 1937. With few exceptions, they mentioned only the names of their supporters. Chu named none of the political officers in the Third, Fourth, or Twelfth Armies, and Mao only two, Chu Yi in the Third and T'ai Tsung-ling in the Twelfth. He told Snow that these men were appointed in 1929, but the date is probably incorrect. Chu Teh dates the events of this period quite definitely in 1930.[22] No political commissars in the new Twentieth, Twenty-first, and Thirty-

[e] Wu was replaced by Lo P'ing-hui sometime during the summer, but information on when this occurred is contradictory. Lo himself told Wales that he took command of the Twelfth Army during the fighting at Nanch'ang in early August, so Wu probably remained in command until that time. (Wales, *Red Dust*, p. 124.)

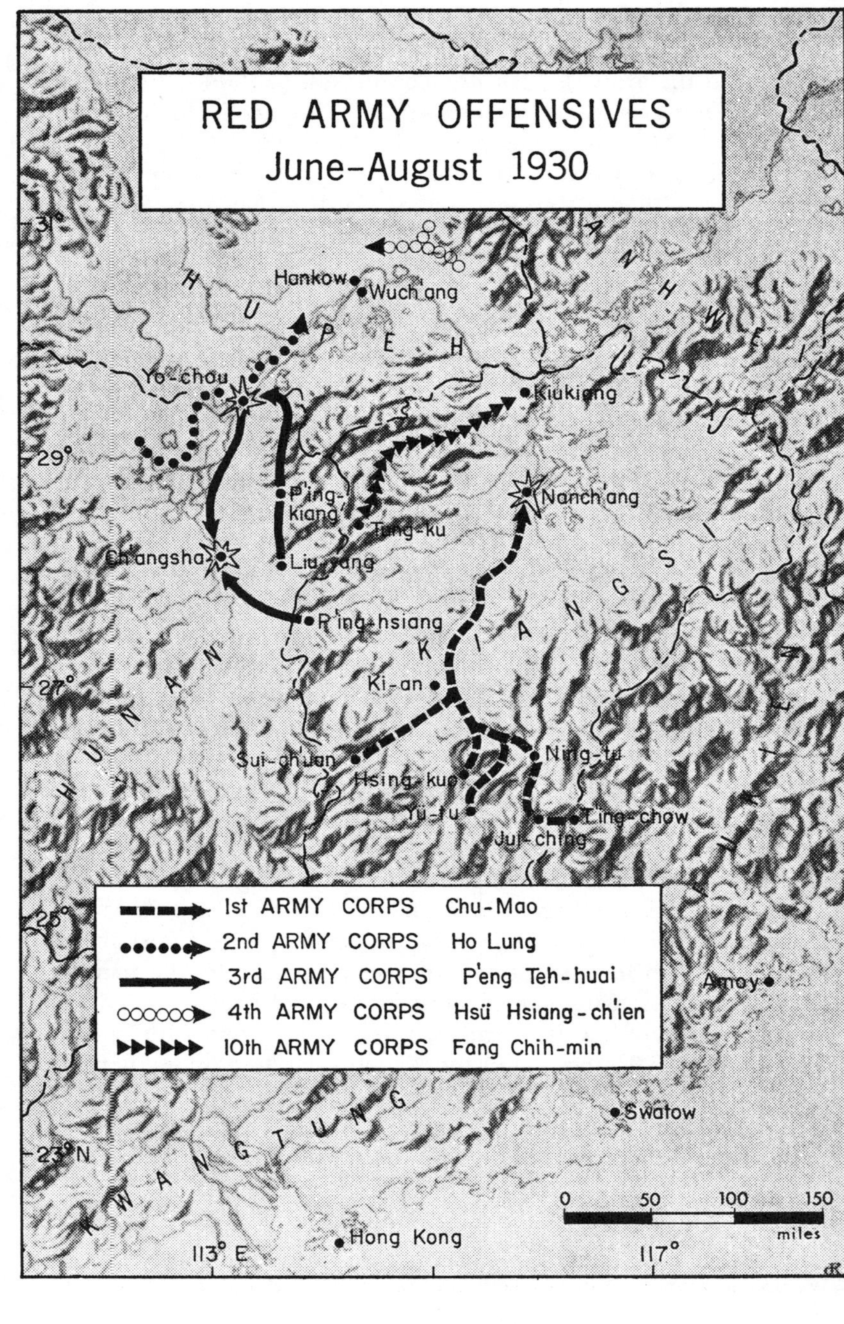

RED ARMY OFFENSIVES
June–August 1930
Hankow
Wuch'ang
Yo-chau
Kiukiang
P'ing-kiang
Tung-ku
Nanch'ang
Ch'angsha
Liu-yang
P'ing-hsiang
Ki-an
Sui-ch'uan
Ning-tu
Hsing-kuo
Yü-tu
Ting-chow
Jui-chin
Amoy
Swatow
Hong Kong
H U P E H
A N H W E I
K I A N G S I
H U N A N
K W A N G T U N G
31°
29°
27°
25°
23° N
113° E
117°
1st ARMY CORPS Chu-Mao
2nd ARMY CORPS Ho Lung
3rd ARMY CORPS P'eng Teh-huai
4th ARMY CORPS Hsü Hsiang-ch'ien
10th ARMY CORPS Fang Chih-min
0 50 100 150
miles

fifth Armies were mentioned. Mao mentioned Liu T'ieh-ch'ao, commander of the Twentieth Army, but only to accuse him of leading the forces that revolted in the Fu-t'ien incident.[f]

At about the same time that Mao and Chu were reorganizing the command structure of the Red Armies in Ting-chow, the small remnants of the Eighth Red Army arrived on the Hunan-Kiangsi border from the East Bank soviet in Kwangsi. This army was commanded by Chang Yün-yi, with Teng Hsiao-p'ing as its political commissar. It and the Fifth Red Army were then reorganized and subordinated to the Third Red Army Corps, in which P'eng Teh-huai held the top military post.[g]

When the reorganization was completed on June 19, the whole First Army took the "Li Li-san oath": "In order to cooperate with the Communist revolution all over China, we must struggle to win the support of the masses in Hunan [at the time the army was still in Fukien] and to capture Ch'angsha and Nanch'ang, and then Hankow and Wuch'ang, and finally to carry on down the Yangtze River to Shanghai!"[23] On June 22, Chu and Mao signed the order of the day directing their troops to march into Kiangsi and assemble near a city in the southern part of the province, then fight their way through enemy territory to Nanch'ang, take it, and proceed on to Kiukiang. At the same time, P'eng Teh-huai's armies were to march from their base in northwestern Kiangsi into central Hunan and take Ch'angsha. From these vantage points all the armies were to converge on Wuhan, where Li counted on the workers to rise in a general strike and take the city from within even before the armies arrived.[24]

The Third Reorganization of the Red Armies

The First Army Corps attacked Nanch'ang on August 1, but failed to capture it. A day later, after losing many men, the armies withdrew and turned westward toward Hunan. In the meantime, P'eng's Third Army Corps had captured Ch'angsha on July 29 and proclaimed a soviet government of three provinces (Kiangsi, Hunan, and Hupeh), with Li Li-san as its chairman *in absentia*. Unable to hold the city, the Third Army Corps withdrew on August 4, after which the leaders of the two defeated armies met in western Kiangsi to consider Li's

[f] Snow, RSOC, p. 82. Liu T'ieh-ch'ao is not accused of this in the contemporary records of the Fu-t'ien incident. I shall treat this discrepancy in more detail below.

[g] Wales, *Inside Red China*, p. 250; Jerome Ch'en, p. 157. In 1932 the Eighth Army was commanded by a Li T'ien-chu, with Wang Cheng as political commissar. Its name was changed to the Sixth Army in September of that year, when Hsiao K'e became its commander. Hsiao traces its old name back to Ching-kang-shan but does not give more of its history. (Wales, *Red Dust*, pp. 99, 138.)

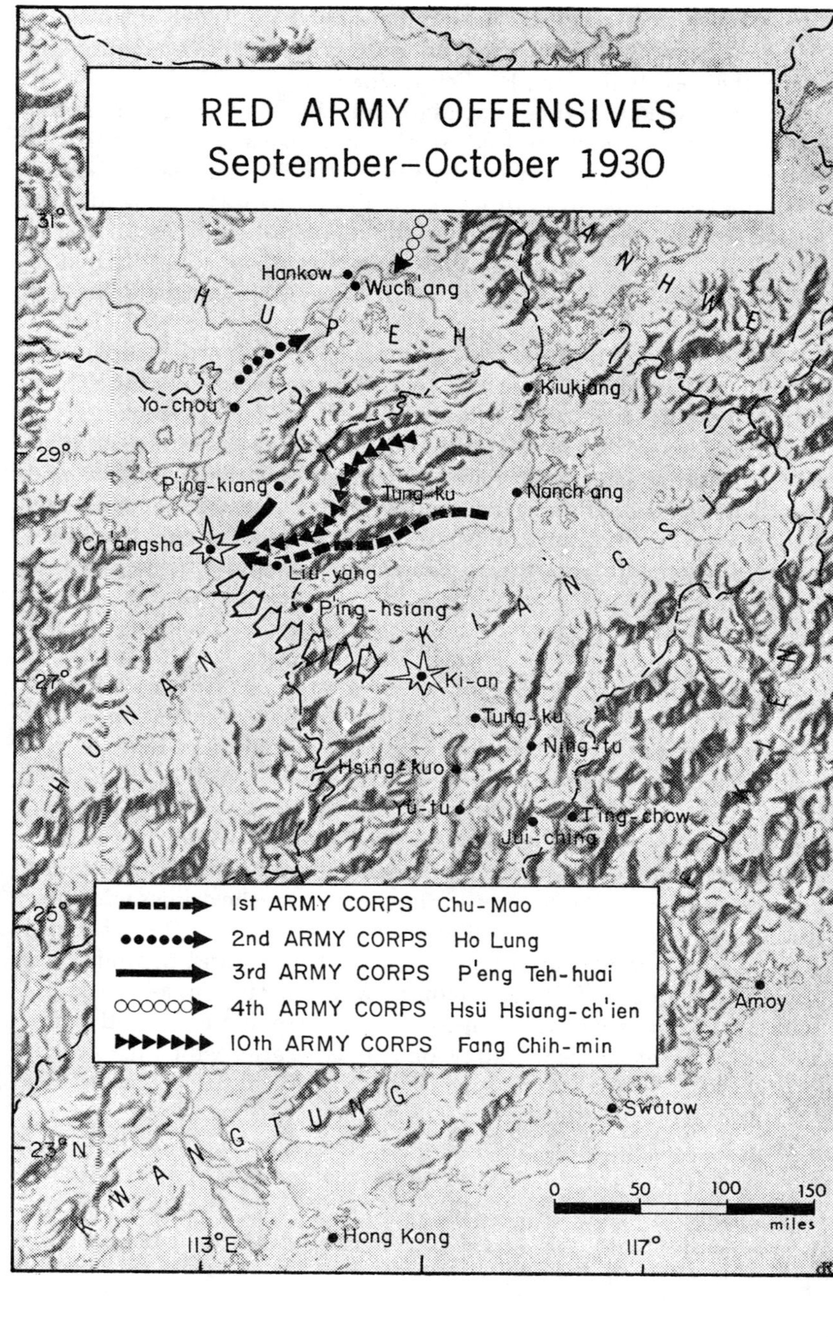

RED ARMY OFFENSIVES
September–October 1930
Hankow
Wuch'ang
HUPEH
ANHWEI
Yo-chou
Kiukiang
P'ing-kiang
Tung-ku
Nanch'ang
Ch'angsha
Liu-yang
P'ing-hsiang
KIANGSI
HUNAN
Ki-an
Tung-ku
Ning-tu
Hsing-kuo
Yü-tu
T'ing-chow
Jui-ching
FUKIEN
Amoy
Swatow
KWANGTUNG
Hong Kong
31°
29°
27°
25°
23° N
113° E
117°
0 50 100 150
miles
1st ARMY CORPS Chu-Mao
2nd ARMY CORPS Ho Lung
3rd ARMY CORPS P'eng Teh-huai
4th ARMY CORPS Hsü Hsiang-ch'ien
10th ARMY CORPS Fang Chih-min

new orders, which called first for a reoccupation of Ch'angsha and then for an assault on the Wuhan cities.[25]

According to Chu, he questioned Li's orders on the grounds that the Red Armies were not yet strong enough to fight positional warfare: "To attack such overwhelming enemy forces and powerful equipment might result in the annihilation of the Red Army and in the crushing of the revolution for decades to come."[26] Mao and P'eng agreed. The objections of the three men were overruled by the Revolutionary Military Council, and the Third, Fourth, Fifth, Eighth, and Twelfth Armies returned for the second attack on Ch'angsha. It began in the first week of September and lasted until September 13, when "Chu and Mao took one of the most serious steps of their careers.... They repudiated the Li Li-san line, which was the policy adopted by the Central Committee of the party of which they were leading members, and ordered their troops to withdraw from Ch'angsha."[27] Their orders were supported by P'eng, and by some, but not all, of the other military commanders. The political commissars denounced them for rebellion against the Central Committee. The troops, however, obeyed their commanders and cursed the political commissars loyal to the Central Committee.[28]

After ordering their troops to disperse and reassemble near Ki-an, Mao and Chu went to P'eng's headquarters in the base in P'ing-kiang and Liu-yang, and then traveled with him to the point where the troops were to assemble for an attack on Ki-an, which fell on October 4.[29]

Sometime in the midst of all this excitement the armies were again reorganized—Mao and Chu disagree on the exact date. According to Mao, the First and Third Army Corps were combined into a First Front Army in August, before the second attack on Ch'angsha.[30] According to Chu, the First Front Army was established a month later, after the second attack on Ch'angsha. Both agreed that Chu became the commander-in-chief and Mao the political commissar. Chu specifies that he retained his old position as commander of the First Army Corps, without indicating whether or not Mao kept his position as its political commissar.[31]

It is likely that there were political reasons, which, if known, would explain this reallocation of the responsibility for the retreat from Ch'angsha. Mao did not mention the retreat in 1936, but did claim general authority over all the armies that converged on Ch'angsha and therefore authority to issue an order for withdrawal. In this light, P'eng would simply have been following orders from the next highest political level in the party, acting as both a good soldier and a disciplined Communist. In his account of a year later, Chu claims that when the retreat was ordered he and Mao did not have legitimate authority to issue the order to all armies—indeed, he does not claim that they did. According to Chu, P'eng willingly cooperated with them in forming the "anti-party group" that in effect brought the Li Li-san line to an abrupt end. Like Mao and Chu, P'eng was guilty of deliberately disobeying the orders of the Central Committee at a crucial time in the history of the party. This looks suspiciously like an attempt on Chu's part to share out the responsibility for a breach in party discipline among all the important survivors.

This reorganization, whether it took place in August or September, placed Mao and Chu in control of a central army headquarters for all the armies in Kiangsi. (The Second and Fourth Army Corps, under Ho Lung and Hsü Chi-shen, respectively, were too far away to be placed under the jurisdiction of Mao and Chu.) According to both accounts, Mao achieved his dominant position because he supported Chu's judgment in military affairs. Opposing the Li Li-san line on purely military grounds and arguing that the Red Army would compose the main force in the coming revolution brought Mao into continuous conflict both with the Central Committee and with most of the political commissars in the armies over which he was extending his control. But by resisting the orders of the Central Committee, never carrying them out fully or enthusiastically, he preserved the Red Army's ability to fight again. His judgment of the relative strength of revolutionary and counterrevolutionary forces in 1930 was certainly more accurate than the official optimism of the Central Committee. Chu Teh and Mao's other supporters in the army and the local party units probably were convinced that Mao was right and the Central Committee wrong.

Conflict Between the General Front Committee and the Kiangsi Provincial Action Committee

While Mao was extending his authority over all Red Armies in Kiangsi, he was also struggling with the Kiangsi Provincial Action Committee, which claimed jurisdiction over all party units in the province. After Ki-an fell on October 4, the Kiangsi provincial soviet government was reorganized under the aegis of the General Front Committee.[32] Most of the leaders of the Kiangsi Provincial Action Committee were excluded from the new government. The Action Committee and the General Front Committee both claimed jurisdiction over all party members in the province, and their struggle precipitated a split in the Kiangsi party. Throughout the year members of the two committees had accused each other of being liquidationists and Trotskyites, but by November Mao would also charge that the leaders of the Action Committee were members of the A-B Corps. In December, at Fu-t'ien, the situation would explode into violence.

By the spring of 1930 the Central Committee had regained some of its control over local party organs. Lines of command ran from the Central Committee down through the provincial and special committees to the local cells. Mao's idea of the local integrating role of the Front Committees had no place in the system. The Front Committee could not control local party units if the Central Committee exercised direct control through regular channels. Proponents of the two systems of organization clashed at the February 7 Conference. The decision to implement Mao's land law was made by the Maoists in the armies despite the opposition of the Southwest Kiangsi Special Party Committee.

Because Li needed the Front Committees to coordinate the uprisings he was planning, rather than abolish them he combined them into the General Front Committee and directed Mao to leave the soviet areas. Li probably hoped to bring all Communist groups in the soviet areas under his control by this maneuver. Li had a relatively strong apparatus loyal to himself in the party, youth corps, and trade unions when he began to plan the insurrection. In April he may have planned to coordinate these groups through the General Front Committee in the soviet areas by placing his own loyal supporters in control of the important positions on the Front Committees. If this was the plan, Mao saw to it that it did not work. Therefore sometime in late May or early June, Li amalgamated the many small factions who did support him into action committees.[h] Their members withdrew from the party, youth corps, and trade union posts they had previously held; the regular organizational structures of these organs were dissolved and their work suspended. According to available records, action committees were organized at the lower levels before August 1, when Li dissolved the central headquarters of the CCP, youth corps, and trade unions, replacing them with the Central Action Committee.[33]

While Tuan Liang-pi and Li Wen-ling were in Shanghai after the February 7 Conference, presenting the Southwest Kiangsi Special Committee's case against Mao to the Politburo, they probably attended the May Conference of Delegates from the Soviet Areas. This

[h] The date the Politburo set up action committees below the provincial level has not been established. None are mentioned in available documents before the May Conference of Delegates.

Conference passed the Li Li-san land law, which forbade the confiscation of fields rich peasants worked themselves as well as the sale, lease, or mortgage of land after redistribution was completed, and which advocated the establishment of collective farms. These provisions had a familiar ring. They had been essential parts of the land policy adopted shortly before the November 1927 Plenum of the Central Committee, which had expelled Mao from the Central Committee. Li Li-san had played a leading role in that Plenum.[34] Li's revival of the November 1927 land policy in May 1930 indicated his continued opposition to Mao's tactic of equal distribution and to Mao's February 7 land law.

Li undoubtedly ordered some of the delegates at the May Conference to organize action committees upon their return to the soviet areas. When Tuan and Li returned to Kiangsi, they co-opted many of Mao's enemies into the new Kiangsi Action Committee. The dominant faction in the new Action Committee was drawn from the old Southwest Kiangsi Special Committee. Since the sole function of the new committee was to carry out the uprising, even the land distribution was halted. The May 1930 land law was provisional, and it is unlikely that Li intended to apply it before the general uprising.

In addition to the dispute over land laws, Mao and the new Action Committee quarreled over three issues: the purge from the CCP of KMT agents known collectively as the A-B Corps,[i] Mao's orders to the peasant partisans to stay behind and protect their own soviets, and the election of delegates from the soviet areas to the First National Congress of the Chinese Soviet Republic.

Since Mao had left three small armies of peasant partisans behind, contrary to the orders of the Central Committee, the new Action Committee probably agitated among the political and military officers of these armies to get them to leave their soviets and march on the cities —if not on Nanch'ang and Ch'angsha, then at least on Ki-an and other large hsien capitals in southern Kiangsi. According to one letter the Action Committee sent in late December, it had urged swift action against the enemy, but Mao had impeded the assault on the

[i] Li Ang, a dissident Communist, believed that there was no such thing as an A-B Corps in the soviet areas and that Mao used the title to cover all opposition to his leadership. But an A-B Corps did exist in Kiangsi. It had been organized in early 1927 to purge Communists from local KMT party units. Its director, Tuan Hsi-p'eng, was a native of Kiangsi and a relative of Tuan Liang-pi. Hsi-p'eng had been a leader of the May Fourth movement in Peking University and had befriended Mao in 1918. (Li Ang [66], p. 152; Snow, RSOC, p. 150; Hsiao, p. 100. A biography of Tuan Hsi-p'eng is included in Chow, *May Fourth Movement,* pp. 75, 121*n*, 148*n*, 164.)

cities by refusing to move all his troops out of the soviet areas.[35] Agitation by Tuan Liang-pi and Li Wen-ling was especially effective among the officers of the 20th Army, which Mao had left in occupation of the base at Tung-ku and Hsing-kuo. Part of this army was to rise against Mao in the Fu-t'ien incident.

The composition of the Southwest Kiangsi soviet government Mao had organized in February was also a fruitful source of conflict. Members of that government had continued to implement Mao's land law at least until the Second Plenum of the Action Committee, in July. From February on both the Maoists and the future members of the Action Committee had been carrying out a purge of the government to rid it of rich peasants and Nationalist agents. In the course of the purge, each faction tended to identify the opposite faction's supporters in lower party echelons as enemy agents, hoping to replace them with men more favorable to itself.

Another factor entered the situation when the May Conference of Delegates appointed a commission to prepare for the All-China Soviet Congress, then scheduled for November 7, 1930. This commission drew up regulations to govern the election of delegates to the Congress. These regulations, which were probably distributed before September 1930, disenfranchised all religious workers. This weakened the Kiangsi Action Committee, which Mao claimed included Taoist priests among the members of some of its local soviet governments (probably because they were among the few literate men available). Henceforth the priests had to be excluded from the soviet governments. They could not vote for the delegates to either the provincial or the national congress of soviets.[36]

While the details are obscure, both the Maoists and the Action Committee attempted to control the selection of delegates, and in the attempt soviet governments were reorganized several times during the summer. By the middle of August, when the Third, Fourth, and Twelfth Armies were all away in Hunan, the Action Committee achieved a dominant position in several hsien, in which it then applied its own agrarian policy. When the armies returned to southern Kiangsi in September, Mao's supporters in the Kiangsi provincial government and the peasant armies he had left behind in June supplied him with the names of most of the comrades who had been supporting Li Li-san's line on agrarian problems. The Kiangsi Provincial Action Committee and the General Front Committee were soon engaged in a far-ranging debate on military and peasant policy. This dispute came to a head in conferences held in Ki-an in November, when the new provincial soviet government was organized.

Although the Third Plenum of the CCP officially abolished all the action committees, as well as the General Front Committee, in late September, this information probably did not reach Kiangsi until the following January. Documentary evidence for this assertion is scanty, but it is not entirely lacking. For instance, on October 10, 1930, the Red Army Academy Party Committee, then located in Ki-an, reprinted the CCP Politburo directive of June 11, which had launched the Li Li-san line. Surely the Committee would not have done so had it known that the directive had already been branded incorrect. Among the many party documents captured by KMT troops in Kiangsi in late 1930 there are no Central Committee circulars or directives issued after the Third Plenum. NTTC never refers to the decisions of the Third Plenum. Finally, the Central Bureau circular officially announcing the demise of the General Front Committee and the Kiangsi Provincial Action Committee is dated January 15, 1931. So it is probably safe to assume that when the conflict between the Maoists and the anti-Maoists split the Kiangsi party neither side knew that the committee each professed to lead had already been officially abolished.

Mao's Version of the Inner-Party Struggle in Kiangsi (October–December 1930)

As soon as Ki-an fell to the Red Armies on October 4, Mao went there to investigate the members of the local soviet. Yang Ch'eng-fu, a Li Li-sanist, was the chairman. In the KMT police files at Ki-an Chu Teh found coded documents listing the members of the A-B Corps in the soviet areas. Although the code itself was not broken for months, the files also held a receipt for money signed by Li Wen-ling's father, a Hsing-kuo landlord. Chu did not then believe that Li Wenling was involved with the A-B Corps, but the receipt certainly implied a connection that had to be investigated between A-B Corps headquarters in Ki-an and landlords in the base area of Tung-ku and Hsing-kuo. A special Committee to Combat the Counterrevolution was organized and ordered to infiltrate the Corps—to make friends with the members of the Corps, join its secret groups, and quietly uncover the entire network of enemy agents.[j] While the Committee was still being organized, Mao left for P'eng Teh-huai's headquarters at Lou-fang in Hsin-yü hsien, north of Ki-an. There, in the last week

[j] Smedley, *Great Road,* p. 280. In Snow, RSOC, Mao gives a different story. In his interview with Wales, Chu does not mention the A-B Corps at all, and none of the others Wales interviewed in 1937 mentioned this incident. (Snow, RSOC, pp. 172, 182; Wales, *Inside Red China,* pp. 250–51; *Red Dust, passim.*)

of October, he conducted an investigation of Hsing-kuo hsien that he uses in NTTC as an excellent illustration of his method of inquiry. He was undoubtedly trying to uncover connections between Li Wen-ling's father, landlord families related to him by marriage or economic ties, and the soviet and party hierarchies in Hsing-kuo. He used eight informants who had been sent from Hsing-kuo to join the Red Army. These informants all came from Yang-feng ch'ü on the border of Hsing-kuo. After recording their life histories, Mao asked them questions about the class structure of Yang-feng's population and the proportion of land held by each class. He also asked about all kinds of exploitation practiced in Yang-feng: rents, taxation, usury, and special assessments. Then he inquired about the struggle for land, eliciting a detailed account of the way in which land distribution was actually carried out. He drew from them a history of two soviet governments at the ch'ü and hsiang levels, as well as the history, organization, and structure of military units in the villages. Of more than nine landlords in Yang-feng, two had welcomed the Red Army when it appeared, brought out their land deeds and assisted in burning them. These two were taken into the Hsing-kuo soviet government, where one became head of the propaganda department and the other chairman of the finance department. Under their auspices the first soviet government of Yang-feng had been filled with gamblers and Taoist priests, some of whom retained their influence even after they lost their official positions in the July purge.[37] Mao's informants did not spell out any relationship between the landlords in the government and the Li and Tuan clans. The surnames Li and Tuan do not appear on Mao's list of members of local soviet governments.[k]

In addition, Mao discovered that one rich peasant from Yang-feng, Hsü Ch'ang-han, had joined the revolution only when the Red Army arrived and left almost immediately for a job at the seat of the Southwest Kiangsi soviet government—clearly a suspicious action. Most of the rich peasants had joined the revolution in February. About 30 percent of the soviet officials were middle or rich peasants until April and May, when the anti-rich-peasant slogan was raised and they were expelled from the soviets. By October only two rich peasants remained in the ch'ü soviet. Many of the rich peasants had been accused of being members of the A-B Corps and arrested as such; some had been killed. No landlords had been arrested, although several were killed attempting to run away.[38] The real object of Mao's survey

[k] Mao does not give a complete list of members of the Hsing-kuo hsien soviet government, nor does he list any nonresident landlords whose homes were located in the hsien capital. It is possible that the Li and Tuan families were in this group.

was to discover which landlords in the area were associated with the A-B Corps and which CCP members and soviet officials had familial or business ties with the landlords and rich peasants, who were most likely to engage in counterrevolutionary activities. Furthermore, a list of landlord and rich peasant families in the area would have helped immensely in deciphering the names in the KMT code book in Ki-an. Whether the investigation of Hsing-kuo achieved this purpose is unknown, but it was certainly about this time that Mao's secret agents successfully began to infiltrate the A-B Corps and lay the groundwork for its destruction.

The Lou-fang Conference

According to NTTC, the investigation of Hsing-kuo was completed on October 30. On the same day the General Front Committee held a conference at Lou-fang and decided to follow the tactic of "luring the enemy to penetrate deep." This is one of the military tactics Mao specifically defends in RSQHP. At the time he first proposed it, it was a maneuver aimed at the destruction of opponents within his own camp as well as of the destruction of the military forces of the enemy. Because the war in the north between Chiang Kai-shek and the northern warlords Feng Yü-hsiang and Yen Hsi-shan had just ended, large numbers of KMT troops were returning south to renew their attack on the soviet areas. They were to be lured deep into the base area and their scattered forces destroyed by separate attacks in which the Red Army would have local, temporary superiority in numbers. Essentially this was a variation of the guerrilla tactics Mao and Chu had developed earlier, i.e., tactics appropriate to a small, weak force facing a powerful enemy.[l]

To implement this strategy the General Front Committee decided to evacuate Ki-an, the seat of the Provincial Action Committee. Some 40,000 troops were to withdraw from southwestern Kiangsi and concentrate on the Kiangsi-Fukien border, east of the base in Tung-ku and Hsing-kuo. This maneuver would lure the enemy troops up the mountain valleys of eastern Kiangsi, where stragglers could be cut off and destroyed. As a maneuver against Mao's enemies in the party it had a double advantage. At the beginning of the campaign it placed

[l] Mao, NTTC, p. 63; SW, IV, 203; HC, III, 984. According to Mao, a small, weak force fighting a powerful enemy can win in the long run if at first it adopts guerrilla tactics. After some success it can move onward to the stage of mobile warfare, of which the Lou-fang tactics were a primitive form. Only forces with absolute superiority can afford to adopt positional warfare. (Mao, SW, I, 219, 212, 222; HC, I, 198, 204, 207.)

their main forces in the base area from which Mao and Chu drew their most solid support. At the same time, it exposed the soviet areas most deeply penetrated by the A-B Corps to the first enemy attacks. Mao's old enemies on the Southwest Kiangsi Special Committee would probably lose the area in which their supporters were concentrated. If they refused to evacuate Ki-an, they might be partially wiped out in the attack on the city that was sure to come.

The decision to abandon Ki-an to the enemy meant losing the only major city the Communists held. The Action Committee wanted not only to hold Ki-an, but also to make another attempt on Nanch'ang and Kiukiang.[39] Under the circumstances this would have meant a frontal assault by a weak force against a much stronger one. If such a last-ditch policy were put into practice, the KMT agents who had been maneuvering against Mao and Chu might suddenly find their own lives endangered. Thus new factional splits among the supporters of the Action Committee might lead Mao to genuine KMT agents. Like many of Mao's policies, "luring the enemy to penetrate deep" was multifunctional. Successfully pursued, it would lure all his enemies into traps and leave his faction supreme in the soviet bases and the Red Army.

Mao's Report on the Conferences in Ki-an (November 1930)

After the decision to adopt this policy had been made at the Lou-fang Conference, Mao returned to Ki-an to plan the retreat. On his way he made a number of investigations to document the manner in which the Action Committee had managed the soviets in and around Ki-an, undoubtedly to prepare for the conferences of the Kiangsi Action Committee and CEC of the Kiangsi soviet government scheduled for mid-November in Ki-an. The problem of land distribution was the chief item on the agendas of these conferences.

In his own words, Mao proceeded as follows:

On November 6, the Red Army moved out of Hsia-chang, forded the Kan River, and moved toward Ying-feng in Nan-ch'eng. To lay out the road of the retreat, I went from Hsia-chang to Ki-an. On the night of November 7, I rested at Tung-t'ang, and on the second day [November 9] I reached Ki-an. On this journey, I made a simple investigation. In my investigation of Li-chia-fang I understood for the first time the circumstances developing, in a few places, in hsiang- and village-level soviet organs in the midst of the agrarian struggle. When I began this investigation, my viewpoint on the many circumstances affecting the agrarian revolution at these two levels was still muddled and confused. It was only during this investigation that I discovered that using the village as a unit in dividing land has serious consequences. [In fact, he had discarded this method by the time of the February 7 Conference.] In the southern part of Kiangsi, more than ten hsien have already divided the land. Proclamations of the higher levels of government have ordered that the hsiang is to be used as the basic unit in dividing land. Up to the present time, all workers in the higher levels have believed that the lower levels were using the hsiang as the basic unit. Actually, very few places have used the hsiang as the unit.

If the method of taking the village as the unit is used, it benefits the rich peasants, but not the poor peasants. This method ought to be changed.[40]

One of the long-standing disagreements between Mao and the Southwest Kiangsi party leaders concerned the optimum size of the unit within which land was distributed. Mao's two early land laws permitted a choice among village, hsiang, or ch'ü. The February 7 land law permitted a choice only between hsiang and ch'ü.[41] In his brief investigations on the road to Ki-an, Mao discovered that the village was still being used as a unit in southwestern Kiangsi. He rejected this procedure because the wealthier men usually dominated the proceedings when only the residents of a single village took part in dividing the land. Large and wealthy villages (in this area usually comprising a single clan with one surname) favored using the village as the unit, while small, poor villages (usually composed of weak clans with fewer members) naturally favored using the hsiang or ch'ü. Mao believed that if hsiang or ch'ü were used, competition among villages and clans could be transformed into class struggle and the rich peasants could then be more readily dispossessed. He felt that the size of the unit within which land was distributed was of the utmost importance, especially at the time of the first division.

Mao's investigations also gave him facts with which to judge the accuracy of reports to be made at the coming meeting by chairmen of the local soviets. He discovered that some comrades were liars. For instance, the chairman of Ju-fang ch'ü in Ki-shui hsien was to report that the village of Hsi-i-t'ing had already undergone a division of land. Mao knew from his own inquiries that land distribution had barely begun there.[42]

On arriving in Ki-an on November 9, Mao immediately began to mobilize his supporters among the delegates. At this point Maoists dominated the Kiangsi Provincial Soviet Central Executive Committee, chaired by Ch'en Cheng-jen, while their opponents dominated the Provincial Action Committee, the action committees in southern and western Kiangsi, and the Ki-an soviet government, all at this time located in Ki-an. The soviet executive had issued orders that Mao's February land law was again to be applied. The leaders of the Action

Committee, as well as Yang Ch'eng-fu, the chairman of the Ki-an soviet, were opposed to this move and still supported the Li Li-san land law.

The first meeting after Mao's arrival in Ki-an was an enlarged meeting of the Southwest Kiangsi Action Committee on November 12. At its first session delegates from 14 hsien in southwestern Kiangsi began to report in detail on the progress of land distribution and the problems of the peasants in their hsien. Mao took notes that were printed (possibly with some emendations) in NTTC.[43] It was at this session that he recorded the lie told by the chairman of Ju-fang ch'ü. It is quite likely that Mao heard a number of other things at this session that he knew or suspected to be downright lies, or at best exaggerations and distortions. But since he does not name the chairmen reporting for each area it is impossible to determine whether any were among those he later arrested.

The Kiangsi Provincial Executive Committee held its first session two days later. While Mao had evidently been only an honored guest at the enlarged meeting of the Action Committee, on this occasion he came as the delegate of the General Front Committee.[44] The only surviving record of this meeting is Mao's biased account in NTTC, "Mistakes Made in the Land Struggle in Kiangsi," which begins with the following statement:

> On November 14, 1930, the Kiangsi Provincial Executive Committee met in Ki-an. In my capacity as secretary of the General Front Committee, I was present as a delegate. After the reports by Comrades Ch'en Yi, Ch'en Cheng-jen, and Ma Ming, I pointed out that from the time of the Second Plenum [of the Kiangsi Provincial Action Committee, in July 1930] everyone in the party in southwestern Kiangsi had continuously taken the line of liquidating the land revolution. After discussion there was unanimous agreement that this line was wrong, and that we must make a resolute struggle against it. Below are a few of the important points I noted down during the reports of Comrades Ch'en Yi, Ch'en Cheng-jen, and Ma Ming. When I recorded these important points, there were very many that only I understood.[45]

Ma Ming, who reported first, said that in Ju-fang all honest comrades had been driven out of party office and the whole party organization was dominated by the A-B Corps, while the economy was dominated by rich peasants. In Yung-hsin hsien the soviet government supported a rich peasant line. The ch'ü party secretaries neglected inspection of the hsiang, and policy made at higher levels was not implemented below. Rich peasants cheated the poor with impunity, threatening them with the return of the White armies.[46]

Ch'en Yi stated that no land had yet been divided in Tung-lu.[m] None had been divided in Nan-lu, either, aside from a few areas in Hsing-kuo and Kan-hsien. In Shang-yü hsien not only had the land not been divided, the grain confiscated from the landlords had not even been distributed to the poor. This state of affairs, Ch'en said, resulted from domination of the party organization by wealthy peasants. In Jui-ching 80 percent of the party members were landlords or rich peasants; of 80 party members in Shang-yü, more than 30 were landlords or rich peasants, including some former members of the *min-t'uan*. All the officers of the Red Vanguards in Hsin-feng were rich peasants. In Yung-hsin the families of those who volunteered for the Red Army were not given help in cultivating their fields, while the families of those who were sent to the army by the soviet were.[47] This phenomenon Ch'en also attributed to the influence of the rich peasants. Evidently the volunteers sided with the Maoists on the issue of equal land distribution, while the Yung-hsin soviet government and its draftees aligned themselves with the Action Committee.

According to Ch'en, these situations arose after the Second Plenum of the Southwest Kiangsi Special Committee. Ch'en specifically accused Li Wen-ling and Ch'en Chih-chung, a member of the Southwest Kiangsi Special Committee, of "liquidating the peasants" and "liquidating the land revolution," i.e., of bringing to a halt all land distribution in areas under their control.[48] Until at least the middle of July, and probably later, Ch'en Yi had been one of the representatives of the Kiangsi soviet government who organized conferences of local soviets to explain the February 7 land law. Shortly after the Second Plenum, members of the Action Committee intervened and countermanded all he had done. Ch'en gave at least two examples of this. On July 15, he had made a report on the land problem to an enlarged conference of soviet chairmen, advocating and explaining Mao's February 7 law. On the basis of his report, the South Kiangsi Revolutionary Committee officially promulgated the law, but the soviet authorities in Jui-ching and Yü-tu refused to implement it. The rich peasants in these hsien had countered with the land law promulgated by the Second Plenum, which enabled them to retain possession of their land.[49] On another occasion Ch'en Yi had attended an enlarged meeting of soviet chairmen in Hsi-ho and held the floor for nine days

[m] Kiangsi was divided into four major military areas, or routes, by the Communists. Each was the area from which an army drew its recruits and supplies, and which it was required to protect. They were *Tung-lu* (east route), *Nan-lu* (south route), *Hsi-lu* (west route), and *Pei-lu* (north route).

explaining the provisions of Mao's land law. On the tenth day Ch'en Chih-chung had arrived, squelched him, and ended the conference.

Although the Second Plenum had adopted the Li Li-san land law, the members of the Action Committee did not intend to implement it until the insurrection had succeeded. Ch'en Yi reported that at a conference held somewhere in Nan-lu on August 14 Li Wen-ling, representing the Action Committee, did not even discuss land problems. When the February 7 law was revived after the retreat from Ch'angsha, the leaders of the Action Committee opposed it. At a meeting of the Southwest Kiangsi Action Committee on October 28, one member had advocated the Maoist provision "take from those who have fertile land and give to those who have poor land," but his proposal was not even discussed.[50]

Ch'en Yi also presented to the meeting several arguments the Southwest Kiangsi Action Committee had used against Mao's land law. One was that confiscation of landlords' land could only be a temporary measure, for it was not the real aim of redistribution. Another was that the use of the criterion of labor power in distributing land, not the criterion of equal distribution to all, was in the interest of the poor peasants. To advocate equal division was a sign of "peasant consciousness." Mao's land law therefore was not a genuinely proletarian land law.[51] Ch'en Yi finally concluded that there were now two lines being followed in southern Kiangsi.

The last report Mao records was made by yet a third Ch'en, Ch'en Cheng-jen, whom Mao had made chairman of the Kiangsi soviet in February. Ch'en reported a clash with Tuan Liang-pi, who had said that he did not believe the land revolution should be "deepened."[52] According to Ch'en, the Southwest Kiangsi Special Committee (the Kiangsi Action Committee's predecessor) had reported to the Central Committee that to deepen and broaden the agrarian revolution at the same time was a policy based on "peasant consciousness." The first part of the report was a direct attack on the Maoist plan to simultaneously deepen and broaden the agrarian revolution by gradually extending the base outward from its mountain center. The second part was an attack on Mao's idea that only Kiangsi could be taken in a year, an idea rejected by the Special Committee and by Li Li-san on the ground that it was conservative. Mao did not advocate the capture of Ch'angsha and Wuhan, and therefore he "cut short the rising tide of the revolution."[53] This report to the Central Committee undoubtedly was made at the May Conference of Delegates from the Soviet Areas, probably by Tuan Liang-pi and Li Wen-ling. After these two had returned to Kiangsi, Ch'en Cheng-jen had discovered what they had reported to the Central Committee. Now he made it known to everyone present at this session of the Kiangsi CEC.

After these three reports were delivered, Mao condemned the line the Second Plenum of the Action Committee had adopted on the ground that it "terminated the agrarian revolution." According to Mao, those present at the Executive Committee meeting agreed that the line had been incorrect and that the party must begin to struggle against it immediately. This had little effect, however, on the members of the Kiangsi Action Committee, for on the following day it resumed its sessions and continued the discussion of land distribution.

Mao attended two enlarged sessions of the Action Committee on that day, the first of which was devoted to a continuation of the detailed reports on land problems.[54] Mao introduces his discussion of the second session with these remarks:

> On November 15, 1930, the Kiangsi Provincial Action Committee held an enlarged meeting in Ki-an. Aside from the regular members of the Provincial Action Committee, those who attended were the hsien soviet chairmen from Yung-hsin, Ki-an, T'ai-ho, Wan-an, Ki-shui, An-fu, Fen-yi, and Hsia-kiang, as well as Comrade Ch'en Yi of the Twenty-second Army. I attended as the delegate of the General Front Committee. The special features of this meeting were the discussions of the problems of compensation and rentals. On the problem of compensation I advocated supporting compensation on a mass basis. On the problem of rentals I denounced the provision "no rents shall be collected in the soviet areas"[n] as a left deviation that is in practice a theory of the rich peasants. Aside from this, I opposed Chiang Han-po's method of dividing land on the basis of labor power, pointing out that his error in fact supports the rich peasants and places obstacles in the poor peasants' path. Before the business of this meeting was completed it dispersed, for the enemy had already reached Hsia-kiang and responsible persons from every hsien returned to prepare for the enemy's arrival. Therefore the problems of mountain groves of trees, ponds, houses, vacated fields, unemployment, and debts, which were on the original agenda, were not discussed. After the meeting ended there was a heavy enemy assault. The Fu-t'ien incident occurred shortly after that. Therefore the Provincial Action Committee has not been able to publish the resolutions of this meeting.[55]

The Retreat from Ki-an

The meeting was ended by a general order for a retreat from the city, which was retaken by KMT troops on November 18. It is highly likely that members of the Kiangsi Action Committee resisted the order to

[n] This was a provision of an anti-Maoist land law (not the Li Li-san land law) that had been advocated or enforced, or both, in southwestern Kiangsi from sometime after Mao left Ching-kang-shan until the February 7 Conference.

retreat, for a few days earlier they had been advocating another drive northward on Nanch'ang. Nevertheless, they did evacuate and the soviet government and Action Committee moved to Fu-t'ien. On November 19, according to Mao,

> [With] Ku Po and Hsieh Wei-chün, my two comrades, I left Ki-an and went to Heng-t'ien, a town under the jurisdiction of Yung-feng hsien, in order to join up there with the main forces of the Red Army. On November 21 we passed through Shui-nan on the way to Po-sha. At Mu-k'uo village we ate our noon meal. There we investigated the class composition of the members of the village government, and the class composition of counter-revolutionary elements killed in the village. In this investigation we discovered that when the land was equally divided, the middle peasants did not lose anything, but in fact improved their position. However, in this violent peasant struggle the rich peasants and small landlords all went over to the counterrevolutionary camp.

Mao reported that the killing of some of the "reactionaries" in Mu-k'uo village was impolitic. Not all had been true reactionaries, and when they were killed the other members of their classes in the village began to oppose the revolution.

> Among the seven reactionaries listed above who were killed in this village, three were small landlords, three were rich peasants, and one was a vagabond. This is evidence that very many small landlords and rich peasants go over to the counterrevolution when the land revolution is deepened. But should every one of these seven persons have been killed? This is a problem.[56]

Although Mao blamed the A-B Corps for these killings, their relation to the whole alleged plot of the A-B Corps is unclear. By this time the Nationalist armies were encircling the soviet areas. Mao and Chu were preparing to strike out at traitors in the ranks of the Red Army. At the same time, political opposition to the Chu-Mao military strategy and land policy continued in the ranks of the Action Committees and their supporters. There is no indication in NTTC that Mao's Committee to Combat the Counterrevolution had yet discovered any connection between the leaders of the Action Committee and the A-B Corps, but the accusations were soon to come.

The Fu-t'ien Incident

The Spark

According to contemporary letters of the General Front Committee, Mao struck his first blow at suspected members of the A-B Corps in late November, arresting some 4,400 officers and men of the Red Army. Some of the officers arrested testified that Tuan Liang-pi, secretary-general of the Kiangsi Action Committee, Li Wen-ling, one of its leading members, and Hsieh Han-ch'ang, political commissar of the Twentieth Army, were all in the A-B Corps. They in turn implicated Ts'ung Yün-chung, head of the Orgburo of the Action Committee, and Chin Wan-pang, another of the Committee members. Others were soon implicated, and before long all but two members of the Committee were under arrest in Fu-t'ien. The two exceptions, Mao's supporters, had probably acted as *agents provocateurs*.[57] The arrest of Hsieh Han-ch'ang must have caused many of the officers of the Twentieth Army to fear for their own safety. According to contemporary records Liu Ti, a battalion political commissar who had presumably been appointed by Hsieh, was contacted by Li Shao-chiu, one of Mao's agents, who informed him that the arrests involved political issues as well as membership in the A-B Corps.[58] Coming from Mao's opponents, this information may be deliberately falsified, but the implication is clear. Mao incited Liu Ti to revolt. Given the tension between the General Front Committee and the Action Committee at the time and the fact that Mao and Chu were using secret agents to ferret out members of the A-B Corps, it is highly probable that Li Shao-chiu intended to provoke Liu Ti into some demonstration of disloyalty. But neither Mao nor Li Shao-chiu realized that the demonstration would take the form of an armed attack on the Kiangsi soviet government. That, however, is what happened.

The Incident

On December 7 or 8, 1930, Liu Ti and the four hundred men under his command revolted in Tung-ku, arrested their commander, Liu T'ieh-ch'ao, and made a forced march to Fu-t'ien. There they attacked the prison, set free Li Wen-ling and some twenty other members of the Southwest Kiangsi Action Committee, overthrew the provincial soviet government, and arrested many of its members.[o]

[o] Hsiao, p. 98. A different story is given in Schwartz, *Chinese Communism*, pp. 174–78, based on Ch'eng Sheng-ch'ang, "The Fu-t'ien Incident and the Internal Divisions in the Party," *Materials of Modern History* [55], III, 265; K'o Ch'eng, "A Record of Mao Tse-tung's Tyranny," *ibid.*, p. 256; Li Ang [66], p. 152; Hatano, *Sekishoku Shina no Kyūmei*, p. 206; Johanson and Taube, p. 246; and Snow, RSOC, p. 182.

The account I have given here follows the story given in the contemporary letters included in Hsiao, using those parts of Schwartz's account that do not contradict the letters. Mao told Snow that the leader of the revolt was Liu T'ieh-ch'ao, who was actually arrested by Liu Ti. He also said that Tseng Shan, the recently elected chairman of the Kiangsi soviet government, was arrested by Liu T'ieh-ch'ao. The contemporary letters state that Tseng escaped. Moreover, Mao attributed the uprising to Li Li-san's supporters. As we shall see, the accusation

At Fu-t'ien more than a hundred of Mao's supporters were killed, and several of them were captured with their relatives. Chu Teh's wife may have been among them.[p] Immediately after Li Wen-ling was released from prison, he summoned a "people's conference" in Fu-t'ien and called for Mao's overthrow. Li and his followers were soon dislodged from Fu-t'ien. They fled to Yung-yang, west of the Kan River, and organized a rival soviet government. They attacked Mao as a "party emperor," undoubtedly believing that they were following the party line and that Mao and Chu had revolted against the Central Committee with practically the whole of the Red Army. In the absence of communications from Shanghai, there must have been many men in the army who believed they might be cutting their ties with the CCP by siding with Mao and Chu against the Action Committee. The Committee dwelt on this theme for the rest of the month, trying to win over the greater part of the Red Army by claiming to support the military leaders—Chu Teh, P'eng Teh-huai, and Huang Kung-lüeh—but not Mao.[59] According to all later published accounts, P'eng, Huang, and Chu supported Mao solidly throughout this period of tension. The political commissars in their armies, however, probably tended to side with the Southwest Kiangsi leaders, at least until news reached them of the demise of the Li Li-san line.

According to Chu Teh, the revolt allowed the KMT troops to occupy Hsing-kuo and Tung-ku. Peasants in these hsien defended themselves but were soon forced to flee to the main body of the Red Army, where many enlisted. The enlarged Red Army was then able to defeat the KMT army in its first campaign of encirclement and annihilation.[60] The Maoists had a propaganda advantage over the Fu-t'ien rebels during this period of battle. They were waging a successful campaign that lasted until the early days of January 1931, and thereby preserved the core of their soviet base on the Kiangsi-Fukien border, while the Action Committee remained west of the Kan River

---

of Li Li-sanism was not the original one brought against the Southwest Kiangsi leaders. It was added to the charges only after news of the 28 Bolsheviks' attack on the Li Li-san line arrived in the soviet districts. Therefore I surmise that in this instance Mao followed the line of the 28 Bolsheviks in his account to Snow. Hsiao's account is based on letters captured by the KMT, the evidence used by Schwartz, and a recent book by Lu Ch'iang, an ex-Communist who alleges he was on the scene. (Lu [74], pp. 33–38.)

p K'ang K'e-ching, Chu Teh's wife, told Wales that at the time she was the director of the headquarters guards regiment at Fu-t'ien and was separated from her husband for a year, beginning shortly before the incident. (Wales, *Red Dust*, pp. 214–15.)

in a relatively peaceful area where few Red Army troops could be exposed to the Committee's agitation.

The Aftermath

In a confidential letter addressed to Chu Teh and other military leaders two weeks after the Fu-t'ien incident, the Action Committee charged Mao with arbitrarily arresting the members of the Kiangsi Action Committee (except his two supporters) on the trumped-up charge of membership in the A-B Corps.[61] To illustrate that Mao was out to dominate the party in the soviet areas, they forwarded to the military leaders a copy of a letter Mao had allegedly written his henchman Ku Po, in which he directed Ku to carry out his mission in western Kiangsi and eliminate the Kiangsi Action Committee in three days, but only after forcing them to confess that Chu Teh, P'eng Teh-huai, Huang Kung-lüeh, and other army commanders were members of the A-B Corps.[62] Chu, P'eng, and Huang immediately branded the letter a forgery and declared their continued agreement with Mao and his policies.

At this point, Mao and Chu ostensibly changed their minds and admitted that the Action Committeemen had not in fact been members of the A-B Corps, but had been guilty of following the liquidationist line, which allowed the rich peasants to exploit the land revolution, and had thereby played into the hands of the A-B Corps.[63] In reply to the original charge, the Action Committee asserted the identity of its policies with those of the Central Committee and denied any connection with the A-B Corps except for the highly respectable one of leading the struggle against it:

> We do not deny that the A-B Corps has a widespread organization in Kiangsi and that it has penetrated into the soviet areas, for in the past we have been active fighters against it ourselves. . . . Comrade Tuan Liang-pi was the first to combat the A-B Corps in the Southwest Kiangsi Special Committee. . . . As late as two weeks ago [December 6?], Comrade Tuan attacked Lo Shou-nan of the Twenty-second Army for compromising with the A-B Corps. . . . Now, two weeks later, Tuan himself is branded a member of the A-B Corps.[64]

Evidently both the Action Committee and the General Front Committee had penetrated the A-B Corps, each with its own counterspies. Each, uncovering a part of the other's underground network, believed it had discovered genuine members of the A-B Corps. The Action Committee's discovery that Lo Shou-nan, one of Mao's men, was a member of the Corps, and the Committee's publicizing of the fact, resulted in several of Mao's counterspies' being arrested and killed either by the KMT underground or by agents of the Action Committee. Perhaps this is what happened in Mu-k'uo village.[q]

In spite of the bitter feuding in the Kiangsi party, neither side acted with the ruthlessness of Stalinists. The Stalinist police system was yet to be imitated in the Chinese soviet areas. The General Front Committee arrested some 4,400 Communists, but very few were shot. Most were released after an investigation and a short period of reeducation.[65] Data on the manner in which the Action Committee treated its prisoners is lacking. No one, however, has accused it of torturing them or of shooting them without trial.

In the last weeks of December, while the Red Army broke the back of the first KMT encirclement and annihilation campaign, the rival committees exchanged nasty messages, but took no further steps toward a final break. Evidently neither side dared to expel the other until there was some indication of the Central Committee's attitude toward the dispute.

The Third Plenum Abolishes the General Front Committee and the Action Committees

Sometime early in January 1931 a welcome letter arrived from the Central Committee announcing that Li Li-san's policies had been "revised" by the Third Plenum of the Central Committee and that action committees had been officially abolished sometime in late September or early October (they had ceased to function in Shanghai even earlier). The General Front Committee was also abolished; its functions were to be taken over by a new Central Bureau for the Soviet Areas. Nine men were named to the new Bureau, on which the Maoist faction was clearly dominant.[66] Its dominance, however, appears to have been largely accidental, dependent upon the fact that of the nine appointees (Chou En-lai, Hsiang Ying, Mao Tse-tung, Chu Teh, Jen Pi-shih, Yü Fei, Tseng Shan, and two others)[67] only Mao, Chu, and Tseng were in the soviet areas. Chou, Hsiang, Yü, and probably Jen were in Shanghai. Even if the "two others" were the men who had carried the letter from Shanghai, the Maoist faction had a majority of the quorum present.

It was clearly the Third Plenum of the Central Committee, held in September 1930, and not the Fourth Plenum, held in January 1931, that created the new Bureau. Several of its members would not

[q] Mao, NTTC, p. 73. See also Smedley, *Great Road*, p. 281, for Chu Teh's story of how Mao's bodyguard was killed by the A-B Corps. Ch'en Yi was the political commissar of the Twenty-second Army, in which Lo was allegedly an officer.

have been appointed by the Politburo Mif and the 28 Bolsheviks set up at the Fourth Plenum. The name of Yü Fei on the list betrays that fact. He had been one of the leaders of the anti-Mif faction at Sun Yat-sen University. In February 1930 Mif had had him expelled from the CCP delegation to the Comintern. When Chou En-lai returned from Moscow in August 1930, he brought with him most of the men Mif had expelled—Ch'ü Ch'iu-pai, Yü Fei, Teng Chung-hsia, and others. This group immediately joined forces with the Li Li-sanists to keep Mif's protégés out of the Central Committee. Since Chou was the highest-ranking delegate to the Comintern, Mif held him responsible for this maneuver. Yü's factional activities in the labor unions were especially distasteful to Mif, and shortly after the Fourth Plenum the 28 Bolsheviks expelled Yü from the Central Committee for assisting Wang K'e-ch'üan and Hsü Hsi-ken to organize opposition to Mif's protégés in the National Labor Federation. Chou En-lai was not expelled, but he was forced to repent of his "cowardly rotten opportunism" in defending Li Li-san at the Third Plenum.[68] A Central Bureau selected by the Mif faction would probably not have included Chou, and certainly not Yü.

The Maoists' dominant position in the soviet areas was officially confirmed, then, by an alliance of old cadres in the Central Committee who refused to bend to the will of a Comintern adviser. As a member of the new Central Bureau, Mao was at last in an authoritative position to settle his old scores with the Action Committee. The second circular issued by the Central Bureau (on January 16, 1931) announced the expulsion from the party of Tuan Liang-pi, Li Po-fang, Hsieh Han-ch'ang, Chin Wan-pang, and Liu Ti, the five leading members of the Action Committee. At last in a secure position, Mao admitted that he did not have a watertight case:

> No doubt the Fu-t'ien incident was in fact an act directed against the party and the revolution. Though it has not yet been proved that they [the Action Committee's leaders] are organizationally all members of the A-B Corps and liquidationists, their action against the party and against the revolution has objectively been in agreement with the reactionary behavior of these groups.[69]

While Mao was of course aware that the Action Committee followed Li Li-san, he did not dare say so until the Fourth Plenum had condemned Li's line. When Hsiang Ying arrived from Shanghai after the Fourth Plenum and took over the administration of the Central Bureau, he berated Mao for having failed to recognize Li's influence on the Action Committee in his investigations and reports on the

Fu-t'ien incident.[70] Mao's failure to note this fact, Hsiang held, was part and parcel of the blindness of old cadres and the ideological poverty of rural soviet areas. But even though Hsiang became secretary of the Central Bureau, the Maoists were not to lose their newly acquired authority until after the Central Committee itself moved to the soviet areas.[r]

[r] This statement is contradictory to earlier findings of Schwartz, *Chinese Communism,* p. 185. It rests on documents from BIC and SSC and on the testimony of Chang Kuo-t'ao and Kung Ch'u. (Hsiao, pp. 151–52.)

CHAPTER XI

The Bolshevik Reconstruction of the Party

In 1931 Mao reached the height of his power in the soviet areas. Three years later he was in prison, as the first phase of his struggle with the 28 Bolsheviks, who represented the Comintern line in China, reached a denouement. The story of these years is one of intrigue and conflict between the interests of the international Communist movement and those of the Chinese Communists.

As 1930 drew to a close, Li Li-san fell and the 28 Bolsheviks rose to power in the CCP. In the process the old CCP cadres outside the soviet areas were almost all destroyed. Concurrently, the revolt at Fu-t'ien split the party in the central soviet districts. In Moscow, Lominadze and Syrtsov circulated a memorandum among the members of the CPSU Central Committee suggesting that Stalin be deposed from his position as general secretary. This perfectly legal plea was labeled the product of a conspiracy, and Lominadze and Syrtsov were imprisoned. The unsuccessful rebellion among the Stalinists opposed to the forced pace of super-industrialization and disheartened by the miseries of the collectivized peasantry soon led the true believers and police agents in the Comintern to tighten their control of the apparatus. This increasing stress on theoretical conformity and the cult of Stalin's personality was to culminate in the bloody purge of Old Bolsheviks six years later.

The Fall of Li Li-san

Pavel Mif and his protégés appeared in Shanghai in the early summer of 1930. Li Li-san did nothing to oppose them until they attacked his June 11 resolution. Then he placed Wang Ming on probation for six months, officially reprimanded Po Ku (Ch'in Pang-hsien), Wang Chia-hsiang, and Ho Tzu-shu, and for several weeks refused to talk to Mif.[1] Mif sent off an urgent letter to Moscow demanding that Li be reproved for his disrespect, but did not immediately get the response he wanted. Lominadze, who was at the time in Stalin's good graces, undoubtedly made the next move—Ch'ü Ch'iu-pai and Chou En-lai, both of whom had been on good terms with Lominadze in 1927, were sent back to Shanghai to review Li Li-san's policies and actions. With them were the Chinese labor leaders Mif had ejected from the Comintern several months earlier. When this unwelcome group appeared in Shanghai, they brought with them a Comintern directive dated July 23 that they used to support Li in his contest with Mif. The directive was ambiguous enough to permit Ho Meng-hsiung, a labor leader opposed to Li who read the new directive without permission from the Politburo, to use it as a basis for *attacking* Li. But with the assistance of Chou and Ch'ü, Li was able to expel Ho from his post as a Central Committee alternate before the Third Plenum convened in September.[2]

When the Plenum met, Chou and Ch'ü insisted that Li was open to criticism only for tactical errors. They directed their main attack at Ho and his followers in the labor union faction. These comrades, Chou and Ch'ü declared, were right deviationists who did not believe in the new revolutionary wave. They underestimated the significance of the soviet areas and the Red Army and failed to recognize the value of armed insurrections.[3] By attacking Ho, Chou and Ch'ü managed to associate Mif with a right deviation. Mif also attacked Ho, but he wanted the Plenum to condemn the left aspects of Li Li-san's line as well. Chou and Ch'ü, however, refused to admit that Li had developed a line of his own contrary to that of the Comintern. Li was reelected to the Politburo along with three of his supporters, Hsiang Chung-fa, Li Wei-han, and Ho Ch'ang, and Ch'ü Ch'iu-pai and Chou En-lai.[4] Fourteen members of the Central Committee and twenty-two others attended the Plenum. Since between nine and seventeen members of the Central Committee had died or been expelled since the Sixth Congress, seven new members of the Central Committee, eight new alternates, and two new members of the Supervisory Committee (which supervised purges) were elected. This brought the total number of comrades in the central organs to twenty-three full members of the Central Committee and eight alternates, and three full members of the Supervisory Committee and two alternates.[5] I have attempted to identify as many members of the new Central Committee as possible, since it was this group of old Communists who led the resistance to Mif and his 28 Bolsheviks in the next three months. Of the thirty-five who may have been members, twenty-six were in Shanghai, four in Moscow, four in the soviet areas, and one in prison in Nanking. Of those in Shanghai only one, Shen Tse-min, was a member of the Mif faction. Six were Li Li-sanists: Li himself, Hsiang Chung-fa, Li Wei-han, Ho Ch'ang, Kuan Hsiang-ying, and Li Ch'iu-shih. Five had just returned from Moscow, where they had opposed Mif: Ch'ü Ch'iu-pai and Chou En-lai, who had previously been labeled left putschists; and Teng Chung-hsia, Yü Fei, and Hsü Hsi-ken, who had been identified with the right-wing labor faction. Also labeled as rightists were Lo Chang-lung, Wang K'e-ch'üan, Wang Feng-fei, Kuo Miao-ken, Ts'ai Po-chen, Ch'en Yu, Wang Chung-i, and P'eng Tse-hsiang. There were six other old Communists in Shanghai whose political tendencies at the time I have not been able to discover: Hsiang Ying, Jen Pi-shih, K'ang Sheng, Lo I-nung (Lo I-yüan?), Yang Pao-an, and Liu Shao-ch'i. None of these six comrades were specifically condemned as Li Li-sanists or rightists by the Fourth Plenum. Mao, Chu Teh, Tseng Shan, and possibly Fang Chih-min may have been elected or reelected to the Central Committee at the Third Plenum, for they were placed on the Central Bureau for the Soviet Areas immediately afterward. They remained aloof from the dispute. Of the four possible members in Moscow—Chang Kuo-t'ao, Ts'ai Ho-shen, Huang P'ing, and Lin Yü-nan—the first three opposed both Mif and Li. The man in Nanking, Yün Tai-ying, had been captured while on a dangerous mission for Li Li-san, who had hoped it would lead to Yün's demise. The mission had partially fulfilled its purpose, and Yün was in prison.[a]

In the face of this broad coalition of old cadres in Shanghai, Mif could not reassert the authority of the Comintern and impose a new leadership on the CCP without assistance from Moscow. He called for help. His appeal was answered on November 16, when a letter arrived from the ECCI condemning both the Li Li-san line and the line adopted by the Third Plenum. Li left for Moscow forthwith. On arrival he was interrogated by a committee of the Far Eastern Department of the Comintern, headed by Otto Kuusinen. The committee then drew up a report on his errors for the Presidium of the ECCI. Li had gone to Moscow with the expectation that there would be some old friends around to assist and defend him, but instead found himself entangled in the Lominadze-Syrtsov affair, with none to befriend him. Lominadze and Syrtsov had circulated their memoran-

[a] In addition to the 32 men named, it is extremely likely that a few Whampoa cadets and military men associated with Chou En-lai were also elected members or alternate members of the Central Committee. Liu Po-ch'eng, Yeh Chien-ying, Kung Ho-ch'ung, and Kung Ch'u, none of whom were in Shanghai, are among the possibilities. Hsiao's list of those removed from the Central Committee after the Fourth Plenum substantiates this. (Hsiao, pp. 125–49.)

dum among the members of the CPSU Central Committee at about the time Li's interrogation began. They were expelled from that body for their audacity on December 2. Since in most of the Communist world those who are guilty must be guilty of the currently fashionable sin, this event altered the course of Li's trial: his line was suddenly condemned as one aspect of the plot against Stalin.

The report of the Far Eastern Department charged that Li had been playing with insurrections again: he had tried to involve the Soviet Union and Outer Mongolia in a general world war by provoking the imperialists to intervene in China. It charged that his orientation toward labor had led him to underestimate the Red Army and the rural bases, and to demand wrongly that the first all-China soviet government and the first regular Red Army be organized in a city. Finally, it reprimanded him for his disrespect to Mif. The report also charged Chou and Ch'ü with having compromised with Li even though they had recognized the contradiction between his line and the Comintern's. Ch'ü was especially treacherous, for he had promised in Moscow to support the Comintern and had then thrown his support to Li in Shanghai. Li and Ch'ü, the report said, had been under the influence of Lominadze since 1927. According to the CCP journal *Bolshevik,* Comrades "Pi" (Piatnitsky?) and Magyar testified before the Presidium of the ECCI that Lominadze's influence on Li was visible in Li's rich peasant policy of distributing land according to labor power and refusing to allot land to coolies and hired farm hands, as well as in certain aspects of his labor policy. Chang Kuo-t'ao was called on to contribute his judgment and disagreed. He asserted that Li had initially formulated his peasant and labor policies under the influence of Borodin and Ch'en Tu-hsiu, and had come under the influence of Lominadze only after the fundamental aspects of his line had been worked out. Therefore, Chang urged, the fight against Li Li-sanism must be a two-front struggle in which the right deviation was treated as the main danger.[6]

The Presidium not only condemned Li, it also condemned Ch'ü for his two-faced double-dealing, his factionalism, and his "wily oriental diplomacy." It asserted that his views on the agrarian and peasant questions were associated not only with those of Borodin, Ch'en Tu-hsiu, and Lominadze, but with those of T'an P'ing-shan as well. If that statement had any historical truth at all, it presumably meant that Ch'ü had at one time or another agreed with each one of the four and was therefore ex post facto guilty of their deviations—right opportunism, left putschism, Trotskyism, and refusal to obey Comintern directives.[7] These conclusions laid the basis for Ch'ü's expulsion from the CCP Politburo in the following month. When the hearings ended, Li was directed to stay in the Soviet Union and study at Lenin University in order to rectify his mistakes. He did not return to China until 1945.

The Reconstruction of the Central Committee

While Li was being tried in Moscow, the coalition of Ch'ü, Chou, and Hsiang repulsed the first attempt of Shen Tse-min and Wang Ming to gain control of the Politburo. Their obduracy could not last, however, and they were soon compelled to confess their errors and reinstate the members of Mif's faction Li had demoted. They also readmitted Ho Meng-hsiung to the Central Committee.[8] Ho, who was not aware of recent events in Moscow, made the fateful error of calling for an emergency conference to reconstitute the party's leading organs, as Lominadze had four years earlier. Unlike Ho, Mif knew that Lominadze had become an outcast, so he and his protégés demanded a regular plenum of the Central Committee to officially expel Li from the Politburo, reconstitute that body, and take adequate measures to overcome the effects of Li Li-san's line. With no one left in Moscow with enough power to restrain them, they got their way, and early in January 1931 the Fourth Plenum convened under Mif's guidance.

At this Plenum the Central Committee was reduced from thirty to sixteen full members and alternates.[9] Although we do not know how many members the Committee had when the Plenum convened, we are fairly sure that there were not many more than 32, so some of the 39 men who attended the Plenum's opening sessions were not Committee members. For some reason, Lo Chang-lung and Ho Meng-hsiung appeared at one of these sessions still demanding an emergency conference. Li Li-san and Ch'ü Ch'iu-pai were expelled from the Central Committee early in the course of the Plenum, as were the men most closely identified with Li Li-san. Those known to have been expelled are Li Wei-han, Ho Ch'ang, Kuan Hsiang-ying, and Li Ch'iu-shih. Ho Meng-hsiung, Lo Chang-lung, Wang K'e-ch'üan, Hsü Hsi-ken, Yü Fei, Kuo Miao-ken, Ts'ai Po-chen, Ch'en Yu, P'eng Tse-hsiang, and others left the Plenum or the party, or were reprimanded for their anti-Comintern activities, before the end of the month. After making groveling confessions, Chou En-lai and Hsiang Chung-fa were reinstated to membership on the Politburo. Mif's protégés Wang Ming, Po Ku, Chang Wen-t'ien (also know as Lo

Fu and Szu Mei), and Shen Tse-min dominated it.[10] After a bitter debate accompanied by name-calling and threats of violence, Ho Meng-hsiung and Lo Chang-lung left the meeting with some of the expelled Li Li-sanists. At subsequent meetings of the Labor Federation and the Kiangsu and Shanghai party committees they continued to call for an emergency conference and accused the 28 Bolsheviks of turning the CCP into "Stalin's China section."[11]

On January 17, a mixed group of leaders of the labor union and Li Li-san factions called a meeting in a Shanghai hotel to reconstitute the party leadership in their own way, beyond Mif's control. Seeking as broad a base as possible, they invited expelled rightists and Trotskyites to attend.[b] Someone informed the British police, who raided the meeting and arrested 25 persons, among them Ho Meng-hsiung, Lin Yü-nan, Li Ch'iu-shih, and Wang Ming's enemy Hu Yeh-p'ing. All were turned over to the KMT and shot in Lung-hua prison on February 7.[12] According to sources hostile to the 28 Bolsheviks, it was Wang who had informed the British police, in a personal vendetta against Hu Yeh-p'ing, who had published an accurate account of the toadying, unprincipled methods Wang had used in his climb to first place among the 28 Bolsheviks. Hu, the husband of the prominent writer Ting Ling, was the leader of the Shanghai rickshaw-pullers' union, a friend of Chou En-lai, and a minor poet to boot.[13] Rumors surrounding his betrayal therefore alienated many old Communists and left-wing writers, artists, and labor leaders, as well as contributing to a general state of confusion and suspicion in the party.

Early in February Wang Ming published *The Two Lines*, his version of the inner-party struggle against Li Li-san, Ch'ü Ch'iu-pai, and the right wing. Wang's main theoretical point in this pamphlet was that all the old cadres in the CCP—Li Li-sanists, rightists, and compromisers—had failed to grasp the fact that Chinese capitalists were counterrevolutionary. These cadres had labeled capitalists and their political representatives a "third group" or an "intermediate camp." Concentrating their main attack on imperialists and feudal remnants,

[b] While Lo Chang-lung was campaigning against "Stalin's China section," Ch'en Tu-hsiu called a conference in Shanghai of all opposition groups, evidently hoping to win the majority of the old Chinese party leaders over to the Trotskyite opposition. This conference set up a nine-man Central Executive Committee that included Ch'en Tu-hsiu, P'eng Shu-chih, Kao Yü-han, Liu Jen-ch'ing, and Ts'ai Chen-te. Wang Chung-i, who may have attended this conference, also maintained contacts with the group advocating an emergency conference. This laid the basis for the new Politburo's accusation that the Ho Meng-hsiung and Lo Chang-lung opposition was in collusion with Trotskyites and expelled rightists. (Brandt, Schwartz, and Fairbank, p. 36; Hsiao, p. 143.)

the old cadres had been blind to the error of forming tactical alliances with capitalists and bourgeois reformers. By this line of analysis Wang opened the way to a united front from below.[c] He denied that Communists could form alliances for any purpose whatsoever with any party, army, or organization against the imperialists or the landlords. Henceforth any Communist who tried to do so or who quietly supported others who tried to do so was a right deviationist or a two-faced, double-dealing compromiser.[14] If applied retrospectively, this formula was general enough to embrace everyone in the CCP except the 28 Bolsheviks, for they alone had been out of China throughout the period when all party members in the country had worked within the KMT. More important, the new line precluded any coalition with any other political party or army against the Japanese, who were soon to invade Manchuria and attempt to drive the Nationalist armies out of Shanghai.

Having placed the 28 Bolsheviks in the Politburo, Mif returned to Moscow to assume command of the Chinese section of the Far Eastern Department of the Comintern. From this position he would be able to give his protégés strong support against anyone willing to attack or resist their regime. At the same time, Chang Kuo-t'ao returned from Moscow to Shanghai, and soon moved to oust the new Politburo before the 28 Bolsheviks could consolidate their control. Early in March, he attempted to replace the Politburo by a new standing committee led by himself, with Hsiang Chung-fa as secretary-general and Chou En-lai as the third man.[15] His attempt failed. At a secret meeting in April the Politburo agreed to split up and move to the soviet areas. Jen Pi-shih set off for Ho Lung's soviet in northwestern Hunan. Shen Tse-min and Chang Kuo-t'ao went to the O-yü-wan soviet in western Anhwei. Chou En-lai, Po Ku, and Chang Wen-t'ien agreed to go to the central soviet districts. This left Liu Shao-ch'i, Hsiang Chung-fa, and Wang Ming in charge of a small Central Bureau in Shanghai.[16]

Then another disaster befell the new Politburo. The KMT police in Hankow captured Ku Shun-chang, a young Communist whom Li Li-san had raised out of the depths of the Shanghai slums to a position of leadership during the general strikes of 1926–27. Angered by the anti–Li Li-san line of the new Politburo and despising those who had opportunistically fallen in with it, he gave the KMT police the underground addresses of Ch'ü Ch'iu-pai, Chou En-lai, Li Wei-han, Hsiang Chung-fa, and others in Shanghai. He also identified Yün Tai-ying, who was still in prison, as a Communist. Yün was immediately

[c] See note *a*, p. 118, for an explanation of the various forms of the united front.

shot. The homes of the Shanghai Communists were raided. Hsiang Chung-fa was captured, and executed on June 24.[17] The others were not at home when the police arrived and so escaped. According to Li Ang, when the Communists discovered Ku's betrayal they took revenge by killing some hundred members of his family, who had served as unwitting hostages against his defection since he had entered the secret service of the CCP. The Ku family had connections throughout the Shanghai labor movement, and by this dreadful act the CCP broke almost every tie it still possessed with the proletariat of Shanghai.[d]

After Hsiang Chung-fa's death, Wang Ming became the acting secretary-general, Chang Wen-t'ien took charge of the Orgburo, Shen Tse-min (who had already arrived in the O-yü-wan soviet area) was appointed head of the Propaganda Bureau, Meng Ch'ing-shu (Wang Ming's wife) took over the Women's Bureau, Po Ku worked with the Youth Corps, and Chou En-lai (the only remaining old leader) continued to head the Military Affairs Committee.[18] This group, or part of it, may have attempted to reach the central soviet districts in the summer of 1931, but the KMT was then in the midst of its third annihilation campaign and had thrown up a blockade that was very difficult to get through. By midsummer the Comintern had endorsed the decisions of the Fourth Plenum and supported the 28 Bolsheviks in their reconstruction of the party. The Comintern's directives, stressing that the right deviation was the main danger, called for a provisional all-China soviet government to be established in the safest soviet base area, and spelled out details for handling the land problem in the soviet areas. On the basis of these directives, the Politburo circulated a letter to all the soviet areas in September calling for the consolidation of a soviet base and an armed attack on the major cities. It condemned the Red Army for clinging to guerrilla warfare and demanded that it organize as a regular army. It called for a new land policy whereby rich peasants should get infertile land and poor peasants the most fertile land, thus countermanding Mao's policy of equal distribution. On the national scene, it called for a major effort to precipitate what it saw as the "imminent collapse" of the KMT regime.[19]

One more reorganization of the Politburo took place before it went

[d] Li Ang [66], pp. 115–16. Li Ang's figures may be exaggerated. According to Dr. Li T'ien-min, who has interviewed the men who were in charge of the Shanghai and Hankow police at the time, only about two dozen people were killed. Four were members of Ku's immediate family and the others people who were living in the same house. (Personal communication—Dr. Li was a visiting scholar at the Hoover Institution in 1965.)

to Jui-ching to direct the First All-China Soviet Congress. Sometime in September, Wang Ming and his wife left Shanghai for Moscow (possibly passing through Jui-ching on their way) and Po Ku took charge of the Politburo. In the same month the Japanese launched their attack on Manchuria. Chinese nationalists inside and outside the Nanking government called for unity against the new threat. The new CCP Politburo now had the opportunity to join in the rising sentiment against the invaders and maneuver for leadership within a united front. Instead of taking advantage of this opportunity, the Politburo refused to form any kind of alliance and called for the defeat of both the KMT and the Japanese. Having thus isolated itself from all other anti-imperialist groups in China and having destroyed its base in Shanghai as well, the Politburo set out to apply in the soviet areas two closely related organizational policies: the fight against the right deviation and the "reform and replenishment of the leading bodies at all levels."[20]

The Attack on the Maoists: The Charges Are Entered

Mao was identified as the leader of the right deviationists in the soviet areas even before the Politburo arrived there. It prepared for a confrontation by attacking all the policies that he advocated and removing his supporters from office. This process, however, took quite a long time—there were only 28 Bolsheviks and Mao had many supporters. All the charges Mao attributes to the leaders of the "third left line" in RSQHP were not made until the party conference held in the southern Kiangsi base in November 1931, shortly before the First All-China Soviet Congress. The new Politburo's prolonged struggle against the old cadres in Shanghai delayed its coming. Mao had plenty of time to unravel the story of its activities in Shanghai and prepare for its arrival. Hsü Meng-ch'iu, Hsü T'e-li, and Ch'en Hui-ch'ing (Teng Fa's wife), whose political leanings at the time are not clear, had arrived in January with accounts of events in Shanghai through the previous October. When Hsiang Ying arrived in March to take charge of the Central Party Bureau in the soviet areas, he related his version of the Fourth Plenum. Several other small groups of comrades arrived at Mao's headquarters before the main body of the new Politburo. Po Ku, Chang Wen-t'ien (Lo Fu), Wang Chia-hsiang, and Chou En-lai arrived in the late summer or early autumn.[e] By that time Mao and Chu had successfully fought three campaigns against the KMT

[e] Interview with Lieberman, cited in McLane, p. 38; Wales, *Red Dust,* pp. 63–64. Wang Ming may not have traveled to the Kiangsi base in 1931. If he did, he left

armies, wiped out most of the A-B Corps, executed the leaders of the Fu-t'ien rebels, consolidated the power of their faction in Fukien, and managed the elections of delegates to the First Soviet Congress in the areas within reach of their own First Front Red Army. They had confidence in themselves, their army, their policies, and their formidable political machine. The coming confrontation with the Politburo would require them either to alter their policies, surrender control of their army, and give up their hard-won political powers, or else to fight the Politburo and thereby flout Comintern discipline.

While Mao was making his preparations for this confrontation, the new Politburo members were making theirs. They reviewed the record of Mao's conduct of party affairs in the soviet districts. They heard Hsiang Ying's report on Mao's attitudes after Hsiang had replaced Mao as chairman of the Central Bureau, and learned that in purging the A-B Corps Mao had executed several Whampoa cadets and a few Li Li-sanists. In November, after drawing up a set of resolutions, they co-opted enough members to ensure themselves a working majority and convened a party conference. The major aim of the conference was to set the line and guide the work of the party fraction—i.e., the new Politburo's fraction—at the First All-China Soviet Congress. The essential purpose of the resolutions the Politburo sponsored at the party conference was to attack the Maoists in the Red Army and soviet governments and set the stage for replacing them at the coming All-China Soviet Congress.[21]

The November 1931 Party Conference

The Political Resolution of the November 1931 Party Conference echoed the Politburo's September letter. It charged that the party's local leaders had avoided adopting a strong "class and mass line" and rebuked them for failing to establish links with other base areas. It attacked the guerrilla tactics of the Fourth Red Army. It charged that the land programs adopted by the Kiangsi and Fukien governments established in February 1930 were contaminated by both left and right opportunism, and specifically attacked Mao's February 7 land law on the grounds that equal distribution to all persons was a rich peasant line. It claimed that both the soviet government and the trade

---

almost immediately and may not have attended the First All-China Soviet Congress. He reportedly delivered a speech to a Moscow meeting of the Profintern at the end of 1931. The text of the speech is in *Krasnyi internatsional profsoiuzov*, Nos. 1–2 (1932), pp. 67–71, cited in McLane, p. 38*n*96. See also North, *Moscow*, p. 158; Mao, HC, III, 968; SW, IV, 185; Hsiao, p. 162.

union apparatus were filled with "class alien" elements and that the program of mass education against counterrevolutionaries carried on by the party apparatus was motivated by "narrow empiricism."[22] The Conference's "Resolution on Party Reconstruction" directed several of these charges against Mao himself, finding him guilty of narrow empiricism, "opportunistic pragmatism," and a "general ideological poverty." It reasserted the dogma that the agrarian revolution must be led by the proletariat.[23] In other words, it was the clear intent of the Conference that Mao's machine should be replaced by new cadres loyal to the 28 Bolsheviks. The "Resolution on the Red Army" rejected the idea that guerrilla warfare should be the mainstay of the army. The immediate aim of the Red Army, it declared, should be to organize revolutionary bases by taking urban areas in one or several provinces. This revived one of Li Li-san's basic ideas. The army should expand, adopt regular forms of warfare, and overcome the conservative notion of guerrillaism that had dominated its councils before 1931.[24] Guerrillaism in this context refers specifically to the Maoist tactics adopted at the Second Mao-ping Conference and the Lou-fang Conference—"luring the enemy to penetrate deep" into the base area.

Thus *all* charges Mao admits were brought against him by the 28 Bolsheviks were made immediately before the First All-China Soviet Congress, which convened on November 7.

The First All-China Soviet Congress

When the Congress convened, the 28 Bolsheviks did not have enough support in the soviet areas to overcome the Maoists; Mao was elected chairman of the Central Executive Committee of the all-China soviet government. He also managed to retain his position as chief political commissar of the First Front Red Army. Hsiang Ying, who had displaced Mao on the Central Bureau in March, was elected vice-chairman of the CEC (under Mao) and commissar for labor. Chang Kuo-t'ao, who was then in the O-yü-wan soviet, was elected second vice-chairman and commissar for justice. Chu Teh became first commissar for war. Ch'ü Ch'iu-pai, who had been expelled from the Central Committee and Politburo at the Fourth Plenum and who was still in hiding in Shanghai, was elected commissar for education. This post was actually filled by Hsü T'e-li, Mao's old teacher, until Ch'ü arrived in the soviet areas more than a year later. Chang Ting-ch'eng, who had been one of Mao's students in the Peasant Department Institute in Canton, was elected commissar for land. Teng Fa, who had been one of the leaders of the Fukien soviet before the arrival of the Politburo, became head of the police. Teng Tzu-hui, one of Mao's old friends, was elected commissar of finance. Ho Shu-heng, who had founded the Hunan Provincial Party with Mao, was elected chief of the Workers' and Peasants' Inspection. Chou I-li, whose provenance is unknown, took charge of the Interior Department.[f] Wang Chia-hsiang was the only one of the 28 Bolsheviks elected to any government position. He became commissar for foreign affairs, an honorary post whose sole functions were to conduct relations with the Comintern and make foreign visitors comfortable, should any arrive. Chou En-lai received no position in the government, although he ranked fourth on the CEC. Wang Ming and Shen Tse-min, neither of whom was present, were elected to the CEC, ranking thirteenth and twentieth on the list. Po Ku and Chang Wen-t'ien, who were there, were not elected to anything. To make his sympathies as clear as possible, Mao saw to it that the rightists Hsü Hsi-ken and Ch'en Yu and the Li Li-sanist Kuan Hsiang-ying, whom the Bolsheviks had expelled from the Central Committee, were elected to the CEC. Hsü outranked Wang Ming and Kuan outranked Shen. Ch'en Yu ranked below the three Bolsheviks elected to the committee, but even he ranked above several members of the new government, including Teng Tzu-hui, Ho Shu-heng, and Chou I-li.

The struggle at the November Party Conference had led almost inevitably to a deadlock. The Maoists had won control of the new soviet government and retained control of the First Front Red Army, but the 28 Bolsheviks still controlled the Politburo. The stage was set for a prolonged struggle between the Maoists and the party faction, or, as Mao delicately phrased it in RSQHP, the prolonged struggle against the third left line (of the Politburo).

In spite of the fact that the Maoists won control of the government, the delegates to the First Congress adopted the soviet constitution and, with minor alterations, the land law, labor law, and resolutions on the Red Army introduced by the Politburo. The alterations in the land law were obviously the work of the Maoist faction. In the final text, the interests of the middle peasants were more carefully protected than in the Politburo draft. If a majority of the middle peasants voted to exempt themselves from the land redistribution, they were not required to participate in it, regardless of the wishes of poor peasants and hired farm hands. The final version of the law also pro-

[f] Chou I-li disappeared before the Second All-China Soviet Congress in January 1934.

tected the interests of the rich peasants by providing that only their excess houses and farm implements should be confiscated, which was a more lenient provision than the Politburo's. This provision was important, since under the new law the rich peasants were to receive the less fertile land and were given the option of having it distributed to them on the basis of their labor power, which included houses, tools, and draft animals. If they could keep more tools and draft animals to cultivate the larger areas of poorer land, the old system of equal distribution (with everyone receiving equal portions of all grades of land) could still be approximated.[25]

An appendix spelling out the privileges of soldiers was added to the Politburo's draft resolution on the Red Army.[26] The Politburo's resolutions on economic policy and the Workers' and Peasants' Inspection may or may not have been passed by the Congress. At any rate, no final versions of these laws have yet come to light.

The Maoist faction won another victory, a great one, when in the last days of the Congress the Ning-tu Uprising occurred and 20,000 officers and men in the KMT's 28th Route Army revolted and came over to the Communists. This provided an excellent example of what might be done if the CCP did not impose on itself the limitations of the policy of a united front from below. The Congress ended in general rejoicing. Delegates from other soviet areas left for their home bases, and Po Ku, Chang Wen-t'ien, and most of the other Politburo members left for Shanghai. Mao, Hsiang Ying, and Chou En-lai remained in the new soviet capital at Jui-ching. The long trial of strength between the Maoists and the Comintern-Stalinist faction had begun.

The Conflict Deepens

One of the first clashes came at an enlarged conference of the Kiangsi Provincial Committee convened immediately after the Congress to discuss and vote on its decisions. The Maoists were very strong in this Committee. They had just completed an egalitarian distribution whereby rich peasants, small landlords, and poor peasants had received equal amounts of all grades of land, and they objected to being called on to reallocate the land to the advantage of the poor peasants, the disadvantage of the rich peasants, and the complete deprivation of the landlords. At the same time as they were asked to thus antagonize the landlords and rich peasants, they were also asked to send more men into the Red Army and to subordinate the previously independent guerrilla units to the regular chain of command, leaving reformed areas relatively undefended. These tasks were not only difficult; many comrades believed they were based on a faulty analysis of local conditions. Mao's reasoning in "Oppose Bookism" had bitten deeply into the consciousness of at least a few of the ruling clique in Kiangsi. Many believed that the Comintern and its agents knew all too little about class relations in Kiangsi and that their directives were completely unsuitable. But the reconstituted Central Bureau of the Politburo, now dominated by the 28 Bolsheviks, asserted that the class basis of the Kiangsi party was very weak. It included all too few genuine proletarians. Its class consciousness was unsteady. Many members, including the leaders, still persisted in the backward, peasant mentality that had characterized the Maoists ever since they had first formed their own faction in the Ching-kang Mountains. Although the Kiangsi Committee accepted the decisions of the Soviet Congress, it did so in such a spirit that the Central Bureau issued a sharp reproof for the Committee's display of pragmatism, narrow empiricism, and bureaucratic routinism, and the inadequate reorientation of its work along the lines prescribed by the Comintern.[27]

Early in 1932, a controversy developed between Mao and Chou En-lai over military strategy and the centralization of the Red Army. Mao continued to advocate mobile guerrilla tactics and the strategy of luring the enemy deep into the base area, where small, scattered enemy units would confront much larger contingents of Red troops. The basic strategy adopted by the Red Army under the political leadership of Chou En-lai after 1932 was to hold the base, fight positional warfare, and carry the fight into enemy territory rather than allow enemy troops to penetrate Red territory. Guerrilla tactics were considered useful, but only behind the enemy lines. Although Mao and Chou assisted each other in planning an assault on Kan-chow in January 1932, it was an unhappy and unfortunate collaboration: as a result of their tactical disagreements the Red Army failed to capture the city, which was strategically necessary to the control of all southern Kiangsi. After this unsuccessful attempt a Red Army expansion drive got under way and continued intermittently until September 1932.[28] Maoists in the soviet administration immediately found a reason why the army should not be expanded: peasants were busy in the fields and would fight better when they had nothing to do at home. This argument, of course, reveals a "peasant mentality" at odds with the Comintern's attitude at that time. Local army recruiters in the soviet administrations dragged their feet and slowed down the army expansion drive in June and July, so at the Ning-tu Conference

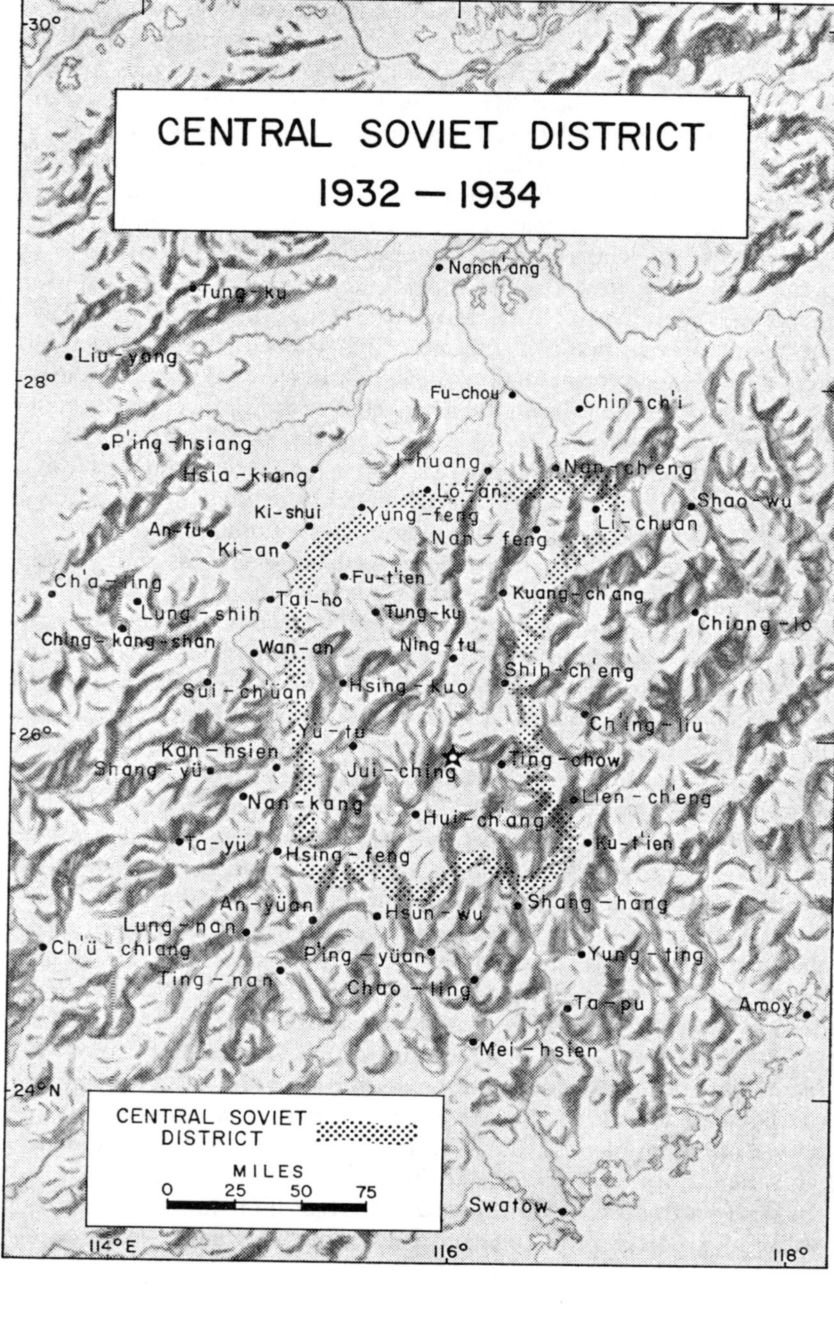
CENTRAL SOVIET DISTRICT
1932 — 1934
Nanch'ang
Tung-ku
Liu-yang
Fu-chou
Chin-ch'i
P'ing-hsiang
Hsia-kiang
I-huang
Nan-ch'eng
Lo-an
Shao-wu
Ki-shui
Yung-feng
Li-chuan
An-fu
Ki-an
Nan-feng
Fu-t'ien
Ch'a-ling
Tai-ho
Kuang-ch'ang
Lung-shih
Tung-ku
Chiang-lo
Ching-kang-shan
Wan-an
Ning-tu
Shih-ch'eng
Sui-ch'üan
Hsing-kuo
Ch'ing-liu
Yü-tu
Kan-hsien
Shang-yü
Jui-ching
Ting-chow
Nan-kang
Lien-ch'eng
Hui-ch'ang
Ta-yü
Ku-t'ien
Hsing-feng
An-yüan
Shang-hang
Hsun-wu
Lung-nan
Ch'ü-chiang
P'ing-yüan
Yung-ting
Ting-nan
Chao-ling
Ta-pu
Amoy
Mei-hsien
Swatow
CENTRAL SOVIET DISTRICT
MILES
0 25 50 75
30°
28°
26°
24°N
114°E
116°
118°

in August Chou took the offensive and forced Mao off the Military Committee of the Central Bureau.[29] From that time onward Mao devoted himself to work in the government, although Chou did not publicly replace him as chief political commissar of the Red Armies until May 1933.

Throughout this debate over centralization and expansion of the Red Army Mao also took issue with the Politburo over the form of the united front. After the Japanese attack on Shanghai in January 1932 he advocated the formation of a coalition government, a united army made up of all existing armies willing to fight the Japanese, and a new volunteer army of armed workers and peasants.[30] Perhaps under pressure from Moscow, the Politburo insisted that all reformist groups were enemies and that all the imperialists were about to unite to attack the Soviet Union. Under these circumstances the Red Army had to be expanded as rapidly as possible in order to achieve victory in one or several provinces before the imperialist attack on the Soviet Union commenced. Only in this way would it be possible for the CCP to come to the defense of the Soviet Union and participate in the final attack on world capitalism. This, the Politburo's view, was a sublime, utopian, apocalyptic vision of the future role of the CCP. The only difficulty with this strategy, according to a recent Communist historian, was that it was based on a complete misunderstanding of the world situation and of the balance of political forces in China. The Maoist policy, however difficult its implementation, would have been much more useful to the CCP in the long run.[31]

As the debate in the inner circle became more furious, Mao, Chu Teh, and Hsiang Ying on April 5, 1932, issued a declaration of war against the Japanese government in the name of the central government of the Chinese soviet republic. The party issued no statement of encouragement. Instead, from that date until August 1, 1935, the soviet government (sometimes in association with the Red Army) and the Politburo issued separate policy statements on the war against Japan and the form of the united front.[32] In other words, the issue was not settled until Mao took over the central party organs at Tsunyi. In the meantime the soviet government followed Mao's line and the 28 Bolsheviks, bound to Moscow by ties of interest and power, followed that of the Comintern.

Learning from the Mistakes of the CCP

By 1932 the Comintern line could be summed up under three simple headings: a struggle on two fronts with the right deviation as the main danger in every section of the Comintern, a united front with the masses against all rival elites of whatever political persuasion, and a subordination of the struggle for power of all Communist parties to the essential task of protecting the Soviet Union—the stern fatherland of the proletariat. In the Maoist reconstruction of history, this was the third left line. As the leader of the 28 Bolsheviks, Wang Ming was assigned the task of applying this line to the Chinese revolution and analyzing deviations in the CCP. He wrote his first major analysis, *The Two Lines,* immediately after the Fourth Plenum. In March 1932 he republished it in Moscow with a new title, *Struggle for the More Complete Bolshevization of the CCP,* adding in a long appendix an analysis of the deviations of leaders in the soviet areas.

RSQHP is a reply to this appendix from the perspective of 1945. Point by point, Mao attacks Wang's theses on five major problems: the intermediate camp or third group, proletarian as opposed to peasant consciousness, the consequences of the Fourth Plenum's line on old and new cadres (the reform of party organs), the capture of large cities, and the struggle on two fronts within the party.

The Intermediate Camp

In both the first edition and the Appendix of *The Two Lines,* Wang criticized the Li Li-sanists and others for failing to realize that all capitalist bourgeois reformers were counterrevolutionary. He insisted that in the stage the Chinese revolution was then in the party should not differentiate between various groups of capitalists and should struggle equally against all imperialists and their agents in China. The party must therefore attack both landlords and rich peasants in the villages and all strata of the bourgeoisie in the cities, for both capitalists and feudal remnants were allied with counterrevolutionary imperialism.

In RSQHP Mao charged that this line had led to the failure to find and use temporary allies. At the time it was being followed, he said, some capitalists and bourgeois reformers had been willing to cooperate with the Communists against the KMT, the CCP's main political and military enemy. This had been especially true after the Japanese invasion of Manchuria.[33] The failure to obtain allies, Mao charged, arose out of the blind inattention of the 28 Bolsheviks to the real situation in China. Their line exaggerated the importance of capitalism in the Chinese economy, and therefore led to insistence on a struggle directed mainly against Chinese capitalists.[34] By exaggerating the necessity of fighting capitalism, the 28 Bolsheviks had overlooked the immediate targets—imperialism and feudalism. Denying the existence of the "third group" or "intermediate camp," they failed to devise workable agrarian policies of their own, and also rejected the provisions for dealing with rich peasants in Mao's February 7 land law. In the face of the Japanese invasion of Manchuria, they had refused to recognize that one imperialist power was more dangerous to China than others. They had refused to form a tactical alliance with the Fukien rebels in 1933 simply because the rebels, though willing to cooperate with the Communists against the KMT and the Japanese, were essentially Chinese capitalists and bourgeois reformers. In the eyes of the 28 Bolsheviks, capitalists and bourgeois reformers were an inseparable part of world imperialism in the "third period," and were therefore the "most dangerous enemies" of the CCP.[35]

Proletarian as Opposed to Peasant Consciousness

In considering the problem of the uneven development of the Chinese revolution, Wang denounced the idea that the peasantry has an unusual revolutionary character in colonial and semicolonial countries, as well as the idea that the peasants could play an independent revolutionary role.[36] He laid heavy emphasis on the leading role of the proletariat and censured CCP members who made light of their role in the Chinese revolution by overstressing that of the peasantry.[37] Mao had been warned against belittling the proletariat when he had been removed from all his party posts in November 1927. Wang reiterated the warning in his pamphlet.

RSQHP pointed out that Wang had erroneously objected to Mao's theory of the "unusual revolutionary character of the peasantry," as well as to his practice of inner-party struggle in defending it.[38] As a result, Wang attacked Mao as a representative of "peasant consciousness" in the party. "Peasant consciousness" had entered the vocabulary of the CCP when Li Li-san had borrowed the term from Stalin's denunciation of A. P. Smirnov for his defense of the interests of the Russian peasants. It was used by the Southwest Kiangsi leaders in their attack on Mao's views immediately before the Fu-t'ien incident; it was used by the A-B Corps; and it was later repeated by the 28 Bolsheviks. Such repetition is excellent testimony to Mao's consistent defense of the revolutionary virtues of the peasantry.

The Reform of Party Organs

In *The Two Lines* Wang claimed that only after the complete reorganization of the party leadership at all levels, the reformation of the Red Army, and the transformation of all party work in the soviet areas would it be possible to defeat the KMT's Fourth Campaign (June 1932–March 1933).[39] RSQHP, on the other hand, held that only the persisting influence of Mao's strategic thinking in the Red Army command had made that defeat possible. The reorganization of the party leadership in the soviet areas (of mid-1933), accomplished when the 28 Bolsheviks gained control of both the party and the army there, had resulted in the utter defeat of the Red Army and the evacuation of the soviet areas at the end of the KMT's Fifth Campaign (October 1933–October 1934).[40] Mao maintained that when positional warfare had replaced his guerrilla strategy, defeat had become inevitable.

The Capture of Large Cities

Wang's attitude toward the capture of large cities changed between the appearance of the first edition of *The Two Lines* and the Moscow edition published one year later. In the first edition the Red Army's capture of Ch'angsha in July 1930 was cited as the point at which Li Li-san turned from right opportunism to putschism. In the Moscow edition Wang admitted that attacking Ch'angsha might have been a mistake at the time, but argued that the failure to hold it did not warrant the conclusion that "key cities should not be taken anyway." He urged that the Red Army be built into a regular army big enough to capture and hold large cities.[41] It was this line that Chou En-lai adopted and employed to expel Mao from the Political Commissariat of the Red Army at the Ning-tu Conference.

According to RSQHP, the Maoists were of the opinion that the principal difference between Li Li-san and the 28 Bolsheviks lay in the fact that although Li desired the help of the Red Army in taking large cities, in the last phase of his line (June–September 1930) he continued to depend heavily on urban workers' uprisings, which the Red Army was to assist, but not to initiate. The 28 Bolsheviks, on the other hand, wanted to use the Red Army to seize the industrial centers directly, with little or no help from the organized workers' movement or the urban CCP organizations.[42] This was a late development in the Bolshevik line; it came only in 1932. The Comintern officials Mif, Magyar, and Kuusinen, under the direction of the CPSU Central Committee, undoubtedly helped Wang work it out after his return to Moscow in 1931. Mao opposed both versions of Wang's views on the taking of large cities.

The Struggle on Two Fronts Within the Party

In the 1931 edition of his pamphlet, Wang implied that the left aspects of the Li Li-san line were attributable to Lominadze's influence and its right aspects to the influence of Borodin and Ch'en Tu-hsiu. In the 1932 edition Wang stressed that the right deviation had been the main danger under Li's regime and continued to be so even after the collapse of the Li Li-san line. Wang's critique of the rightists in the party was directed chiefly against "certain people" in the soviet areas who, misinterpreting the policy of the Central Committee, perceived the policy of consolidating the base areas as a "retreat line." These people did not hope to capture large cities at all and refused to believe that the conditions would soon develop under which urban centers could be taken. Finally, when the enemy attacked they resorted to "retreat," "flight," or "escape" toward the center of the base areas.

In his counterattack on Wang's ideas in 1945, Mao wrote that while Wang *had* criticized the Li Li-san line's left aspects, in the main he had attacked its right aspects.[43] Mao did not mention that Wang criticized the left aspects of Li Li-sanism in 1931, or that the struggle against its right aspects really began only after Wang's return to Moscow and the publication there of the 1932 Appendix. According to Mao, the 28 Bolsheviks attempted to discredit all those who doubted the wisdom or practicability of their line, or who executed it half-heartedly. Such people they labeled "right opportunists," "two-faced persons," and advocates of the "rich peasant line" or the "compromising line." They were attacked not as comrades, but as criminals and enemies. After the Politburo moved to the central soviet districts in 1932, all of these errors were identified with the proponents of the "Lo Ming line."[44] The position of the Maoist faction was undermined in the assault on the Lo Ming line, and Mao himself was placed on probation for persisting in his errors.

The Attack on the Maoists: The Second Phase

In late 1932 or early 1933, Po Ku, Chang Wen-t'ien, Wang Chia-hsiang, and the other members of the Politburo who had previously been in Shanghai arrived in Jui-ching. They were accompanied by a Comintern military adviser, a German known as Li T'e.[g] With his assistance they began their struggle to replace the right-wing Maoists in the party and army with men more willing to submit to orders, place their trust in Comintern analyses, and take the protection of the Soviet Union as the pivot around which all strategic planning of civil

[g] In March 1964, an article appeared in the East German daily *Neues Deutschland* in which the author, one Otto Braun, identified himself as Li T'e. He also used the aliases "Wagner" (by his own testimony) and "Albert" (according to Hsiao, p. 331).

and class warfare in China must revolve. The program the Central Committee was then advocating bore a remarkable resemblance to the Li Li-san line. In accordance with Wang Ming's analysis, the Committee concluded that the mistakes that had been made at Ch'angsha did not warrant the deduction that large cities were not to be taken. The Red Army should be expanded to that end, as Wang had recommended.[45] After the Twelfth Plenum of the ECCI had confirmed Wang's judgment in September 1932, the CCP and the soviet government had begun preparing in the soviet areas for an all-out offensive against the cities.[46] Economic mobilization conferences were called immediately. In early 1933 a land investigation drive was started and preparations begun to elect delegates to the second All-China Soviet Congress.[47]

The Lo Ming Line

A year after Chou En-lai had deposed Mao from his position as chief political commissar of the Red Army, the Politburo arrived to renew the attack on Mao and his supporters. The emergence of the Lo Ming line provided an occasion for a reorganization of the military leadership. Lo Ming was one of the old commanders in the Fukien base who continued to follow the military strategy Chu and Mao had devised on Ching-kang-shan even in 1933. In February of that year, with the backing of the Comintern, the Politburo had ordered the Red Army expanded to a million men, the incorporation of all local militia into the regular army, and a general mobilization of all economic resources.[48] Lo Ming opposed this "Bolshevik forward and offensive line," and in face of the almost complete identity of the new official line with that of Li Li-san, a number of Maoists supported him.

Rather naturally, those who resisted the new line were strongest in guerrilla areas that had never become firmly consolidated bases. Party and army units in the Kiangsi-Fukien and Kiangsi-Kwangtung border regions, and in border hsien in Kiangsi—such as Nan-feng, Kuan-ch'ang, I-huang, Lo-an, Yung-feng, Chi-shui, T'ai-ho, Hui-ch'ang, Hsün-wu and An-yüan—all contributed their quota of Lo Ming partisans.[49] According to an article printed in *Struggle* in July 1933, T'an Ch'en-lin, who had been one of the members of Mao's Front Committee in the Ching-kang Mountains, was then a follower of the Lo Ming line. At that time he was in charge of the party units in the Red Army in Fukien. He is now vice-minister of rural work in the People's Government. According to the same article, four men in the army and party leadership in Kiangsi also supported the Lo Ming line. These were Mao Tse-t'an, Mao Tse-tung's brother; Ku Po, who had helped Mao engineer the Fu-t'ien incident; Hsieh Wei-chün, who had also worked closely with Mao at the time of the incident; and Teng Hsiao-p'ing, who was supporting the Chu-Mao line among the troops on the Kwangtung border. Ku Po and Hsieh Wei-chün disappear from history at about this time. Mao Tse-t'an survived for a time, but was left behind when the Long March began and was captured and executed with Ch'ü Ch'iu-pai in March 1935. Teng is now secretary-general of the CCP. Other men attacked for supporting the Lo Ming line were Teng Tzu-hui, Hsiao Ching-kuang, Ch'en T'an-ch'iu, Yü Tse-hung, Li Shao-chiu, and Yang Wen-chung.[50] The first three survived, Teng and Ch'en to become members of the Central Committee in 1945 and Hsiao to be elected an alternate. Yü Tse-hung, Li Shao-chiu, and Yang Wen-chung disappeared. That those who survived attack as adherents of the Lo Ming line were promoted to high positions after Mao took over the party clearly indicates that they were his supporters.

The Land Investigation Drive

While the campaign against the Lo Ming line led to a purge of Communists working in the Red Army and the other military organizations of the soviet government, the need for money to pay for the expansion of the Red Army led to a change in peasant policy and to a new land investigation drive. The Politburo prepared for this drive in May by calling an enlarged meeting of party cadres in Jui-ching. Kung Ch'u has reported that Chou En-lai opened the meeting by announcing that the party had decided to alter its peasant policy. Henceforth the CCP was to eliminate the landlords entirely, attack the rich peasants, neutralize the middle peasants, and ally itself only with the poor peasants and landless laborers. Landlords were to be herded into camps and all their property confiscated. Rich peasants were to be penalized by extra taxes that would be used to enlarge the army and thus contribute to the protection of the Soviet Union. Kung Ch'u and Ho Ch'ang, who was an old Li Li-sanist, spoke in opposition to these new measures. Chou then announced that the new policy was supported by the Comintern. Kung and Ho continued to argue against it, supported by a majority of those present. They argued that the Russian policy of dividing the peasants into rich, middle, and poor was not valid in China. Some of the "poor" peasants of Russia were richer even than some Chinese landlords. Chou again invoked

Comintern authority and finally achieved a reluctant majority. When the meeting was over, Hsiang Ying took Kung home to dinner and told him that under the circumstances it was unwise for him to defend his position so vociferously. Kung replied that the CCP still operated under democratic centralism and that he had every right to voice his dissent until a decision had been reached. But Kung realized at this time that in fact the system had changed—the majority of elected party representatives had been coerced by the Comintern rather than allowed to make decisions on the basis of free debate.[h]

On June 1, Mao launched the land investigation drive. In his view the drive was necessary to support the war effort, but was not to be allowed to alienate a large proportion of the peasants and thereby narrow the base of popular support in the soviet areas. It was to correct inequities in the previous land distributions, not initiate a new policy altogether.[51] The Central Bureau directive to party cadres in the soviet government issued one day later attributed the failure of the soviet government to solve the land problem in the past to Mao's incorrect, egalitarian line.[52] Conflict between the adherents of the two lines was soon apparent. Kung Ch'u was recalled to Jui-ching in August, and Chou En-lai, in the presence of Li Teh, Po Ku, and Chu Teh, suspended Kung's membership in the CCP for six months.[53] Many of the lower-level cadres who still supported Mao and his land policy suffered similar fates before the end of the drive that autumn.

The situation had become very tense by November, when the KMT armies were again closing in on the central soviet district, in their Fifth Encirclement Campaign. The Red Army had suffered heavy losses, and a scarcity of salt had caused a great deal of illness. Then the outbreak of the Fukien revolt suddenly gave the Red Army a chance to reach the coast through the territory of a friendly government.

The Fukien Revolt

On November 20, 1933, the KMT's Nineteenth Route Army, commanded by Ch'en Ming-shu, revolted in Fukien. The following day the rebels called a "provincial conference of delegates of the Chinese people" in Fuchow. Hoping to negotiate an agreement, delegates from the Nineteenth Route Army had contacted Communist representatives in Shanghai before the revolt. The Shanghai Communists asked Moscow for advice and were instructed to cooperate with the

[h] Kung returned to his post an unhappy man. In December 1934, as the Long March began, he deserted from the Red Army.

rebels on a military but not a party basis. They might work with the rebels against both the Japanese and the Nanking government of Chiang Kai-shek, but were to continue to criticize the political line of the Third Party and left KMT members of the rebel government. On October 26, 1933, a military alliance was concluded between the central soviet government and the Red Army on the one hand, and the Fukien provincial government and the Nineteenth Route Army on the other. Although the content of the agreement probably did not go beyond Moscow's instructions, the fact that a political agent representing the Chinese soviet government had signed the agreement in that government's name undoubtedly did.[54]

Throughout the Fukien revolt the Central Bureau attacked the Fukien rebels as sham democrats and simple military conspirators who were akin to the European Social Democrats. In contrast, telegrams from Chu and Mao expressed cautious hope that the Fukien rebels and the Red Army could work out a genuine basis for cooperation and that the rebel leaders would grant freedom to the people of Fukien. The soviet government and the CCP Central Committee issued no joint statements about either the revolt or the anti-Japanese united front in Fukien.[55] As the Second All-China Soviet Congress convened in Jui-ching, the revolt in Fukien was put down by troops loyal to Nanking. By January 20 it had collapsed. After the opportunity for the CCP to form a united front with a friendly army had passed, Mao joined the Politburo in denouncing the rebels.

The Second All-China Soviet Congress

In spite of the continuing attacks on the Maoist faction in the party, the Red Army, and the soviet government from 1931 to 1934, Mao was reelected as chairman of the soviet government in January 1934. The 28 Bolsheviks intended him to serve only as a figurehead, however, playing the role of Kalinin to Po Ku's Stalin. To this end they rearranged the power structure of the all-China soviet government. At the First Congress Mao had been elected chairman of both the Central Executive Committee and the Council of People's Commissars. No one had shared his power, not even his two vice-chairmen, for Chang Kuo-t'ao was not present in the central soviet areas and Hsiang Ying was, at least by reputation, a weak and incapable man. After the change in 1934, however, the Central Executive Committee was led by a 17-member Presidium that had the power to elect the chairman from among its own members. The 28 Bolsheviks probably had a majority of the Presidium on their side and therefore could afford to elect Mao: they could always depose him if he proved uncooperative. Meanwhile, Chang Wen-t'ien became chairman of the Council of People's Commissars, with no deputies or presidium to control him. Chang became the equivalent of the premier of the government, with almost unlimited power, while Mao held the honorary and essentially powerless post of chairman of the Central Executive Committee.[56] If Mao was playing Kalinin, Chang was Molotov.

At the Second All-China Soviet Congress, Mao delivered a report on the activities of the Central Executive Committee and the Council of People's Commissars. If the usual Communist practice was followed, the text of this speech had previously been approved by the Fifth Plenum of the Central Committee, held immediately before the Second Congress. Only the part of this report dealing with economic policy is found in HC.[57] After a short floor discussion of his official report, Mao made some concluding remarks. About one quarter of the text of these remarks, the part that seems to express his own views, is included in HC. His remarks on the attitudes of the party and government toward the Fukien rebellion are not included, but his attack on the 28 Bolsheviks' bureaucratic methods of leadership is, as is his defense of the work of his own supporters, some of whom had been purged in the drive against the Lo Ming line.[58] He first stressed the fact on which all were in agreement: that the work of mobilizing the masses for revolutionary war was the CCP's central task. But, he stated, before the masses could be effectively mobilized the party and government must provide for them the minimum necessities of life. He pointed with pride to the way the comrades in Chang-kang and Tsai-ki hsiang had solved urgent problems facing the people, and he condemned the work of the comrades in Ting-chow for failing to do the same.[59]

Ting-chow, Fukien, was one of the largest cities then held by the Communists. It is highly probable that the 28 Bolsheviks dominated its soviet government. Chang-kang and Tsai-ki may have been strongholds of the Maoist faction: the evidence is incomplete, but the available facts point toward that conclusion. Chang-kang was in Hsing-kuo, Kiangsi, and Tsai-ki in Shang-hang, Fukien. Both Hsing-kuo and Shang-hang were model hsien created by their respective soviet governments shortly after the First All-China Soviet Congress in 1931, in the period before the 28 Bolsheviks gained control of the leading organs of the soviet governments. As discussed above, Mao's investigation at the end of October 1930 had uncovered small nests of A-B Corpsmen in the hsiang and ch'ü soviets of Hsing-kuo.[60] In the aftermath of the Fu-t'ien incident, Mao's faction had wiped out all local opposition and achieved firm control over this area. Shang-hang had a similar history; there the alleged A-B Corps had been obliterated slightly later than in Hsing-kuo.[61] In defending himself, Lo Ming had specifically mentioned Shang-hang as an area in which he thought the Chu-Mao guerrilla tactics should continue to be used in fighting the enemy. One of Lo Ming's closest associates and fellow purgees, Yang Wen-chung, had also been active in Shang-hang in 1933.[62]

In his concluding remarks, Mao defended and praised the Communists working in Hsing-kuo and Shang-hang. He also praised the Communists who had been successfully utilizing guerrilla tactics against the encircling KMT troops and were therefore doubtful of the applicability to their particular areas of the Central Committee's forward line.[63]

It is not possible to show that Mao's henchmen had been dominant in *all* the areas he singled out for praise, or that members of his faction had been persecuted with particular vigor in some of the places he condemned, but the evidence points in that direction. Those who attended the congress, however, knew the areas in which each faction had been dominant. Certainly they understood the import of where Mao's praise and blame fell.

The Nadir of Mao's Fortunes

As the summer of 1934 approached, the Politburo continued along its suicidal course. The land investigation drive, which had been halted in September or October 1933, recommenced. A new recruitment drive began. And the Bolsheviks and the Maoists began to destroy one another in a fight for their very existence. Mao was put on probation: he was excluded from party meetings and either imprisoned or kept under house arrest at Yü-tu, a hsien capital some 60 miles west of the Communist capital of Jui-ching. According to Kung Ch'u, the order to place Mao on probation originated in Moscow and resulted from his actions during the Fukien rebellion. The Moscow order followed the adoption of a new line by the Thirteenth Plenum of the ECCI in December 1933 that called on all Communists to support the fight against fascism—the united front from below. The new line emphasized in particular the struggle against Social Democrats, who were known at the time as "social fascists."[64]

Thus from sometime in July 1934 until the beginning of the Long March in October Mao was stripped of power, on probation, and probably imprisoned. He had arrived at this sorry state thanks to the combined efforts of Po Ku in Jui-ching and Wang Ming in Moscow. Mao's description of the organizational procedures of the party's leaders in 1934 is graphic, bitter, and accurate. Very few anti-Communists have written more revealing descriptions of the struggles at party meetings during the first year of the great purges. Irrespective of circumstances, he said in RSQHP, the exponents of the third left line

> invariably attached . . . damaging labels to all comrades in the party who, finding the erroneous line impracticable, expressed doubts about it, disagreed with it, resented it, supported it only lukewarmly, or executed it only halfheartedly. Labels like "right opportunism," "line of the rich peasants," "Lo Ming's line," "line of conciliation," and "double-dealing" [were used, for the leftists] waged "relentless struggles" against [their opponents] as if . . . they were criminals and enemies. Instead of regarding the veteran cadres as valuable assets to the party, the sectarians persecuted, punished, and deposed large numbers of these veterans in the central and local organizations. . . . Large numbers of good comrades were wrongly indicted and unjustly punished; this led to the most lamentable losses inside the party.[65]

Amends should be made, he said. "Comrades who upon investigation are proved to have died as victims of a miscarriage of justice should be absolved from false accusations, reinstated as party members, and forever remembered by all comrades."[66]

He went on to recall the memory of four comrades who had died at the hands of the KMT. Three had been captured in January 1931, in the raid supposedly engineered by Wang Ming to destroy the group in the CCP attempting to organize opposition to the 28 Bolsheviks. These were Li Ch'iu-shih, who had worked in the CCP's Propaganda Department in 1927–28, Lin Yü-nan, director of the Wuhan Labor Union Secretariat and secretary-general of the All-China Federation of Trade Unions in 1927–28, and Ho Meng-hsiung, leader of the Kiangsu Provincial Committee and a secretary to its Peasant Department in 1927. The other was Ch'ü Ch'iu-pai, who was left behind at the beginning of the Long March. Ch'ü had been the major opponent of the 28 Bolsheviks before their seizure of power. The Fourth Plenum had permanently ended his successful career, although he survived and continued to work in the party for four years more.[67] In choosing to revive the memory of these men and posthumously reinstate them as party members, Mao challenged the legitimacy of the power and authority of the 28 Bolsheviks, and thereby of the Comintern apparatus that had supported their pretensions. He intimated that the Bolsheviks had seized power by double-dealing, by betraying comrades to the enemy police even before the first Russian Communist had been shot for meeting secretly with Trotsky.

It is no wonder Mao wrote that the Bolsheviks' struggles in the Chinese party had "violated the fundamental principle of democratic centralism, eliminated the democratic spirit of criticism and self-criticism, turned party discipline into mechanical regulation, fostered tendencies toward blind obedience and parrotry, and thus jeopardized and obstructed the development of vigorous and creative Marxism."[68]

Learning from the Mistakes of the CPSU

By the time the Red Armies set out on the Long March, Mao had every reason to feel a deep repugnance for Stalinist methods of controlling non-Soviet parties. In 1931, when Mao was at the height of his power, after he had overcome his opponents in southwestern Kiangsi and successfully led the Red Armies against the first three KMT campaigns of encirclement and annihilation, the 28 Bolsheviks had begun their struggle against his ideas on political and military strategy. By 1934, with the support of the Comintern, they had removed him and his most active supporters from all influential positions in the party, army, and government. They had rejected and condemned his agrarian and military policies and replaced them with policies modeled after the practice of the Soviet government and the CPSU. In implementing their "further bolshevization of the CCP" they had adopted the terroristic policies of the Soviet political police and anticipated in the small soviet districts of South China the great purges in the Soviet Union.

When the Maoist faction took control of the Party Secretariat and the Revolutionary Military Council at the Tsun-yi Conference in January 1935, its only justification was that the strategy of the 28 Bolsheviks had proved itself a dismal failure.[69] The statement of Mao's strategic formulae in terms of Marxist categories still lay in the future. But the protection of the Soviet Union would no longer be the primary purpose of the CCP and the Chinese Red Army. Instead of attempting to copy the Russian Bolshevik model, the party, under Mao, set out to create for itself a strategy based on the requirements of the Chinese revolution.

CHAPTER XII

The Maoist Reconstruction of the Party

On October 15, 1934, one hundred thousand men and thirty-five women gathered around Jui-ching in preparation for the evacuation of the central soviet district. Eighty thousand men were army regulars; twenty thousand were government and party cadres. The women were wives of the highest party and government functionaries. All the other men who had wives and children left them behind. The thirty-five important leaders who took their wives with them, however, were not spared entirely the agonies of separation from dear ones. All their children too young to march were left behind in the care of peasant families. Although prolonged and painstaking searches were carried out when the area was reoccupied by the People's Liberation Army in 1949, not one of these children has ever been reclaimed. Mao himself left two children behind. These were Communists and dedicated revolutionaries, but they were also human, and the bitterness of that departure echoes in the controversies among them even now.[1]

The exodus followed a year of frustrating defeats. Chiang Kai-shek had launched the fifth and last encirclement and annihilation campaign against the soviet districts in October 1933. Interrupted by the revolt of the Nineteenth Route Army in Fukien, the campaign continued after that revolt was suppressed in late January 1934. Encircling the whole of the central soviet district with blockhouses and using a force of five hundred thousand men, the Nationalists had drawn a tight ring around the soviet area. The Red Army was neither large enough nor well enough armed to withstand this assault. Early in the year, as has been discussed, Mao and some of his military supporters had urged that the Red Army should break through the encirclement, split into small units, and fight a guerrilla war in the plains to the north and east of the Nationalist lines. Li T'e rejected this strategy as guerrillaism, insisting that the Red Army must defend the base in the same way the KMT attacked it—with positional warfare, complete with trenches and blockhouses. The Red Army followed this strategy throughout the first half of 1934, but it could not withstand the overwhelming force the Nationalists brought to bear. In April the Red Army lost Kuang-ch'ang, its key fortification north of Jui-ching; by midsummer the Communists held only six hsien. To break through the KMT lines now became imperative if the whole Red Army was not to be annihilated. The army was slowly being crushed. Its greatest success all year was a negative one, when Fang Chih-min's Anti-Japanese Vanguard broke through the enemy lines in July. Under Li T'e, the Revolutionary Military Council continued to reject Mao's guerrilla strategy even after these massive defeats. Instead, it decided that the main forces of the Red Army should break through the encirclement as a united force. Defense of soviet territory to the last man had become opportunistic.

By September there were only 126,000 men left in the Red Army, 20,000 of whom were wounded. All the wounded, and 6,000 others, were to be left behind to harass the Nationalists during the evacuation of the main force. Few were expected to survive.

Li T'e was the man chiefly responsible for organizing the evacuation, which he carried on with the assistance of Po Ku, who acted as his interpreter. As the new premier of the soviet government, Chang Wen-t'ien gave the first public notice of the impending emergency in an article published in *Red Flag* on October 1. When the evacuation began, the members of the Revolutionary Military Council were Chou En-lai, Teng Fa, Chu Teh, Yeh Chien-ying, and Wang Chia-hsiang. Chou replaced Chu as chairman of the Council immediately before the orders were given to evacuate the base. Chu was the only Maoist on the Council; Chou and Yeh were leaders of the Whampoa cadet faction. Teng was in charge of a police force whose independent powers endangered the life of any Red Army commander who dissented from the prevailing line. His men had guarded Mao when he was under house arrest in Yü-tu. Wang Chia-hsiang represented the 28 Bolsheviks. In fact, the Military Council appears to have been subordinated to Li T'e, who, following the principle of one-man direction in battle, took on himself the responsibility for command of the retreating army.

Many of Mao's old friends and supporters were left behind in command of the troops who were to defend the base. The main exception was Hsiang Ying, the first representative of the Politburo to arrive in the soviet districts after the Fourth Plenum and probably one of Mao's rivals for power throughout the whole soviet period. He was

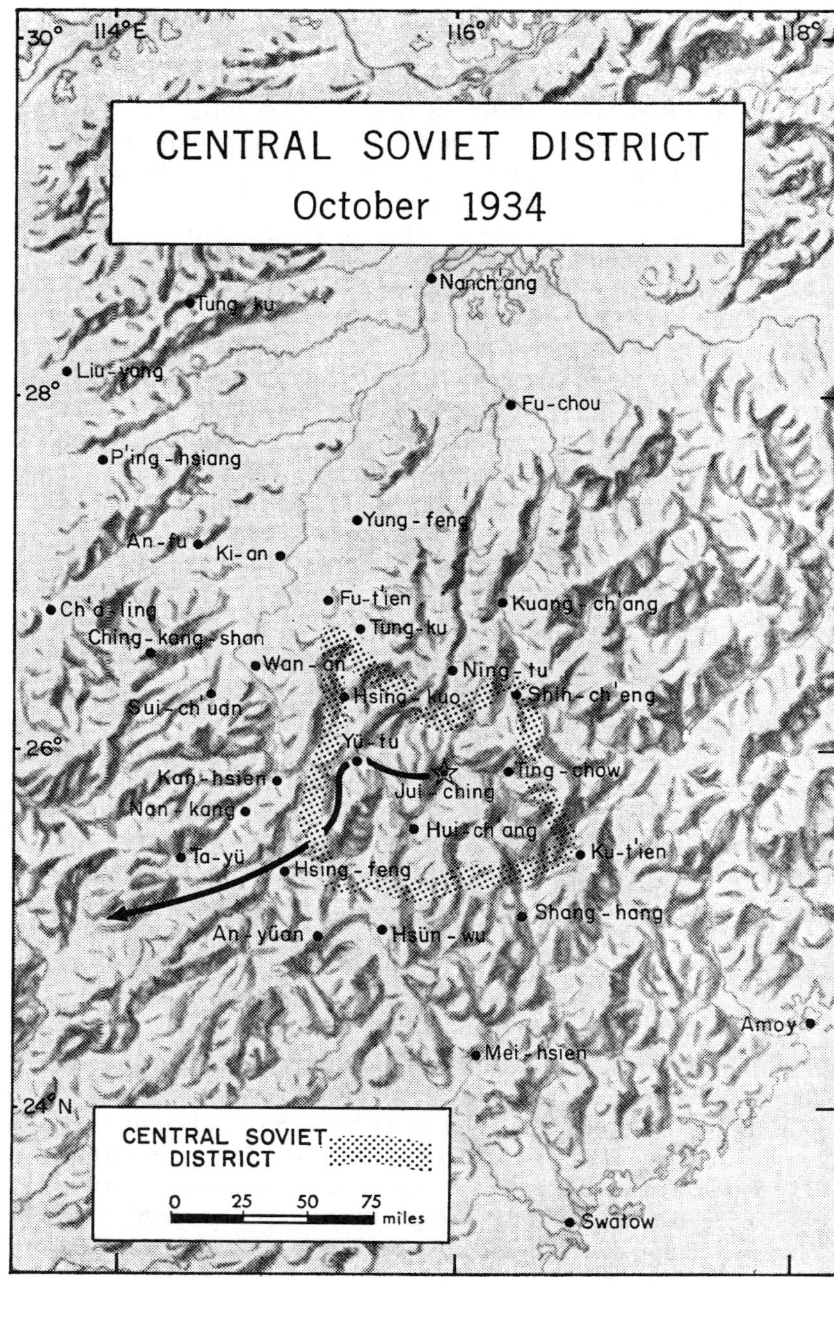
CENTRAL SOVIET DISTRICT
October 1934
30°
114°E
116°
118°
28°
26°
24°N
Nanch'ang
Tung-ku
Liu-yang
Fu-chou
P'ing-hsiang
Yung-feng
An-fu
Ki-an
Fu-t'ien
Ch'a-ling
Kuang-ch'ang
Tung-ku
Ching-kang-shan
Wan-an
Ning-tu
Hsing-kuo
Shih-ch'eng
Sui-ch'uan
Yü-tu
Ting-chow
Kan-hsien
Jui-ching
Nan-kang
Hui-ch'ang
Ta-yü
Ku-t'ien
Hsing-feng
Shang-hang
An-yüan
Hsün-wu
Amoy
Mei-hsien
CENTRAL SOVIET DISTRICT
0
25
50
75
miles
Swatow

appointed commander-in-chief of the remaining troops. Almost all the other major figures left behind can be identified as Maoists. Among them were Fang Chih-min, the peasant organizer who had supported Mao at the Ku-t'ien Conference, and Su Yü, Fang's chief of staff. Fang was then in command of the Anti-Japanese Vanguard Unit that had fought its way out of the base in August 1934. He was captured and executed by the KMT in 1935; Su is now on the Central Committee.[2] Ch'en Yi, chief of the Political Department, Kung Ch'u, Hsiang's chief of staff, and T'an Chen-lin, chief of the security police, had all been with Mao in Ching-kang-shan. Others left behind were Ho Shu-heng, who had helped Mao found the Hunanese CCP; Hsiao Hua, who had been in the New People's Study Society; Fang Fang and Chang Ting-ch'eng, who had studied under Mao at the KMT Peasant Institute in 1926; Liu Hsiao, Chang Yün-yi, and Ku Ta-ts'un, peasant guerrilla leaders who had been in Ching-kang-shan or had joined Mao during his first year in Fukien; Ch'en Cheng-jen, a member of Mao's November 1928 Front Committee; Teng Tzu-hui, who had been expelled from the CEC the previous year for supporting Mao in the Lo Ming period; and Ch'ü Ch'iu-pai, who had been expelled from the Politburo at the Fourth Plenum and then remained in hiding in Shanghai for two years before coming to the soviet area—these men were ordered to remain in the base area. At the time it definitely appeared that those who marched stood a greater chance of surviving than those who remained behind. Ho and Ch'ü were captured and shot by the KMT within the year. Kung Ch'u, oppressed by the security regime instituted by the 28 Bolsheviks, deserted the Red Army and fled to Hong Kong before the Tsun-yi Conference. The few others listed here survived to become leaders of the New Fourth Army organized in 1937, thus strengthening the Maoist faction in the guerrilla bases behind the Japanese lines. All those who survived the Anti-Japanese War became members of the Central Committee in 1945.

The 28 Bolsheviks and the Whampoa cadet faction dominated the party and army when the evacuation began, but they were faced with continuous opposition from the Maoist faction as well as from the older military officers who had graduated from other military academies.[a] If all the ranking army officers and leading government cadres

[a] The leaders of the Whampoa clique were Chou En-lai and Yeh Chien-ying. Probable members of the clique on the Long March were Hsiao Ching-kuang, P'an Tzu-li, Li Ta, and Ch'en Keng. Lin Piao, though a Whampoa graduate, had already joined the Maoist faction. Known members of the 28 Bolsheviks' faction

had been allowed to select their own leaders before the retreat began, these opposition elements probably would have been victorious. The morale of the troops was very bad at the beginning of the retreat, and it was not to improve until the leadership was revamped three months later at Tsun-yi.[3]

According to Hsü Meng-ch'iu, the initial objective of the retreat was to reach Ho Lung's soviet base in northwestern Hunan, but the KMT armies effectively blocked this move. The next plan Li T'e devised was to march straight across mountains and rivers to unite with Hsü Hsiang-ch'ien's troops in northern Szechwan. Following this plan, the disheartened troops retreated across Kweichow toward the Yangtze. Early in January 1935 they reached Tsun-yi, a small town in northern Kweichow. There Mao, supported by dissident military leaders, insisted that an enlarged conference of the Politburo be called for the purpose of reorganizing the Revolutionary Military Council. The conference was held, and Mao was elected chairman of the Council, replacing Chou En-lai, who remained on it but with greatly decreased powers. Yeh Chien-ying was dropped, as was Teng Fa, the head of the security police. No one was appointed to the new Council to represent the police. Liu Po-ch'eng replaced Yeh as chief of staff; Chu Teh continued as commander-in-chief and Wang Chia-hsiang as political commissar. Most important, Li T'e lost his power to direct operations and the reorganized Military Council took over.[4]

According to Mao, the major steps taken at the Tsun-yi Conference were this reorganization of the Revolutionary Military Council and an accompanying reorganization of the Politburo, in which Po Ku was replaced as secretary by Chang Wen-t'ien and Mao became its chairman. We know that the arguments at the Conference were essentially over military strategy, but the details of the debate are still

---

on the March were Chang Wen-t'ien, Po Ku, Wang Chia-hsiang, Wu Liang-p'ing, Liang Pai-t'ai, and Hsü Meng-ch'iu. Ts'ai Shu-fan, Wu Hsiu-ch'uan, and Ch'en Yün were possibly members of the faction. Chu Teh and Liu Po-ch'eng led the military opposition. The other military leaders outside the Whampoa clique included P'eng Teh-huai, Lo Jung-huan, Lo P'ing-hui, Teng Hsiao-p'ing, T'an Cheng, and T'eng Tai-yüan. The Li Li-sanist Li Wei-han and the "rightist" Ch'en Yu, who had been expelled from the Central Committee in 1931 for opposing the Bolsheviks, were among those selected to go with the main body of the army. The core of the Maoist faction consisted of Mao himself, his brother Mao Tse-min, Hsieh Chüeh-tsai, Hsü T'e-li, Li Fu-ch'un, Ts'ai Ch'ang, and Lin Po-chü. All except Mao were relatively minor political figures at the time—old members of the Hunan provincial party branch. Liu Shao-ch'i, who was soon to become Mao's major supporter, may or may not have begun the March: there is evidence for both propositions. (*Asia Who's Who,* p. 737; Smedley, *Great Road,* p. 309.)

wrapped in obscurity.[b] Only two sentences from the resolutions Mao offered to the Conference have ever been published. In the first he argued for "the utilization of every conflict inside the reactionary camp by taking active steps to widen the cleavage."[5] In other words, he felt the time had come to abandon the united front from below and to work with any group opposed to both the Japanese imperialists and the central armies of Chiang Kai-shek. Others in the world Communist movement were taking the same position at this time, Thorez, Browder, and Dimitrov among them. Stalin, however, had

b At the Conference the Maoists raised two major charges against Po Ku's party leadership: he had failed to support the Fukien revolt in 1933 and he had mistakenly switched from guerrilla to positional warfare. These errors, the Maoists held, had led directly to the defeat of the Red Army in the KMT's final campaign against the central soviet base. In the earliest non-Communist reports on this dispute (Snow's interviews with various Red Army leaders in mid-1936) these errors were attributed not to Po Ku and Wang Ming, but to Li T'e. In an inner-party debate toward the end of 1936, Mao attributed the errors to unnamed "left opportunists" (Mao, HC, I, 153). Ten years later Lu Ting-yi, the chief contact for foreigners in Yenan, told Anna Louise Strong only that those responsible had been "dogmatists" (Strong, *Chinese Conquer China,* p. 35). Not until 1947 were Wang Ming and the 28 Bolsheviks named as responsible for the mistakes of the whole Kiangsi period (Hu Ch'iao-mu [57], p. 37; Mao, HC, I, 157; SW, I, 153). I interpret this sequence of names for Mao's opponents as follows: Li T'e opposed Mao's takeover at Tsun-yi, and continued opposing him until at least mid-1936 and possibly late 1937, when Li returned to Moscow.

This conflict with the Comintern representative and with Comintern discipline—a conflict that the Snow interviews made public—kept Mao in a precarious position in the CCP throughout this period. Wang Ming very probably used his positions on the Comintern Secretariat and the ECCI to attack Mao before returning to China in late 1937. Wang was deposed and his ideology was denounced during the first party rectification movement, but the dispute may have broken out again in 1947, for in that year the Maoists publicly attacked Wang and the 28 Bolsheviks, not an undefined group of "dogmatists" or "opportunists," as the faction that had incorrectly opposed Mao's policies from 1931 onward.

Although there was considerable tension between Mao and the authorities in Moscow in both 1936 and 1947, conditions required that Mao react in different ways. In 1936 it was relatively safe for the Maoists to name the Comintern represensative to the CCP as their chief opponent, for the great purge was then decimating the Comintern apparatus and attacks launched from China might effectively terminate the career of an unfriendly comrade. By 1947, the Comintern had been replaced by the CPSU bureau for conducting relations with foreign Communist parties. If Mao opposed orders or suggestions from the CPSU in 1947, he could not safely attack its representatives, so instead he turned on his old opponents in the CCP and publicly associated them with opposition to his strategy—a strategy he believed would shortly carry the CCP to power in all China and should, he felt, be adopted by all Communist parties in countries with a history of colonialism. (See Strong, "Thought of Mao Tse-tung," p. 161.) By this means he could, without appearing to challenge Moscow directly, exhort his supporters in the CCP to follow his chosen strategy in spite of Moscow's refusal to support him.

not yet made up his mind, and Manuilsky, Kuusinen, Mif, and Wang Ming were still supporting the united front from below. When Mao triumphed at the Tsun-yi Conference, he triumphed over and replaced Stalin's men. Stalin himself did eventually embrace Mao's position, but not until August 1935, seven months after the Tsun-yi Conference, when he selected Dimitrov and Wang Ming to announce the adoption of a new popular front strategy at the Seventh Congress of the Comintern.[c]

Tsun-yi was the great turning point in Mao's career. Although he had previously held governmental and military positions of great consequence, just three months before he had been under house arrest. Now, for the first time, he had become the dominant figure in the Politburo. His victory was not unopposed. Mao became boss, but not the undisputed boss. He was to be seriously challenged on several occasions before his Congress of Victors in 1945.

The new military command that took over at Tsun-yi rejected the strategy of Li T'e and returned to the strategic line Mao and Chu had worked out in Ching-kang-shan. At the close of the Conference Mao summed up the basic feature of that line, a summation he later quoted approvingly in RSQHP: "Amass superior forces to attack the enemy's weak spots so that we can assuredly eliminate a part, small or large, of the enemy's forces by picking them off one at a time."[6] This was the aim of "luring the enemy to penetrate deep," of "circling around in a whirling motion," and of the other tactics adopted by the tiny armies on Ching-kang-shan. In China, where political parties had their own armies, this was the only way in which the weaker side could become stronger. Mao argued that positional warfare and attacks on the enemy's strongpoints—the strategy of Li T'e—was stupid. By employing it, the Communists had almost destroyed their army and received no lasting benefits in exchange.

Some members of the former ruling cliques were persuaded. At least they were willing to give Mao and Chu a chance to try their generalship—perhaps secretly hoping that they too would fail. In retrospect, Tsun-yi is the point at which the mass flight of the Red Armies was stemmed and the Long March began: when Chu Teh's superb generalship and Mao Tse-tung's political acumen united to turn defeat into victory. In the legend of the Long March, it was at

[c] Ravines, pp. 113–16, 145–46. Franz Borkenau states that Manuilsky was the leading exponent of the new line and that within the Comintern Piatnitsky and Bela Kun opposed any change. (Borkenau, p. 123; see also McKenzie, pp. 155–56.)

Tsun-yi that the Red Army began its march to meet the Japanese invaders, and then on to the liberation of all China.

Rectification of Error Among Communists

After the Tsun-yi Conference, Mao put into practice the organizational scheme he had first proposed at Ku-t'ien. He drew all factions together around himself, creating a coalition of the party leaders who had survived the 28 Bolsheviks' purge in 1931. At about this time the security police began to lose their autonomous power in the Red Army. Mao and his supporters in the party, government, and army had suffered too long from their special attention. It is unlikely that the police lost all their powers in the army, but the process was begun that finally stripped them of most of their autonomy in the investigation and arrest of political deviators. Their power was checked in the Chinese Red Army at the very point at which Kirov's assassins were being arrested in the Soviet Union and Stalin was allotting sufficient power to the OGPU to destroy the old Bolsheviks and anyone else in the CPSU who had ever in any way dissented from his line. The gradual decrease of control by brute force in the CCP led to, or was accompanied by, increasing emphasis on political education and ideological remolding of party members. This became Mao's favorite method of party reconstruction.

The experience of the CPSU had been imitated blindly by the 28 Bolsheviks during their period in power. They had led the CCP to the brink of disaster and beyond. Rigid application of Comintern directives had led to the evacuation of the central soviet base. Rigid imitation of the police methods of the Soviet Union had led to Mao's imprisonment. In reaction, many leaders of the CCP had come to agree with Mao's arguments against "bookism." He had argued that Stalin's tactical notions and Comintern directives were correct not simply because they issued from the mouth of authority, but because they could successfully be put into practice. If Stalin's strategy failed when applied to Chinese conditions, a better, more correct substitute must be devised. The only way to correct strategy was to make a new analysis of the situation. Investigation to discover the facts, Mao had said, must precede analysis and strategic planning. Only the man on the scene has the necessary intimate knowledge of the facts. His knowledge and experience are therefore essential. Stalin had not consulted the right men and had erected a faulty strategy for China on the foundation of general theory and his own quite different experience. In other words, Stalin had not made a correct analysis of the situation. He had not suggested to his Chinese comrades the correct forms of struggle and organization. He had not correctly utilized "every fissure in the camp of the opponents." His choice of Chinese allies had been less than brilliant. He had looked to the manipulation of leaders to make a revolution rather than relying on the masses of peasants and workers.

Mao's analysis of the situation, on the other hand, was correct. He had suggested to the Central Committee that it should rely more on the peasants. The most important aspect of his political line, which he places first in RSQHP, is that: "The peasants' fight for land is the basic feature of the anti-imperialist and anti-feudal struggle in China. . . . The Chinese bourgeois-democratic revolution is in essence a peasant revolution . . . the basic task of the Chinese proletariat in the bourgeois-democratic revolution is therefore to give leadership to the peasants' struggle." Stalin had pointed out that "the task of the Chinese revolution at its present stage is to fight imperialism and feudalism." Mao, "in line with Comrade Stalin," developed this general formula and worked out the tactical means by which it could be applied in China.[7] To do this he took account of the peculiar balance of class forces in China and worked out his thesis on the leading role of the peasantry in the bourgeois-democratic phase of the Chinese revolution. Mao does not cite anything Stalin wrote to support his contention that his thesis on the role of the peasantry was "in line with Comrade Stalin." Instead he cites four of his own works: "Report on an Investigation into the Peasant Movement in Hunan" (March 1927), "Why Can China's Red Political Power Exist?" (October 1928), "The Struggle in the Ching-kang Mountains" (November 1928), and the April 1929 letter from the Front Committee in the Ching-kang Mountains to the Central Committee.[8]

What Stalin had to say about the Chinese revolution in 1926 and 1927 was mainly determined by the fact that he was fighting the United Opposition for control of the CPSU. If they held one position, Stalin took the opposite one. His theses on the Chinese revolution were not based on careful analysis of the local situation in China, or on sound judgment of the ebb and flow of the Chinese revolutionary movement. In fact, when Stalin made his speech to the Seventh Plenum of the ECCI on November 30, 1926, he was overruling proposals made by men who had recently returned from China and who therefore knew much more about the alignment of class forces within the united front than he did. Nevertheless, he decided against them—not because their theses were actually incorrect estimates of the Chinese situation, but because some of their proponents were linked with the United Opposition. The remarks Stalin made on the Leninist tactical code on August 1, 1927, served a similar function. They were a defense of his interventions in the direction of the Chinese revolution in 1926–27. He made them after all the KMT leaders had broken with the Communists, when, in many parts of China, Communists were fleeing the KMT terror. Even at that time Stalin refused to admit that the CCP-KMT alliance was doomed, simply because the United Opposition in Moscow had seen the light and advocated a complete break with the KMT.

Stalin's Foresight and Analyses

Stalin had shown great foresight in handling his opponents in Moscow. He had shown very little astuteness in judging the political sympathies of KMT generals in China. Correct judgment on that matter was of intense concern to the Chinese Communist leaders in the period of the united front if they were to prepare in time for a strategic retreat. The broader the base of organized support at the disposal of the Chinese Communist leaders when retreat became necessary, the greater the number of organizations and party members they would be able to salvage for use when the revolutionary wave rose again. This, it seems to me, is the whole point of Mao's stress on the correctness of his views on the organization of the peasant movement in the first half of 1927. The greater the strength and militancy of mass organizations supporting the Communists when the KMT leadership defected from the united front, the greater their power to resist in the ensuing period. The policy Stalin's directives forced on the Chinese party in the first half of 1927 had failed to preserve mass organized support for the Communists. Mao believes that the policies he suggested to the Central Committee in February and March of 1927 were correct. They were based on an intimate knowledge of the alignment of class forces among the KMT generals as well as a knowledge of the actual and potential organized strength of the peasant movement. Had his policies been adopted, the Chinese Communists could have begun their strategic retreat with a much broader base of support outside the party. When a strategic retreat must be organized, the most important task of party leaders is to preserve the party's cadres. In this task, Stalin's policy had failed. Had Mao's policy on the peasant movement been followed, more cadres might have been preserved.

Mao's theses on the role of the peasantry in the bourgeois-democratic revolution in China were not acceptable to the Central Committee in March and April of 1927, when Mao first published them, or even after they were accepted by the All-China Peasant Association and he asked the Central Committee to reconsider them. Moreover, in November 1927, early in the period in which he claims to have developed his theses, he had been removed from all his party posts. He knew his position in the party was very tenuous until he was informed of his reappointment to the Front Committee in November 1928. Yet, even though Mao developed his theses in isolation, not knowing whether the Comintern and the new leaders of the CCP to be elected at its Sixth Congress would approve of them, in RSQHP he claimed to have developed them "in line wtih Comrade Stalin."

In the Marxist-Leninist terminology, correct development is dialectical. In thought and in argument the developer moves from thesis to antithesis, and finally reintegrates the two in a higher synthesis. Correct integration, however, is validated only by the development of history, and history itself may protract the period in which the thesis and antithesis remain opposed to each other. According to Stalin, the ability to state correctly the developed formulation of a classic thesis, i.e., its antithesis, depends on the ability to make a "concrete analysis of concrete conditions."[9] Correctness of foresight depends on the ability to discover which existing historical conditions must be abolished before the tension between the thesis and its present historical antithesis can be resolved in a new synthesis. The validity of the statement of the antithesis and the predicted future synthesis in practice depends on correctly calculating strategy and tactics whereby history may be piloted in accordance with the prediction. When Mao states that he has correctly developed Stalin's theses on the Chinese revolution, he implies that he has formulated their antitheses. When he points out that he has correctly developed Stalin's interpretation of Leninist strategy and tactics, he implies that he has modified Stalin's general formulations by taking into account certain concrete historical conditions in China. As far as Mao is concerned, Stalin's theses on the Chinese revolution and his formulations of Leninist strategy and tactics are abstract formulae. Mao's theses on the Chinese revolution are correct because they are conditioned by historical realities. His strategy and tactics are correct for the Chinese party because they are conditioned by Chinese circumstances. They are a development of, different from, and antithetical to Stalin's theses and formulae because they are not abstractions. Tested in revolutionary practice, they have become correct.

The CCP would be able to overcome the historical conditions that created a gap between Stalin's and Mao's theses only by adhering to Mao's antithetical lines. His theses alone could lead to the transformation of the historical conditions that made the existing contradictions between the two lines necessary and inevitable. This was Mao's line. Never once in RSQHP does Mao state that Stalin's theses were *correct*; indeed, he implies that Stalin's direction of the Chinese revolution separated theory and practice. It was not Stalin but Mao who, through struggle and opposition in both theoretical and practical work, finally succeeded in reintegrating theory and practice for the Chinese revolution.

The fact that the only period in which Mao acknowledges help and guidance from the Comintern and from Stalin predates the break with the KMT in 1927 reinforces this interpretation.[10] He does acknowledge political and organizational guidance from the Comintern before 1927, and RSQHP stresses the fact that the Chinese party received very many brilliant directives from both the Comintern and Stalin in the first half of 1927, immediately prior to the failure of the first Great Revolution.[11] His writing about the directives received from Moscow in that half year indicates that he thoroughly disapproved of the bulk of them. It was the policies they contained that led to major disaster for the CCP. After July 1927, the Comintern and Stalin drop into obscurity and the stage is occupied by the bitter struggle between Mao and the trio of Li Li-san, Wang Ming, and Po Ku. The Moscow patrons of Li, Wang, and Po remain discreetly in the background.[12]

Mao Becomes the Philosopher

After Mao and his henchmen took power in the party's central organs at Tsun-yi, Mao had to defend his position and policies against attacks by Wang Ming and Po Ku, and perhaps by their supporters in Moscow. While his opponents set ideological and political traps for him, Mao was forced to restate his political theses and develop their philosophical underpinnings to prove that his policies not only worked in short-run practice but were also theoretically sound. His ideological views were elaborated in the course of this bitter struggle. After his enemies were defeated, Mao no longer claimed that his ideological position was a development or a creative application of

Stalin's. In RSQHP he never claims that his ideology is dependent upon Stalin's.[d] In fact, Mao's ideology is a defense of all those positions he held between 1927 and 1935. It is a defense against all epithets with which his political opponents labeled him: "representative of peasant consciousness in the party," "double-dealing in practical work," and "narrow empiricism." He uses Marxist-Leninist theoretical principles in bold justification of his methods of analysis of the Chinese revolution. In Mao's theses, according to RSQHP, Marxist-Leninist principles and the actual practice of the Chinese revolution are united. This integration is theoretically sound and a practical success. Mao has proven himself, both theoretically and in practice, to be the best leader for the Chinese party.

Inherent in Mao's ideology is an attack on Wang Ming and Po Ku, Mao's strongest opponents in the CCP and the men backed by the Comintern for the longest period of time. From late 1931 until late 1937, Wang represented the CCP in Moscow. After Mao's initial triumph at the Tsun-yi Conference, Moscow became the center of power for his opponents. If Wang returned from Moscow with orders to reorganize the central organs of the CCP, his old comrades might regain their positions of power. Wang's presence in Moscow until late 1937 prolonged and intensified the dispute in Yenan. When Wang finally did return in December 1937, he acted as if he had such orders from Stalin to take over control of the CCP Politburo.[13] According to Chang Kuo-t'ao, Stalin told Wang immediately before he returned to China that in the future orders from the Comintern would not necessarily be binding on the CCP. The implication was that Stalin would send orders directly to Wang. This would have been sensible under conditions existing in the Comintern apparatus at that date. Piatnitsky, chief of the organization section of the Comintern apparatus, Mirov-Abramov, his chief assistant in the technical section, and such left extremists as Bela Kun and Heinz Neumann were all liquidated in late 1937. It is reported that they were removed on account of their united front tactics and their previous association with Zinoviev.[14] As a result of this turmoil, the Comintern was unable to serve as a reliable vehicle for the transmission of Stalin's policies.

In his struggle with Wang, Mao was on the defensive from 1935 until late 1938, when his position as leader of the CCP Politburo was at last recognized by Moscow. After the Sixth Plenum of the Central Committee of the CCP, in October-November of that year, he was on

[d] He does trace several of his *political* theses to Stalin's, but never his military, organizational, or ideological theses. These are basic distinctions in RSQHP.

the offensive—he could express his distaste for Wang in a more open and systematic manner. Wang remained prominent in party circles until 1940. In December 1939, when Yenan was completely isolated from the rest of China by the Chungking government's ban on travel into the region, and while Communist periodicals in Nationalist China were subject to rigorous censorship, Wang was still urging that the Communists support the constitutional government movement initiated by Chungking. From 1935 to 1940, the central political issue dividing Mao and Wang concerned the strategy the CCP should pursue in the united front with the KMT. Mao's struggle with Wang and others over this issue led directly into the party rectification movement and the "study" of party history. In these two movements, Wang's theses on the united front and on bolshevization of the party through the dual struggle against right and left deviations were undermined. Mao's theses replaced them.

Mao was ably assisted in the contest by Liu Shao-ch'i. While Mao elaborated his theses on new democracy and political strategy, Liu elaborated new lines to be pursued in inner-party struggle.[15] As far as the internal organization of the party's leading bodies was concerned, Mao's position on inner-party struggle was the central issue in dispute. The line on party reform that Liu developed in the essays and speeches he wrote in the early 1940's reflects the determination of the men around Mao to emerge victorious, and yet to refrain from imitating the Stalinist style of party purges. Their solution to the problem of how to deal with their political opponents on the Chinese Central Committee was to tell them they were sick, to convince them they were sick, and then to help them get well—to reeducate them. In order to disassociate the ideology and teachings of the Maoists' opponents from the influence of Moscow, Liu asserted that all forms of Chinese Menshevism except for Ch'en Tu-hsiu's Trotskyism were indigenous to China. Chinese Menshevism, Liu held, had no connections at all with European or Russian forms of this heresy. This solution neatly avoided the connection between the Comintern's line and the lines pursued by Wang Ming, Po Ku, and Li Li-san. It ignored Stalin's direction of the CCP through the agencies subordinate to him. In 1943, Liu drew the expedient conclusion: under Chinese conditions, the Comintern line was Menshevist! Those Chinese who had supported Stalin's line had relied on books and set phrases, ignoring Chinese realities.[16] These individuals were Wang, Po, and their supporters. In 1943, Liu did not call them comrades, he called them idealists. In *form,* Liu holds, they appeared before the masses of the Chinese party as "Leninists," "Bolsheviks," and representatives of the "international line."[17] In this Liu is perfectly correct. They did. They were the representatives in the Chinese party of the line laid down in Moscow. They were the 28 Bolsheviks, the "Russian faction" in the CCP.

In RSQHP, Mao attacked the pamphlet Wang wrote in 1931 and 1932 on the proper conduct of inner-party struggle: "That pamphlet, considered both at the time and for more than ten years afterwards to have played a 'correct programmatic role,' contained in fact . . . a completely erroneous left opportunist general program for 'combating right deviation.' "[18] To replace Wang's pamphlet on inner-party struggle, Mao and Liu rescued from obscurity four sections of the first chapter of the *Ku-t'ien Resolutions,* dated December 1929. By making those resolutions the basis for his policy in combating deviations in the party, Mao reached back to the period before Wang Ming became important, before Stalin completely dominated the Comintern. By 1945, when the *Ku-t'ien Resolutions* were circulated to the whole of the Red Army, Mao was ready to assert that the CCP had from its birth used Marxism as its guide and had attempted to integrate the universal truths of Marxism-Leninism with Chinese revolutionary practice. Its first attempts were frequently in error; Mao's major works are a critique of the manner in which earlier leaders of the CCP had attempted to integrate Marxist-Leninist theory with their revolutionary practice. His major conclusion was that the Chinese revolution had been in the "new democratic stage" ever since the founding of the CCP. Mao had arrived at this conclusion independently. In fact, he summed up his theses on the Chinese revolution under the name of "new democracy" only in 1940, five years after he assumed leadership of the party and nineteen years after it was founded. However, while he did not present all of his theses in a systematic manner in a single essay until 1940, all of them had been worked out, written down, and presented to official party meetings before the end of 1936. Most of them had been worked out before 1931, when he had become chairman of the all-China soviet government. In other words, they were proposed and given their initial test in practice before the supporters of Po Ku and Wang Ming took over the party organs in the soviet districts.

The earliest and one of the most important of his theses, that on the major role of the peasantry in the Chinese revolution, was presented to the Central Committee before the collapse of the first united front with the KMT.[19] Mao's assessment of the predominant role of the Chinese peasant in the development of the revolution is one of the most fundamental aspects of his theses on the new democratic stage of the Chinese revolution.[20] While RSQHP traces the general outlines of Mao's definition of the new democratic stage of the Chinese revolution back to his years in Ching-kang-shan and to the first period of the Agrarian Revolutionary War (1927–1930), the period when he opposed the three left lines of the Chinese Central Committee, he did not pull all of the various strands together and weave them into a single whole until the 1939–41 controversy with Wang Ming and his supporters. This controversy led directly into the 1941–44 campaign to study party history and the party rectification campaigns of the same years. In other words, Mao's systematic critique of the manner in which the exponents of the three left lines "integrated theory and practice" was not entirely worked out until the early 1940's.[21]

Mao claims in RSQHP that in his creative application of the scientific theory of Marxism-Leninism he has "brilliantly developed Lenin's and Stalin's theses on the revolutionary movement in colonial and semicolonial countries, as well as Stalin's theses on the Chinese revolution."[22] In fact, throughout the whole of RSQHP Mao does not once mention or cite any of Lenin's theses, or any drafted by Stalin before Lenin's death. Mao confines himself entirely to Stalin's theses and directives in the final period of the first united front with the KMT. Moreover, he at no point affirms that Stalin's theses were *correct,* in spite of his alleged dependence on them. This, perhaps, is the reason why Mao has been able to "creatively" apply Marxist-Leninist principles to the Chinese situation and "brilliantly develop" Stalin's theses on the Chinese revolution.

Finally, Mao does not mention or cite any theses or directives issued either by the Comintern or by Stalin after the end of 1927. Thereafter, Russian agents no longer play a leading role in the direction of the CCP and the Chinese revolution. The stage is dominated by the inner-party struggle between the erroneous line taken by the Chinese Communist leaders appointed by the Comintern (with the implicit or explicit approbation of Stalin) and the correct line of Mao Tse-tung.

Mao did not have the opportunity to test his ideas thoroughly, and he had not discovered a way to justify his strategic notions on Marxist grounds before he became the leader of the CCP. But he knew that directives from Stalin and the Comintern had twice led the CCP to disaster, and he had repeatedly asserted that investigation and analysis of local conditions must precede strategic planning. Sometime after he took power at Tsun-yi he began to emphasize the simple maxim that had been repeated ad nauseam ever since Marxists had begun to apply and revise Marxist ideas: "Marxism is not a dogma but a guide to action." He would not treat everything that Marx or Lenin or Stalin had said or written as universal truth. He would use their method of thought—dialectical materialism—to devise for the Chinese Communists a set of general principles they could use to solve their own revolutionary problems. Mao then proceeded to distill from Marxism every notion arising from the fact that Marx had been a European who lived in the middle of the nineteenth century and from Leninism and Stalinism every concept arising out of the Russian national environment. The precious residue was the essence of Marxism and Leninism. But while its truths were universal, that essence contained no strategic formulae relevant to the Chinese revolution. It was Mao's task as a Chinese Marxist to apply these few remaining fundamentals to the analysis of the class structure, economic relations, history, and politics of China, and then to devise a new strategy that would finally lead the CCP to power.

Mao's revision of Marxism was a delicate business, for he worked out his own theories and strategies and got them accepted by other leaders of the CCP while Stalin and his supporters were insisting that Stalin's own exposition of dialectical and historical materialism must be treated as dogma. All Communists must believe that Stalin's official version of the history of the Bolsheviks provided Communists with a knowledge of the general laws of social development and political struggle that were applicable everywhere and at all times. Paradoxically, it was the publication of this history, the *Short Course,* in 1938 that finally provided Mao with the opportunity to justify his past deviations, present his strategic theories within the framework of Marxist principles of thought, and win acceptance of his analysis of the correct relation between Marxist theory and Chinese practice.

Shortly after the publication of the *Short Course,* Mao began to search for acceptable reasons for *not* using it as a model for the CCP. As early as November 1938 he expounded his major reasons for rejecting the political strategy of the Russian Social Democratic Labor Party (RSDLP) before the October Revolution as the model for the political program of the CCP before it seized political power. In a short passage omitted entirely from SW, Mao contrasted the tasks of the CCP and those that faced the RSDLP between the 1905 Revolution and the October Revolution. The passage reads:

The central task of revolution and its highest form is an armed struggle for political power. War settles the question. This Marxist-Leninist principle is universally true both in China and in foreign countries. It is true in all places.

But under this universal principle we must speak of the various conditions under which the party of the proletariat will put this principle into effect. These conditions may be basically unlike or not completely identical with each other.

In every capitalist country, in a period when there is no Fascism and no war, where conditions are such that within the country there is no feudal regime, if there is a bourgeois-democratic regime, if there is no colonial exploitation from without, and if the people oppress other peoples—if there are these special conditions—the duty of the party of the proletariat in such capitalist countries is to go through a long period of legal struggle, educating the workers, gathering strength, preparing for the final overthrow of capitalism. In this long period of legal struggle there is the possibility of using parliamentary platforms, there is the duty of engaging in economic and political strikes, there is the task of organizing labor unions and educating the workers. Where it is legal to carry on an organizational struggle, there is no bloodshed. On the problem of war, the Communist party should oppose imperialist war by its own country; and should such a war break out, the political tactic of the party should be to cause the defeat in battle of its own reactionary government. "The only war we wish to prepare for is civil war." [Annotated to Lenin and the *Short Course*.] But in that kind of war, if the capitalist class has not truly reached the point of exhaustion, if the great majority of the proletariat is not prepared for an armed uprising, if for them the time to begin the war has not arrived, if the peasants are not already voluntarily willing to help the proletariat, uprisings and wars should not be started. *When the time for uprisings and wars has arrived, cities should be taken first, and only later the villages, not the opposite.*

All of these directives, all are for Communist parties in capitalist states to follow. This has been confirmed and the Russian October Revolution bears testimony to the truth of this pattern.

In China it is different. China is not an independent democratic state, but a semicolonial and semifeudal country: internally there is no democratic regime; but her people suffer the oppression of a feudal regime; externally there is no national independence, but her people suffer the oppression of imperialism. Because of these facts, there is no legislative assembly to make use of, no legal right to organize the workers to strike. Here the fundamental task of the Communist Party is not to go through a long period of legal struggle before launching an insurrection or civil war. *Its task is not to seize first the big cities and then the countryside, but to take the road in the opposite direction.*[e]

---

[e] Mao, HC, II, 542. The first four paragraphs of this article have not been translated in SW. The English translation begins with the last paragraph of the Chinese version in HC, except that the first five characters ("In China it is different") have been omitted. See SW, II, 267. Italics mine.

The need to approach the final struggle for political power by going in the opposite direction from that taken by the Russian party was Mao's justification for his practice of encircling the cities by the countryside, launching peasant insurrections before the proletariat was ready to rise, neglecting the organization of the proletariat, and depending on the unique revolutionary character of the peasantry as the motivating force of the Chinese revolution.

After Wang Ming returned from Moscow toward the end of 1937, he went to Hankow, together with Po Ku, Chou En-lai, Hsiang Ying, Yeh T'ing, and other prominent Communists, to discover some way to improve the then semi-legal status of the Communist party. Mao and Chu remained in Yenan. Between his return in 1937 and the Sixth Plenum in November 1938, Wang argued that Hankow should become China's Madrid—that the Communists should enter a coalition government with the Nationalists and, after a period of legal struggle, use the strength of the proletariat to achieve hegemony within that government. His underlying assumption was that the society of China, like that of Spain, had already become capitalist, and that the proletariat would therefore be ready to overthrow its class enemies toward the end of the war with Japan. At that point the Chinese Communists could follow the example of the Russian Bolsheviks in 1917.

Mao opposed this strategy on the grounds that China was not yet fundamentally capitalist, but was still semifeudal and semicolonial. The internal contradiction between peasants and landlords was therefore still more important than that between proletariat and capitalists. Moreover, the external contradiction between the whole Chinese people (including the petty and national bourgeoisie) and the Japanese imperialists was more antagonistic than that between any of the indigenous Chinese social classes. Therefore Wang's analogy between Hankow and Madrid was false. Nor would the strategy Lenin had developed for Europe during the First World War be useful in China's war against Japan. There would be no seizure of power in the capital, no attempt to subvert the Nationalist armies with Communist agitators, and no Brest-Litovsk. In China, the war would take another course.

At the Sixth Plenum, Mao attempted to give some theoretical justification for abandoning the model of the October Revolution, and to place his own heretical strategy within the framework of Marxist thought. But though he now had a general theoretical position on the differences between the tasks of the RSDLP and the CCP before the final seizure of power, and though he had attacked Wang Ming for attempting to apply the lessons of the Russian Revolution too dogmatically, he still had not made explicit his reasons for rejecting Wang's analysis of deviations in the history of the CCP, including Mao's own deviations. Mao agreed with Wang that the Chinese party should be bolshevized—its higher organs reconstructed and its membership purified—but the procedures he advocated differed entirely from the "merciless blows" at all deviators advocated by Wang and Po. In 1938, Mao proposed that the only way to bolshevize the party was first to examine party history and then, carefully avoiding the mistakes of the past, to take up the job of building the party in the light of present and future tasks.[23]

The leaders of the CCP had failed in the past because they had not been educated in the right kind of Marxism-Leninism. Now the CCP must develop the correct ideology for its situation. The lessons taught by Stalin's *Short Course* must not be blindly applied in China. After 1938, Mao had to differentiate his ideas from those of the opposition leaders in the CPSU who had been felled in Stalin's purges, while maintaining the essential correctness of his ideas during the period in which he had been in opposition to the Comintern line. Once he had shown that he was capable of making the necessary distinctions, comrades who had committed the ideological error of blindly following Stalin in the past could be cured by allowing Dr. Mao to remold their ideology. Survival for themselves and victory for the CCP was dependent on accepting the advice of the doctor with the right medicine. Mao's offer to assume the role of chief physician was most attractive because he held out the hope that anyone could be cured if he would—hence Russian-type purges could be avoided in China. The men and women who refused to follow Mao's prescription for the longest period were the leaders of the 28 Bolsheviks, the men who in the past had believed that they were the best doctors, with the authoritative prescription.

Mao's prolonged struggle with the 28 Bolsheviks was an excellent education in how to resist the application of Stalinist ideas on politics and party organization and still survive. Wang Ming and Po Ku were tactically clever, ruthless, energetic opponents, with considerable means at their disposal until 1938, when the purges made the backing of the Comintern a less important factor. After 1938 the two main issues added to the dispute between Mao and Wang were on how the *Short Course* should be evaluated and on how inner-party disputes should be conducted. On both issues the Maoists triumphed.

They rejected the Stalinist history of the CPSU as the model for their own political and organizational program, and they determined that the CCP should learn from the mistakes of the CPSU and carry on the Chinese revolution using Mao's thought as their guide. They also rejected the mass purge, replacing it with the party rectification movement. Mao was elected chairman of the CCP at the Seventh National Congress in 1945. The new constitution of the CCP adopted at that Congress designated Maoism as the guiding ideology of the CCP. At the Congress Liu Shao-ch'i declared that the CCP had become a proletarian party of a completely new type, built on Mao's new principles of ideological rectification for strengthening the party organization. Stalin's name is completely absent from the 1945 constitution—Mao's thought and Mao's leadership dominate the stage.

On the basis of the evidence presented above, I believe that Mao was less opposed to Stalin as a person than to the little imitators of Stalin who applied his methods to control the CCP. Stalin the man may have been dangerous, but he was far away from China. His personal directives could be treated with appropriate respect and quietly subverted. The application of identical political and organizational directives in all Communist parties—a feature of the Stalinist system of control over non-Soviet parties—was dangerous and mistaken. Imitation of the history of the Russian party or of directives given to other parties, without a critical evaluation of their usefulness, would certainly lead to failure in China. By 1945 the CCP leaders knew that this need not occur. In Mao they had a leader with a strategic formula that worked. They could win on their own. When the CCP accepted Mao's thought as its sole guide, it acknowledged that every time Mao had opposed the party line in the past he had been right, even when the fundamentals of that line had been laid down by Stalin or his agents.

Some years ago Benjamin Schwartz developed the thesis that the Maoist strategy is a "heresy in act never made explicit in theory."[24] In other words, Schwartz held that Mao's strategy essentially consisted of the imposition of a Leninist type of party organization on a purely peasant mass base. His view is that Mao rejected in practice, if not in theory, the basic Marxist principle that the Communist party must never be completely divorced from its natural class base, the proletariat. Under Mao's leadership the CCP became simply a core of professional revolutionaries who used the dynamics of peasant discontent to rise to power. Thus Maoism is a Marxist heresy *in action* on the relation of party to class.[25] Not only that, but it is a heresy for which Mao has never offered any theoretical justification.

I agree that under Mao's leadership the CCP shifted from a proletarian to a peasant class base, and that the Maoists were essentially a core of professional revolutionaries with no necessary relation to any particular class. The development of Mao's theory of contradictions, however, provides evidence contrary to the conclusion that Maoist strategy was never made explicit in theory. I am offering here the hypothesis that Mao definitely did attempt to raise his revolutionary strategy to the theoretical level. In the process, he explicitly rejected the Marxist principles that bind the Communist party to the proletariat and asserted that in semifeudal, semicolonial countries a revolutionary Leninist party could successfully carry out the revolution and remain Marxist without relying upon the proletariat. He also rejected the Stalinist theory of the inevitability of increasing class conflict in the transition to socialism and communism, and the related Stalinist practice of violent party purges.

Mao became anti-Stalinist in the course of his struggle with his opponents in the CCP Central Committee. His claims to ideological originality and creativity are based directly on the deviations for which he was attacked before 1945. In spite of pressure to conform to Stalinist orthodoxy, he maintained to a large extent his distinctive ideological viewpoint between the time of his visit to Moscow in 1949–50 and Stalin's death in 1953.

In the present split in the world Communist movement, many Western observers, following the lead of Soviet and Yugoslav party leaders, cast the Chinese in the role of Stalinists: Mao Tse-tung, chairman of the Chinese Communist Party, is the Stalin of today. This characterization is altogether too simple. The Chinese do not assert that Mao is one of the few surviving loyal comrades-in-arms of Stalin: he is held to be an independent, creative Marxist theoretician in his own right. The cult of Mao focuses not on his personality, but on the correctness of his thought. His theories on the Chinese revolution are held to be the only correct application of Marxist-Leninist principles to the objective realities of modern China. The Chinese now refer to themselves as the only true Marxist-Leninists and denounce Khrushchev and his successors—the Russian heirs of the October Revolution—as modern revisionists. Khrushchev, however, was not the first Soviet leader to revise Marxism-Leninism. Revision of Marxist-Leninist revolutionary principles began under Stalin himself. Chinese and Russians can concur on that fact. After Khrushchev's "de-Stalinization" speech in 1956, the Chinese agreed that in the latter half of his life Stalin took pleasure in the cult of the individual, violated the system of democratic centralism, fell victim to "one-sided subjectivism," and cut himself off from and lost contact with the masses.[26] As the Central Committee put it,

> [He placed] blind faith in personal wisdom and authority. He would not investigate and study complicated conditions seriously or listen carefully to the opinions of his comrades and the voice of the masses. As a result some of the policies and measures he adopted were often at variance with objective reality. He often stubbornly persisted in carrying out these mistaken measures over long periods and was unable to correct his mistakes in time. . . . [He] deviated partly, but grossly, from the dialectical materialist way of thinking and fell into subjectivism.[27]

No party leader can entirely avoid subjectivist views, the Committee continued, for none is infallible. Mistakes arising from subjectivist views, however, can remain isolated and remediable if party leaders maintain their contact with and rely on the masses, if they strictly follow the principles of dialectical materialism in their thinking, and if they observe the rules of democratic centralism in guiding the work of the party. In all three respects, Stalin's leadership was faulty. More than that, he was a great-nation chauvinist.[28]

In judging Stalin, the CCP's Central Committee applied Mao's theory of contradictions. The Committee concluded that although Stalin's mistakes harmed the Soviet Union and the international Communist movement, under his leadership the socialist system was strengthened in the Soviet Union and the socialist bloc became a force to be reckoned with. In spite of his gross errors, Stalin always remained a Communist and Marxist-Leninist who should not be condemned as an enemy of the socialist system, but viewed as a great Marxist-Leninist leader who made mistakes in the course of his work. To treat his leadership in an entirely negative manner confuses two different types of contradictions: *antagonistic* contradictions between Communists and their enemies, and *non-antagonistic* contradictions within Communist ranks.

According to Khrushchev, the ill effects of Stalin's willful dogmatism had become fully evident in the Soviet party by 1934. Mao traces his own difficulties with doctrinaire Communists back to the summer of 1927. In spite of everything that the CCP's Central Committee could say in defense of Stalin's leadership, it had to admit that by enforcing Stalin's directives and imitating his mistakes all CCP leaders before Mao Tse-tung—Ch'en Tu-hsiu, Ch'ü Ch'iu-pai, Li Li-san,

Wang Ming, and Po Ku—had led the Chinese party into great difficulties. Stalin's directives, the Committee noted, were dictatorially enforced by Ch'en Tu-hsiu from 1924 to 1927, when he acted as front man for the erroneous right opportunist line stemming directly from Moscow.[29] Then, throughout the first civil war (1927–1935), in the three periods of left opportunism, the leaders of the CCP derived their tactical policies from Stalin's strategic formula "the main blow should be so directed as to isolate the middle-of-the-road social and political forces."[30] The same formula underlay the putschism of late 1927, the Li Li-san line of 1930, and the Wang Ming line of 1931–34. Only after the Maoist faction took over the Central Committee in January 1935 was the development of incorrect lines thwarted, although Wang Ming attempted to impose an erroneous right line when he returned from Moscow in 1937.[31]

Lacking the ability to think critically, creatively, and independently, these leaders of the CCP crudely imitated Stalin's "gross subjectivist" mistakes and enforced his directives in an arbitrary, doctrinaire manner. As a result, the CCP failed to isolate the main enemy and suffered very heavy losses.[32] The heaviest of these occurred in 1927, when the first united front with the KMT disintegrated; in 1930, when the Red Armies were defeated at Ch'angsha; and in 1934, when the Communists gave up the old soviet bases in South China. In all these cases of opportunism, right and left, Stalin's formula of directing the main effort against the intermediate forces was applied. In the two periods of right opportunism, Stalin himself directed the CCP to form an alliance with right-wing forces led by Chiang Kai-shek against the non-Communist left. When the party's Central Committee formulated its position on "de-Stalinization" in 1956, it stated that the Maoist faction had always opposed the indiscriminate, doctrinaire application of this strategic formula in China:

> Our experience teaches us that the main blow of the revolution should be directed at the chief enemy to isolate him. As for the middle forces, a policy of both uniting with them and struggling against them should be adopted, so that they are at least neutralized; and, as circumstances permit, efforts should be made to shift them from their position of neutrality to one of alliance with us, for the purpose of facilitating the development of the revolution.[33]

The Maoist cult—the cult of Maoist ideology—was built on a struggle against the doctrinaire, mechanical imposition of Stalin's formulae to revolutionary China. The struggle eliminated Stalin's best-known disciples from all positions of actual power in the Chinese

Communist Party. Mao accomplished this astounding feat by 1945, but his triumph in this dangerous inner-party struggle led neither to a split in the Chinese party nor to a reign of terror in China. Nor did Mao allow the many tactical differences between Stalin and himself to develop into an open break between Moscow and Peking. Mao was an adept politician who knew the difference between antagonistic and non-antagonistic contradictions, and Stalin was apparently also willing to live with the non-antagonistic variety as long as it remained far enough from Moscow. Khrushchev was not as skillful in keeping contradictions within the Socialist bloc from developing into political antagonism among Communists. Nor have his successors been able to achieve a reconciliation.

Since Stalin's death Mao has frequently appeared to play the role of a Stalinist, especially in recent debates with Soviet leaders, Khrushchev in particular. Khrushchev, however, accused Mao not of being a terrorist or of carrying out mass purges, but of claiming the role of chief ideologue in the world Communist movement. Mao is a Stalinist in that he claims to have inherited Stalin's mantle, including the right to creatively add to and subtract from Marxist-Leninist principles. Although Khrushchev cast Mao in the role of a doctrinaire Stalinist, Mao is a peculiar Stalinist. He has officially rejected those features of Stalin's practice that isolated the leaders of the CPSU from the masses. Mao values his ties with the masses. He places much more stress on democracy in the party and on criticism from below than Stalin ever did. The value he attributed to the Soldiers' Soviets while in Ching-kang-shan, his emphasis on the close relations between leaders and followers in the *Ku-t'ien Resolutions,* and the revival of these materials as documents for the study of party history after the Seventh Congress point up this contrast between Mao and Stalin. Mao's present insistence that China has the right to devise its policies independently of Moscow is a continuation of the line he developed long before Stalin's death, in opposition to Stalin and his methods.

But it is much more than that. The Maoists are not merely asserting that Chinese interests take priority over those of the USSR within a certain circumscribed field, that the CCP knows best how to devise its own strategies and plan its own internal development without interference from the CPSU, or that the CCP deserves a voice equal to that of all other ruling parties in the planning of policy for the Communist bloc of states and a proper deference in the world Communist movement owing to its position as one of the two chief ruling parties. Guided by an ancient Chinese passion for universal history,

Mao aspires to be the Communist philosopher-king, the master of *t'ien-hsia*—all under heaven—who, like the good king of Mencius, draws the people to himself because his knowledge and virtue are evidenced in his actions. Mao, I believe, would like to be recognized as the man who has moved Communism away from its European proletarian origins, applied the essential elements of Marxism to the mastery of another historical epoch, and restated its fundamentals in universal categories that can be applied in the analysis of any stage of human history and used to incite or inspire revolutionary change in any human society.

Under Mao's guidance, the CCP has become a revolutionary party ready to help other Communist parties struggling for power. The Maoist program for the remolding of thought has a much broader appeal to Communists in all parties than either the historical dictatorship of the proletariat under Stalin or Khrushchev's scurrilous debunking of the Stalin myth. Mao's balanced rejection of those parts of Soviet experience that arose out of pre-Soviet history is to many Communists a more analytic and scientific approach than Khrushchev's attribution of all faults in the Soviet system to the cult of personality. Once upon a time the Ching-kang Mountains were Mao's little world; the world of Ching-kang-shan, he called it. In the end the whole world became his Ching-kang-shan. The guerrilla tactics Mao first devised in Kiangsi were applied in Cuba's Sierra Maestra, and later in South Vietnam and the lands to the west of Kilimanjaro. Ten years after Mao's final triumph in China his appeal was worldwide. And the philosophical notions and revolutionary strategies he devised seem likely to trouble both the Communist and non-Communist portions of the world for a long time to come.

APPENDIX A

Note on the Delegates to the First Congress of the CCP and on the Party's Membership at the Time

Organization of Communist groups in China began under Comintern guidance in 1920. According to Chow Tse-tsung, a secret conference was held in Shanghai in May 1920 to organize the embryo party. Among those who attended this meeting, by Chow's account, were Ch'en Tu-hsiu, Tai Chi-t'ao, Li Han-chün, Shen Ting-i, Shao Li-tzu, Ch'en Wang-t'ao, Li Ta, Shih Ts'un-t'ung, Yü Hsiu-sung, and Yüan Hsiao-hsien. Voitinsky and Yang Ming-chai probably also attended. This conference adopted a provisional party constitution, established a provisional central organization, and elected Ch'en Tu-hsiu as its secretary.[1]

According to Tung Pi-wu, Ch'en Tu-hsiu and Li Ta-chao founded the central organization of the CCP in Shanghai in May 1921.[2] If his date is a year late, he may well be referring to this secret conference in May 1920. Mao told Snow that the central organization elected at the First Congress comprised Ch'en Tu-hsiu, Chang Kuo-t'ao, Ch'en Kung-po, Shih Tsung-tung (Shih Ts'un-t'ung), Sun Yüan-lu (Sun Hsüan-lu, Shen Ting-i), Li Han-tsen (Li Han-chün), Li Ta, and Li Sun (Li Sen, Li Ch'i-han). These men may also have been those who worked in the provisional central organization in Shanghai after the meeting in May 1920.[3]

In the same month, according to Fang Wen-ping, the Chinese Socialist Youth Corps held a meeting and decided to join the Communist Youth International. The founders of this branch of the CYI were Chang T'ai-lei, Shih Ts'un-t'ung (the same man who attended the organizational meeting of the CCP), Hui Tai-yung, Hsiao Ch'u-nu, and four others.[4]

In the following year groups were organized in Shanghai, Peking, Canton, Shantung, Hunan, Hupeh, and Japan. Branches of the Socialist Youth Corps (renamed the Young China Communist Party in January 1921) were also organized in Paris and Moscow.

The first local Communist group was organized in Shanghai in September 1920 by Ch'en Tu-hsiu and Voitinsky. According to Hatano, those who attended its founding meeting were Ch'en Tu-hsiu, Tai T'ien-ch'iu (Tai Chi-t'ao), Shen Ting-i (Sun Hsüan-lu), Ch'en Wang-tao, Li Han-chün, Shih Tsung-tung (Shih Ts'un-t'ung), Yüan Hsiao-hsien, Yang Ming-chai, Chang T'ai-lei, Chou Fu-hai, Chang Tung-sun, and Shao Li-tzu.[5]

According to Chow Tse-tsung, at least three others—Li Ta, Li Ch'i-han (Li Sen, Li Sun), and Yü Hsiu-sung—joined the group before the First Congress assembled.[6] Ch'en Tu-hsiu's two sons, Ch'en Ch'iao-yen and Ch'en Yen-nien, probably also joined the group.

In Peking there were eleven members in the first group, only nine of whom are known by name. These were Li Ta-chao, Chang Kuo-t'ao, Ho Meng-hsiung, Liu Jen-ch'ing, Lo Chang-lung, Teng Chung-hsia, Huang Ling-shuang, Kao Chün-yü, and Kao Yü-han. The two men whose names are not known were anarchists, as was Huang Ling-shuang.

In Canton, the members of the first group were Ch'en Kung-po, T'an P'ing-shan, Pao Hui-seng (Pao Hui-sheng), T'an Chih-t'ang, Ch'ü Sheng-pai (an anarchist), Chang T'ai-lei, Liu Erh-sung, Su Chao-cheng, Lin Wei-min, and Lin Po-chü (Lin Tsu-han).

In Ch'angsha, the first members were Mao Tse-tung, Ho Shu-heng, Ch'en Ch'ang, Hsia Hsi, and Kuo Liang.

In Wuhan, they were Tung Pi-wu, Ch'en T'an-ch'iu, Yün Tai-ying, and Hsiao Ch'u-nu.

In Tsinan: Wang Ching-mei and Teng En-ming.

In Japan: Chou Fu-hai and P'eng P'ai.

Among those who attended the founding meeting of the Young China Communist Party in Paris, in January 1921, or who joined it shortly thereafter, were Chou En-lai, Wang Jo-fei, Li Li-san, Ts'ai Ho-shen, Li Fu-ch'un, Li Wei-han, Ts'ai Ch'ang, Hsiang Chin-yü, Chang K'un-ti, Lo Hsüeh-tsan, Ssu Yang (Shih Yang, Chao Shih-yen), Wu Yü-chang (probably), Ch'en Yi, Teng Hsiao-p'ing, Fu Chung, and Jen Cho-hsüan (Yeh Ch'ing).

Among those in the first Moscow group were Hsiao Ching-kuang, Jen Pi-shih, Liu Shao-ch'i, Lo I-nung, and P'eng Shu-chih.

According to the accounts published, the delegates to the First Congress of the CCP in July 1921 represented 57 members, organized into seven groups, in Shanghai, Peking, Canton, Wuhan, Ch'angsha, Tsinan, and Japan. Paris and Moscow were not represented. So these lists of the members of the seven groups represented, totaling 47 members of the CCP, are still incomplete. Hui Tai-yung, a member of the CYI but not on any of these CCP lists, brings the total known to 48.

Accounts of the Congress given both by those who attended it and by later Chinese Communist historians disagree on whether there were 11, 12, or 13 delegates present. Ch'en Kung-po, a delegate, said in 1924 that there were 12.[7] The 1926 edition of the *Brief History of the Chinese Communist Party* states that there were 11.[8] In midsummer 1936 Mao told Snow that there were 12.[9] Then in October 1936 Ch'en T'an-ch'iu, who was a delegate, wrote an article stating that there were 13—a number that was repeated to Nym Wales the following year by another delegate, Tung Pi-wu.[10] This is the number used by Hatano, North, Schwartz, and others.[11] Since 1949 orthodox Chinese Communist histories have stated that there were 12 delegates.[12]

There are three possible resolutions of these discrepancies. First, Chang Kuo-t'ao has said in his unpublished autobiography that although 13 delegates were originally appointed, Mao sent Ho Shu-heng back to Ch'angsha before the Congress started. Thus only 12 may actually have attended. Second, Jerome Ch'en has recently pointed out that Hu Hua says there was only one delegate from Canton. Since all accounts agree that Ch'en Kung-po did attend, representing Canton, we might well assume that Pao Hui-sheng did not.[13] Finally, it is possible that Chang and Jerome Ch'en are both correct—that neither Ho nor Pao attended—and that there were only 11 delegates, as recorded in the 1926 edition of the *Brief History*.

Jerome Chen's conclusion, which substantiates the accounts of Ch'en Kung-po, Mao himself, and official Chinese Communist sources seems to me the most likely to be correct. I accordingly conclude that there were 12 delegates, representing seven Communist groups, as follows.

Shanghai:	Li Ta, Li Han-chün
Peking:	Chang Kuo-t'ao, Liu Jen-ch'ing
Canton:	Ch'en Kung-po, Pao Hui-sheng
Ch'angsha:	Mao Tse-tung
Wuhan:	Tung Pi-wu, Ch'en T'an-ch'iu
Tsinan:	Wang Ching-mei, Teng En-ming
Japan:	Chou Fu-hai

APPENDIX B

Excerpt from the CCP Politburo's "Resolution on Political Discipline" (November 14, 1927)

This is C. Martin Wilbur's translation of this excerpt, as it appears in "The Ashes of Defeat" (*China Quarterly*, No. 18, pp. 53–54). The disciplinary actions described here were taken against the leaders of the Nanch'ang Uprising at the November Plenum, the same Plenum at which Mao was expelled from the Central and Front Committees for his role in the Autumn Harvest Uprisings (see pp. 80–81 for the Plenum's condemnation of Mao). The treatment accorded Mao and that given the Nanch'ang leaders, and the reasons given for them, are interestingly parallel.

The Enlarged Conference of the Provisional Central Political Bureau has decided upon the following punishments for Party executive organs and responsible comrades for the above errors of execution and policy [i.e., those made during the Nanch'ang Uprising].

1. Comrade T'an P'ing-shan, in his actions and proposals, completely opposed the policy of land revolution from the time he became Minister of Agriculture in the Nationalist Government after the Fifth [CCP] Congress down till after the Nanch'ang Revolt. His acts were frequently independent actions separate from the Party, the most evident being that in July of this year, when the Wuhan Kuomintang and Government began pushing out the Communists, he secretly negotiated with Teng Yen-ta and others, advocating the dissolution of the Chinese CP and the organizing of a separate Third Party, and made propaganda among intellectual comrades to oppose Central and organize a Third Party. At the same time, he disregarded the Party's decision and without receiving Central's permission he privately requested Wang Ching-wei for leave of absence, while in his letter petitioning for leave he repeatedly cursed the thorny matter of the peasant movement. In conversations with Wang Ching-wei's delegate, Ch'en Ch'un-pu, he even more fervently cursed our Party Central and the peasant movement, and finally when the Central Political

Bureau decided he should go to Russia he did not accept orders and go. When he got to Kiukiang and Nanch'ang he even more completely developed his individual activity. In Kiukiang, because of his agreement in conversation with Ho Lung that Ho should oppose Chang [Fa-k'uei], in meetings of responsible comrades he stirred up an anti-Party atmosphere of disregarding Central, disregarding the Party, and acting on their own. When he got to Nanch'ang he continued his propaganda among the comrades and Kuomintang members for a Third Party. Later in the Revolutionary Committee his behavior was often to act first and inform the Front Committee later or not even inform it at all. He often prevented the carrying out of such policies as slaughtering bullies and gentry, or expropriation. These were all actions disobedient to our Party organization and he should be removed from the Party rolls immediately.

2. Comrade Chang Kuo-t'ao was entrusted by the Central Standing Committee to go to Nanch'ang and direct the revolt, but after Comrade Kuo-t'ao arrived at Kiukiang and Nanch'ang he did not execute Central's orders but on the contrary doubted the revolt should be advocated, going so far as to oppose it. After the Nanch'ang Incident he advocated negotiating with Chang Fa-k'uei. He also opposed the program of expropriating all land. The results of this disobedience to Central policies and its commission in sending him to the front to direct matters was to give the comrades at the front an even more injurious and even more rightist influence, and the Front Committee became even more wavering because of it. Comrade Kuo-t'ao should be removed from his positions as an alternate member of the Provisional Political Bureau and as a Central Executive Committee member.

3. Because of the extremely great errors of leadership committed by the Front Committee the comrades of the entire Front Committee should be given a Warning.

4. Comrade Hsü Kuang-ying, when he was Chief of the Public Security Bureau in Swatow, suppressed laborers, arrested them without authority, and even executed three poor folk who were looting. He should be punished by undergoing Party Observation for one year.

5. For the errors of the Southern Bureau and the Kwangtung Provincial Committee directing peasant revolts, in not understanding fully the slogans of the Policy on the Land Problem and in not arousing the peasant masses but merely taking military actions, the entire group should be given a Warning.

APPENDIX C

Excerpt from the CCP Politburo's Letter to Comrade Chu Teh (Late November 1927)

This letter appeared in *Central Political Newsletter,* No. 16 (November 30, 1927), [16], pp. 81–88. David Tseng of the Hoover Institution at Stanford University kindly made this translation, which I have altered in some minor respects.

The main armed forces of the workers' and peasants' uprising must be organized spontaneously by the workers and peasants themselves. No workers' and peasants' uprising can take place without the broad participation of the masses, merely on the strength of a band or group of bands of insurgents armed with a few rifles. Even if such isolated armed forces succeeded in killing a large number of the gentry, officials, and labor racketeers, in distributing the property of the capitalists and the rich, and in burning the houses of the landlords and the mortgage deeds of the creditors, little would come of it. In the eyes of the masses such acts are at best only a Liang-shan-po[a] type of chivalry aimed at righting the wrongs suffered by the people. They do not help to deepen the land revolution. Furthermore, isolated insurgent bands cannot withstand attack by the full military force of the ruling class; in the face of such an attack they either take to the hills or, worse still, suffer total collapse. They cannot hide themselves among the masses, to say nothing of being able to broaden the participation of the masses and extend the area of the uprising in order to resist the reactionary forces. Therefore, a force that has been split off from the reactionaries to aid the workers' and peasants' uprisings can only be

[a] The bandit heroes of the famous Chinese novel *The Water Margin,* assembled in the Liang-shan area in Shantung. Like Robin Hood, they took from the rich and gave to the poor, but did not change the social system. (*The Water Margin* was translated into English by Pearl S. Buck under the title *All Men Are Brothers,* New York, Grosset and Dunlap, 1933.)

regarded as ancillary to the armed might of the workers and peasants. Such a force must not become a band of roving insurgents standing in the way of uprisings. The present situation in which your troops find themselves and the mission entrusted to you are of such an ancillary nature to the workers' and peasants' uprisings.

APPENDIX D

The Land Law of February 7, 1930

This land law appears in *Red Bandit Reactionary Documents* [51], III, 912–18. The translation is my own.

Land Confiscation and Redistribution

I. After the uprising overthrows the regime of village bosses, gentry, and landlords, all land belonging to individuals or organizations—village bosses, gentry, landlords, ancestral shrines, temples, associations, or rich peasants—shall be immediately confiscated and become the public property of the soviet government. This includes cultivated, forested, residential, and water-covered land. The soviet government shall redistribute the land to peasants who have little or none of their own and to other poor people in need of land to cultivate. Where no soviets have been established, existing peasant associations shall have the power to confiscate and redistribute.

II. Village bosses, gentry, landlords, and the dependents of reactionaries [or perhaps—the original is ambiguous—"Dependents of village bosses, gentry, landlords, and reactionaries"] who, after investigation by the soviets, are permitted to remain in their townships, and who then have no other means of livelihood, may have an appropriate portion of land distributed to them.

III. Officers, soldiers, coolies, and persons actively engaged in revolutionary work shall also receive land, and the soviets shall send persons to help their dependents to cultivate it.

IV. Villagers engaged in industry, handicraft, commerce, or studies who are thereby able to maintain their livelihood shall not receive land; those who are unable to live from such occupations shall have sufficient land to maintain life distributed to them.

V. Hired farm laborers and jobless idlers shall receive land if they wish. Land distributed to a jobless idler shall be reclaimed by the soviet if he does not rid himself of such bad habits as opium smoking and gambling.

VI. Villagers working in other places shall not receive a share of the land redistributed [in their home villages].

VII. The hsiang shall be the unit for land redistribution. The peasants shall pool all the land they cultivate in their own and in neighboring hsiang for common redistribution. If three or four hsiang adjoin each other, and if some hsiang have many fields and others few, and if those with few fields will not be able to support all their inhabitants if the hsiang is taken as the unit, and if there are no other forms of production that can sustain life, then three or four hsiang may form one unit for the purpose of redistribution. But such mergers must be requested by the hsiang soviets and approved by the ch'ü soviets.

VIII. To satisfy the demands of the great majority of the people, and to enable the peasants to obtain land immediately, *the land shall be distributed equally among everyone living in a village. Men and women, old and young, shall each receive an equal share.*[a] The criterion of ability to work shall not be adopted.

IX. In principle, merchants and workers in cities shall not participate in the redistribution of land. However, if unemployed workers or the urban poor demand shares of land, it may be distributed to them, insofar as circumstances permit.

X. In order to destroy feudal forces and deal a blow to the rich peasants immediately, *the policies of "take from those who have much to help those who have little" and "take from those who have fertile land to help those who have poor land" shall be followed in redistributing land.*[b] Landlords and rich peasants shall not be allowed to conceal their land by not declaring it, nor shall they be allowed to withhold fertile land for themselves. After redistribution has been completed, the soviets shall place a wooden marker in each field indicating its average annual yield and the name of the person who is to cultivate it.

XI. All title deeds held by village bosses, gentry, landlords, and

[a] This provision appeared in the Ching-kang-shan land law of December 1928 and the Hsing-kuo land law of April 1929. It was condemned by the 28 Bolsheviks after the Fourth Plenum of the Central Committee of the CCP in January 1931. In RSQHP, Mao claims that it was correct. Italics mine.

[b] These policies were also advocated in the Ching-kang-shan and Hsing-kuo land laws, condemned by the 28 Bolsheviks after the Fourth Plenum, and defended in RSQHP. They appear again, in abbreviated form, in Article XI of the *Agrarian Reform Law of the People's Republic of China* (Peking: Foreign Languages Press, 1950, p. 11). Italics mine.

rich peasants, as well as deeds to public lands held by ancestral shrines and temples, shall be surrendered to the hsiang soviets or the hsiang or ch'ü peasant associations within a specified time. They shall then be publicly burned.

XII. After redistribution of land, the hsien or ch'ü soviets shall issue cultivation certificates.[c]

XIII. When anyone within a hsiang dies, moves away, or changes his occupation, the land distributed to him shall be reclaimed by the soviets for further redistribution. Upon the birth or immigration of a person into a hsiang, the soviet shall distribute land to him, but not until after the harvest following his arrival.

XIV. If land redistribution following an uprising occurs after seeds have been planted, the plants shall be cultivated and the harvest reaped by the peasant to whom the land is distributed. The sower shall have no claim to the harvest.

XV. Tea plantations, river banks, and waste land [on which grain other than rice can be cultivated] shall be redistributed. Large ponds, which cannot easily be divided, shall remain in the possession of the soviets, which shall manage them or lease them out at a fixed rate.

XVI. The equivalence of bamboo and tung-oil forests to rice land shall be computed according to their respective yields. The forests shall then be redistributed together with the land. However, if such forests have already become industrial capital—if workshops have been established and labor employed—the soviets may lease them out; they need not be redistributed.

XVII. Pine, fir, and similar forests shall be managed or leased out by the soviet government. However, if the people of a hsiang need wood for the construction of ponds, ditches, or other public utilities, or to repair and rebuild houses burned by the reactionaries, they may cut and use trees after receiving permission from the soviet government.

XVIII. Firewood mountains shall be closed or opened to the public at the discretion of the soviet government.

XIX. To satisfy the demands of the poor and miserable peasants, all land confiscated shall be redistributed to them. The soviet government shall not hold back any [for its own use]. But under certain circumstances—if there is a small amount of land left over after redistribution, for instance—the extra land may be used to establish

[c] Cultivation certificates granted individual peasants the right to cultivate individual plots of land. Only the right of use was granted; the land remained the property of the soviet government.

a model farm or temporarily leased out. At the same time, a portion [ten percent] of the houses confiscated shall be retained for use by public institutions.

Cancellation of Debts

XX. All outstanding debts that workers, peasants, and poor people owe to village bosses, gentry, landlords, and rich peasants shall not be repaid. All promissory notes shall be surrendered to the soviet government or the peasant associations within a specified time and shall be publicly burned.

XXI. All outstanding debts, old and new, that village bosses, gentry, landlords, and merchants owe to the public or to workers, peasants, and poor people shall be repaid.

XXII. All debts of workers, peasants, and poor people to merchants, if incurred before the uprising, shall not be repaid, irrespective of whether such debts resulted from usurious business transactions or personal loans.

XXIII. All debts that workers, peasants, and poor people owe to each other, if incurred before the uprising, as a rule shall not be repaid. Only loans extended without interest, for the purpose of friendly assistance, and which the debtors are willing to repay, shall be excepted from this provision.

XXIV. Workers, peasants, and poor people who have mortgaged or pawned articles or houses to village bosses, gentry, landlords, rich peasants, or pawnbrokers shall have their securities returned with no conditions attached.

XXV. All money and grain associations [two forms of mutual aid societies common in the villages of South China] shall be abolished.

XXVI. Loans at usurious interest rates shall be forbidden. Hsien soviets shall fix appropriate rates of interest, taking the local financial situation into account. The rates fixed shall not exceed the local interest rates on ordinary capital under ordinary economic conditions.

Land Taxes

XXVII. To provide the necessary funds to suppress counterrevolution (e.g., to expand the Red Army and the Red Guards, and finance the agencies of political power) and to promote the interests of the masses (e.g., to establish schools and clinics, provide relief for the disabled, the old, and the young, and repair roads, ponds, and ditches) the soviets shall collect land taxes from the peasants.

XXVIII. The land tax shall be based on the principles of protecting the poor peasants, winning over the middle peasants, and striking a blow at the rich peasants. It shall be levied only after the soviets have been established, the masses have received actual benefits, and permission has been granted by the higher-level soviets.

XXIX. A peasant's land tax shall be assessed according to the average annual rice yield of the land redistributed to him. The assessment shall be graduated in the following manner:

1. A person harvesting less than five piculs of rice shall be exempt from the land tax.
2. A person harvesting six piculs shall pay a tax of one percent of the harvest.
3. A person harvesting seven piculs shall pay a tax of one and one-half percent.
4. A person harvesting eight piculs shall pay a tax of two and one-half percent.
5. A person harvesting nine piculs shall pay a tax of four percent.
6. A person harvesting ten piculs shall pay a tax of five and one-half percent.
7. A person harvesting eleven piculs shall pay a tax of seven percent.
8. A person harvesting twelve piculs shall pay a tax of eight percent.

For each additional picul of rice harvested per person an additional one and one-half percent of the harvest shall be collected as land tax.

XXX. Collection and disbursement of land taxes shall be controlled by the higher-level soviet government. Lower-level government agencies shall not collect and disburse land taxes at their own discretion. The higher-level government shall determine the criteria for disbursement according to the total amount of taxes collected and the urgency and importance of the needs of the government at all levels.

Wages

XXXI. Wherever the wages of handicraft workers and hired farm hands in the villages have been too low in the past, they shall be raised. Wage rates shall be determined by the soviet government in accordance with two criteria: variations in the costs of daily necessities [excluding food produced in the villages] and variations in the quantity of rice harvested per person per year. Before setting wage rates, the hsiang and ch'ü soviets must obtain the approval of the hsien or provincial soviet.

APPENDIX E

Mao Tse-tung's "Fan-tui pen-pen-chu-i" (Oppose Bookism) (May 1930)

This essay is from *Selections from the Works of Mao Tse-tung* (Peking, People's Publishing Co., 1964 [83], I, 17–28). Dennis Doolin of the Hoover Institution at Stanford University kindly made this translation for me. I have altered it in a number of minor respects. The "idealism" (*wei-hsin-chu-i*) against which Mao inveighs here is identical to that in his "Dialectical Materialism," "On Practice," and "On Contradiction." The footnotes are all in the Chinese edition.

Without Investigation, There Is No Right to Speak

If you have not made an investigation of a particular problem, your right to speak on it is suspended. Is this too drastic? Not at all. If you have not made an investigation of the actual and historical conditions of the particular problem you are discussing, if you do not know its background, you will inevitably be talking through your hat. Since we all know that such talk cannot solve problems, there is no injustice in suspending your right to speak. Many of our comrades talk all day long with their eyes shut. This is a shameful thing for Communist party members, for how can there be Communists who talk through their hats?

Undesirable!
Undesirable!
Stress investigation!
Oppose irresponsible talk!

Investigation Is the Way to Solve Problems

Are you unable to solve a certain problem? Then you must investigate its current condition and its history! Once you have made a thorough investigation, you will have the means for its solution. All conclusions come after investigation, not before. Only an idiot racks his brain for the means to solve a problem without first investigating, either on his own or by getting a group of people together. Such a person will be unable to think of a good means. In other words, he inevitably comes up with the wrong means.

Many inspectors, guerrilla leaders, and newly assigned work cadres like to declare their political opinion the moment they arrive on the scene. After seeing some superficialities, some side issues, they gesticulate and criticize, pointing out mistakes and errors. Such subjective, irresponsible talk is most reprehensible. One who talks this way will inevitably ruin the matter and lose mass support, and he will not be able to solve the problems.

Many doing leadership work only sigh when confronted with difficult problems, instead of solving them. They become frustrated and ask for a transfer on the grounds that their "talent is too small for the job." These are the words of a coward. Stretch your legs, take a walk around your work area, and learn the Confucian way of "inquiring into everything."[a] Then, no matter how small your talent, you will be able to solve problems. Though your mind may be blank when you go out, it will no longer be so by the time you return: it will be filled with the facts you need for the solution of the problems, and in this manner they will be solved. Must you go out? Not necessarily. You may call an investigative meeting of those who understand the situation, and by this means locate the "source" of a problem that you consider difficult and clarify its "present conditions." The problem is then easily solved.

Investigation is the "ten-month gestation"; solution of the problem is the "one-day delivery." Investigation is the way to solve problems.

Oppose Bookism

"Anything in the books is right." This is a psychology still extant among the peasants of culturally backward China. Even when discussing problems in the Communist party, there are those who always say "Let's look at the book." But when we say that a directive issued by the higher leadership organ is accurate, this is not simply because the directive comes from the higher organ, but because the contents of the directive are compatible with, and required by, the objective and subjective conditions of the struggle. Blind enforcement [of directives] without discussion and observation according to practical conditions is an erroneous, formalist attitude built on the naïve "higher level" concept. Such formalism prevents the party's strategic line from

[a] "Confucius enters the Imperial Ancestral Temple and inquires into everything." "*Pa-hsiu*, No. 3," *The Analects*.

penetrating the masses. Blind, superficial, and inflexible enforcement of a directive from a higher level is not its true implementation, but is actually resistance to such implementation, or the most ingenious way of subverting it.

The bookish method of studying social science is most dangerous, and may even lead to the road of counterrevolution. That many Communist party members in China who relied on books in their study of social science have turned counterrevolutionary, group by group, is clear proof of this. When we say that Marxism is right, this is definitely not because Marx was a "sage," but because his theory has been verified in our practice and our struggle. We need Marxism in our struggle. We welcome his theory, but we do so without any formalistic ideas or sense of mystery. Many who have studied Marxist books have turned against the revolution, while illiterate workers have often successfully mastered Marxism. Marxist books should be studied, but their study must be coordinated with actual conditions in our country. We need books, but we must correct the error of bookism, the reliance on books without reference to practical conditions. How is bookism corrected? Only by investigating practical conditions.

In the Absence of Practical Investigation, Idealism Will Govern Class Analysis and the Direction of Work: Adventurism, If Not Opportunism, Will Result

Do you question this conclusion? The facts will convince you. Try to assess the political conditions and direct struggle-work apart from practical investigation, and won't you find it to be nothing but empty idealism? Can such empty, idealistic political assessments and work guidance result in anything save opportunist or adventurist errors? Errors are inevitable. Errors come not from lack of planning prior to action, but from neglect of practical social conditions prior to planning. This often happens with the Red Army guerrillas. Officers of the Li K'uei type[b] take foolish summary actions every time they discover their men doing anything wrong. The wrongdoers become dissatisfied, many disputes result, and the leaders lose all their prestige. Don't we often encounter such occurrences in the Red Army?

We must eliminate the idealistic spirit and prevent all opportunist

[b] Li K'uei was a heroic figure in the peasant war toward the end of the Northern Sung dynasty in China's famous novel *The Water Margin* [translated into English by Pearl S. Buck under the title *All Men Are Brothers,* New York, Grosset and Dunlap, 1933]. Simple and straightforward, he was devoted to the peasant revolutionary cause, but too hasty in handling matters.

and adventurist errors from occurring before we can complete the task of fighting for the masses and defeating the enemy. We must strive to make practical investigations before we can eliminate the idealistic spirit.

Social and Economic Investigation Is for the Purpose of Arriving at a Correct Class Assessment and a Correct Revolutionary Strategy

Why must we investigate social and economic conditions? We reply in this manner. The objects of our social and economic investigation are all classes in society, not fragmentary social phenomena. The comrades of the Fourth Red Army have recently been giving attention to investigative work, but many of them are using the wrong method.[c] The result of their sort of investigation is a deceptive account, like the tall tales a villager hears when he goes to town, or the panoramic view of people and cities seen from the summit of a high mountain. Such investigation is of little use. It will not enable us to reach our principal goal, which is to clarify the political and economic conditions of the social classes. We want our investigation to yield [a correct analysis of] the history and current condition of class relations. For example, when investigating the social status and class position [*ch'eng-fen*] of the peasantry, we must collect statistics on the social and economic conditions of the different types of peasantry, not merely as distinguished by their tenure relations, such as the land-owning, semi-land-owning, and tenant farmers, but even more important as distinguished by their classes and strata such as the rich, middle, and poor peasants. When investigating the mercantile elements, we must know the statistics of the social and economic conditions of the different trades, such as grain, clothing, medicine . . . [ellipsis in original], but even more those of the small, middle, and large merchants. We must investigate not only the economic conditions of the trades, but even more the class conditions within the trades. We must investigate not only relations among the trades, but even more the rela-

[c] Comrade Mao Tse-tung has always given serious attention to investigative work; he has considered social investigation the primary task of leadership and the foundation of policy formulation. It was at his instigation that the investigative work of the Fourth Red Army was gradually expanded, and it was he who developed social investigation into a systematic work procedure. The Red Army's Political Department worked out detailed investigation forms, including such items as the conditions of the mass struggle, reactionary factions, economic life, and land tenure by the various classes in the villages. Upon arriving in an area, the Red Army would first clarify class relations before proposing slogans suited to mass needs.

tions among the classes. The principal method of our investigative work is the dissection of the many types of social classes, and our ultimate goal is to clarify relations among them. Thus we can make a correct assessment, determining which classes are the major forces of the revolutionary struggle, which ones we should strive to gain as our allies, and which ones should be overthrown, and then decide on our correct struggle strategy. All this must be done before we can achieve our goal.

What social classes should be given attention in our investigation? They are the industrial proletariat, the handicraft workers, the tenant farmers, the poor farmers, the urban poor, the lumpenproletariat, the handicraftsmen, the small merchants, the middle farmers, the rich farmers, the landlord class, the mercantile bourgeoisie, and the industrial bourgeoisie. The conditions of these classes (some of which are strata) are what we must give attention to in our investigations. Except for the industrial proletariat and the industrial bourgeoisie, which are absent in our [present] temporary work area, we encounter all of them regularly. Our struggle strategy is our strategy toward all these classes and strata.

Our former investigations had a great defect: overemphasizing the rural while neglecting the urban. Hence many comrades are hazy about our strategy toward the urban poor and the mercantile bourgeoisie. The development of the struggle has made us leave the mountaintop and proceed to the plains.[d] But though our bodies have left the mountain, our thoughts remain there. As we understand the countryside, so we must understand the cities, or we will fail to adapt ourselves to the needs of the revolutionary struggle.

The Victory of China's Revolutionary Struggle Depends on Our Comrades' Comprehension of China's Conditions

The goal of our struggle is to shift from democracy to socialism. The first steps in our task are to win over a majority of the working class, activate the peasantry and the urban poor, overthrow the landlord class, the imperialists, and the Kuomintang regime, and thus complete the democratic revolution. As the struggle develops, we must begin the work of the socialist revolution. The completion of

[d] "Mountaintop" refers to the Ching-kang-shan area on the Kiangsi-Hunan border, "plains" to the plains in southern Kiangsi and western Fukien. In January 1929, Comrade Mao Tse-tung led the major force of the Fourth Army down from Ching-kang-shan to march on southern Kiangsi and western Fukien, where they set up two great revolutionary bases.

our great revolutionary task will not be simple or easy, and it will depend entirely on the correctness and firmness of the struggle strategy of the proletarian political party. An erroneous or hesitant and vacillating struggle strategy on the part of the proletarian political party will inevitably lead the revolution to temporary defeat. We must realize that the bourgeois political party also discusses its strategy daily. Its problems are how to spread the reformist influence among the workers and thus deceive them into withdrawing support from the Communist party's leadership, how to get the rich peasantry to suppress the uprisings of the poor peasantry, how to organize the lumpenproletariat to suppress the revolution, and so on. Under the conditions of the increasingly acute class struggle, with fighting going on at close quarters, the victory of the proletariat depends entirely on the correctness and firmness of the struggle strategy of its political party—the Communist party.

A correct and firm struggle strategy on the part of the Communist party definitely cannot be produced by a few persons sitting together in a room; it can only be produced in the process of the mass struggle; i.e., in practical experience. Hence we must constantly clarify our view of social conditions and continually pursue practical investigations. Some comrades with inflexible, conservative, formalistic, and empty optimistic minds consider that our current struggle strategy cannot be excelled, that the "book" of the Sixth All-China Party Congress assures permanent victory, and that we are invincible because we follow its predetermined method.[e] These ideas are completely wrong; they are totally inconsistent with the ideological line of Communist party members who create new situations through struggle; they result in entirely conservative lines. If such conservative lines are not completely discarded, they will bring harm to the comrades who hold them and cause a great loss to the revolution. There are apparently some comrades in the Red Army who are satisfied with their present relations [with the masses] and do not seek to penetrate deeper [into the masses]. With empty-headed optimism, they erroneously excuse their laziness by saying "This is the way of the proletariat" (*wu-ch'an-chieh-chi chiu-shih che-yang*). They sit, with full stomachs, dozing in the office, and never deign to go among the masses

[e] The "book" refers to the resolutions passed at the Sixth All-China Congress of the Chinese Communist Party in July 1928, which dealt with the organization of political power and with politics, the peasantry, land, and other problems. At the beginning of 1929, the Vanguard Committee of the Fourth Army printed these resolutions in pamphlet form and issued them to the Red Army and local party organizations.

to make some investigations of society. Their conversation is limited to a few platitudes that only bore the listener. We must shout at the top of our voices to awaken them:

Immediately change your conservative thinking!

Adopt the progressive struggle thinking of a Communist party member!

Take part in the struggle!

Go among the masses! Make practical investigations!

The Technique of Investigation

1. Discussions must be held at investigative meetings. Only thus will we obtain accurate data and reach correct conclusions. The method of relying on one's individual experiences, without holding discussions at investigative meetings, easily results in error. Casual questioning without proposing the central issue for discussion at the meeting table will not lead to correct conclusions.

2. Who should come to the investigative meeting? Persons with a profound understanding of social and economic conditions. As to age, old people are best, because they possess rich experience and understand causes and effects as well as current conditions. Young people with experience in the struggle should also be included, for their thinking is progressive and their powers of observation are keen. As to occupation, the meetings should include workers, farmers, merchants, and intellectuals, and sometimes soldiers and tramps. Naturally, those unconnected with a problem need not be present at a meeting discussing it. For example, those in industry, agriculture, or academic work need not attend a discussion of commerce.

3. Should the number of participants be large or small? This depends on the leadership ability of the investigator concerned. A capable investigator can handle meetings of a dozen or two dozen people. Such a large number makes for greater accuracy in assessing data (for example, on the percentage of poor peasants in a village) and for more knowledgeable conclusions (for example, on whether land should be equally or differentially allocated). Of course, large meetings also have a disadvantage. Investigators with little leadership ability will be unable to keep order. Hence the meeting's size depends on the ability of the investigator. But there should be no fewer than three persons present, for otherwise one's view may become restricted and the investigation may become incompatible with the actual conditions.

4. Preparation and use of an outline for investigations. An investi-

gative outline must be prepared beforehand, and the investigator must follow it in asking his questions, which the participants must answer orally. Debates should be held on points that are unclear or doubtful. The outline must contain both general categories and their subdivisions. For example, "commerce" is the general category; "piece goods," "food grains," "sundry goods," and "medicines" are its subdivisions; and "piece goods" is further subdivided into "foreign fabrics," "native cotton cloth," "silk and satin," etc.

5. Personal attendance is required. All who supervise work, from the chairman of the hsiang soviet to the chairman of the Central Government, from the battalion leader to the commander-in-chief, and from the secretary of a party branch to the secretary-general of the party, must personally engage in the practical investigation of the social economy, instead of simply relying on written reports. Personal investigation and written reports are two different matters.

6. Penetration of the masses is required. Those first entering into investigative work must do intensive investigation once or twice. In other words, they must understand thoroughly the background of one area (e.g., a village or a city) or one problem (e.g., the grain problem or the currency problem). A profound understanding of one area or one problem will make it easier to investigate other areas and other problems in the future.

7. The investigator must do the recording personally. Not only must he serve as chairman of the meeting, so as to conduct it properly, but he must also do the recording himself and write down the outcome of the investigation. The duty of recording must not be delegated.

Notes

Notes

Complete publication data are given in the Bibliography, pp. 355–69. Abbreviations used are explained in the List of Abbreviations, p. xiii. Works in Chinese are referred to by English translations of their titles and keyed to the list of Chinese sources in the Bibliography by bracketed numbers.

I. Introduction

1. See Franz Borkenau, *European Communism* (New York: Harper and Brothers, 1953), pp. 170, 226–29, for the creation of the OGPU's Spanish section; see also Walter Krivitsky, *I Was Stalin's Agent* (London: H. Hamilton, 1940), p. 109.

2. Mao Tse-tung, *Selected Works* (New York: International Publishers, 1954–62, 5 vols.), IV, 171–218; the Chinese version is *Mao Tse-tung hsüan-chi* (Peking: People's Publishing Co., 1951–61, 4 vols.) [84], III, 955–1002. Hereafter Mao's *Selected Works* will be abbreviated SW and his *Hsüan-chi* will be abbreviated HC.

3. Mao, SW, I, 153; HC, I, 138.

4. This is the conclusion reached by Charles B. McLane after an extensive search of Russian-language sources. See McLane, *Soviet Policy and the Chinese Communists: 1931–1946* (New York: Columbia University Press, 1958), p. 34.

5. Mao, SW, IV, 157–218; HC, III, 941–1002.

6. *Cheng-feng wen-hsien* (Party Rectification Papers—hereafter CFWH) (Shanghai: Liberation Press, 1949) [12], pp. 61–66. See also the English translations of the Chinese documents in Boyd Compton, *Mao's China: Party Reform Documents, 1942–44* (Seattle: University of Washington Press, 1952), *passim*.

7. Mao, SW, IV, 171–218; HC, III, 955–1002.

8. Liu Shao-ch'i, *On the Party* (Peking: Foreign Languages Press, 1952) [73]. The Chinese edition is *Lun tang* (Peking: People's Publishing Company, 1950) [72]. Liu's other *Lun tang* (Hua-pei: New China Bookstore, 1946) [71] is a completely different work, made up of articles reprinted from CFWH. Citations are to the 1950 original [72] and its 1952 translation [73].

9. Mao, SW, IV, 218. Liu, *On the Party* [73], pp. 143–47; *Lun tang* [72], pp. 147–50.

10. McLane, p. 176.

11. The best exposition of this thesis is found in Zbigniew Brzezinski, *The Soviet Bloc* (Cambridge: Harvard University Press, 1960), especially Chapter 16, "Ideology and Power in Relations Among Communist States," pp. 383–408.

12. Stuart R. Schram, *The Political Thought of Mao Tse-tung* (New York: Praeger, 1963), p. 92.

13. Chang Kuo-t'ao, interview with H. R. Lieberman, Hong Kong, 1952 [2].

14. Kung Ch'u, *The Red Army and I* (Hong Kong: Southwind Publishing Company, 1954) [63], pp. 395–400.

15. Mao, SW, IV, 178; HC, III, 962.

16. All these accusations are cited in Tso-liang Hsiao, *Power Relations within the Chinese Communist Movement, 1930–1934* (Seattle: University of Washington Press, 1961), pp. 164–69, from documents adopted by party conferences in the soviet districts in October and November 1931.

17. Wang Ming's *The Two Lines* [100] was first issued in Shanghai by the Proletarian Bookstore in February 1931. A second edition, bearing the same title, was published in Moscow in March 1932. A third edition, with a new title, *Struggle for the More Complete Bolshevization of the Chinese Communist Party,* was issued in Yenan in July 1940. This book is based on a Comintern letter of July 23, 1930, and the Comintern directive of November 16, 1930, both addressed to the Chinese Politburo. The Moscow and Yenan editions are identical, containing an appendix that does not appear in the Shanghai edition. According to Hsiao, "The importance lies in the part of the book called postscript inserted in the second edition published in Moscow in 1932, but not the first edition published in Shanghai in 1931 as the Mao machine would have us believe. The postscript contains virtually all the major points which Mao and his group in the 1945 'Resolution on Some Historical Problems' [RSQHP] severely attacked." Hsiao, p. 203. Hsiao here substantiates a point at which I arrived independently, that it was the Moscow formulations of Wang Ming that Mao attacked.

18. Mao, HC, III, 986–87; SW, I, 206.

II. The Beginning of Mao's Party Career

1. Mao, SW, IV, 171; HC, III, 955.

2. The quotation is "in order to lead, one must foresee." Mao, SW, IV, 209; HC, III, 989.

3. Mao, SW, IV, 190.

4. *Ibid.,* p. 193.

5. *Ibid.,* p. 197.

6. *Ibid.*, pp. 190, 193, 197.

7. In Chinese this adjective is *ying-ming*.

8. Mao, SW, IV, 197.

9. Mao, HC, III, 956. My translation.

10. This analysis was altered in 1956, when the CCP discovered right opportunist error even in the period between 1924 and 1927, i.e., the whole period of the Stalin-Bukharin alliance.

11. Mao, SW, IV, 174–75.

12. Chang Kuo-t'ao, interview with Hsiao Tso-liang, Hong Kong, October 1959, cited in Hsiao, pp. 296–97.

13. Kung [63], pp. 395–400.

14. Edgar Snow, *Red Star Over China* (hereafter RSOC—New York: Modern Library, 1944), p. 169; Central Committee of the CCP, resolution quoted in *Kuo-wen Weekly*, V, Nos. 2 and 3 (Jan. 8 and 15, 1928), as cited in Conrad Brandt, *Stalin's Failure in China* (Cambridge: Harvard University Press, 1958), p. 167. A more extensive translation of the part appearing in the January 15, 1928, issue can be found in Karl A. Wittfogel, "The Legend of 'Maoism,'" Part 2, *China Quarterly*, No. 2 (Apr.–June, 1960), pp. 32–33. *Central Newsletter* [46], No. 13 (Nov. 30, 1927), p. 41, confirms the accuracy of the *Kuo-wen Weekly* version and gives the only version published by the CCP.

15. U.S., Congress, House, Committee on Un-American Activities, "Constitution of the Communist International" (adopted by the Sixth Congress in 1928), in *The Communist Conspiracy* (Washington, D.C.: U.S. Government Printing Office, 1956), Part 1, Section C, pp. 228–33.

16. The list of delegates to the Congress appears in Communist International, *Der I. Kongress der Kommunistischen Internationale: Protokoll der Verhandlungen in Moskau, vom 2. bis zum 19. März 1919* (Petrograd: 1920), pp. 4–5. Cf. Jane Degras, *The Communist International, 1919–1943* (London: Oxford University Press, 1956, 2 vols.), I, 452. An excellent recent account of the First Congress can be found in James W. Hulse, *The Forming of the Communist International* (Stanford: Stanford University Press, 1964), pp. 17–19. The best summaries of the First Congress are in Olga Hess Gankin, "The Bolsheviks and the Founding of the Third International," *Slavonic and Eastern Review*, XX (1941), 88–101; Edward Hallett Carr, *A History of Soviet Russia* (New York: Macmillan, 1950–64, 8 vols.), *The Bolshevik Revolution*, III, 119–26; and Stanley W. Page, *Lenin and World Revolution* (New York: New York University Press, 1959), pp. 125–33.

17. Degras, I, 138. Italics mine.

18. *Ibid.*, I, 138–39; Hulse, pp. 201–2.

19. Brandt, pp. 4–5; Degras, I, 139; Hulse, pp. 201–2; Communist International, *The Second Congress of the Communist International: Report of the Proceedings of the Petrograd Session of July 17th and of the Moscow Sessions of July 23rd–August 7th, 1920* (Moscow, 1920), pp. 577–79.

20. Degras, I, 143.

21. *Ibid.*

22. *Ibid.*

23. Xenia Joukoff Eudin and Robert C. North, *Soviet Russia and the East, 1920–27* (Stanford: Stanford University Press, 1957), pp. 25–30.

24. Carr, *The Bolshevik Revolution*, I, 314–29; William H. Chamberlin, *The Russian Revolution* (New York: Grosset and Dunlap, 1965), II, 418–29.

25. Brandt, p. 13.

26. Degras, I, 453.

27. Günther Nollau, *International Communism and World Revolution* (New York: Praeger, 1961), pp. 132–34, 178–81; Isaac Deutscher, *Stalin* (New York: Vintage, 1960), pp. 228ff.

28. Nollau, pp. 86–87.

29. C. Martin Wilbur and Julie Lien-ying How, eds., *Documents on Communism, Nationalism, and Soviet Advisers in China, 1918–1927* (New York: Columbia University Press, 1959), pp. 79–137; Carr, *History of Soviet Russia, Socialism in One Country*, III, Part 2, 987–97; Brandt, pp. 34–39, 126–29.

30. Snow, RSOC, pp. 144, 147–48.

31. *Ibid.*, p. 144; Howard L. Boorman, "Mao Tse-tung: The Lacquered Image," *China Quarterly*, No. 16 (Oct.–Dec. 1963), p. 7; Schram, *Political Thought*, p. 12.

32. Trans. in Schram, *Political Thought*, p. 12.

33. Schram, *Political Thought*, p. 12; Boorman, "Mao Tse-tung," pp. 2–6; Snow, RSOC, pp. 121–48.

34. Li Jui, *Comrade Mao's Early Revolutionary Activities* (Peking: Chinese Youth Publishing Co., 1957) [67], pp. 48–54.

35. Boorman, "Mao Tse-tung," p. 7.

36. Snow, RSOC, pp. 144–45. Li Jui (pp. 71–72) identifies one of the ultra-reactionaries as Ch'en Ch'ang.

37. Boorman, "Mao Tse-tung," p. 7; Snow, RSOC, pp. 145–47.

38. Snow, RSOC, pp. 146–47.

39. *Ibid.*, p. 147.

40. *Ibid.*, p. 150.

41. Siao-yu, *Mao Tse-tung and I Were Beggars* (Syracuse: Syracuse University Press, 1959), p. 166; Snow, RSOC, p. 151.

42. Li Jui, p. 91.

43. Boorman, "Mao Tse-tung," pp. 8–9.

44. Snow, RSOC, pp. 155–56.

45. Boorman, "Mao Tse-tung," pp. 10–12.

46. Chow Tse-tsung, *The May Fourth Movement: Intellectual Revolution in Modern China* (Cambridge: Harvard University Press, 1960), p. 249; *Research Guide to the May Fourth Movement* (Cambridge: Harvard University Press, 1963), pp. 120–21.

47. Conrad Brandt, Benjamin Schwartz, and John K. Fairbank, *A Doc-*

umentary History of Chinese Communism (Cambridge: Harvard University Press, 1952), p. 29; Chow, *May Fourth Movement,* pp. 40, 249; Robert A. Scalapino and George T. Yu, *The Chinese Anarchist Movement* (Berkeley: Center for Chinese Studies, University of California, 1961), pp. 49–55; Snow, RSOC, p. 137; Nym Wales, *The Chinese Labor Movement* (New York: John Day, 1945), pp. 26, 38.

48. Boorman, "Liu Shao-ch'i: A Political Profile," *China Quarterly,* No. 10 (Apr.–June 1962), p. 4.

49. Brandt, pp. 37–38.

50. Boorman, "Liu Shao-ch'i," pp. 5–6.

51. Wales, *Labor Movement,* pp. 25–26; Jean Chesneaux, *Le Mouvement ouvrier chinois de 1919 à 1927* (Paris: Mouton, 1962), pp. 205–10.

52. Chesneaux, p. 260; Wales, *Labor Movement,* p. 32.

53. Boorman, "Liu Shao-ch'i," pp. 5–6.

54. Wales, *Red Dust* (Stanford: Stanford University Press, 1952), pp. 83–89.

55. Snow, RSOC, p. 159.

56. Harold R. Isaacs, *The Tragedy of the Chinese Revolution,* rev. ed. (Stanford: Stanford University Press, 1951), p. 59. Citations are to the revised edition unless otherwise noted. See also Wilbur and How, pp. 83–84, 493*n25*.

57. Wilbur and How, p. 88.

58. Boorman, "Mao Tse-tung," p. 13; Jerome Ch'en, *Mao and the Chinese Revolution* (London: Oxford University Press, 1965), p. 92; Li Jui [67], p. 237; Snow, RSOC, p. 156.

59. Wilbur and How, p. 86.

60. Brandt, pp. 35–38. Brandt's account is based on an interview with Chang Kuo-t'ao and on Ts'ai Ho-shen's story in Ts'ai, "History of Opportunism in the CCP," *Problemy Kitaia,* No. 1 (Moscow, 1929) [97], p. 5. Jerome Ch'en (p. 98) states that Mao quarreled with Yeh Ch'u-ts'ang, then the head of the KMT Organization Department in Shanghai, who became a leader of the Western Hills faction after Sun Yat-sen's death.

61. Chang Kuo-t'ao's interview with Brandt, in Brandt, pp. 36–38; partial confirmation in Mao's interviews with Snow, RSOC, p. 159.

62. Brandt, p. 37.

III. The Destruction of the United Front

1. Eudin and North, p. 267.

2. *Ibid.,* p. 268.

3. Shinkichi Eto, "Hai-lu-feng—The First Chinese Soviet Government" (Part 2), *China Quarterly,* No. 9 (Jan.–Mar. 1962), p. 153.

4. *Ibid.,* pp. 156–57.

5. Snow, RSOC, p. 160; *Materials of Modern History* (Shanghai: Hai-t'ien

Publishing Co., 1934–35, 4 vols.) [55], I, 136, and IV, 344–45. At that time Shen Yen-ping (better known by the pen name of Mao Tun) was Mao's secretary. His brother was one of the 28 Bolsheviks, Shen Tse-min.

6. Snow, RSOC, p. 158.

7. Eto (Part 2), p. 155.

8. Wilbur and How, p. 229.

9. Eto, "Hai-lu-feng" (Part 1), *China Quarterly,* No. 8 (Oct.–Dec. 1961), pp. 179–82.

10. Deutscher, *Stalin,* pp. 302–8; Eudin and North, pp. 290–97; Leonard Schapiro, *The Communist Party of the Soviet Union* (New York: Random House, 1959), pp. 296–303; Carr, *Socialism,* III, Part 2, pp. 736–72.

11. *Kommunisticheskii Internatsional,* No. 12 (49), Dec. 1925, pp. 30–31, cited in Carr, *Socialism,* III, Part 2, 749.

12. Wilbur and How, pp. 211–12.

13. *Ibid.,* pp. 186-99, 212.

14. *Ibid.,* pp. 206–9.

15. *Ibid.,* pp. 217–18.

16. O. Edmund Clubb, *Twentieth Century China* (New York: Columbia University Press, 1964), pp. 130–32.

17. Carr, *Socialism,* III, Part 2, 767–69.

18. *Ibid.,* pp. 769–72. Quote cited on p. 772.

19. Li Jui [67], p. 177.

20. Snow, RSOC, pp. 160–61.

21. Mao, HC, I, 3; SW, I, 13.

22. Mao, "Analysis of Various Classes of the Chinese Peasantry" [79], *Chinese Peasant,* No. 1 (Jan. 1, 1926), pp. 13–20; "Analysis of Various Classes in Chinese Society" [80], *Chinese Peasant,* No. 2 (Feb. 1, 1926), pp. 1-13.

23. As quoted in Schram, *Political Thought,* p. 144.

24. *Ibid.,* p. 176.

25. Kung [63], pp. 35–36.

26. Mao, "Classes of the Peasantry" [79], p. 20.

27. *Ibid.,* pp. 19–20.

28. Carr, *Socialism,* III, Part 2, 743.

29. Wilbur and How, pp. 217, 229; Jerome Ch'en, p. 104.

30. Isaacs, p. 197.

31. Wilbur and How, pp. 377–79.

32. Leon Trotsky, *The Stalin School of Falsification* (New York: Pioneer Publishers, 1937), pp. 164–73; Joseph Stalin, *Works* (Moscow: Foreign Languages Publishing House, 1951–55, 13 vols.), X, 18.

33. Wilbur and How, pp. 375–81.

34. Boorman, "Mao Tse-tung," p. 16.

35. Hua Kang, *A History of the Chinese National Liberation Movement* (Shanghai: 1947, 2 vols.) [59], II, 211; *The Peasant Movement in the Period of the First Revolutionary War,* in *Chinese Modern History Documentary*

Archive (Peking: 1953) [44], p. 274; *People's Tribune* [93], July, 30, 1927, p. 3. This last report comes from a signed article by Anna Louise Strong.

36. *People's Tribune* [93], July 30, 1927, p. 3.
37. *Ibid.*, pp. 2–3.
38. Wilbur and How, p. 428.
39. *Ibid.*, pp. 381–84.
40. *Ibid.*, pp. 386–88, 396–401.
41. Isaacs, pp. 126, 143; Wilbur and How, p. 534.
42. Isaacs, pp. 130–36.
43. *Ibid.*, pp. 126–27.
44. Wilbur and How, pp. 396–99.
45. Isaacs, pp. 143–53.
46. *Ibid.*, pp. 143–53, 163; Chesneaux, pp. 497–99, 503–6.
47. Isaacs, pp. 175–85; Chesneaux, pp. 512–14.
48. *The Hai-lu-feng Soviet* (n.p. [Shanghai?]: 1928) [52], p. 11.
49. *Ibid.*, pp. 13–16.
50. This is from the translation in Eudin and North, pp. 350–56, of Stalin's "On the Prospects of the Revolution in China," a speech to the Chinese Commission of the Seventh Enlarged Plenum of the ECCI, Nov. 30, 1926.
51. *Ibid.*, pp. 354–55.
52. Mao Tse-tung, "Report of an Investigation into the Peasant Movement in Hunan" [81]; *Guide Weekly*, No. 191 (Mar. 12, 1927); Central Bimonthly, No. 7 (Mar. 28, 1927); *Chinese Correspondence*, II, No. 8 (May 15, 1927).
53. Snow, RSOC, pp. 161–63.
54. Liu Chih-hsün, "Recollections of the Horse-Day Incident," *Pu-erh-shih-wei-k'o* (Bolshevik), No. 20 (May 30, 1928). Quoted in *Modern Chinese History Documentary Archive* [44], p. 384.
55. *People's Tribune* [93], May 6, 1927, p. 4; June 11, p. 2.
56. Liu Chih-hsün, p. 384.
57. Wales, *Red Dust*, p. 47. This is Hsieh Chüeh-tsai's story.
58. *Materials of Modern History* [55], I, Part 2, p. 179. This story has recently been retold in Jerome Ch'en, pp. 115–16.
59. Ts'ai Ho-shen, "Opportunism in the CCP" [97], p. 42; trans. in Robert C. North and Xenia J. Eudin, *M. N. Roy's Mission to China* (Berkeley: University of California Press, 1964), p. 106.
60. M. N. Roy, *Revolution and Counterrevolution in China* (Calcutta: Renaissance Publishers, 1946), pp. 551–52.
61. *Materials of Modern History* [55], I, Part 2, p. 179.
62. Wittfogel, "Legend of 'Maoism,'" Part 2, pp. 16–34; Eto, Part 2, pp. 161–62; *People's Tribune* [93], July 29, 1927, p. 4.
63. Agnes Smedley, *The Great Road: The Life and Times of Chu Teh* (New York: Monthly Review Press, 1956), pp. 199–201.

64. *Ibid.*, pp. 200–201.

65. C. Martin Wilbur, "The Ashes of Defeat," *China Quarterly*, No. 18 (Apr.–June 1964), pp. 9–10.

66. *Ibid.*, p. 35.

67. North and Eudin, pp. 125–26.

68. Wilbur, pp. 45–47.

69. *Ibid.*, p. 46.

70. *Ibid.*, pp. 46–47.

71. *Ibid.*, p. 35.

72. *Ibid.*, pp. 11, 46.

73. *Ibid.*, p. 52. Italics mine.

74. Brandt, pp. 151–52.

75. Brandt, Schwartz, and Fairbank, p. 35. The extent of Stalin's responsibility for the final breakdown of the united front between the KMT and the CCP has been one of the main points of contention among the many scholars who have studied this confusing and complex period. The question has been discussed at length in Brandt, *Stalin's Failure*; Isaacs, *Tragedy of the Chinese Revolution*; Robert C. North, *Moscow and Chinese Communists* (Stanford: Stanford University Press, 1953); North and Eudin, *Roy's Mission*; Benjamin Schwartz, *Chinese Communism and the Rise of Mao* (Cambridge: Harvard University Press, 1951); Wittfogel, "Legend of 'Maoism,'" Part 1, *China Quarterly*, No. 1 (Jan.–Mar., 1960), pp. 72–86; and Schwartz, "The Legend of the 'Legend of Maoism,'" *China Quarterly*, No. 2 (Apr.–June 1960), pp. 35–42.

76. As rendered in Schram, "On the Nature of Mao Tse-tung's 'Deviation' in 1927," *China Quarterly*, No. 18 (Apr.–June 1964), pp. 58–59. Minor changes have been made in punctuation and orthography.

77. Li Jui [67], pp. 214–15; *Historical Documents Concerning the Revolutionary Struggles Under the Leadership of the CCP in Kiangsi* (Nanch'ang: Kiangsi People's Publishing Co., 1958) [45], I, 60; Snow, RSOC, p. 163.

78. Hua Kang [59], II, 251. As rendered by Jerome Ch'en, p. 132, with minor stylistic changes.

79. Li Jui [67], pp. 214–15; Snow, RSOC, pp. 163–64; Jerome Ch'en, pp. 131–33.

80. See the debate between Schwartz and Wittfogel on this issue in the first two numbers of *China Quarterly* (1960). Cf. Snow, RSOC, p. 167.

81. *Pravda*, July 25, 1927, cited in Isaacs, p. 279.

82. Brandt, Schwartz, and Fairbank, pp. 97–122.

83. *Inprecor*, 1927, pp. 1075 ff., cited in Wittfogel, "Legend," Part 2, p. 24.

84. Wittfogel, "Legend," Part 2, p. 24; Schwartz, "Legend of the 'Legend,'" pp. 40–41.

85. Isaacs, pp. 281 ff.; Li Ang, *Red Stage* [66], cited in North, *Moscow*, p. 117.

86. Hsiao, p. 40. Chang testifies that if Moscow exerted influence over the decision to organize soviets, its communication must have been sent in September.

87. Brandt, Schwartz, and Fairbank, p. 34; Snow, RSOC, pp. 167–69.

88. *Pravda,* Sept. 30, 1927, cited in Isaacs, p. 281.

89. Snow, RSOC, pp. 166–69; Smedley, pp. 199–201, 213–15.

90. Smedley, p. 200.

91. Snow, RSOC, pp. 167, 169.

92. Eto, Part 2, pp. 168–71.

93. Snow, RSOC, pp. 169–70; Mao, SW, I, 99–100.

94. Wilbur, pp. 22–23.

95. Cited in Schwartz, *Chinese Communism,* p. 104, from Hu Hua, *Lectures on the History of the Chinese Revolution* (Peking: 1959) [58], pp. 220–22.

96. CCP Politburo Resolution on Political Discipline (Nov. 14, 1927), as translated in Wittfogel, "Legend," Part 2, pp. 32–33, with minor modifications. See Appendix B, pp. 296–97, for an excerpt from this Resolution.

IV. Mao's Struggle in the Ching-kang Mountains

1. Mao, SW, I, 80, 82; HC, I, 66–67; *Selected Works of Mao Tse-tung (Supplement)*—hereafter cited as HC (*hsü-pien*) (n.p.: CCP Chin-ch'a-chi Central Bureau, Dec. 1947) [87], p. 55.

2. Snow, RSOC, pp. 169–70.

3. Brandt, Schwartz, and Fairbank, pp. 96–97.

4. Mao, SW, I, 73; HC, I, 61.

5. Mao, SW, I, 73.

6. Mao, HC (*hsü-pien*), pp. 74–75.

7. Mao, SW, I, 99–100.

8. *Ibid.*

9. Smedley, *Great Road,* pp. 213–14.

10. Robert Payne, *Mao Tse-tung: Ruler of Red China* (New York: Schuman, 1950), p. 102.

11. *Ibid.,* pp. 208–210, 213, 224.

12. Smedley, *Great Road,* pp. 214–15.

13. Leon Trotsky, *Problems of the Chinese Revolution* (New York: Pioneer Publishers, 1932), pp. 291–92; Isaacs, p. 282; Li Ang, *Red Stage* [66], chap. 4, cited in North, *Moscow,* p. 117.

14. Smedley, *Great Road,* pp. 215 ff.

15. Brandt, Schwartz, and Fairbank, p. 34.

16. Kung [63], pp. 89–91.

17. *Ibid.,* pp. 91–92.

18. *Ibid.*, pp. 103–4.

19. "Letter from the CCP Politburo to Comrade Chu Teh," *Central Political Newsletter*, Nov. 30, 1927, No. 16, [16], pp. 81–88.

20. Eto, Part 2, pp. 167–68.

21. "Resolution on the Chinese Question," *Inprecor*, Mar. 15, 1928, pp. 321–22, cited in North, *Moscow*, p. 120.

22. *Ibid.*

23. *Ibid.*

24. *Ibid.*

25. Brandt, p. 166; Snow, RSOC, p. 167; and the debate between Schwartz and Wittfogel in *China Quarterly*, Nos. 1, 2.

26. Mao, SW, I, 73.

27. *Ibid.*, p. 97.

28. Mao, HC (*hsü-pien*), p. 64. My translation.

29. Smedley, *Great Road*, p. 228.

30. *Ibid.*

31. *Ibid.*, p. 229.

32. *Ibid.*, pp. 221–22, 229; Snow, RSOC, pp. 170–71; Kung [63], pp. 132–36; Mao, SW, I, 82–83, 88–91, 100.

33. Mao, SW, I, 102.

34. *Ibid.*, pp. 75, 102.

35. *Ibid.*, pp. 75, 97, 102; Mao, HC (*hsü-pien*), p. 66.

36. Mao, SW, I, 102.

37. Snow, RSOC, p. 170.

38. Mao, SW, I, 102–3.

39. *Ibid.*, pp. 75–79.

40. *Ibid.*, p. 96.

41. *Ibid.*, pp. 93–94.

42. *Ibid.*, p. 97.

43. *Ibid.*, pp. 97, 98.

44. Wilbur and How, p. 534*n151*; Mao, SW, I, 309*n1*.

45. Mao, SW, I, 117.

46. Mao, SW, I, 104–5, 106–8, and IV, 178, 195, 203–4.

47. Borkenau, p. 109.

48. Kermit E. McKenzie, *Comintern and World Revolution, 1928–1943* (New York: Columbia University Press, 1964), p. 137.

49. "Conclusion of the Political Discussion at the Third Enlarged Plenum —Item No. 12 on the Agenda of the Third Plenum" [21], Sept. 1930. This account, written by Ch'ü Ch'iu-pai under the pseudonym Chih Fu, is in the Bureau of Investigation Collection (a collection of CCP documents from the Shanghai police files, hereafter BIC). A short English summary is given in Hsiao, pp. 66–68.

50. Hsiao, p. 61.

51. Brandt, Schwartz, and Fairbank, pp. 138–40.

52. *Ibid.*, p. 139.

53. "Resolution on the Chinese Question," *Inprecor,* March 15, 1928, pp. 321–22, cited in North, *Moscow,* pp. 120–21; cf. Schwartz, *Chinese Communism,* pp. 109–26.

54. Schwartz, *Chinese Communism,* p. 113.

55. Mao, SW, IV, 177; HC, III, 961.

56. *Ibid.*

57. Mao, SW, IV, 176–77; HC, III, 960–61; Brandt, Schwartz, and Fairbank, pp. 130–32.

58. Mao, SW, IV, 177; HC, III, 961; Brandt, Schwartz, and Fairbank, pp. 140–43.

59. Mao, SW, IV, 177; HC, III, 961.

60. Mao, SW, IV, 190; HC, III, 973.

61. Mao, SW, IV, 191; HC, III, 973–74. Mao is quoting himself in SW, I, 122–23; HC, I, 106.

62. Mao, SW, IV, 191; HC, III, 974.

63. Mao, SW, IV, 341*n16*; HC, III, 1001*n15*.

64. Mao, SW, IV, 191; HC, III, 974.

65. *Ibid.*

66. Mao, SW, IV, 197; HC, III, 979, cited from Stalin, "Comments on Current Affairs," *Stalin on China* (Bombay: People's Publishing House, 1951), p. 59.

67. Mao, SW, IV, 177–78; HC, III, 961-62.

68. Mao, SW, I, 98. "Why Can China's Red Political Power Exist?" (SW, I, 63–70) is an excerpt from this resolution. The resolution has not been published in its entirety.

69. Smedley, *Great Road,* p. 224.

70. Mao, SW, I, 98.

71. Mao, HC (*hsü-pien*), p. 64.

72. *Ibid.*, pp. 74, 98.

73. *Ibid.*, p. 98.

74. *Ibid.*, p. 68.

75. *Ibid.*, p. 89.

76. *Ibid.*, pp. 87, 89.

77. *Ibid.*, p. 97.

78. Mao, SW, I, 97.

79. Anonymous letter from Kiangsi titled "The Workers' and Peasants' Revolution in Kiangsi," *Bolshevik,* probably published in Shanghai, Nov. 1928, cited in North, *Moscow,* p. 126.

80. Mao, NTTC, pp. 91–95. My translation.

81. Brandt, Schwartz, and Fairbank, p. 158; Mao, SW, I, 90, 307–8*n21*.

82. Mao, SW, I, pp. 87–89.

V. The Leftward Turn in the Comintern

1. Stalin, "The Initial Results of the Grain Collection Campaign," trans. Robert V. Daniels, *The Conscience of the Revolution* (Cambridge: Harvard University Press, 1960), p. 325.

2. *Ibid.*

3. *Ibid.*, p. 326.

4. *Ibid.*, p. 328.

5. *Ibid.*, p. 330.

6. *Ibid.*, p. 331.

7. *Ibid.*, p. 330.

8. *Ibid.*, pp. 337–44, 347, 363–64.

9. *Ibid.*, pp. 356–59.

10. See Daniels, pp. 360–62, for a short summary of the political side of the controversy, and Gustav A. Wetter, *Dialectical Materialism* (New York: Praeger, 1958), pp. 128–36, for a more elaborate account of its philosophical aspects.

11. Stalin, "The Right Deviation in the Communist Party of the Soviet Union," *Selected Writings* (New York: International Publishers, 1942), pp. 94, 98, 101, 108, 122, 129, 131, 133. A more complete text is to be found in Stalin's *Works*, XII, 3–91.

12. Wetter, pp. 175–76.

13. "Resolution of the Tenth Plenum of the ECCI on Bukharin" (July 3, 1929), *Pravda*, August 21, 1929, trans. Daniels, p. 368. The month's delay before the first publication of the resolution on Bukharin's removal may indicate that Bukharin's supporters in the Comintern apparatus were able to rally their forces for a last stand after the Tenth Plenum ended.

14. Stalin's speech to the Chinese Commission of the Seventh Enlarged Plenum of the ECCI, Nov. 30, 1926, cited in Eudin and North, p. 351; *Asia Who's Who*, 1958 (Hong Kong: Pan-Asia Newspaper Alliance, 1958), p. 681; Robert C. North, *Kuomintang and Chinese Communist Elites* (Stanford: Stanford University Press, 1952), p. 111.

15. Gene O. Overstreet and Marshall Windmiller, *Communism in India* (Berkeley: University of California Press, 1959), pp. 25–37, 74–98. Cf. North and Eudin, especially chapters 1 and 6.

16. Overstreet and Windmiller, pp. 98–99.

17. *Ibid.*, pp. 106–7.

18. *Ibid.*, pp. 102–4.

19. Stalin, "The Right Deviation in the CPSU (b)," *Works*, XII, 27–28.

20. *Inprecor*, IX (Aug. 21, 1929), 887; cited in Overstreet and Windmiller, p. 140.

21. Snow, RSOC, p. 165.

22. Brandt, pp. 143, 151.

23. *Ibid.*, p. 148.

24. North, *Elites,* p. 111.

25. Brandt, p. 214*n96,* information obtained from Chang Kuo-t'ao and Boris Souvarine.

26. North, *Moscow,* p. 120.

27. North, *Elites,* p. 111.

28. Borkenau, *European Communism,* pp. 65, 69, 75, 78, 80, 109–10.

29. Part of this story appears in the "Resolution on the Question of the Action of the Delegation of the CCP Central Committee to the Communist International in 1929–30" adopted by the CCP Politburo on Feb. 20, 1931, which is summarized in Hsiao, pp. 143–45. Cf. Hsiao's Oct. 1959 interview with Chang Kuo-t'ao, pp. 144–45.

VI. Conflict Between Mao and Li Li-san, 1928–29

1. *Political Activities After the Sixth Congress,* trans. Schwartz, *Chinese Communism,* p. 128.

2. *Ibid.*

3. Schwartz, *Chinese Communism,* p. 137. Italics mine.

4. Mao, SW, IV, 178; HC, III, 962.

5. Smedley, *Great Road,* pp. 238–39; Snow, RSOC, pp. 172–77.

6. Snow, RSOC, pp. 172–73, 177.

7. *Ibid.,* p. 171.

8. Smedley, *Great Road,* p. 252.

9. Mao, HC (*hsü-pien*), p. 90, used *wei-hsin-kuan-nien;* HC, I, 103, used *chu-kuan-chu-i.*

10. Mao, SW, I, 128; HC, I, 110.

11. Mao, HC, I, 110*n6.* This note does not appear in SW.

12. Mao, SW, I, 122–23; HC, I, 106–7.

13. Smedley, *Great Road,* p. 253.

14. North, *Moscow,* p. 129.

15. Brandt, Schwartz, and Fairbank, pp. 154, 161–65.

16. Mao, SW, I, 122–23; HC, I, 106. This is the retranslation in Hsiao, p. 7. With the exception of one character, which is of no political importance, this passage is identical to that in HC (*hsü-pien*), p. 94.

17. Mao, SW, I, 123; HC, I, 107.

18. Mao, SW, I, 118–19; HC, I, 103–4.

19. Smedley, *Great Road,* pp. 254–55.

20. Isaac Deutscher, *The Prophet Outcast* (London: Oxford University Press, 1963), p. 32.

21. Deutscher, *Stalin,* pp. 84–100.

22. Mao, SW, I, 126–27; HC, I, 108–9.

23. Mao, SW, I, 126; HC, I, 109.

24. Mao, SW, I, 119; HC, I, 103–4.

25. Eto, Part 2, p. 179.

26. Mao, SW, I, 127–28; HC, I, 109–10.

27. Mao, SW, I, 101–4; HC, I, 81–83.

28. Mao, SW, I, 126–28, IV, 198–99; HC, I, 108–10, III, 980.

29. Smedley, *Great Road,* p. 255; Snow, RSOC, p. 177; Mao, NTTC, pp. 94–95.

30. Mao, NTTC, pp. 91, 94–95.

31. *Ibid.,* p. 95.

32. *Ibid.,* p. 93.

33. *Ibid.,* p. 95; Brandt, Schwartz, and Fairbank, p. 150.

34. Mao, NTTC, p. 95.

35. Snow transliterates his name as Wang Kung-lu. RSOC, p. 177.

36. Snow, RSOC, pp. 171–72, 177; Wales, *Red Dust,* pp. 120–23.

37. Snow, RSOC, p. 177; Smedley, *Great Road,* pp. 273–75.

38. Smedley, *Great Road,* pp. 255–67.

39. Eto, Part 2, pp. 176–77, 180.

40. Isaacs, p. 303; Schwartz, *Chinese Communism,* pp. 127–63; Brandt, Schwartz, and Fairbank, pp. 179–84; North, *Moscow,* pp. 122–46; Wittfogel, *A Short History of Chinese Communism* (unpublished manuscript on file in the Far Eastern and Russian Institute, University of Washington, 1956), Chap. 5, cited in Hsiao, pp. 24, 374.

41. "Letter of the ECCI to the CC, CCP on the Peasant Question, June 1929," in Pavel Mif, ed., *Strategiia i taktika Kominterna v natsional'no-kolonial'noi revoliutsii na primere Kitaia* (*Strategy and Tactics of the Comintern in the National-Colonial Revolution, Primarily in China*) (Moscow: 1934), pp. 236–44. At the conclusion of the "Letter on the Peasant Question," Mif notes that it was first published in *Kung-ch'an* (*The Commune*) in November 1929. This letter was translated for me by Professors Marin Pundeff and Noel Voge of San Fernando Valley State College; I have altered their translation slightly.

42. McLane, pp. 30–31.

43. Mif, p. 237.

44. Brandt, Schwartz, and Fairbank, p. 147.

45. *Ibid.*

46. *Ibid.,* p. 157.

47. Mif, pp. 240–41. In the translation used by McLane the phrase "letter *from the CC to Mao Tse-tung*" has been translated "letter *from Mao Tse-tung to the CC*" (italics mine). See McLane, pp. 30–31.

48. Mif, p. 241.

VII. The Struggle in Shanghai, June–November 1929

1. Nollau, pp. 136, 141–42, 148.

2. *Ibid.,* p. 148.

3. *Ibid.,* p. 171.

4. See North, *Moscow*, pp. 123–25.

5. Wales, *Red Dust*, pp. 120–23, relates Lo P'ing-hui's guarded account of the circumstances that led to the decision to precipitate an insurrection.

6. Brandt, Schwartz, and Fairbank, pp. 172–73.

7. Wales, *Red Dust*, pp. 46–47; Li Ang, *The Red Stage* (Taipeh: Victory Publishing Co., 1953) [66], p. 97.

8. Brandt, Schwartz, and Fairbank, pp. 171–73.

9. *Ibid.*, p. 172.

10. *Ibid.*, pp. 170–73; Mao, SW, I, 119; HC, I, 102–3.

11. Brandt, Schwartz, and Fairbank, p. 175.

12. *Ibid.*, p. 169.

13. Mao, SW, I, 99; HC, I, 80.

14. Brandt, Schwartz, and Fairbank, p. 167.

15. *Ibid.*, pp. 167, 169–70.

16. *Ibid.*, pp. 167, 173.

17. Mao, NTTC, pp. 91–95; *Provisional Land Law* adopted by the National Congress of Delegates from the Soviet Areas, in *A Collection of Red Bandit Documents* (Nanch'ang: 1933–34, 4 vols.) [50], I, 11–17. In the Shih Sou Collection (a microfilmed collection of documents from the files of Vice-President Ch'en Ch'eng in Taiwan—hereafter SSC).

18. Brandt, Schwartz, and Fairbank, pp. 150–51, 172–73; Mif, pp. 236–37.

19. Brandt, Schwartz, and Fairbank, p. 172.

20. Mif, p. 237; cf. p. 241.

21. Mao, SW, IV, 177–79; HC, III, 961–63.

22. Mif, p. 236.

23. See Hsiao, p. 27, for reference to his interview with Chang Kuo-t'ao in October 1959. Chang did not state what the substance of Ts'ai's article was, and I have been unable to locate any article attributed to Ts'ai. I have interpreted Chang's report in the light of the contents of the June "Letter on the Peasant Question" and the testimony against Li published after his trial. See "Remarks of Ts'ai Ho-shen," Hsiao, p. 85; "Remarks of Bela Kun," p. 87; "Remarks of Comrade P'i," p. 89; and especially the "Remarks of Chang Kuo-t'ao," pp. 83–84. For the 1931 Chinese translation of the proceedings of Li's trial, see *Pu-erh-shih-wei-k'o (Bolshevik)*, IV, No. 3 (May 10, 1931), 1–75.

24. Isaacs, p. 362.

25. Brandt, Schwartz, and Fairbank, pp. 175–77.

26. North, *Moscow*, p. 123.

27. "Letter of Ch'en Tu-hsiu to the Central Committee" (Aug. 1929), in Ch'ü Ch'iu-pai, *Liquidationism and Opportunism in China* (Moscow: 1930) [47], Appendix, p. 44.

28. "Resolution Concerning the Expulsion of Ch'en Tu-hsiu and Approving the Expulsion by the Kiangsu Provincial Committee of P'eng Shu-chih, Wang Tse-chieh, Ma Yü-fu, and Ts'ai Chen-te," Nov. 15, 1929, [17]. In BIC.

29. Ch'en Tu-hsiu, *A Statement of Our Political Views* (Shanghai: 1929) [11], pp. 16–20.

30. Hsiao, pp. 9–13.

VIII. The Ku-t'ien Conference

1. "Resolutions and Spirit," trans. in Brandt, Schwartz, and Fairbank, pp. 176–77. Italics mine.

2. Mao, SW, I, 305*n3*, 306*n10*; HC, I, 84*n3*, 85*n11*.

3. Mao, SW, I, 116–18, and IV, 204–6; HC, I, 101–11, and III, 985–87; Liu, *On the Party* [73], pp. 25, 87, 92; Payne, p. 112; Smedley, *Great Road,* pp. 267–69; Snow, RSOC, pp. 173–74.

4. HC, I, 87–99; SW, I, 105–15.

5. Snow, RSOC, pp. 173–74; Smedley, *Great Road,* pp. 267–69.

6. Mao, SW, IV, 177; HC, III, 961.

7. Payne, p. 112.

8. Mao, HC (*hsü-pien*), p. 90.

9. Mao, SW, IV, 205; HC, III, 987; Liu, *On the Party* [73], pp. 25, 87, 92.

10. Wetter, pp. 166–74.

11. Mao, SW, I, 112; HC, I, 94; *Resolutions for the Ninth Conference of Delegates from the Chinese Communist Fourth Red Army, Dec. 1929, Western Fukien, Ku-t'ien Conference* (Hong Kong: New Democracy Publishing Co., 1949—hereafter *Ku-t'ien Resolutions*) [78], pp. 11–12. This is the *Ku-t'ien Resolutions* of which four sections are reprinted in CFWH. Compton, pp. 244–45. The section of the resolutions cited is retitled *Chu-kuan-chu-i* (*Subjectivism*) in HC, I, 94–95.

12. Snow, RSOC, pp. 173–74.

13. *Ibid.*, p. 174.

14. Mao, *Ku-t'ien Resolutions* [78], p. 16.

15. *Ibid.*, pp. 16–17.

16. *Ibid.*, p. 17.

17. *Ibid.*

18. *Ibid.*, p. 18.

19. *Ibid.*, p. 17.

20. *Ibid.*, p. 18.

21. *Ibid.*, pp. 18–19.

22. See "The Party Constitution of the Chinese Communist Party," trans. in Paul M. A. Linebarger, *The China of Chiang Kai-shek* (Boston: World Peace Foundation, 1943), p. 360.

23. Mao, *Ku-t'ien Resolutions* [78], p. 19.

24. *Ibid.*

25. *Ibid.*, p. 20; Linebarger, p. 360.

26. Mao, *Ku-t'ien Resolutions* [78], pp. 19–20.

27. *Ibid.*, p. 19.
28. *Ibid.*, pp. 48–49. My translation.
29. *Ibid.*, p. 49.

IX. Mao's Agrarian Policy in 1930

1. Schwartz, *Chinese Communism*, p. 140; Hsiao, p. 18.
2. "The Chinese Soviet Political Program," in *A Collection of Red Bandit Secret Documents* (First Bandit-Suppression Propaganda Department, Headquarters, Commander-in-Chief, Land, Sea, and Air Forces, Jun.–Oct. 1931) [48], II, 1–2, in SSC.
3. Cf. Victor A. Yakhontoff, *The Chinese Soviets* (New York: Coward-McCann, 1934), p. 131; Schwartz, *Chinese Communism*, p. 141; and North, *Moscow*, p. 135.
4. "The New Revolutionary High Tide and Preliminary Successes in One or Several Provinces," resolution of the CCP Politburo, June 11, 1930, [20], reproduced by the Red Army Academy Party Committee, Ki-an, Kiangsi, Oct. 10, 1930; in *Collection of Red Bandit Secret Documents* [48], III, 12–24. This was the version available to Mao. The resolution was first published in *Hung-ch'i (The Red Flag)*, No. 121 (special issue, July 19, 1930), pp. 1–4. An English translation appears in Brandt, Schwartz, and Fairbank, pp. 184–200.
5. Brandt, Schwartz, and Fairbank, p. 188.
6. *Ibid.*, pp. 196–97.
7. "Letter from the Central to the Front Committee of the Fourth Army—for Transmission to the General Front Committee of the Third, Fourth, and Fifth Armies," Apr. 26, 1930, [19], in BIC; Hsiao, pp. 16–18, 94, 106.
8. Mao, SW, IV, 208; HC, III, 988.
9. "A Reply of the General Front Committee," in *A Collection of Reactionary Documents* (KMT Headquarters, 14th Division of the Army, Mar. 1, 1932) [49], III, 10–16, in SSC; Hsiao, pp. 105–7.
10. Snow, RSOC, pp. 174–75; Hsiao, pp. 7–8, 21, 99, 106, 107, 109, 165, 180. In 1936–37 Mao was the only Communist who mentioned this conference in interviews with foreign correspondents. No mention of it is to be found in either Smedley or Wales.
11. Snow, RSOC, pp. 178–79; Smedley, p. 279.
12. Snow, RSOC, pp. 174–75.
13. "Political Resolution Adopted by the First Party Congress of the [Central] Soviet Area," printed by the Central Bureau of the Soviet Areas, Nov. 1931, [38], in SSC. My translation.
14. "Circular Note Number 2 of the Central Bureau—Resolution on the Fu-t'ien Incident," Jan. 16, 1931, [26], reprinted by the CCP branch in the Fourth Army, Jan. 23, 1931, in SSC; also "Resolution and Reports Adopted by the First Enlarged Meeting of the CCP Central Bureau in the Soviet

Areas," late March (?) 1931, reproduced by the CCP Wan-t'ai-tung Committee, May 8, 1931, [27], in SSC; Hsiao, pp. 108–9, 152–53.

15. Brandt, Schwartz, and Fairbank, pp. 222–26; "Directive Letter of the Central to the Soviet Areas," Sept. 1, 1931, [28], in SSC; "Political Resolution Adopted by the First Party Congress of the [Central] Soviet Area," Central Bureau of the Soviet Areas, Nov. 1931, [38], in SSC; Hsiao, pp. 159–61, 164–65.

16. *Red Documents* (n.p.: Liberation Press, Feb. 1938) [60], p. 397, in SSC; Hsiao, p. 8.

17. Mao, SW, I, 90, 307*n21*; HC, I, 71, 86*n21*.

18. *Red Documents* [60], p. 397; Hsiao, p. 8.

19. Mao, SW, I, 97; HC, I, 78; North, *Moscow,* p. 126.

20. Mao, SW, I, 100, 307*n19*; HC, I, 80–81, 85–86*n19*.

21. Mao, SW, I, 97; HC, I, 78.

22. Brandt, Schwartz, and Fairbank, pp. 146, 158.

23. In "The Struggle in the Ching-kang Mountains" Mao refers to the practice of allotting more land to those with capital (tools, draft animals, etc.) as the use of "productive power" (*sheng-ch'an li*) as the criterion to determine the size of land allotments. He distinguishes this scheme from the plan he attributes to the Central Committee, which calculated allotments in terms of ability to work in the fields (*lao-tung li*) (Mao, SW, I, 90; HC, I, 73). In NTTC both practices are referred to as *lao-tung li* (ability to work) (Mao, NTTC, pp. 91, 94). There is no evidence in either NTTC or contemporary documents that the land laws of the early 1930's made any terminological distinction between the two concepts. Thus in NTTC the two plans are easily confused.

24. Mao, SW, I, 90, 91, 307–8*n21*; HC, I, 73, 86*n21*.

25. Mao, NTTC, pp. 91, 94.

26. *A Collection of Red Bandit Reactionary Documents* (Taipeh: 1935, reprinted 1960, 6 vols.) [51], III, 913–14, in SSC.

27. Hsiao, pp. 99, 106.

28. Edgar Snow, *Random Notes on Red China* (Cambridge: Harvard University Press, 1957), p. 18; Li Ang, *Red Stage* (Chungking: Victory Publishing Co., 1942; also published in Taipeh: Victory Publishing Co., 1953—these are not the same company) [66], p. 122 (citations are to the Chungking edition unless otherwise noted); *Asia Who's Who,* p. 762.

29. Hsiao, p. 106.

30. This list of names has been drawn from Hsiao, pp. 105–6; *Materials of Modern History* [55], III, 267; Mao, NTTC, p. 84.

31. "A Confidential Letter of the Rebels" (Yung-yang: Kiangsi Provincial Action Committee, Dec. 20, 1930), in *A Collection of Reactionary Documents* [49], III, 16–18; Hsiao, p. 103.

32. *Reactionary Documents* [49], III, 10–16.

33. Smedley, *Great Road,* p. 275.

34. Mao, NTTC, p. 79.
35. *Red Bandit Reactionary Documents* [51], III, 913–14.
36. Mao, NTTC, pp. 47–51, 77–78, 83, 92, 95.
37. *Ibid.*, p. 83.
38. *Ibid.*, pp. 47–52.
39. *Ibid.*, pp. 49, 85–86.
40. *Red Bandit Reactionary Documents* [51], III, 913–15.
41. Mao, NTTC, p. 86.
42. *Ibid.*, p. 87.
43. *Ibid.*, pp. 86–88.
44. Snow, *Random Notes*, p. 18; Mao, HC, I, 79; SW, I, 98; *Asia Who's Who*, pp. 677–78.
45. Mao, NTTC, pp. 79, 89.

X. *The General Front Committee*

1. Wales, *Inside Red China* (New York: Doubleday, 1939), p. 131; *Red Dust*, p. 123.
2. Wales, *Inside Red China*, p. 249.
3. Mao, HC (*hsü-pien*), p. 90.
4. Mao, SW, I, 116–17, 309*n1*; HC, I, 101–2, 110*n1*.
5. Snow, RSOC, p. 177, gives the date of the formation of this army as "early in 1929," but in all other sources the date is given as 1930. Cf. Wales, *Inside Red China*, p. 249; *Red Dust*, p. 123; Smedley, *Great Road*, p. 270.
6. Smedley, *Great Road*, pp. 269–70; Wales, *Inside Red China*, pp. 249–50.
7. Schwartz, *Chinese Communism*, pp. 173–74, 176.
8. "Letter from the Central to the Front Committee of the Fourth Army," April 3, 1930, [18], in BIC; Hsiao, pp. 14–16; "Letter from the Central—for Transmission," April 26, 1930, [19], in BIC; Hsiao, pp. 16–18.
9. "Letter from the Central," April 3, 1930, [18], in BIC; Hsiao, pp. 14–16.
10. Smedley, *Great Road*, pp. 273–75; Snow, RSOC, pp. 178–79.
11. Hsiao, p. 16.
12. Smedley, *Great Road*, pp. 273–79.
13. Mao, "Oppose Bookism," *Selections from the Works of Mao Tse-tung* (Peking: People's Publishing Co., 1964) [83], I, 17–28. See also Appendix E.
14. *Ibid.*, pp. 21–22.
15. *Ibid.*, pp. 24–28.
16. Smedley, *Great Road*, pp. 273–74.
17. *Ibid.*, p. 274.
18. Snow, RSOC, pp. 178–79, 181–82.
19. Smedley, *Great Road*, pp. 274–75.
20. *Ibid.*; Wales, *Inside Red China*, p. 250.
21. Smedley, *Great Road*, pp. 275–76.

22. Snow, RSOC, p. 177; Smedley, *Great Road,* p. 274; Wales, *Inside Red China,* pp. 249–50, *Red Dust,* p. 124.

23. This version of the oath is given in Wales's interview with Lo P'ing-hui, *Red Dust,* pp. 123–24.

24. Smedley, *Great Road,* p. 276.

25. *Ibid.,* pp. 278–79.

26. *Ibid.,* p. 278.

27. *Ibid.,* pp. 278–79.

28. *Ibid.,* p. 279.

29. *Ibid.,* pp. 279–80.

30. Snow, RSOC, p. 179.

31. Wales, *Inside Red China,* pp. 250–51.

32. "The Central Soviet Area in Kiangsi," Sept. 3, 1931, *Red Flag Weekly,* No. 24 (Nov. 27, 1931), [13], pp. 39–50.

33. "The Current Political Situation and the Tasks of the Party in Preparation for Armed Uprisings," an address delivered by Li Li-san before the Central Action Committee, Aug. 6, 1930, *Red Flag Daily,* Nos. 2–4 (Aug. 16–18, 1930), Shanghai, [68]; "Minutes of the Enlarged Politburo Meeting," Nov. 22, 1930, [22], in BIC; Hsiao, pp. 32–33, 93–94.

34. "Provisional Land Law," *Red Bandit Secret Documents* [48], I, 11–17. *Central Newsletter,* No. 7 (Oct. 30, 1927), p. 20, stated "No one may buy or sell land."

35. *Reactionary Documents* [49], III, 16–18; Hsiao, pp. 102–4.

36. "Proclamation of the Plenum of the Central Preparatory Commission for the First National Congress of the Chinese Workers', Peasants', and Soldiers' Council [Soviet]," and "Regulations Governing the Election of Delegates to the First National Congress of the Chinese Workers', Peasants', and Soldiers' Council," in *The Chinese Soviets* [36], vol. I (n.p. [Shanghai?]: Central Preparatory Commission for the National Soviet Congress, Nov. 7, 1930), in BIC, both summarized in Hsiao, pp. 44–45; cf. NTTC, pp. 53–57.

37. Mao, NTTC, pp. 7, 21–62, 53–55.

38. *Ibid.,* pp. 30–34.

39. *Ibid.,* p. 82.

40. *Ibid.,* p. 63.

41. *Red Bandit Reactionary Documents* [51], III, 913–14.

42. Mao, NTTC, pp. 69, 75.

43. *Ibid.,* pp. 74–78.

44. *Ibid.,* p. 79.

45. *Ibid.*

46. *Ibid.*

47. *Ibid.,* pp. 79–80.

48. *Ibid.,* p. 80.

49. *Ibid.,* pp. 80–81. Ch'en does not identify the members of the Action Committee who aroused the rich peasants in Jui-ching and Yü-tu.

50. *Ibid.*, p. 81.
51. *Ibid.*
52. *Ibid.*, p. 82.
53. *Ibid.*
54. *Ibid.*, p. 74.
55. *Ibid.*, p. 83.
56. *Ibid.*, pp. 71, 73.
57. "Reply of the General Front Committee," and "Letter from the Central Bureau to Comrades of the West Route," *Reactionary Documents* [49], III, 10–16, 19–30; "Central Bureau Resolution on the Fu-t'ien Incident" [26], in SSC.
58. "A Secret Letter of the Rebels," in *Reactionary Documents* [49], III, 16–18.
59. Hsiao, p. 98; Smedley, *Great Road,* p. 287.
60. Smedley, *Great Road,* pp. 287–88.
61. "Secret Letter of the Rebels," in *Reactionary Documents* [49], III, 16–18.
62. "Letter from Mao Tse-tung to Ku Po" (probably a forgery), Dec. 10, 1930, *Reactionary Documents* [49], III, 18.
63. "An Open Letter From Chu Teh, P'eng Teh-huai, and Huang Kung-lüeh to Tseng Ping-ch'un and Others" (Ning-tu, Kiangsi: Dec. 18, 1930), reprinted by the Hsing-kuo hsien soviet government at P'ing-chuan, Kiangsi, [43], in SSC.
64. "Secret Letter of the Rebels," in *Reactionary Documents* [49], III, 16–18. See also the translation in Hsiao, p. 103.
65. Hsiao, pp. 105, 107; Smedley, *China's Red Army Marches* (New York: Vanguard Press, 1934), p. 279.
66. "Circular No. 1 of the CCP Central Bureau of the Soviet Areas—Establishment of the Central Bureau of the Soviet Areas and its Tasks," Jan. 15, 1931, [25], in SSC.
67. *Ibid.*
68. Hsiang Ying, "Open Fire on the Rightist Faction," Jan. 19, 1931, *Party Reconstruction,* No. 1 (Jan. 25, 1931), [54], pp. 23–24; Isaacs, 1st ed., p. 407.
69. "Central Bureau Resolution on the Fu-t'ien Incident" [26], in SSC.
70. "Resolution and Reports Adopted by the First Enlarged Meeting of the CCP Central Bureau of the Soviet Areas" [27], reproduced by the Wan-t'ai-tung CCP Committee, May 8, 1931, in SSC, summarized in Hsiao, pp. 152–53. It is possible that the Wan-t'ai-tung Committee was one of the offshoots of the Action Committee located east of the Kan River in Wan-an and T'ai-ho hsien. If so, it must have reproduced this resolution with considerable satisfaction. According to NTTC, Wan-an and T'ai-ho had been among the Action Committee's centers of strength before November 1930. Mao, NTTC, pp. 76–77, 83.

XI. The Bolshevik Reconstruction of the Party

1. "Central [Politburo] Resolution Rescinding the Punishment of the Four Comrades Ch'en Shao-yü, Ch'in Pang-hsien, Wang Chia-ch'iang, and Ho Tzu-shu," *Party Reconstruction,* No. 1 (Jan. 25, 1931), [23], pp. 29–30, in BIC.

2. "Central [Politburo] Resolution Concerning the Question of Comrade Ho Meng-hsiung," *Party Reconstruction,* No. 1 (Jan. 25, 1931), [24], pp. 30–31, in BIC.

3. Schwartz, *Chinese Communism,* p. 154.

4. Brandt, Schwartz, and Fairbank, p. 36.

5. Hsiao, pp. 59, 73.

6. "Discussion of the Li-san line by the Presidium of the ECCI," Dec. 1930, *Bolshevik,* IV, No. 3 (May 10, 1931), [62], 66–75, in BIC.

7. *Ibid.,* pp. 43–47.

8. "Minutes of the Enlarged Politburo Meeting," Nov. 22, 1930, in Hsiao, pp. 93–95.

9. *Ibid.,* p. 155.

10. North, *Moscow,* p. 158*n41*; Brandt, Schwartz, and Fairbank, p. 36.

11. "Open Fire on the Rightist Faction," *Party Reconstruction,* No. 1 (Jan. 1931), [54], pp. 23–24.

12. Schwartz, *Chinese Communism,* p. 166; Hsiao, p. 130.

13. Li Ang, *Red Stage* [66], English trans., Chap. 12; Isaacs, 1st ed., p. 407.

14. Ch'en Shao-yü (Wang Ming), *The Two Lines* [100], Shanghai edition.

15. North, *Moscow,* p. 158.

16. Hsiao, pp. 161–62.

17. "Order of the Council of People's Commissars of the Soviet Provisional Central Government to Arrest the Deserter of the Revolution Ku Shun-chang," Dec. 10, 1931, *Red Flag Weekly,* No. 27 (Dec. 17, 1931), [33].

18. Brandt, Schwartz, and Fairbank, p. 36.

19. "A Directive Letter of the Central to the Soviet Areas," Sept. 1, 1931, [28], in SSC.

20. Mao, SW, IV, 182; HC, III, 961.

21. Mao, SW, IV, 185; HC, III, 968–69.

22. Hsiao, p. 165.

23. "Resolution on the Question of Party Reconstruction of the First Party Congress of the [Central] Soviet Areas," Nov. 1931, [39], in SSC.

24. "Resolution on the Problem of the Red Army Adopted by the First Party Congress of the [Central] Soviet Areas," Oct. 1931, [37], in SSC.

25. See Hsiao, pp. 178–79, for another interpretation of the effects of the final draft on the rich peasants' interests.

26. "Draft Resolution of the First National Soviet Congress on the Question of the Red Army," *Draft Resolutions Introduced by the CCP Central*

Committee to the First National Soviet Congress (Political Department, Third Army Corps, Chinese Workers' and Peasants' Red Army, n.d. [1931?]) [40], in SSC.

27. "Letter from the CCP Central Bureau of the Soviet Areas to the CCP Kiangsi Provincial Committee," Jan. 19, 1932, in *Documents of or Concerning the Enlarged Conference of the Provincial Committee of the Kiangsi Soviet Area* (n.p. [Jui-ching?]: Kiangsi Provincial Committee, Feb. 7, 1932) [29], in SSC.

28. Hsiao, p. 214.

29. *Ibid.,* pp. 210–11, 214; Mao, SW, IV, 185.

30. Ho Kan-chih, *A History of the Modern Chinese Revolution* (Peking: Foreign Languages Press, 1959) [53], pp. 156–61.

31. *Ibid.*

32. McLane, pp. 266–71, gives a complete list of the declarations on these subjects appearing in Russian and Comintern sources between those dates.

33. Mao, SW, IV, 181; HC, III, 965.

34. *Ibid.*

35. Mao, SW, IV, 191; HC, III, 974.

36. *Ibid.*

37. See Hsiao, pp. 204–5, for his summary of Wang's points on this issue.

38. Mao, SW, IV, 192; HC, III, 974.

39. Hsiao, pp. 205–6.

40. Mao, SW, IV, 185–86; HC, III, 968–69.

41. Hsiao, p. 206.

42. Mao, SW, IV, 195–96; HC, III, 978.

43. Mao, SW, IV, 181; HC, III, 964.

44. Mao, SW, IV, 206; HC, III, 986–87; Hsiao, pp. 206–7.

45. Wang Ming, *The Two Lines* [100], 2d ed., Appendix, Chap. 1, Sect. B-2.

46. The full text of the resolution confirming Wang's line was translated into Chinese and published in *Struggle* (Shanghai), No. 31 (Dec. 31, 1932), leaves 2–8, cited in Hsiao, p. 233. This *Struggle,* officially the organ of the CCP, continued to be published in Shanghai until May 1934. Another journal called *Struggle,* officially the organ of the Central Bureau of the Soviet Areas, was published in Kiangsi from Feb. 1933 to Sept. 1934.

47. Mao, "Smashing the KMT Fifth 'Campaign' and the Task of Soviet Economic Reconstruction," in Hsiao, pp. 221–22; SW, I, 129–37. For Mao's line on the investigation drive of 1933, see SW, I, 138–40; for the investigations he made in 1933 see NTTC, pp. 96–133.

48. "Urgent Tasks of the Party in the Decisive Fight Against the Enemy's Fourth 'Campaign' " (Central Bureau, CCP, Feb. 8, 1933), *Struggle* (Kiangsi), No. 2 (Feb. 4—probably a misprint of Feb. 14—1933), [31], pp. 1–3, in SSC.

49. Jen Pi-shih, "What is the Forward and Offensive Line?" dated Feb. 19, 1933, *Struggle* (Kiangsi), No. 3 (Feb. 23, 1933), [61], pp. 15–18, in SSC.

50. Kung [63], pp. 242, 245, 267, 272; Hsiao, pp. 234, 239–47 (for a summary of the articles in the Kiangsi *Struggle*); Isaacs, 2d rev. ed., pp. 347–48, for information on Teng Hsiao-p'ing; Mao, NTTC, p. 71, for information on one of his trips with Ku Po and Hsieh Wei-chün, on Nov. 18, 1930.

51. "Instruction No. 11 of the Council of People's Commissars of the Provisional Central Government of the Chinese Soviet Republic—Launching an Extensive and Intensive Land Investigation Drive," dated June 1, 1933, *Red China,* No. 87 (June 20, 1933), [34], p. 5, in SSC.

52. "Resolution of the Central Bureau on the Land Investigation Drive," June 2, 1933, *Red China,* No. 87 (June 20, 1933), [32], p. 2, in SSC.

53. Kung [63], pp. 378–81.

54. Lei Hsiao-ch'en, *Thirty Years of Turmoil in China* (Hong Kong: Asia Press, 1955, 2 vols.) [65], I, 212–16.

55. McLane, p. 271; Hsiao, pp. 248–60; Snow, RSOC, 1st ed., pp. 381–82. The comments of Mao and others on the Fukien revolt in these chapters were completely rewritten in the second edition.

56. "Proclamation of the Central Executive Committee of the Chinese Soviet Republic, No. 1," dated Feb. 5, 1934, *Red China,* Feb. 12, 1934, [35], p. 1.

57. Mao, SW, I, 141–46; HC, I, 125–30.

58. Mao, SW, I, 147–52; HC, I, 131–36.

59. Mao, SW, I, 148–49; HC, I, 132–33.

60. Mao, NTTC, pp. 7–62.

61. Smedley, *China's Red Army Marches,* p. 269.

62. Hsiao, p. 236.

63. Mao, SW, I, 151–52; HC, I, 135.

64. Kung [63], pp. 395–400; "Fascism, Danger of War, and the Tasks of the Communist Parties in the Various Nations—Resolution of the ECCI 13th Plenum on the Report of Comrade Kuusinen," in Hsiao, pp. 223–24.

65. Mao, SW, IV, 206–7; HC, III, 986–87.

66. Mao, SW, IV, 207; HC, III, 987.

67. Mao, SW, IV, 240, 340, 341; HC, III, 999–1000; Isaacs, 1st ed., p. 407; Li Ang [66], p. 112.

68. Mao, SW, IV, 206; HC, III, 986.

69. Mao, SW, IV, 188; HC, III, 971.

XII. The Maoist Reconstruction of the Party

1. Smedley, *Great Road,* p. 309.

2. Chalmers Johnson, *Peasant Nationalism and Communist Power* (Stanford: Stanford University Press, 1962), p. 74.

3. Wales, *Red Dust,* pp. 127–28.

4. *Ibid.,* p. 67. This is based on Hsü Meng-ch'iu's story. I assume that his list of new members is complete, although he does not explicitly say so.

5. Mao, SW, IV, 198; HC, III, 980.
6. Mao, SW, IV, 203; HC, III, 984.
7. Mao, SW, IV, 190.
8. Citations are listed in Mao, SW, IV, 341.
9. Cf. Commission of the Central Committee of the CPSU (b), ed., *History of the Communist Party of the Soviet Union (Bolshevik), Short Course* (Moscow: Foreign Languages Press, 1949), p. 442; also V. I. Lenin, *Sochineniya* (*Collected Works*) (Moscow: State Publishing House, 1950), XXXI, 143, cited in Mao, SW, I, 320*n8*.
10. Mao, SW, IV, 207–8; HC, III, 988.
11. Mao, SW, IV, 172–73; HC, III, 956–57.
12. Mao, SW, IV, 174–211; HC, III, 958–91.
13. Chang Kuo-t'ao, "Mao—A New Portrait of an Old Colleague," *New York Times Magazine,* August 2, 1953, [3], p. 47. Also Chang's interview with H. R. Lieberman, Hong Kong, 1952, [2].
14. Borkenau, *European Communism,* pp. 123, 227.
15. Mao, SW, III, 106–56, 215–24; HC, II, 655–704, 759–67; Liu Shao-ch'i, "On the Training of a Communist Party Member," *Guide to the Resist-Japan People's United Front,* No. 8 (July 1940), [70], pp. 59–142; "Liquidation of Menshevist Thought in the Party," written in commemoration of the 22nd anniversary of the CCP, July 1943, in CFWH, pp. 210–22; "On Inner-Party Struggle," originally a speech delivered at the Central Committee Party School, July 2, 1941, in CFWH, pp. 166–209.
16. Liu, "Liquidation of Menshevist Thought," trans. Compton, pp. 263–65; CFWH, pp. 218–19.
17. Liu, "Liquidation of Menshevist Thought," in Compton, p. 263.
18. Mao, SW, IV, 182; HC, III, 966.
19. See Mao, SW, I, 21, and IV, 341; HC, I, 13, and III, 1000.
20. There is general agreement among scholars on this point. See Schwartz, *Chinese Communism,* for one of the first and best expositions of this thesis.
21. Mao, SW, III, 106–56, and IV, 189–211; HC, II, 655–704, and III, 972–91.
22. Mao, HC, III, 955–56. My translation.
23. Mao, SW, II, 258–61; HC, II, 521-23.
24. Schwartz, *Chinese Communism,* p. 191.
25. *Ibid.,* pp. 189, 199, 202.
26. "On the Historical Experience of the Dictatorship of the Proletariat," editorial in *People's Daily,* Apr. 5, 1956, written on the basis of a discussion at an enlarged meeting of the CCP Politburo, reprinted in *On the Historical Experience of the Dictatorship of the Proletariat* (Peking: Foreign Languages Press, 1959) [92], pp. 8–9.
27. "More on the Historical Experience of the Dictatorship of the Proletariat," editorial in *People's Daily,* Dec. 29, 1956, in *Historical Experience* [92], pp. 37–38.
28. *Historical Experience* [92], pp. 36, 57.

29. *Ibid.*, p. 17.
30. *Ibid.*, p. 15.
31. *Ibid.*, p. 17.
32. *Ibid.*, p. 15.
33. *Ibid.*

A. Note on the Delegates to the First Congress of the CCP

1. Chow Tse-tung, *May Fourth Movement*, p. 248.
2. Wales, *Red Dust*, p. 39.
3. Snow, RSOC, p. 157.
4. Wales, *Inside Red China*, p. 98.
5. Hatano Ken'ichi, *Shina Kyōsantō Shi (History of the Chinese Communist Party*) (Tokyo: Jiji Tsushin Sha, 1961, 7 vols.), I, 29.
6. Chow, *May Fourth Movement*, pp. 248, 256.
7. Ch'en Kung-po, *The Communist Movement in China* (New York: Columbia University East Asian Institute, 1960), p. 81.
8. Wilbur and How, p. 81.
9. Snow, RSOC, p. 157.
10. Ch'en T'an-ch'iu, under the pseudonym Chen Pan-tsu, "Reminiscences of the First Congress of the Communist Party of China," *Communist International*, Oct. 1936, pp. 1361–66; Wales, *Red Dust*, pp. 39–40.
11. Hatano, "Shina Kyōsantō Shi" (History of the Chinese Communist Party), in *Azia Mondai Kōza* (Tokyo: 1940), p. 24; *Shina Kyōsantō Shi* (1961), I, 29; North, *Moscow*, p. 56; Schwartz, *Chinese Communism*, p. 217*n24*.
12. Ho Kan-chih, *A History of the Modern Chinese Revolution* (Peking: Foreign Languages Press, 1959) [53], p. 40; Hu Hua, *Lectures on the History of the Chinese Revolution* (Peking: 1959) [58], p. 53.
13. Jerome Ch'en, pp. 79*n31*, 361–62.

Chronology

1893–1920

1893 Dec. 26th. Mao is born in the village of Shao-shan, Hsiang-t'an hsien, Hunan.

1898 Failure of the Hundred Days Reform.

1900 Boxer Uprising quelled by the Great Powers.

1905 Russo-Japanese War fought in Manchuria. First Russian Revolution. Formation of Sun Yat-sen's T'ung-meng hui (Alliance Society) in Tokyo.

1910 Mao enters Tung-shan Primary School in Hsiang-hsiang, where he meets the Hsiao brothers, Hsiao Yu (Siao-yu) and Hsiao San.

1911 Summer. Mao enters Hsiang-hsiang Middle School in Ch'angsha.

Oct. Revolt in Hankow begins the Republican Revolution. Mao joins the revolutionary army in Ch'angsha.

1912 Mao leaves the army, enters a school of commerce, is admitted to Hunan First Middle School, drops out, and spends most of the rest of the year reading in the Hunan Provincial Library.

1913 Mao admitted to Hunan Fourth Normal School, which is merged with Hunan First Normal School in the autumn.

1914 Mao studies Paulsen's *System of Ethics* under Yang Chang-ch'i, his future father-in-law.

1915 Ch'en Tu-hsiu founds the journal *Hsin Ch'ing-nien* (*New Youth*). Mao becomes one of the leaders of a student campaign against peculation by First Normal's headmaster, and is elected secretary of the Ch'angsha Students' Society.

1916 Spring. Mao distributes pamphlets attacking President Yüan Shih-k'ai.

Summer. Mao and Siao-yu travel through central Hunan as beggars.

1917 Mao becomes chairman of the Students' Society. His first published article—"A Study of Physical Culture"—appears in *New Youth.*

1918 Spring. First Marxist study groups formed in Peking by Li Ta-chao.

April. Mao establishes Hsin-min hsüeh-hui (New People's Study Society).

June. Mao graduates from First Normal.

Sept. Mao goes to Peking and works as an assistant in the Peking National University Library under Li Ta-chao.

Nov. Chang Ching-yao becomes governor of Hunan.

1919 Feb. Mao visits Shanghai, watches the first contingent of work-study students from Hunan depart for France, and returns to Ch'angsha.

Mar. Comintern organized; First Congress held, March 2d–6th. Mao begins to teach primary school in Ch'angsha.

May. May Fourth Movement begins in Peking in protest against the decision of the Paris Peace Conference to give Shantung to Japan.

Summer. Mao becomes editor of the *Hsiang River Review,* organ of the Hunan Student Association. It is suppressed by Chang Ching-yao, after which Mao takes over and reorganizes another student journal, *Hsin Hu-nan* (*New Hunan*).

Dec. Mao helps organize a student-teacher strike against Chang. Chang retaliates by suppressing all student organizations, including Mao's journal. Mao flees to Peking.

1920 Jan. Mao agitates against Chang Ching-yao in Peking and begins to read Marxist books.

Spring. Voitinsky arrives in Peking. Chinese Communist Youth Corps is formed in France. Mao (by now a confirmed Marxist) visits Shanghai, continues agitation against Chang Ching-yao, and meets Ch'en Tu-hsiu.

May–June. War breaks out in Hunan. T'an Yen-k'ai becomes governor.

July 19th–Aug. 7th. Second Congress of the Comintern held in Petrograd and Moscow.

July. Mao is appointed director of the primary section of Hunan First Normal School.

Aug.–Sept. First Chinese Socialist Youth Corps founded in Shanghai. Founding of Chinese Communist Party discussed. Mao returns from Shanghai to Hunan, begins to work in the labor movement, recruits members of first Communist group in Hunan.

1921

June 22d–July 12th. Third Congress of the Comintern held in Moscow.

July Early in month. First Congress of the CCP held in Shanghai, with Mao among the founding participants. Chinese Labor Secretariat established shortly thereafter.

Oct. Hunan branch of the CCP established with Mao as its secretary. Mao takes over as director of primary section of First Normal.

Dec. Maring establishes contact with Sun Yat-sen.

1922

Jan. Hong Kong seamen's strike begins. Communists and future Communists take part.

May An-yüan Workers' Club opens with Li Li-san as its director.

May–June Second Congress of the CCP. Mao does not attend.

Aug. Central Committee of the CCP, under Maring's direction, agrees that Communists will join the KMT as individuals.

Sept. Liu Shao-ch'i and Mao direct a strike in An-yüan mines.

Nov. Mao resigns as director of primary section of the First Teachers' Normal School. Shortly thereafter, he is elected chairman of the Association of Trade Unions of Hunan.

5th. Fourth Congress of the Comintern convenes, meets until Dec. 5.

1923

Jan. 23d. Sun Yat-sen and Adolph Joffe publish a Joint Manifesto in Shanghai on Sino-Soviet relations, and on the impossibility of practicing Communism in China in the near future.

Feb. 7th. Communist-instigated Peking-Hankow Railroad workers' strike bloodily suppressed by Wu P'ei-fu. End of collaboration between Wu and the Communists.

Apr. Chao Heng-t'i orders Mao's arrest. Mao flees Hunan.

May Mao works in CCP headquarters in Shanghai.

June Third Congress of the CCP held in Canton. Mao attends, is elected to the Central Executive Bureau of the CCP (there was no Politburo until after the Fifth Congress) shortly afterward.

July Mao, back in Shanghai, begins to work as liaison officer between the CCP and the KMT, working with Wang Ching-wei and Hu Han-min.

Sept. Borodin arrives in Canton as a political adviser to Sun Yat-sen.

Dec. Mao goes to Canton to attend the First Congress of the KMT.

1924

Jan. First Congress of the KMT convenes in Canton. Approves reorganization of party on democratic-centralist lines, admission of Communists to regular membership, alliance with the Soviet Union, and support for workers and peasants. Three Communists elected full members of CEC; four, including Mao, elected alternate members.

Feb.–Mar. Mao returns to Shanghai to work in CCP Orgburo and continue liaison with Shanghai branch of the KMT.

May Founding of Whampoa Military Academy in Canton with Chiang Kai-shek as President and Chou En-lai as Political Commissar. Galen (Blücher) becomes Chiang's chief military adviser.

June Soviet Union establishes diplomatic relations with Peking. 7th–July 8th. Fifth Congress of the Comintern meets in Moscow.

Nov. Mao, allegedly ill, leaves the Orgburo and returns to Hunan.

1925

Jan. Fourth Congress of the CCP meets in Canton. Mao loses his position on the Central Executive Bureau.

Spring Mao begins to organize the peasants of Hsiang-t'an, Hsiang-hsiang, and Ch'angsha.

Mar. Sun Yat-sen dies in Peking.
21st. Fifth Plenum of the ECCI convenes in Moscow, meets until April 6th.

May 1st–7th. Second Congress of the All-China Labor Federation meets in Canton.

30th. British police fire on a demonstration of workers and students in Shanghai. May 30th Movement begins with anti-British demonstrations, strikes, and a boycott of Hong Kong. Shanghai General Labor Federation organized.

June After a massive demonstration in Ch'angsha, Mao flees Hunan for Canton.

Aug. Mao first works in the peasant movement in Canton, then becomes secretary of the Propaganda Department of the KMT under Wang Ching-wei and editor of *Political Weekly,* the official journal of the KMT.

Nov. Western Hills faction of KMT meets outside of Peking and votes to expel leftists from party.

Dec. Mao goes to Shanghai to agitate against Chao Heng-t'i. Ch'en Tu-hsiu refuses to publish Mao's article against Chao in *Hsiang-tao* (*Guide Weekly*), the official journal of the CCP.

1926

Jan. Mao's "Analysis of the Various Classes of the Chinese Peasantry" published in *Chung-kuo nung-min* (*Chinese Peasant*). Second Congress of the KMT meets in Canton. Seven Communists elected to full membership of the CEC; 24, including Mao, elected alternate members.

Feb. Mao's "Analysis of All Classes in Chinese Society" published in *Chinese Peasant.*

Mar. 20th. Chiang Kai-shek carries out a coup against the Chinese Communists and some of the Soviet advisers in Canton.

Apr. Mao becomes head of the KMT training school for peasant agitators, a post he holds until October.

May 1st–15th. Third Congress of the All-China Labor Federation meets in Canton.

15th. Resolution of the CEC of the KMT bars Communists from office in KMT central and provincial headquarters.

July Northern Expedition begins.

Nov. 25th. Mao's "The Bitter Sufferings of the Peasants in Kiangsu and Chekiang, and Their Movements of Resistance" published in *Guide Weekly,* the official organ of the CCP.

29th–Dec. 16th. Seventh Enlarged Plenum of the ECCI meets in Moscow.

Dec. Conference of peasant delegates meets in Ch'angsha, and is addressed by Mao. Shortly thereafter land confiscation begins in Hunan.

1927

Jan. Mao investigates the peasant movement in Hunan.

Feb. Mao writes his "Report of an Investigation into the Peasant Movement in Hunan." Membership of the Hunan Peasant Associations climbs to more than 2,000,000.

Mar. 21st. Shanghai workers begin the insurrection that drives the warlord forces from the city and prepares for the arrival of Chiang Kai-shek and the KMT armies.

Apr. 12th. Anti-Communist coup in Shanghai launched by Chiang Kai-shek. Execution of Communists and left KMT members begins in territory newly occupied by armies under Chiang's control.

27th. Fifth Congress of the CCP convenes in Hankow.

28th. Li Ta-chao and other CCP leaders in the north executed by Chang Tso-lin.

May 20th–26th. Eighth Plenum of the ECCI meets in Moscow to consider events in China.

21st. Hsü K'o-hsiang begins massacre of Communists and left KMT members in Ch'angsha.

June 19th–28th. Fourth Congress of the All-China Labor Federation convenes in Hankow.

July 3d. CCP continues to follow a conciliatory policy toward the left KMT and Wuhan government.

13th. CCP members withdraw from Wuhan government. Ch'en Tu-hsiu ceases to act as head of the CCP. Politburo reorganized under Chang Kuo-t'ao.

Late in month. Communists gather in Nanch'ang and Kiukiang. Borodin and Roy prepare to leave China. Lominadze arrives to replace Roy.

Aug. 1st. Nanch'ang Uprising begins.

7th. Emergency Conference condemns Ch'en Tu-hsiu's policies and Ch'ü Ch'iu-pai becomes Secretary-General of the CCP.

Sept. 5th–18th. Autumn Harvest Uprisings in Hunan.

25th–30th. Communist troops from Nanch'ang led by Yeh T'ing, Ho Lung, Chou En-lai, and T'an P'ing-shan occupy Swatow.

Oct. 4th. P'eng P'ai organizes soviets in Hai-lu-feng.

Nov. Mao organizes a soviet in Ch'a-ling, then moves into the Ching-kang Mountains.
10th–15th. The November Plenum of the CCP Central Committee removes Mao from the Central Committee, Hunan Provincial Committee, and Front Committee.

Dec. 11th–14th. Canton Commune organized on instructions from the ECCI.

1928

Jan. South Hunan Uprisings begin under leadership of Chu Teh.

Feb. 9th–25th. Ninth Plenum of the ECCI in Moscow. Proceedings on China dominated by Stalin, Bukharin, Li Li-san, and Hsiang Chung-fa.

Mar. Messenger reaches Ching-kang-shan with news of November Plenum. Mao's Front Committee abolished and replaced by a Special Committee.

Apr. Chu Teh's troops join Mao's in Ching-kang-shan. Fourth Red Army established.

June–July Three letters from the Hunan Provincial Committee arrive at the Ching-kang Mountain base condemning Mao and urging renewed attacks in southern and eastern Hunan.

July P'eng Teh-huai leads the P'ing-kiang Uprising. Yang K'ai-ming replaces Mao as secretary of the Ching-kang-shan Special Committee. Fourth Red Army evacuates the mountains and marches into southern Hunan.
Sixth Congress of the Comintern and Sixth Congress of the CCP convene in Moscow, meet through August. Mao reappointed to the Front Committee.

Aug. Mao leads a small army to assist Chu Teh's troops at Kuei-tung. The two armies return to Ching-kang-shan.

Sept. Mao replaces Yang as secretary of the Special Committee.

Nov. Series of conferences at Mao-ping in Ching-kang-shan. Message arrives notifying Mao of his reappointment to the Front Committee, which is then revived as the main directing organ of the party and army.

Dec. P'eng Teh-huai arrives in Ching-kang-shan. Mao's first land law adopted. Preparations are begun for evacuation of the area by a part of the Red Army.

1929

Jan. Mao's and Chu's troops descend from Ching-kang-shan and invade southern Kiangsi.

Feb. Central Committee under Li Li-san's direction writes to Mao, attacking his policies and giving new orders on the disposition of his troops.

Mar. Chu-Mao army captures Tingchow in Fukien. A second land law is promulgated in Hsing-kuo.

Apr. Mao replies to the Central Committee's letter and disagrees with Li Li-san on tactical and strategic problems.

June Second Plenum of the Central Committee of the CCP meets in Shanghai and approves all Politburo directives issued since Sixth Congress.

27th. Soviet Consulate in Harbin raided by Chinese troops. CCP urged to adopt slogans calling for protection of Soviet interests in China.

July 3d. Tenth Plenum of the ECCI convenes in Moscow. Bukharin expelled.

Sept. Ch'en Tu-hsiu begins to form groups in opposition to Li Li-san in Shanghai. Central Committee writes Mao and the Front Committee demanding a purge and reorganization of the Red Army.

Nov. 15th. Ch'en Tu-hsiu and his followers expelled from the CCP as Trotskyites.

Dec. Mao drafts resolutions to be presented to Ku-t'ien Conference.

1930

Jan. Ku-t'ien Conference convenes. Shortly afterward, Mao sends a letter to Lin Piao (now called "A Single Spark Can Start a Prairie Fire") commenting on the policy of the Central Committee.

Feb. 7th. Mao attends a conference in southwestern Kiangsi at which the Southwest Kiangsi soviet government is organized and the February 7 land law promulgated.

Mar. Red Armies attack Kanchow.

Apr. Li Li-san writes Mao two letters urging him to come to Shanghai to attend the Conference of Delegates from the Soviet Areas. One of the letters establishes the General Front Committee, with Mao as secretary.

May Conference of Delegates from the Soviet Areas convenes in

Shanghai and sets up a committee to prepare for the formation of an all-China soviet government. Mao does not attend. Mif and the 28 Bolsheviks arrive in Shanghai.

June 11th. CCP Politburo calls for attacks on large cities, formally launching the Li Li-san line.

19th. Reorganization of Red Armies completed. Every Red soldier takes Li Li-san oath of allegiance to the revolution.

July 27th. P'eng Teh-huai's Third Army occupies Ch'angsha, holding it until August 11.

Aug. 1st. First Army Corps under Chu and Mao attacks Nanch'ang. General Action Committee formed in Shanghai.

Chou En-lai, Ch'ü Ch'iu-pai, and others return to Shanghai from Moscow.

Sept. Ho Meng-hsiung and others attack the Li Li-san line. Politburo attacks on Ho begin on or before September 10 and continue through the Third Plenum.

1st–13th. Second attack on Ch'angsha, ending in withdrawal forced by Mao and Chu without permission from the Politburo.

24th–28th. Third Plenum of the CCP Central Committee meets and condemns Li Li-san's tactics, but denies that his line is contrary to the Comintern's. Action Committees and Front Committees officially abolished.

Oct. Early in month. Red Armies capture Kian. Kiangsi soviet government organized.

30th. Front Committee Conference at Lou-fang adopts Mao's strategy of "luring the enemy to penetrate deep" into the soviet areas of southeastern Kiangsi.

Nov. 14th–15th. Conferences of the Kiangsi Provincial Government and the Kiangsi Action Committee held in Kian. Mao's military tactics and land policies are debated.

16th. Politburo receives a letter from the ECCI attacking Li Li-san's line. Li departs for Moscow.

18th. Red Armies evacuate Kian. Kiangsi soviet government moves to Fu-t'ien.

Dec. Li Li-san's "trial" before the Comintern Far Eastern Department and the ECCI in Moscow. Lominadze and Syrtsov circulate a petition to members of the Central Committee of the CPSU demanding Stalin's removal as Secretary-General.

8th. The Fu-t'ien incident. Twentieth Red Army rebels against Mao's Front Committee. Leaders of Kiangsi Action

Committee freed from Fu-t'ien prison. Overthrow of Kiangsi soviet government.

9th–30th. Mao and Chu defeat Fu-t'ien rebels. First Encirclement Campaign of the KMT armies beaten back from the central soviet areas.

1931

Jan. Fourth Plenum of the CCP Central Committee meets in Shanghai. Mif and the 28 Bolsheviks, under Wang Ming and Po Ku, take over and expel Ho Meng-hsiung, Li Li-san, and their supporters. Orders from the Politburo elected at the Third Plenum are received in the central soviet areas. Front Committee and Action Committees abolished, Central Bureau of the Soviet Areas established in their stead.

Feb. Opponents of the 28 Bolsheviks are arrested at a meeting in Shanghai by the KMT and shot. First version of Wang Ming's *The Two Lines* circulated in Shanghai. Second Encirclement Campaign begins.

Mar. Hsiang Ying arrives in the central soviet areas and takes over the Central Bureau.

Apr. Third Encirclement Campaign begins. Ku Shun-chang arrested, gives KMT secret addresses of leading Communists. Chang Kuo-t'ao returns from Moscow to Shanghai. Eleventh Plenum of the ECCI convenes in Moscow.

June Hsiang Chung-fa arrested and executed. Wang Ming becomes Secretary of CCP Central Committee.

Sept. Japanese invade Manchuria. Third Encirclement Campaign ends. Wang Ming returns to Moscow and Po Ku becomes Secretary of the CCP Politburo.

Nov. First Party Congress of the central soviet areas held.

7th–27th. First National Soviet Congress meets in Jui-ching.

1932

Jan. Politburo calls for attacks on large cities, partially returning to the Li Li-san line.

Feb. Red Armies fail to capture Kanchow. Dispute between Mao and Chou En-lai over military strategy begins.

Mar. Revised version of Wang Ming's *The Two Lines* published in Moscow.

Apr. 15th. Central soviet government declares war on Japan.

June Fourth Encirclement Campaign begins.

Aug. Ning-tu Conference held. Mao probably loses his official control of the Red Army and his position on the Revolutionary Military Committee of the Central Bureau of the Soviet Areas immediately afterward.

Sept. Twelfth Plenum of the ECCI held in Moscow. Wang Ming's line confirmed.

Oct. O-yü-wan and Hsiang-o-si soviets collapse. Red Armies stationed there march to Szechwan. Central soviet orders urgent mobilization for war.

Dec. Soviet Union resumes diplomatic relations with KMT government.

1933

Jan. CCP Central Bureau moves from Shanghai to Jui-ching and calls for an armistice with the KMT.

Feb. Struggle against the Lo Ming line begins.

Mar. Fourth Encirclement Campaign called off as Japanese take Jehol. Chinese soviet government issues declaration protesting Japanese occupation of Jehol and invasion of Peking-Tientsin area.

May 8th. Chou En-lai becomes General Political Commissar of the Red Army.

June 1st. Land Investigation Drive begins. Mao actively participates.

Aug. 1st. Anniversary of the Nanch'ang Uprising first celebrated as Founding Day of the Red Army.
Economic mobilization conferences held in Kiangsi soviet districts.

Sept. 27th. Li-ch'uan, a strategic city in eastern Kiangsi, falls to the KMT Armies as the Fifth KMT Encirclement Campaign begins. Land Investigation Drive ends.

Oct. Military alliance signed between the Red Army and the planners of the Fukien Revolt.

Nov. 20th. Fukien Revolt against KMT government in Nanking.

Dec. Thirteenth Plenum of the ECCI convenes in Moscow, continues extreme left line.

1934

Jan. KMT troops suppress Fukien Revolt.
18th–22d. Fifth Plenum of the CCP Central Committee.
22d. Second All-China Soviet Congress convenes in Jui-ching, meets until February 1.

Feb. 3d. Mao reelected chairman of Central Executive Committee of soviet government, but loses chairmanship of Council of People's Commissars and almost all his power to Chang Wen-t'ien.

Debate within CCP Politburo and soviet government over responsibility for the failure of the alliance with the Fukien rebels.

Mar. Land Investigation Drive revived.

Apr. 28th. Kuangch'ang falls to KMT armies. Jui-ching threatened.

June Fang Chih-min's Anti-Japanese Vanguard breaks out of the encirclement and marches to the Anhwei border.

July Hsiao K'e's army breaks out of the encirclement and marches westward to join Ho Lung in western Hunan.

Aug. Mao reported under house arrest at Yü-tu after a dispute over his role in the soviet government's negotiation with the Fukien rebels.

Oct. The Long March begins.

Nov. KMT troops occupy Jui-ching.

1935

Jan. Tsun-yi Conference held. Mao takes over the Revolutionary Military Committee and the Secretariat of the CCP.

Glossary of Chinese Terms

cheng-feng 整風 rectification

ch'eng-fen 成份 social status and class position of an individual

ch'i-i 起義 uprising in a righteous cause

ch'ü 區 an administrative unit between the hsien and the hsiang

chu-kuan-chu-i 主觀主義 subjectivism

hsiang 鄉 a rural administrative unit of three to five villages, a township

hsien 縣 county

jen-min wei-yüan-hui 人民委員會 people's council

kung-nung-ping tai-piao-hui 工農兵代表會 council of workers', peasants', and soldiers' delegates

lao-tung li 勞動力 labor power

min-t'uan 民團 private troops employed by local gentry

pao-tung 暴動 insurrection

sheng-ch'an li 生產力 productive power

shan 山 mountain

shih-pien 事變 incident

su-wei-ai 蘇維埃 soviet

t'ien-hsia 天下 the world

wei-hsin-chu-i 唯心主義 idealism

wei-hsin-kuan-nien 唯心觀念 idealism, idealistic concepts

ying-ming 英明 brilliant, shrewd, clever

Bibliography

I. CHINESE SOURCES

Chinese sources are arranged alphabetically, with the exception of some documents that are grouped under the headings "Chinese Communist Party Documents," "Chinese Soviet Republic Documents," and "Documents of the CCP, Soviet Republic, and Red Army Compiled by the Kuomintang." These headings themselves are in the alphabetical sequence, but the documents listed under them are in chronological order.

[1] Bureau of Investigation Collection (BIC). A collection of CCP documents from the Shanghai police files. Some items in this collection are also available in SSC.

[2] Chang Kuo-t'ao. Interview with H. R. Lieberman. Hong Kong, 1952. A manuscript summary of this interview is available at the Hoover Library, Stanford University.

[3] ———. "Mao—A New Portrait of an Old Colleague," *New York Times Magazine,* Aug. 2, 1953.

[4] Chang Tzu-sheng. "Kuo-min ke-ming-chün pei-fa chan-cheng chih ching-kao" (Chronicles of the Northern Expedition of the National Revolutionary Army), *Tung-fang tsa-chih* (*Eastern Miscellany*), Aug. 10, Aug. 25, and Sept. 10, 1928.

[5] Ch'en Po-ta. Mao Tse-tung on the Chinese Revolution. Peking: Foreign Languages Press, 1953.

[6] ———. Notes on Mao Tse-tung's "Report of an Investigation into the Peasant Movement in Hunan." Peking: Foreign Languages Press, 1954.

[7] ———. Ssu-ta-lin ho Chung-kuo ke-ming (Stalin and the Chinese Revolution). Shanghai: July 1952.

[8] ———. Stalin and the Chinese Revolution: In Celebration of Stalin's Seventieth Birthday. Peking: Foreign Languages Press, 1953. This is the English translation of the work listed above.

[9] ———. A Study of Land Rent in Pre-Liberation China. Peking: Foreign Languages Press, 1958.

Ch'en Shao-yü. See Wang Ming.

[10] Ch'en T'an-ch'iu. "Reminiscences of the First Congress of the Communist Party of China," *Communist International,* Oct. 1936.

[11] Ch'en Tu-hsiu. Wo-men ti cheng-chih i-chien-shu (A Statement of Our Political Views). Shanghai: 1929.

[12] Cheng-feng wen-hsien (Party Rectification Papers). Shanghai: Chieh-fang-she, 1949.

[13] "Chiang-hsi ti chung-yang su-ch'ü" (The Central Soviet Area in Kiangsi), dated Sept. 3, 1931, *Hung-ch'i chou-pao* (*Red Flag Weekly*), No. 24 (Nov. 27, 1931), pp. 39–50. See also Chinese Soviet Republic Documents (Kiangsi Soviet and Central Soviet Areas).

[14] Chiang Kai-shek. Soviet Russia in China. New York: Farrar, Straus, 1957.

[15] China's Revolutionary Wars. Peking: Foreign Languages Press, 1951.

CHINESE COMMUNIST PARTY DOCUMENTS

Central Committee and Politburo

[16] "Chung-kuo kung-ch'an-tang chung-yang ta Chu Teh t'ung-chih hsin" (Letter from the CCP Central [Politburo] to Comrade Chu Teh), *Chung-yang cheng-chih t'ung-hsün* (*Central Political Newsletter*), No. 16 (Nov. 30, 1927), pp. 81–88.

[17] K'ai-ch'u Ch'en Tu-hsiu tang-chi ping pi-chun Chiang-su sheng-wei k'ai-ch'u P'eng Shu-chih Wang Tse-chieh Ma Yü-fu Ts'ai Chen-te szu-jen chüeh-i-an (Resolution Concerning the Expulsion of Ch'en Tu-hsiu and Approving the Expulsion by the Kiangsu Provincial Committee of P'eng Shu-chih, Wang Tse-chieh, Ma Yü-fu, and Ts'ai Chen-te). Adopted by the Politburo, Nov. 15, 1929. In BIC.

[18] Chung-yang chih szu-chün ch'ien-wei hsin (Letter from the Central to the Front Committee of the Fourth Army). Apr. 3, 1930. In BIC.

[19] Chung-yang chi szu-chün ch'ien-wei—ping chuan san szu wu chün tsung-ch'ien-wei—ti hsin (Letter from the Central to the Front Committee of the Fourth Army—for Transmission to the General Front Committee of the Third, Fourth, and Fifth Armies). Apr. 26, 1930. In BIC.

[20] Hsin ti ke-ming kao-ch'ao yü i-sheng huo chi-sheng shou-hsien sheng-li i-chiu-san-ling nien liu yüeh shih-i jih cheng-chih-chü hui-i t'ung-kuo mu-ch'ien cheng-chih jen-wu ti chüeh-i (The New Revolutionary High Tide and Preliminary Successes in One or Several Provinces—Resolution on the Present Political Tasks Adopted by the CCP Politburo on June 11, 1930). Ki-an, Kiangsi: Red Army Academy Party Committee, Oct. 10, 1930. In SSC.

[21] San chung k'uo-ta ch'üan-hui cheng-chih t'ao-lun ti chieh-lun—san-chung ch'üan-hui ts'ai-liao ti-shih-erh hao (Conclusion of the Political Discussion at the Third Enlarged Plenum—Item Number Twelve on the Agenda of the Third Plenum). Sept. 1930. Written by Ch'ü Ch'iu-pai, under the pseudonym Chih Fu. In BIC.

[22] Cheng-chih-chü k'uo-ta-hui chi-lu (Minutes of the Enlarged Politburo Meeting). Nov. 22, 1930. In BIC.

[23] "Chung-yang kuan-yü ch'ü-hsiao Ch'en Shao-yü, Ch'in Pang-hsien, Wang Chia-ch'iang, Ho Tzu-shu szu-t'ung-chih ti ch'u-fen wen-t'i ti chüeh-i" (Central [Politburo] Resolution Rescinding the Punishment of the Four Comrades Ch'en Shao-yü, Ch'in Pang-hsien, Wang Chia-ch'iang, and Ho Tzu-shu), *Tang ti chien-she* (*Party Reconstruction*), No. 1 (Jan. 25, 1931), pp. 29–30. In BIC.

[24] "Chung-yang kuan-yü Ho Meng-hsiung t'ung-chih wen-t'i ti chüeh-i" (Central [Politburo] Resolution Concerning the Question of Comrade Ho Meng-hsiung), *Tang ti chien-she* (*Party Reconstruction*), No. 1 (Jan. 25, 1931), pp. 30–31. In BIC.

[24a] K'ang-chan i lai chung-yao wen-chien hui-chi (Collection of Important Documents from the Beginning of the Resistance War to the Present). CCP Central Committee Secretariat, July 1942. One copy, signed by Central Committee member Li Po-chien, is available at the Hoover Library at Stanford University.

For other Central Committee and Politburo documents see entries [12], [28], [36], [46], [60], [68], [72], [77]–[90], [94], [96].

Central Bureau of the Soviet Areas

[25] Chung-kung su-ch'ü chung-yang-chü t'ung-kao ti-i hao—su-wei-ai ch'ü chung-yang-chü ti ch'eng-li chi ch'i jen-wu (Circular No. 1 of the CCP Central Bureau of the Soviet Areas—Establishment of the Central Bureau of the Soviet Areas and Its Tasks). Jan. 15, 1931. In SSC.

[26] Chung-yang-chü t'ung-kao ti-erh-hao — tui Fu-t'ien shih-pien ti chüeh-i (Circular No. 2 of the Central Bureau—Resolution on the Fu-t'ien Incident). Jan. 16, 1931. In SSC.

[27] Chung-kung su-ch'ü chung-yang-chü ti-i-tz'u k'uo-ta-hui i-chüeh-an yü pao-kao (Resolution and Reports Adopted by the First Enlarged Meeting of the CCP Central Bureau of the Soviet Areas). Adopted perhaps late in March 1931, reproduced by the Wan-t'ai-tung Committee, May 8, 1931. In SSC.

[28] Chung-yang tui su-ch'ü chih-shih hsin (A Directive Letter of the Central to the Soviet Areas). Sept. 1, 1931. In SSC.

[29] Chung-kung su-ch'ü chung-yang-chü chih chung-kung Chiang-hsi sheng-wei hsin (Letter from the CCP Central Bureau of the Soviet Areas to the CCP Kiangsi Provincial Committee), dated Jan. 19, 1932, in *Chiang-hsi su-ch'ü sheng-wei k'uo-ta hui-i wen-chien (Documents of or Concerning the Enlarged Conference of the Provincial Committee of the Kiangsi Soviet Area)*. N.p. [Jui-ching?]: Kiangsi Provincial Committee, Feb. 7, 1932. In SSC.

[30] Fan ti-kuo-chu-i tou-cheng yü wu-chuang pao-hu su-lien chih nan-chen (A Guide to the Anti-Imperialist Struggle and the Armed Protection of the Soviet Union). N.p.: Propaganda Department, Central Bureau, Soviet Areas, CCP; Sept. 18, 1932. In SSC.

[31] "Kuan-yü tsai fen-sui ti-jen szu-tz'u 'wei-chiao' ti chüeh-chan ch'ien-mien tang ti chin-chi jen-wu" (The Urgent Task of the Party in a Decisive

Fight Against the Enemy's Fourth 'Campaign'), Central Bureau, CCP, dated Feb. 8, 1933, *Tou-cheng* (*Struggle*) (Kiangsi), No. 2 (Feb. 4—probably a misprint for Feb. 14—1933), pp. 1–3. In SSC.

[32] "Chung-yang-chü kuan-yü ch'a-t'ien yün-tung ti chüeh-i" (Resolution of the Central Bureau on the Land Investigation Drive), dated June 2, 1933, *Hung-se chung-hua* (*Red China*), No. 87 (June 20, 1933), p. 2. In SSC.

CHINESE SOVIET REPUBLIC DOCUMENTS (KIANGSI SOVIET AND CENTRAL SOVIET AREAS)

Central Executive Committee and Council of People's Commissars

[33] "Su-wei-ai lin-shih chung-yang cheng-fu jen-min wei-yüan-hui t'ung-ling wei t'ung-ch'i ke-ming p'an-t'u Ku Shun-chang shih" (Order of the Council of the People's Commissars of the Soviet Provisional Central Government to Arrest the Deserter of the Revolution Ku Shun-chang), dated Dec. 10, 1931, *Hung-ch'i chou-pao* (*Red Flag Weekly*), No. 27 (Dec. 17, 1931).

[34] "Chung-hua su-wei-ai kung-ho-kuo chung-yang chih-hsing wei-yüan-hui ti shih-i hao hsün-ling—kuan-yü k'uo-ta ho shen-ju ti ch'a-t'ien yün-tung" (Instruction No. 11 of the Council of People's Commissars of the Provisional Central Government of the Chinese Soviet Republic—Launching an Extensive and Intensive Land Investigation Drive), dated June 1, 1933, *Hung-se chung-hua* (*Red China*), No. 87 (June 20, 1933), p. 5. In SSC.

[35] "Chung-hua su-wei-ai kung-ho-kuo chung-yang chih-hsing wei-yüan-hui pu-kao, ti-i hao" (Proclamation of the Central Executive Committee of the Chinese Soviet Republic, No. 1), dated Dec. 1, 1931, *Hung-se chung-hua (Red China),* No. 1 (Dec. 11, 1931), p. 2. In SSC.

Congresses

[36] Chung-kuo su-wei-ai, ti-i-chi (The Chinese Soviets, vol. I). N.p. [Shanghai?]: Central Preparatory Commission for the National Soviet Congress, Nov. 7, 1930. In BIC.

[37] Su-ch'ü tang ti-i-tz'u tai-piao ta-hui t'ung-kuo hung-chün wen-t'i chüeh-i-an (Resolution on the Problem of the Red Army Adopted by the First Party Congress of the [Central] Soviet Areas). Oct. 1931. In SSC.

[38] Su-ch'ü tang ti-i-tz'u tai-piao ta-hui t'ung-kuo cheng-chih chüeh-i-an (Political Resolution Adopted by the First Party Congress of the [Central] Soviet Areas). Central Bureau, Soviet Areas; Nov. 1931. In SSC.

[39] Su-ch'ü tang ti-i-tz'u tai-piao ta-hui t'ung-kuo tang ti chien-she wen-t'i chüeh-i-an (Resolution on the Question of Party Reconstruction of the First Party Congress of the [Central] Soviet Areas). Nov. 1931. In SSC.

[40] "Ch'üan-kuo su-wei-ai ti-i-tz'u tai-piao ta-hui hung-chün wen-t'i chüeh-i-an ts'ao-an" (Draft Resolution of the First National Soviet Congress on the Question of the Red Army), *Chung-kuo kung-ch'an-tang chung-yang wei-yüan-hui t'i-ch'u ch'üan-kuo su-wei-ai ti-i-tz'u tai-piao ta-hui ts'ao-an*

(Draft Resolutions Introduced by the CCP *Central Committee to the First National Soviet Congress)*, Political Department, Third Army Corps, Chinese Workers and Peasants Red Army, n.d. [1931?], pp. 1–7. In SSC.

[41] Chung-hua su-wei-ai kung-ho-kuo ti-erh-tz'u ch'üan-kuo tai-piao ta-hui wen-hsien (Documents of the Second Soviet Congress of the Chinese Soviet Republic). Jui-ching: Council of People's Commissars, Mar. 1934. In SSC.

———

Ch'in Pang-hsien. See Po Ku.

Chu Hsin-fan. See Li Ang.

[42] Chu Teh P'eng Teh-huai Huang Kung-lüeh wei Fu-t'ien shih-pien hsüan-yen (Statement by Chu Teh, P'eng Teh-huai, and Huang Kung-lüeh on the Fu-t'ien Incident). Huang-p'i, Kiangsi: Dec. 17, 1930. In SSC.

[43] Chu Teh P'eng Teh-huai Huang Kung-lüeh chi Tseng Ping-ch'un teng i-feng kung-k'ai ti hsin (An Open Letter from Chu Teh, P'eng Teh-huai, and Huang Kung-lüeh to Tseng Ping-ch'un and Others), Dec. 18, 1930, Ning-tu, Kiangsi. Reprinted by the Hsing-kuo hsien soviet government, at P'ing-chuan, Kiangsi. In SSC.

[44] Chung-kuo hsien-tai-shih tzu-liao ts'ung-k'an (Modern Chinese History Documentary Archive). Ti-i-tz'u kuo-nei ke-ming chan-cheng shih-ch'i ti nung-min yün-tung (The Peasant Movement in the Period of the First Revolutionary War). Peking: 1953.

[45] Chung-kuo kung-ch'an-tang tsai Chiang-hsi ti-ch'ü ling-tao ke-ming tou-cheng ti li-shih tzu-liao (Historical Documents Concerning the Revolutionary Struggles under the Leadership of the CCP in Kiangsi), vol. I. Kiangsi jen-min ch'u-pan-she, 1958.

[46] *Chung-yang t'ung-hsün* (*Central Newsletter*), Aug. 1927–July 1928. Beginning with No. 14 the name of this periodical was changed to *Chung-yang cheng-chih t'ung-hsün* (*Central Political Newsletter*).

[47] Ch'ü Ch'iu-pai. Chung-kuo ch'ü-hsiao-chu-i ho chi-hui-chu-i (Liquidationism and Opportunism in China). Moscow: 1930.

DOCUMENTS OF THE CCP, SOVIET REPUBLIC, AND RED ARMY COMPILED BY THE KUOMINTANG

[48] Ch'ih-fei chi-mi wen-chien hui-pien (A Collection of Red Bandit Secret Documents). Compiled by First Bandit-Suppression Propaganda Department, Headquarters of the Commander-in-Chief of the Land, Sea, and Air Forces; June–Oct. 1931. 6 vols. In SSC.

[49] Fan-tung wen-chien hui-pien (A Collection of Reactionary Documents). Compiled by KMT Headquarters, 14th Division of the Army, Mar. 1, 1932. 4 vols. In SSC.

[50] Ch'ih-fei wen-chien hui-pien (A Collection of Red Bandit Documents). Compiled by the 4th and 2d Departments, Nanch'ang Headquarters, Chairman of the Military Council; July 1933–Oct. 1934. 4 vols. In SSC.

[51] Ch'ih-fei fan-tung wen-chien hui-pien (A Collection of Red Bandit Reactionary Documents). Compiled under General Ch'en Ch'eng. Taipeh: 1935, reprinted 1960. 6 vols. In SSC.

For other KMT-compiled Communist documents see entries [1], [95].

———

[52] Hai-lu-feng su-wei-ai (The Hai-lu-feng Soviet). N.p. [Shanghai?]: 1928.

[53] Ho Kan-chih. A History of the Modern Chinese Revolution. Peking: Foreign Languages Press, 1959.

[54] Hsiang Ying. "Hsiang yu-p'ai k'ai-huo" (Open Fire on the Rightist Faction), Jan. 19, 1931, *Tang ti chien-she* (*Party Reconstruction*), No. 1 (Jan. 25, 1931), pp. 23–25.

[55] Hsien-tai shih-liao (Materials of Modern History). Hai-t'ien Publishing Co., ed. Shanghai: Hai-t'ien Publishing Co., 1934–35. 4 vols.

[56] Hu Ch'iao-mu. Chung-kuo kung-ch'an-tang san-shih nien (Thirty Years of the Chinese Communist Party). Peking: Jen-min ch'u-pan-she, 1951.

[57] ———. Thirty Years of the Chinese Communist Party. Peking: Foreign Languages Press, 1952. This is the English translation of the book listed above.

[58] Hu Hua. Chung-kuo ke-ming-shih chiang-i (Lectures on the History of the Chinese Revolution). Peking: 1959.

[59] Hua Kang. Chung-kuo min-tsu chieh-fang yün-tung-shih (A History of the Chinese National Liberation Movement). Shanghai: 1947. 2 vols.

[60] Hung-se wen-hsien (Red Documents). N.p.: Chieh-fang-she, Feb. 1938. In SSC.

[61] Jen Pi-shih. "Shih-ma shih chin-kung lu-hsien" (What is the Forward and Offensive Line?), dated Feb. 19, 1933, *Tou-cheng* (*Struggle*) (Kiangsi), No. 3 (Feb. 23, 1933), pp. 15–18. In SSC.

Kiangsi Soviet. See Chinese Soviet Republic Documents.

[62] Kung-ch'an kuo-chi chih-wei chu-hsi-t'uan tui-yü Li-san lu-hsien ti t'ao-lun (Discussion of the Li-san Line by the Presidium of the ECCI), Dec. 1930. Chinese version in *Pu-erh-shih-wei-k'e* (*Bolshevik*), IV, No. 3 (May 10, 1931), 1–75. In BIC.

[63] Kung Ch'u. Wo yü hung-chün (The Red Army and I). Hong Kong: Southwind Publishing Company, 1954.

[64] "Kuo-chi tung-fang-pu kuan-yü chung-kuo tang san-chung ch'üan-hui yü Li Li-san t'ung-chih ti ts'o-wu ti pao-kao" (Report of the Comintern Eastern Department on the Errors of the Chinese Party's Third Plenum and of Comrade Li Li-san), dated Dec. 1930, *Pu-erh-shih-wei-k'e* (*Bolshevik*), IV, No. 3 (May 10, 1931), 66–75.

Land Investigation Drive. See entries [32], [34].

[65] Lei Hsiao-ch'en. Sa nien tung-luan chung-kuo (Thirty Years of Turmoil in China). Hong Kong: Asia Press, 1955. 2 vols.

[66] Li Ang (Chu Hsin-fan). Hung-se wu-t'ai (The Red Stage). Chungking: Sheng-li ch'u-pan-she, 1942. Also published in Taipeh: Victory Pub-

lishing Company, 1953. Citations are to the 1942 edition except where otherwise noted.

There is no published English translation, but I have consulted and cited a translation by Wen Shun-chi in the possession of Professor Robert C. North at Stanford University.

[67] Li Jui. Mao Tse-tung t'ung-chih ti ch'u-ch'i ke-ming huo-tung (Comrade Mao's Early Revolutionary Activities). Peking: Chung-kuo ch'ing-nien ch'u-pan-she, 1957.

[68] Li Li-san. "Mu-ch'ien cheng-chih hsing-shih yü tang tsai chun-pei wu-chuang pao-tung chung ti jen-wu" (The Current Political Situation and the Tasks of the Party in Preparation for Armed Uprisings), Aug. 6, 1930, *Hung-ch'i jih-pao* (*Red Flag Daily*), Shanghai, Nos. 2–4 (Aug. 16–18, 1930).

[69] Lien-kung (pu) chung-yang t'e-she wei-yüan-hui. Lien-kung (pu) tang shih chien-ming, chiao-ch'eng. Shanghai: Chieh-fang-she, September 1949. [This is the Chinese edition of: Commission of the Central Committee of the CPSU (b), ed. History of the Communist Party of the Soviet Union (Bolshevik), Short Course. Moscow: Foreign Languages Press, 1949.]

[70] Liu Shao-ch'i. "Lun kung-ch'an-tang yüan ti hsiu-yang" (On the Training of a Communist Party Member), *K'ang-jih min-tsu t'ung-i chan-hsien chih-nan* (*Guide to the Resist-Japan People's United Front*), No. 8 (July 1940), pp. 59–142.

[71] ———. Lun tang (On the Party). Hua-pei: Hsin-hua, 1946. This is not Liu's report on the revision of the Party Constitution, which was also published under this title, but a reprint of Liu's articles in CFWH.

[72] ———. Lun tang (On the Party). Peking: Jen-min ch'u-pan-she, 1950. This is Liu's report on the revision of the Party Constitution.

[73] ———. On the Party. Peking: Foreign Languages Press, 1952. This is the English translation of Liu's report on the revision of the Party Constitution.

[74] Lu Ch'iang. Ching-kang-shan shang ti "ying-hsiung" (The "Hero" of Ching-kang-shan). Hong Kong: Liberty Press, 1951.

[75] "Lun Kuo-min-tang kai-tsu-p'ai ho Chung-kuo kung-ch'an-tang ti jen-wu" (Concerning the Kuomintang Reorganizationists and the Tasks of the CCP), *Hung-ch'i* (*Red Flag*), No. 16 (Feb. 15, 1930), pp. 9–11. This is a Comintern letter to the CCP Central Committee.

[76] Mao Ssu-ch'eng. Min-kuo shih-wu-nien i-ch'ien chih Chiang Chieh-shih hsien-sheng (Mr. Chiang Kai-shek before 1926). Shanghai: 1936.

[77] Mao Tse-tung. Chung-kuo ke-ming chan-cheng ti chan-lüeh wen-t'i (Strategic Problems of China's Revolutionary War). Hong Kong: Hsin-min ch'u-pan-she, 1949.

[78] ———. Chung-kuo kung-ch'an-tang hung-chün ti-ssu-chün ti-chiu-tz'u tai-piao ta-hui chüeh-i-an i-chiu-erh-chiu nien, shih-erh yüeh, Min-hsi, Ku-t'ien hui-i (Resolutions for the Ninth Conference of Delegates from the Chinese Communist Fourth Red Army, Dec. 1929, Western Fukien, Ku-t'ien Conference). Hong Kong: Hsin-min-chu ch'u-pan-she, 1949.

[79] Mao Tse-tung. "Chung-kuo nung-min ko-chieh-chi ti fen-hsi chi ch'i tui-yü ke-ming ti t'ai-tu" (Analysis of Various Classes of the Chinese Peasantry and Their Attitude toward the Revolution), *Chung-kuo nung-min* (*Chinese Peasant*), No. 1 (Jan. 1, 1926), pp. 13–20.

[80] ———. "Chung-kuo she-hui ko-chieh-chi ti fen-hsi" (Analysis of Various Classes in Chinese Society), *Chung-kuo nung-min* (*Chinese Peasant*), No. 2 (Feb. 1, 1926), pp. 1–13.

[81] ———. Hu-nan nung-min yün-tung k'ao-ch'a pao-kao (Report of an Investigation into the Peasant Movement in Hunan). Central China: Chieh-fang-she, 1949. Also published in *Hsiang-tao* (*Guide*), No. 191 (Mar. 12, 1927), and *Chung-yang fu-k'an* (*Central Bi-monthly*), No. 7 (Mar. 28, 1927).

[82] ———. Izbrannye Proizvedeniia (Selected Works). Moscow: State Publishing House, 1953–54. 4 vols.

[83] ———. Mao Tse-tung chu-tso hsüan-tu (Selections from the Works of Mao Tse-tung). Peking: Jen-min ch'u-pan-she, 1964. 2 vols.

[84] ———. Mao Tse-tung hsüan-chi (Selected Works of Mao Tse-tung). Peking: Jen-min ch'u-pan-she, 1951–61. 4 vols. The English translation is Mao Tse-tung: Selected Works. New York: International Publishers, 1954–62. 5 vols. Published at the same time in London, by Lawrence and Wishart, and in Bombay, by the People's Publishing House, Ltd. Another English translation has been published in Peking as Selected Works of Mao Tse-tung. Peking: Foreign Languages Press, 1961–65. 4 vols.

[85] ———. Mao Tse-tung hsüan-chi (Selected Works of Mao Tse-tung). Chin-ch'a-chi Jih-pao-she (Shansi-Chahar-Hopei Daily), ed. N.p.: Chin-ch'a-chi New China Book Company, May 1944. This, the earliest collection of Mao's writings available in the United States, may be found at the Yenching Library at Harvard University and at the Library of the Hoover Institution at Stanford University.

[86] ———. Mao Tse-tung hsüan-chi. N.p.: CCP Chin-ch'a-chi Central Bureau, Mar. 1947.

[87] ———. Mao Tse-tung hsüan-chi (hsü-pien) [Selected Works of Mao Tse-tung (Supplement)]. N.p.: CCP Chin-ch'a-chi Central Bureau, Dec. 1947.

[88] ———. Nung-ts'un tiao-ch'a (Rural Survey). Yenan: Chieh-fang-she, Apr. 1941; N.p.: Hsin-hua shu-tien, 1949. Citations are to the 1949 edition.

[89] ———. "Pien-cheng-fa wei-wu-lun" (Dialectical Materialism), *Min-chu* (*Democracy*), Shanghai, Mar. 1940.

[90] ———. Yu-chi chan-cheng ti chan-lüeh wen-t'i (Strategic Problems of Guerrilla Warfare). Hong Kong: Hsin-min-chu ch'u-pan-she, 1949.

[91] New China Information Committee. Friction Aids Japan: Documents Concerning Instances of Friction, 1939–40. Chungking: New China Information Committee (Bulletin No. 14), 1940.

[92] On the Historical Experience of the Dictatorship of the Proletariat. Peking: Foreign Languages Press, 1959.

[93] People's Tribune, Hankow, Jan.–Aug. 1927. This was an English-language journal, allegedly controlled by the Borodin faction.

[94] Po Ku (Ch'in Pang-hsien). "Chung-kuo kung-ch'an-tang chung-yang wei-yüan-hui ti-wu-tz'u ch'üan-hui tsung-chieh" (Conclusion of the CCP Central Committee Fifth Plenum), *Tou-cheng* (*Struggle*) (Kiangsi), No. 48 (Feb. 23, 1934), pp. 1–6.

[95] Shih Sou Collection (SSC). A microfilmed collection of documents from the files of Vice-President Ch'en Ch'eng in Taiwan. It is available at the libraries of the University of Washington and the Hoover Institution at Stanford University, and at several other major university libraries.

[96] *Tang ti chien-she* (*Party Reconstruction*). Shanghai. A CCP journal, twelve issues of which are in BIC.

[97] Ts'ai Ho-shen. "Istoriia opportunizma Kommunisticheskoi partii Kitaia" (History of Opportunism in the Chinese Communist Party), *Problemy Kitaia,* No. 1 (1929), pp. 1–77. Chinese translation in Li Min-hun, Ch'ih-se tang-an (Affairs of the Red Party), Peking: 1929.

[98] Wan Yah-kang. The Rise of Communism in China, 1920–50. Hong Kong: Chung-shu Publishing Co., 1952.

[99] Wang Ming (Ch'en Shao-yü). "Chung-kuo kung-ch'an-tang shih Chung-kuo fan-ti yü t'u-ti ke-ming chung ti wei-i ti ling-hsiu" (The CCP Is the Only Leader in the Anti-Imperialist and Agrarian Revolution in China), *Tou-cheng* (*Struggle*), No. 66 (June 30, 1934), pp. 1–12.

[100] ———. Liang t'iao lu-hsien (The Two Lines). First ed. Shanghai: Wu-ch'an-chieh-chi shu-tien, Feb. 1931. Second ed. Moscow: no publisher given, Mar. 1932. Third ed. retitled Wei chung-kung keng-chia pu-erh-shih-wei-k'e-hua erh tou-cheng (Struggle for the More Complete Bolshevization of the Chinese Communist Party). Yenan: no publisher given, July 1940. This book is based on a Comintern letter of July 23, 1930, and the Comintern directive of Nov. 16, 1930, both of which are addressed to the Chinese Politburo. The Moscow and Yenan editions are identical and contain an appendix that does not appear in the first edition.

[101] ———. "Ts'u-chin hsien-cheng yün-tung nu-li ti fang-hsiang" (Promote Our Vigorous Direction of the Constitutional Government Movement), *K'ang-jih min-tsu t'ung-i chan-hsien chih-nan* (*Guide to the Resist-Japan People's United Front*), No. 10 (Aug. 1940), pp. 6–11.

[102] Wang Ming (Ch'en Shao-yü) and Kan Sing (Kang Sheng). Revolutionary China Today. Moscow: Foreign Languages Press, 1934.

II. OTHER WORKS

The Asia Who's Who. Hong Kong: Pan-Asia Newspaper Alliance, 1958.

Boorman, Howard L. "Liu Shao-ch'i: A Political Profile," *China Quarterly,* No. 10 (Apr.–June 1962), pp. 1–22.

———. "Mao Tse-tung: The Lacquered Image," *China Quarterly,* No. 16 (Oct.–Dec. 1963), pp. 1–55.

Borkenau, Franz. European Communism. New York: Harper, 1953.

Borkenau, Franz. World Communism. New York: Norton, 1939.

Brandt, Conrad. Stalin's Failure in China. Cambridge: Harvard University Press, 1958.

Brandt, Conrad, Benjamin Schwartz, and John K. Fairbank. A Documentary History of Chinese Communism. Cambridge: Harvard University Press, 1952.

Brière, O. Fifty Years of Chinese Philosophy. London: Allen and Unwin, 1956.

Brzezinski, Zbigniew K. The Soviet Bloc. Cambridge: Harvard University Press, 1960.

Carr, Edward Hallett. A History of Soviet Russia. New York: Macmillan, 1951–64. 8 vols. The three parts completed are: The Bolshevik Revolution, The Interregnum, and Socialism in One Country.

Chamberlin, William H. The Russian Revolution. New York: Grosset and Dunlap, 1965. 2 vols.

Ch'en, Jerome. Mao and the Chinese Revolution. London: Oxford University Press, 1965.

Ch'en Kung-po. The Communist Movement in China. New York: Columbia University East Asian Institute, 1960.

Ch'en T'an-ch'iu (under the pseudonym Chen Pan-tsu). "Reminiscences of the First Congress of the Communist Party of China," *Communist International,* Oct. 1936, pp. 1361–66.

Chesneaux, Jean. Le mouvement ouvrier chinois de 1919 à 1927. Paris: Mouton, 1962.

China: The March Toward Unity. New York: Workers' Library, 1937.

Chow Ching-wen. Ten Years of Storm. New York: Holt, Rinehart and Winston, 1960.

Chow Tse-tsung. The May Fourth Movement: Intellectual Revolution in Modern China. Cambridge: Harvard University Press, 1960.

———. Research Guide to the May Fourth Movement. Cambridge: Harvard University Press, 1963.

Clubb, O. Edmund. Twentieth Century China. New York: Columbia University Press, 1964.

Cohen, Arthur. The Communism of Mao Tse-tung. Chicago: University of Chicago Press, 1964.

Columbia University Russian Institute, ed. The Anti-Stalin Campaign and International Communism. New York: Columbia University Press, 1956. This is a collection of documents including Khrushchev's secret speech to the Twentieth Party Congress of the CPSU.

Commission of the Central Committee of the CPSU (b), ed. History of the Communist Party of the Soviet Union (Bolshevik), Short Course. Moscow: Foreign Languages Press, 1949. The Chinese version is Lien-kung (pu) chung-yang t'e-she wei-yüan-hui. Lien-kung (pu) tang shih chien-ming, chiao-ch'eng. Shanghai: Chieh-fang-she, Sept. 1949.

Communist International. Der I. Kongress der Kommunistischen Internationale: Protokoll der Verhandlungen in Moskau vom 2. bis zum 19. März 1919. Petrograd, 1920.

———. The Second Congress of the Communist International: Report of the Proceedings of the Petrograd Session of July 17th and the Moscow Sessions of July 23rd–August 7th, 1920. Moscow: 1920.

Compton, Boyd, ed. Mao's China: Party Reform Documents, 1942–44. Seattle: University of Washington Press, 1952.

Conquest, Robert. Power and Policy in the USSR. New York: St. Martin's, 1961.

Dallin, David J. Soviet Russia and the Far East. New Haven: Yale University Press, 1948.

Daniels, Robert V. The Conscience of the Revolution. Cambridge: Harvard University Press, 1960.

Dedijer, Vladimir. Tito. New York: Simon and Schuster, 1953.

Degras, Jane, ed. The Communist International, 1919–1943: Documents. London: Oxford University Press, 1956 & 1960. 2 vols.

Deutscher, Isaac. The Prophet Outcast. London: Oxford University Press, 1963.

———. Stalin: A Political Biography. New York: Vintage, 1960.

Dinerstein, Herbert S. War and the Soviet Union. New York: Praeger, 1959.

Djilas, Milovan. Conversations with Stalin. New York: Harcourt, 1962.

Doolin, Dennis J., and Peter J. Golas. " 'On Contradiction' in the Light of Mao Tse-tung's Essay on 'Dialectical Materialism,' " *China Quarterly*, No. 19 (July–Sept. 1964), pp. 38–46.

Elegant, Robert S. China's Red Leaders. London: Bodley Head, 1952.

Eto, Shinkichi. "Hai-lu-feng—The First Chinese Soviet Government," *China Quarterly*, No. 8 (Oct.–Dec. 1961), pp. 161–84; No. 9 (Jan.–Mar. 1962), pp. 149–81.

Eudin, Xenia Joukoff, and Robert C. North. Soviet Russia and the East, 1920–27. Stanford: Stanford University Press, 1957.

Feis, Herbert. The China Tangle. Princeton: Princeton University Press, 1953.

Gankin, Olga Hess. "The Bolsheviks and the Founding of the Third International," *Slavonic and Eastern Review*, XX (1941), 88–101.

Guillermaz, J. "The Nanch'ang Uprising," *China Quarterly*, No. 11 (July–Sept. 1962), pp. 161–68.

Harrison, James P. "The Li Li-san Line and the CCP in 1930," *China Quarterly*, No. 14 (Apr.–June, 1963), pp. 178–94.

Hatano, Ken'ichi. Sekishoku Shina no Kyūmei (A Study of Red China). Tokyo: Daito Shuppan Sha, 1941.

———. "Shina Kyōsantō Shi" (History of the Chinese Communist Party), *Azia Mondai Koza* (Tokyo: 1940).

———. Shina Kyōsantō Shi (History of the Chinese Communist Party). Tokyo: Jiji Tsushin Sha, 1961. 7 vols.

Hsiao, Tso-liang. Power Relations within the Chinese Communist Movement, 1930–1934. Seattle: University of Washington Press, 1961.

Hsieh, Alice L. Communist China's Strategy in the Nuclear Era. Englewood Cliffs, New Jersey: Prentice-Hall, 1962.

Hsüeh Chun-tu. The Chinese Communist Movement, 1921–1937. Stanford, Calif.: Hoover Institution, 1960. An annotated bibliography of selected materials in the Chinese Collection of the Hoover Institution at Stanford University.

Hulse, James W. The Forming of the Communist International. Stanford: Stanford University Press, 1964.

Isaacs, Harold R. The Tragedy of the Chinese Revolution. First ed., London: Secker and Warburg, 1938. Revised ed., Stanford: Stanford University Press, 1951. Second revised ed., Stanford: Stanford University Press, 1961. Citations refer to the 1951 edition unless otherwise noted.

Johanson and Taube. Soviety v Kitai (Soviets in China). Moscow: Partiinoe Izdatyel'stvo, 1934.

Johnson, Chalmers A. Peasant Nationalism and Communist Power. Stanford: Stanford University Press, 1962.

Klein, Donald W. Who's Who in China; Biographical Sketches of 542 Chinese Communist Leaders. New York: 1959. 3 vols.

Krivitsky, Walter. I Was Stalin's Agent. London: H. Hamilton, 1940. Also published as In Stalin's Secret Service. New York: Harper, 1939.

Leites, Nathan. A Study of Bolshevism. Glencoe, Illinois: Free Press, 1953.

Lenin, V. I. What Is to Be Done? New York: International Publishers, 1929.

Linebarger, Paul M. A. The China of Chiang Kai-shek. Boston: World Peace Foundation, 1943.

McKenzie, Kermit E. Comintern and World Revolution, 1928–1943. New York: Columbia University Press, 1964.

McLane, Charles B. Soviet Policy and the Chinese Communists: 1931–1946. New York: Columbia University Press, 1958.

Meyer, Alfred G. Marxism, the Unity of Theory and Practice. Cambridge: Harvard University Press, 1954.

Mif, Pavel, ed. Strategiia i taktika Kominterna v natsional'no-kolonial'noi revoliutsii na primere Kitaia (Strategy and Tactics of the Comintern in the National-Colonial Revolution, Primarily in China). Moscow: 1934. This is a collection of Comintern documents on Chinese policy.

Mills, Harriet C. "Lu Hsün and the Communist Party," *China Quarterly*, No. 4 (Oct.–Dec. 1960), pp. 17–27.

Nollau, Günther. International Communism and World Revolution. New York: Praeger, 1961.

North, Robert C. Kuomintang and Chinese Communist Elites. Stanford: Stanford University Press, 1952.

———. Moscow and Chinese Communists. Stanford: Stanford University Press, 1953. 2d ed. Stanford: Stanford University Press, 1965. Citations are to the 1st edition.

North, Robert C., and Xenia J. Eudin. M. N. Roy's Mission to China. Berkeley: University of California Press, 1963.

Overstreet, Gene D., and Marshall Windmiller. Communism in India. Berkeley: University of California Press, 1959.

Page, Stanley W. Lenin and World Revolution. New York: New York University Press, 1959.

Payne, Robert. Mao Tse-tung: Ruler of Red China. New York: Schuman, 1950.

Perleberg, Max. Who's Who in Modern China (from the Beginning of the Chinese Republic to the End of 1953). Hong Kong: Ye Olde Printerie, 1954.

Pringsheim, Klaus H. "Chinese Communist Youth Leagues (1920–1949)," *China Quarterly,* No. 12 (Oct.–Dec. 1962), pp. 75–91.

Ravines, Eudocio. The Yenan Way. New York: Scribner, 1951.

Rosenthal, M. M., and P. Yudin. Kratky filosofsky slovar (Short Philosophical Dictionary). Moscow: State Publishing House, 1955. The Chinese version is Lo-ching-t'ai-erh, M. M., and P. Yu-chin. Chien-ming che-hsüeh tz'u-tien. Translated by Sung Yeh-fang. Hong Kong: Hsin Chung-kuo Shu-ch'u, 1949. Shanghai: Sheng-huo Tu-shu, Mar. 1940. N.p.: Hsin-hua Shu-tien, Sept. 1948. Hua-pei (North China): Hsin-hua shu-tien, Aug. 1948. Peking: San-lien Shu-tien, Apr. 1950. An English version is the Short Philosophical Dictionary, edited by Howard Selsam. New York: International Publishers, 1949.

Rosinger, Lawrence K. China's Wartime Politics, 1937–1944. Princeton: Princeton University Press, 1944.

Roy, M. N. Revolution and Counterrevolution in China. Calcutta: Renaissance Publishers, 1946.

Scalapino, Robert A., and George T. Yu. The Chinese Anarchist Movement. Berkeley: Center for Chinese Studies, Institute of International Studies, University of California, 1961.

Schapiro, Leonard. The Communist Party of the Soviet Union. New York: Random House, 1959.

Schram, Stuart R. The Political Thought of Mao Tse-tung. New York: Praeger, 1963.

———. "On the Nature of Mao Tse-tung's 'Deviation' in 1927," *China Quarterly,* No. 18 (Apr.–June 1964), pp. 55–66.

Schwartz, Benjamin I. Chinese Communism and the Rise of Mao. Cambridge: Harvard University Press, 1952.

———. "The Legend of the 'Legend of Maoism,'" *China Quarterly,* No. 2 (Apr.–June 1960), pp. 35–42.

———. "A Marxist Controversy on China," *Far Eastern Quarterly,* XIII (Feb. 1954), 143–53.

Schwartz, Benjamin I. "On the 'Originality' of Mao Tse-tung," *Foreign Affairs,* XXXIV (Oct. 1955), 67–76.

Siao-yu (Hsiao Yü). Mao Tse-tung and I Were Beggars. Syracuse, N.Y.: Syracuse University Press, 1959.

Smedley, Agnes. China's Red Army Marches. New York: Vanguard, 1934.

———. The Great Road: The Life and Times of Chu Teh. New York: Monthly Review Press, 1956.

Snow, Edgar. The Other Side of the River: Red China Today. New York: Random House, 1962.

———. Random Notes on Red China. Cambridge: Harvard University Press, 1957.

———. Red Star Over China. New York: Random House, 1938; Modern Library, 1944. Citations refer to 1944 edition unless otherwise noted.

Stalin, Joseph. Economic Problems of Socialism in the USSR. New York: International Publishers, 1952.

———. "Prospects of the Revolution in China," *Inprecor,* No. 90 (Dec. 23, 1926), pp. 1581–84.

———. Selected Writings. New York: International Publishers, 1942.

———. Stalin on China. Bombay: People's Publishing House, 1951.

———. Works. Moscow: Foreign Languages Publishing House, 1951–55. 13 vols.

Steiner, H. Arthur. "Maoism or Stalinism for Asia?" *Far Eastern Survey,* XXII, No. 1 (Jan. 14, 1953), 1–5.

———. " 'On the Record' with Mao and His Regime," *Journal of Asian Studies,* XVII, No. 2 (Feb. 1958), 215–22.

Strong, Anna Louise. The Chinese Conquer China. Garden City, N.Y.: Doubleday, 1949.

———. "The Thought of Mao Tse-tung," *Amerasia,* XI, No. 6 (June 1947), 161–74.

Trotsky, Leon. Problems of the Chinese Revolution. New York: Pioneer Publishers, 1932.

———. Stalin. London: Hollis and Carter, 1947.

———. The Stalin School of Falsification. New York: Pioneer Publishers, 1937.

———. The Third International after Lenin. New York: Pioneer Publishers, 1936.

U.S., Congress, House, Committee on Foreign Affairs. "Communism in China," Supplement III C of *Strategy and Tactics of World Communism,* 80th Cong., 2d Sess., 1949. House Document No. 154.

U.S., Congress, House, Committee on Un-American Activities. "Constitution of the Communist International" (adopted by the Sixth Congress in 1928), in *The Communist Conspiracy,* Part I, Section C. Washington, D.C.: U.S. Government Printing Office, 1956.

U.S., Department of State. United States Relations with China: With Special Reference to the Period 1944–1949. Far Eastern Series, No. 30. Washington, D.C.: U.S. Government Printing Office, 1949.

Vinacke, Harold M. A History of the Far East in Modern Times. 6th ed. New York: Appleton, 1959.

Wales, Nym (Helen Foster Snow). The Chinese Labor Movement. New York: John Day, 1945.

———. Inside Red China. New York: Doubleday, 1939.

———. Red Dust: Autobiographies of Chinese Communists (as told to Nym Wales). Stanford: Stanford University Press, 1952.

Wetter, Gustav A. Dialectical Materialism. New York: Praeger, 1958.

Whiting, Allen S. China Crosses the Yalu. New York: Macmillan, 1960.

———. "Rewriting Modern History in Communist China: A Review Article," *Far Eastern Survey,* XXIV, No. 11 (Nov. 1955), 173–74.

Whiting, Allen S., and Sheng Shih-ts'ai. Sinkiang: Pawn or Pivot? East Lansing: Michigan State University Press, 1958.

Wilbur, C. Martin. "The Ashes of Defeat," *China Quarterly,* No. 18 (Apr.–June 1964), pp. 3–54.

Wilbur, C. Martin, and Julie Lien-ying How, eds. Documents on Communism, Nationalism, and Soviet Advisers in China, 1918–27. New York: Columbia University Press, 1959.

Wittfogel, Karl A. "The Legend of 'Maoism,'" *China Quarterly,* No. 1 (Jan.–Mar. 1960), pp. 72–86; No. 2 (Apr.–June 1960), pp. 16–34.

———. Oriental Despotism. New Haven: Yale University Press, 1957.

———. The Russian and Chinese Revolutions: A Socio-Historical Comparison. London: Stevens & Sons, 1961.

Wright, Arthur F., ed. Studies in Chinese Thought. Chicago: University of Chicago Press, 1953.

Wu, Eugene. Leaders of Twentieth-Century China: An Annotated Bibliography of Selected Chinese Biographical Works in the Hoover Library. Stanford: Stanford University Press, 1956.

Yakhontoff, Victor A. The Chinese Soviets. New York: Coward-McCann, 1934.

Zagoria, Donald S. "Strains in the Sino-Soviet Alliance," *Problems of Communism,* X (May–June 1960), 1–11.

Index

Index

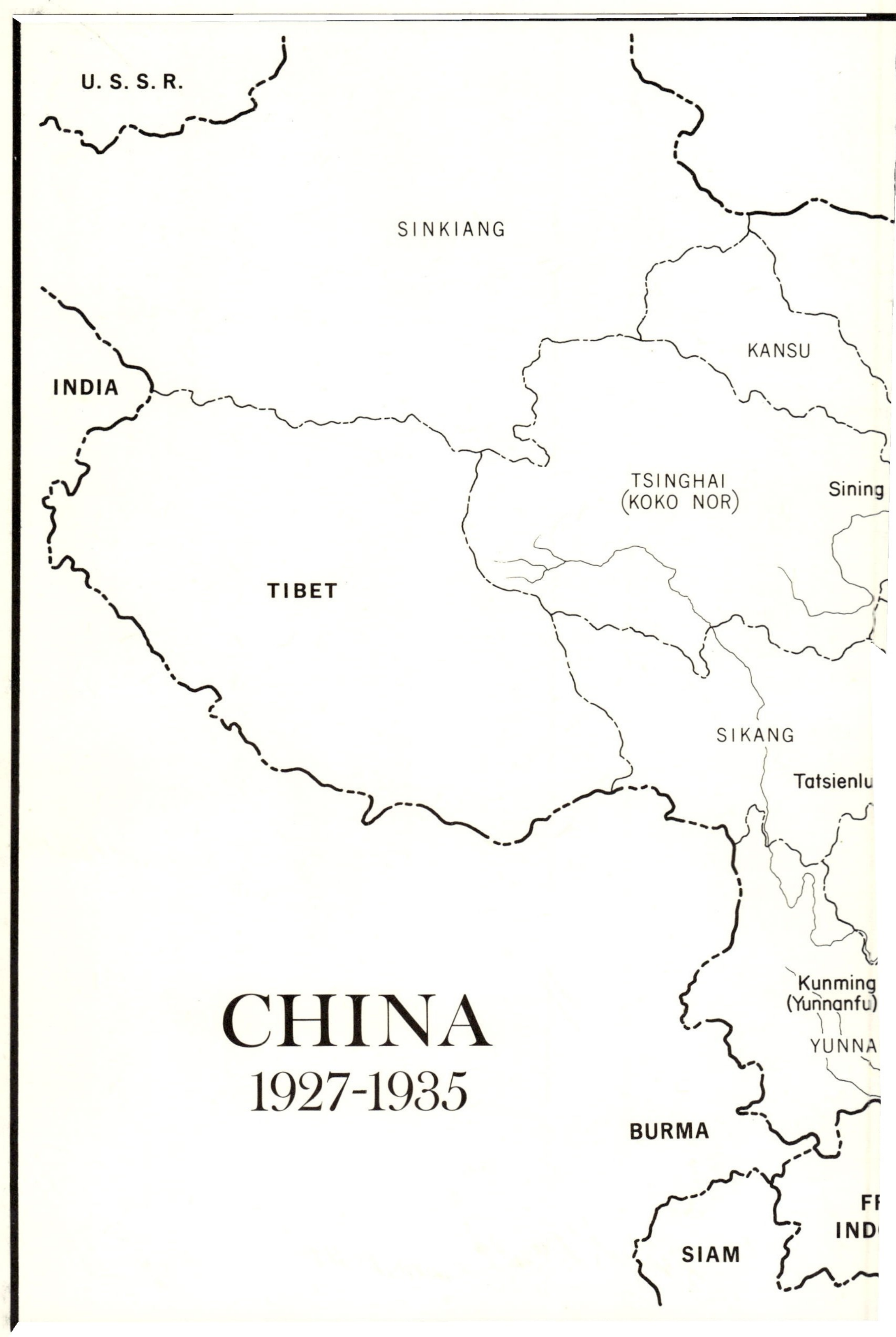

CHINA
1927-1935